Religion
American Style

Religion
American Style

EDITED BY

Patrick H. McNamara
THE UNIVERSITY OF NEW MEXICO

HARPER & ROW, PUBLISHERS
NEW YORK, EVANSTON, SAN FRANCISCO, LONDON

Sponsoring Editor: Alvin A. Abbott
Project Editor: Ralph Cato
Designer: June Negrycz
Production Supervisor: Stefania J. Taflinska

Religion American Style

Standard Book Number: 06-044377-4
Library of Congress Catalog Card Number: 73-10686

FOR JOAN AND
OUR TWO CONSTANT COMPANIONS
LAURA AND AMY

CONTENTS

✣ vii ✣

PREFACE

Religion is concerned with the deepest dimensions of human experience, with the problem of man's wholeness. How can we keep those issues out of the classroom without hopelessly distorting the very subject we are attemping to teach?

Religion is always concerned with the link between subject and object, with the whole that contains them and forms their ground. Though religion is not primarily subjective, it is not objective either.

These are the words of Robert Bellah, and a dozen semesters of teaching the sociology of religion leaves me in complete agreement with them. I find myself in full sympathy with Bellah's "symbolic realism," with the concept of religion as both a cognitive and noncognitive symbolic world. This perspective suggests that one take this world seriously, in conducting both one's life and one's classes, and that the importance of this world be respected in the developing consciousness of students. Religion thus becomes a way of apprehending and constructing, through symbols, a reality that is both "inner" to the individual and "outer" in the sense of familiar institutional forms. I do not deny the difficulty of maintaining the "double vision" of which Bellah speaks—holding fast to canons of scientific inquiry and analysis, eschewing advocacy of any particular religious tradition, yet attempting to understand, as a teacher, the meaning and value of religious understanding and to communicate this understanding to one's students.

I have edited this reader, then, with a dual purpose: (1) to provide a sociologically sound and consistently analytical set of basic readings covering salient relationships of religion and American society, and (2) to illuminate the "inner meaning" or subjectively apprehended aspects of these relationships through informal essays and personal accounts. The material directed toward this second purpose should, through illustration, enable students to better understand the principles, perspectives, and themes set forth in the more formal readings. Thus, Bellah's "Civil Religion in America" is followed by a sermon by Billy Graham ("The Unfinished Dream") and a satirical essay by Cornish Rogers ("Sports, Religion and Politics"), both of which illustrate the intertwining of religion and national culture known as civil religion. Again, Marshall Sklare's "The Sociology of the American Synagogue" analyzes the functions of a key Jewish religious institution, while Danny Siegel's highly personal "The Essence of My Commitment" accents the conflict between tradition and radical moral imperatives experienced by many American Jews. Jeffrey Hadden's "Clergy Involvement in Civil Rights" analyzes conflicts whose opposing sides find colorful expression both in J. Howard Pew's indignant "Should the Church 'Meddle' in Civil Affairs?" and in Francine du Plessix Gray's "The Berrigans."

The question inevitably arises: Why treat only religion in the United States? In answer, I can only reply that my teaching experience strongly suggests that students more quickly grasp material embedded in familiar cultural settings. I am further persuaded that America in the late 1960s and 1970s displays a wider variety of religious expression than perhaps any other contemporary culture. I have tried to capture this variety, which includes an attempt to relate religion to the recent popular movements of ecological awareness and women's liberation.

I would not argue that *Religion American Style* ought to supplant exposure of students to the giants of our tradition—Weber, Troeltsch, Durkheim, Otto, Malinowski—or to pioneers in this country such as Sorokin, Parsons, Merton, Niebuhr, Lenski, and others. In this respect, I have tried to keep in mind those wishing to use the book as a sole text in, for example, a course on American religion. An introductory chapter on functional definitions has therefore been included in order to provide some theoretical discussion. In addition, each chapter introduction briefly outlines some general themes relevant to the chapter topic. I personally feel the reader's maximum benefit lies in conjunctive use with an introductory text as well as some readings from classic authors—many of which are available in other readers or in reprints. I have therefore chosen not to cover some familiar basic themes such as Weber's Protestant Ethic, distinctions between magic and religion, and relationships between religion and social stratification. *Religion American Style* may not be every instructor's cup of tea, but it does leave sufficient freedom to the instructor to cover, in whatever way he or she chooses, those themes deemed essential to the course being taught. Therefore the book's contents need not be read serially, and the book should lend itself easily to selective usage by individual instructors.

I have found teaching the sociology of religion an exciting experience. I know that many of the colleagues with whom I have shared these experiences at regional and national conferences, in settings both formally analytical and highly informal, feel equally enthusiastic. I welcome their comments and suggestions regarding *Religion American Style*, and I hope it may enrich their own teaching experiences by encouraging students to enter thoughtfully both the inner-subjective and outer-objective worlds that comprise the inexhaustible study of religion and society.

Patrick H. McNamara

ACKNOWLEDGMENTS

My students have contributed much more than they realize to this volume. Their response to my experimental mixing of the formal and the informal launched this venture. I am especially pleased to include personal essays by two of my former students, Reid Cole's "Ritual Among Track Athletes" and Paul Carnes' "Yoga Made Plausible: A Personal Account." I owe a great deal as well to the staff of Ghost Ranch, Abiquiu, New Mexico. The United Presbyterian Church deserves commendation for maintaining their virtual Shangri-la for wandering scholars seeking quiet days and nights in which to spin out their creations. I am grateful as well to the editor-in-chief and staff of Harper & Row's College Department, who have been extremely helpful and thorough in the editing of this reader.

Final praise goes to my wife for her patience, help, and enthusiasm. Joan shares so much of the credit for this final product.

Religion
American Style

PART ONE

Religion and Society: Exploring the Relationships

CHAPTER 1

❖❖❖❖❖❖❖❖❖❖❖❖❖❖❖❖❖❖❖❖❖❖

Functionalism:
Variations and Critiques

Try to define religion and you invite an argument. Yet every sociologist of religion feels compelled to construct his own definition or to cite someone else's with appropriate critical evaluation. Keep in mind that sociologists, unlike, say, theologians or psychologists of religion, always have an eye on the relationship of religion to society when defining religion. Religion, for the sociologist at least, is not just pure individual experience of God or the holy, nor is it a description, however carefully catalogued, of the religious belief and worship system of a particular society or grouping of societies. Sociologists search for universal features of religion found in whatever society one may be considering.

Functionalism is the name given to the attempt to state in comprehensive theoretical terms what religion *does* in human society, how it relates to the ongoing, usually changing social scene. In this quest social scientists are indebted to Emile Durkheim, who focused on one important function of religion as he studied it in primitive societies: Religion is "a unified system of beliefs and practices relative to sacred things which unite into one single moral community all those who adhere to them."[1] In other words, religion is a cohesive, unitive force binding together those who profess and worship from the same religious world view. Durkheim's views, of course, are far more complex than this simple summary, and are generally treated in standard texts. The important point, however, is that his perspective alerted sociologists to seek, as well, *other* functions that religion might perform.

In contemporary sociology, the functions that religion performs are usually seen as rooted in certain fundamental needs or concerns shared universally by people living together. These are well expressed by J. Milton Yinger:

> How shall we respond to the fact of death? Does life have some central meaning despite the suffering and the succession of frustrations and tragedies it brings with it? How can we deal with the forces that press in upon us, endangering our livelihood, our health, and the survival and smooth operation of the groups in which we live—forces that our empirical knowledge cannot handle adequately? How can we bring our capacity for hostility and our egocentricity sufficiently under control to allow the groups within which we live—without which our life would indeed be impossible—to be kept together?[2]

As Yinger views them, these questions represent first of all *emotional* needs— these events occur and stimulate a quest, even a demand, for answers to the questions they raise. And every society presents some (in our pluralistic society, many) overarching schemes of meaning to interpret and handle these questions. Our first working definition, then, is Yinger's own formulation of religion in the context of the above discussion:

> Religion, then, can be defined as a system of beliefs and practices by means of which a group of people struggles with these ultimate problems of human life. It expresses their refusal to capitulate to death, to give up in the face of frustration, to allow hostility to tear apart their human associations. The quality of being religious, seen from the individual point of view, implies two things: first, a belief that evil, pain, bewilderment and injustice are fundamental facts of existence; and second, a set of practices and related sanctified beliefs that express a conviction that man can ultimately be saved from those facts.[3]

Notice that this definition makes no reference to God (or gods) or to the supernatural. Nor does it insist that every individual without exception must have a religion, in the above sense. Yinger, agreeing with many, if not most, contemporary students of religion, acknowledges the possibility of "ultimate answers" that are not grounded in theism or belief in the supernatural. Liberal humanism, communism, socialism, some expressions of Unitarianism, Ethical Culture, some forms of nationalism may well qualify, for some people at some point in history, as satisfactory interpretative schemes for the questions of fundamental concern.

Yinger's rather broad definition, however, poses some difficulties. Durkheim laid great stress on a distinction, which he claimed to be universal in human societies, between the realm of the *sacred* and that of the *profane.*

> The major distinguishing characteristic of religion, Durkheim noted, is that it deals with *sacred*, not *profane*, things. Sacred things are "set apart and forbidden," whereas profane objects are ordinary. Moreover sacredness may be

imputed to almost anything; sacred character, that is, resides not in the object, but in the mind of the beholder.[4]

This idea of the world of the sacred was expanded by Rudolph Otto in his classic *The Idea of the Holy*. The presence of the sacred, whether in the form of a person or a consecrated animal or object, evokes the primary experience underlying the genuinely religious stance: awe in the presence of the "wholly other," an experience which, if prolonged and repeated, can bring conviction that there does indeed exist a world lying beyond the visible one.

But if "natural" worldviews are admitted as capable of constituting religions, does not the important element of the sacred disappear? Andrew Greeley aptly suggests a compromise. One may suggest a *tendency* for man to sacralize his value systems, however secular they may appear.

> Even if one excluded the possibility of a transcendent or supernatural, one nonetheless is very likely to treat one's system of ultimate explanation with a great deal of jealous reverence and respect and to be highly incensed when someone else calls the system of explanation to question or behaves contrary to it.[5]

Thus a communist may well treat his doctrine and its prophets—Lenin, Mao, Castro, Ché Guevara, or Ho Chi Minh—with all the reverence a devout Jew might accord the Torah and may act with "religious" devoutness during great ritual celebrations, for example, on May 1, the anniversary of the Revolution.

The first reading, Clifford Geertz's "Religion as a Cultural System" deserves careful attention, for it takes into account all the elements and definitional features discussed above. As an anthropologist, Geertz is aware of the great variety of cultural expressions of religion. Wherever it is found, however, religion always provides a scheme of meaning set forth in an interrelated set of symbols that evoke authority in the minds of its devotees. Following Durkheim, Geertz points to ritual as an occasion of intense participation of the believers in the symbolic world of the sacred. Ritual is particularly important in times of crisis, for it is then that symbolic "reminders" and interpretative schemes are needed to reassure, comfort, and put men in touch with the "really real."

Notice, too, that Geertz places himself in a functionalist tradition by suggesting three critical and recurring human experiences that threaten "to break in upon man" and create chaos: bafflement, suffering, and inability to make sound moral judgments. A religious system attempts to cope with these. Geertz acknowledges the roles of other meaning systems as well—common sense, science, art—and contrasts them with the unique function of the religious symbol system.

The importance of ritual is well demonstrated in Geertz's account of the Navaho curing rites or "sings." Besides providing "a mode of action through which [suffering] can be expressed, being expressed, understood, and being understood, endured," the rites also perform the Durkheimian function of identification with "the Holy People, and thus with cosmic order generally." More importantly, in ritual participation the world of the sacred is made capable of inducing the "long-lasting moods and motivations in men" by fusing together "the world as lived and the world as imagined" so that "they turn out to be the same world." In other words, "the dispositions which religious rituals induce thus have their most important impact—from a human point of view—outside the boundaries of the ritual itself as they reflect back to color the individual's conception of the established world of fact. From this perspective, then, it is no exaggeration to say that religion gives shape to the everyday world in which men live and act."

In "Religion as Autobiography and Story," Michael Novak presents a striking portrayal of religion in its function of quest for personal meaning. He underlines the primacy of action, or life-in-process, as the chief "fashioner" of a person's faith, and invites the reader to make explicit to himself the story line of the life he is living. He echoes Geertz in stressing the role of culture that "burns its heroes and archetypes deeply into one's psyche." Notice, too, that Novak manages to evoke a religious mood by utilizing the symbolic vocabulary of an existentialist approach so widespread today—words and phrases such as "liberation," "a pilgrimage, a search in a labyrinth," "responsible for one's identity," "a personal story." For many, again in Geertz's framework, these sets of symbols do not merely interpret social processes in some cosmic framework (a function of philosophy); they are a template or shaper of the "really real" world.

"Ritual Among Track Athletes" by Reid Cole illustrates a number of functions performed by ritual (including several not previously stated). He supports Geertz's conviction that ritual creates a kind of identification between the world as lived and the world as imagined: The athletes take their warmup rituals very seriously and are convinced of their necessity in "attuning" the world to their advantage.

Richard Fenn's thoughtful essay challenges received concepts of an important functionalist viewpoint and articulates a contemporary (and future) version of secularization. His targets are three assumptions: (1) that religious symbols can lend a basis for cultural integration of societies at large; (2) that even in the midst of rapid societal change, religious symbols maintain a "creative tension" and will adapt eventually to whatever changes society as a whole experiences; (3) that societies need a religious basis for cultural integration if they are to survive. Religious values, however they may be acknowledged or alluded to as in the civil religion conception (presented in the following chapter), "seem to have little *demonstrable* relationship to what people actually do in work and politics. The President of the U.S. may as well be a Quaker as a Catholic; a computer programmer may as well be a Zen Buddhist as a Protestant. In either case political or occupational performance cannot be deduced from the religious values of the actor." Changes in society may have occurred so rapidly that no change in religious symboliza-tion will have any effect on other societal institutions. As for survival, modern societies may rely on socializing techniques rather than on religious training in order to help people prepare to participate in the occupational system. "Finally, legitimacy in these most advanced societies depends on the capacity to meet most popular demands for participation in the polity and for high levels of consumption rather than on the manipulation of religious symbols." This does not mean that religion has no place in a society. Fenn sees two possible arenas for religious relevance: For ethnic or minority groups, religion may serve to define boundaries and/or to legitimate demands for greater control over political and educational institutions. Second, religion may serve *expressive* functions for groups and for individuals, fulfilling personal and interpersonal needs. In this context, discussed in considerable detail by Fenn, religion is neither "compensatory" (as, in a sense, it is in Geertz's formulation) nor "legitimating" (as it partially is in Bellah's essay). Religious activity becomes an end in itself, that is, "a search for 'truth' or 'transcend-ence,' " and is reminiscent of Luckmann's religion as a "private universe of ultimate significance."

Thus Fenn's essay is no simplistic claim that "modern society no longer needs religion" or that "secularization has driven religion to the boundaries." Religion, in the contexts stated by Fenn, may be more necessary than ever precisely because other spheres—political and economic, among others—seem to have their own autonomous rationales.

The brief selection from a speech by Senator George McGovern, Democratic candidate for the Presidency in 1972, is an insistence that religion (in this instance, Christianity) ought to play the role of informing and inspiring one's political stances—a popularly stated counterthesis to Fenn's assertion of the autonomy of religion and the polity.

Andrew Greeley's colorful essay, "Superstition, Ecstasy, and Tribal Con-sciousness," locates recent resurgences of religion as play, celebration, to-getherness. Supporters of Fenn's thesis may raise eyebrows at Greeley's assertion that political and social crises of recent years, along with disenchant-ment with the church, "have raised a demand for new interpretative schemes and new religious communities that can provide meaning and belonging for human life." In Fenn's view, however, these functions are operative for "certain strata or for particular individuals." But religion has no wider societal function. In his succinct formulation, "secularization therefore does not drive religion from modern society, but rather fosters a type of religion which has no major functions for the *entire* society." (See Chapter 11 for further dis--cussion of new cultic forms.)

The double reading from Thomas Luckmann and Peter Berger is in close kinship with Fenn's viewpoint. Persons inhabiting complex, urban, mobile societies are confronted with a variety of religious options. "Official" religious systems, promulgated by the churches or, as in the case of civil religion discussed in Chapter 2, by our political representatives and institutions, find themselves in competition with worldviews formed in the "private sphere" of family, friends, neighbors, clique associates. To be sure, individuals may borrow from creedal formulations and beliefs of churches to which they belong, but, with the disappearance of sanctions formerly wielded by religious institutions, they are free to construct an amalgam stemming partly from church tradition and partly from the many sources mentioned in the reading itself.

The impact of Luckmann and subsequent writers of kindred convictions such as Fenn is to shift religious functions away from society-wide roles—institutional differentiation has allegedly resulted in political, economic, judicial, and cultural realms each guarding its own set of "rational" norms—to supportive (that is, provision of meaning, comfort, and belonging) functions for individuals both alone and in small groupings. Peter Berger, whose theory of religion's function in society is spelled out fully in his *The Sacred Canopy*, shows *how* individuals in the absence of compelling society-wide religious systems sustain worldviews in a social milieu teeming with Luckmann's "assortment of religious representations available to potential consumers." Berger uses a kind of sociology of knowledge perspective to stress the crucial importance of interaction with "confirming others." Only thus can a worldview remain believable. As he sees it, without the massive institutional support of the kind Geertz predicates of simpler societies, religious beliefs and practices stand or fall according to the extent of support from one's community of reference.

In Selection E, Paul Carnes offers a student's autobiographical view of involvements in a series of Berger's "plausibility structures." Conversion and deconversion occur among changing scenarios of significant others. He concludes by broaching the question that occurs to any critical student of this perspective: *Can* one transcend the influence of a network (or networks) of significant others and arrive at a worldview which is "really mine"?

In Selection F, philosopher Walter Kaufmann relentlessly challenges the notion that everyone must have some "ultimate" commitment or concern. His strictures are a sharp reminder that no sociological theory of religion should be interpreted as postulating of *all* men some overarching interpretation of the cosmos. In the tradition celebrated by Sigmund Freud, modern (even primitive?) man may choose to be one "who goes no further, but humbly acquiesces in the small part which human beings play in the great world—such a man is . . . irreligious in the truest sense of the word."[6]

NOTES

[1] EMILE DURKHEIM, *The Elementary Forms of the Religious Life* (New York: Free Press, 1947), p. 62.

[2] J. MILTON YINGER, *The Scientific Study of Religion* (New York: Macmillan, 1970), p. 6.

[3] Ibid., p. 7.

[4] N. J. DEMERATH III and PHILLIP E. HAMMOND, *Religion in Social Context* (New York: Random House, 1969), p. 24.

[5] ANDREW M. GREELEY, *The Denominational Society: A Sociological Approach to Religion in America* (Glenview, Ill.: Scott, Foresman, 1972), p. 9.

[6] SIGMUND FREUD, *The Future of an Illusion*, rev. ed. (Garden City, N.Y.: Doubleday Anchor Books, 1964), p. 52.

RELIGION AS A CULTURAL SYSTEM

CLIFFORD GEERTZ

...As we are to deal with meaning, let us begin with a paradigm: viz. that sacred symbols function to synthesize a people's ethos—the tone, character, and quality of their life, its moral and aesthetic style and mood—and their world-view—the picture they have of the way things in sheer actuality are, their most comprehensive ideas of order (Geertz, 1958). In religious belief and practice a group's ethos is rendered intellectually reasonable by being shown to represent a way of life ideally adapted to the actual state of affairs the world-view describes, while the world-view is rendered emotionally convincing by being presented as an image of an actual state of affairs peculiarly well arranged to accommodate such a way of life. This confrontation and mutual confirmation has two fundamental effects. On the one hand, it objectivizes moral and aesthetic preferences by depicting them as the imposed conditions of life implicit in a world with a particular structure, as mere common sense given the unalterable shape of reality. On the other, it supports these received beliefs about the world's body by invoking deeply felt moral and aesthetic sentiments as experiential evidence for their truth. Religious symbols formulate a basic congruence between a particular style of life and a specific (if, most often, implicit) metaphysic, and in so doing sustain each with the borrowed authority of the other. . . . Without further ado, then, a *religion* is:

(1) a system of symbols which acts to (2) establish powerful, pervasive, and long-lasting moods and motivations in men by (3) formulating conceptions of a general order of existence and (4) clothing these conceptions with such an aura of factuality that (5) the moods and motivations seem uniquely realistic.

1. *a system of symbols which acts to . . .*

Such a tremendous weight is being put on the term "symbol" here that our move must be to decide with some precision what we are going to mean by it. This is no easy task, for, rather like "culture," "symbol" has been used to refer to a great variety of things, often a number of them at the same time.

Reprinted with permission from Michael Banton, ed., *Anthropological Approaches to the Study of Religion.* © 1966 Tavistock Publications, Ltd., London.

Clifford Geertz is a member of the faculty of Social Sciences at the Institute for Advanced Study, Princeton University.

In some hands it is used for anything which signifies something else to someone: dark clouds are the symbolic precursors of an oncoming rain. In others it is used only for explicitly conventional signs of one sort or another: a red flag is a symbol of danger, a white of surrender. In others it is confined to something which expresses in an oblique and figurative manner that which cannot be stated in a direct and literal one, so that there are symbols in poetry but not in science, and symbolic logic is misnamed. In yet others, however (Langer, 1953, 1960, 1962), it is used for any object, act, event, quality, or relation which serves as a vehicle for a conception—the conception is the symbol's "meaning"—and that is the approach I shall follow here. . . . Cultural acts, the construction, apprehension, and utilization of symbolic forms, are social events like any other; they are as public as marriage and as observable as agriculture.

·   ·   ·

So far as culture patterns, i.e., systems or complexes of symbols, are concerned, the generic trait which is of first importance for us here is that they are extrinsic sources of information (Geertz, 1964a). By "extrinsic," I mean only that—unlike genes, for example—they lie outside the boundaries of the individual organism as such in that intersubjective world of common understandings into which all human individuals are born, in which they pursue their separate careers, and which they leave persisting behind them after they die (Schutz, 1962). By "sources of information," I mean only that—like genes—they provide a blueprint or template in terms of which processes external to themselves can be given a definite form (Horowitz, 1956). As the order of bases in a strand of DNA forms a coded program, a set of instructions, or a recipe, for the synthesization of the structurally complex proteins which shape organic functioning, so culture patterns provide such programs for the institution of the social and psychological processes which shape public behavior. Though the sort of information and the mode of its transmission are vastly different in the two cases, this comparison of gene and symbol is more than a strained analogy of the familiar "social heredity" sort. It is actually a substantial relationship, for it is precisely the fact that genetically programmed processes are so highly generalized in men, as compared with lower animals, that culturally programmed ones are so important, only because human behavior is so loosely determined by intrinsic sources of information that extrinsic sources are so vital (Geertz, 1962). To build a dam a beaver needs only an appropriate site and the proper materials—his mode of procedure is shaped by his physiology. But man, whose genes are silent on the building trades, needs also a conception of what it is to build a dam, a conception he can get only from some symbolic source—a blueprint, a textbook, or a string of speech by someone who already knows how dams are built, or, of course, from manipulating graphic or linguistic elements in such a way as to attain for himself a conception of what dams are and how they are built.

This point is sometimes put in the form of an argument that cultural patterns are "models," that they are sets of symbols whose relations to one another "model" relations among entities, processes or what-have-you in physical, organic, social, or psychological systems by "paralleling," "imitating," or "simulating" them (Craik, 1952). The term "model" has, however, two senses—an "of" sense and a "for" sense—and though these are but aspects of the same basic concept they are very much worth distinguishing for analytic purposes. In the first, what is stressed is the manipulation of symbol structures so as to bring them, more or less closely, into parallel with the pre-established non-symbolic system, as when we grasp how dams work by developing a theory of hydraulics or constructing a flow chart. The theory or chart models physical relationships in such a way—i.e., by expressing their structure in synoptic form—as to render them apprehensible: it is a model *of* "reality." In the second, what is stressed is the manipulation of the non-symbolic systems in terms of the relationships expressed in the symbolic, as when we construct a dam according to the specifications implied in an hydraulic theory or the conclusions drawn from a flow chart. Here, the theory is a model under whose guidance physical relationships are organized: it is a model *for* "reality." For psychological and social systems, and for cultural models that we would not ordinarily refer to as "theories," but rather as "doctrines," "melodies," or "rites," the case is in no way different. Unlike genes, and other non-symbolic information sources, which are only models *for*, not models *of*, culture patterns have an intrinsic double aspect: they give meaning, i.e., objective conceptual form, to social and psychological reality both by shaping themselves to it and by shaping it to themselves. . . .

. . . The inter-transposability of models *for* and models *of* which symbolic formulation makes possible is the distinctive characteristic of our mentality.

2. . . . *to establish powerful, pervasive, and long-lasting moods and motivations in men by* . . .

So far as religious symbols and symbol systems are concerned this inter-transposability is clear. The endurance, courage, independence, perseverance, and passionate willfulness in which the Plains Indian practices the vision quest are the same flamboyant virtues by which he attempts to live: while achieving a sense of revelation he stabilizes a sense of direction (Lowie, 1924). The consciousness of defaulted obligation, secreted guilt, and, when a confession is obtained, public shame in which Manus' seance rehearses him are the same sentiments that underlie the sort of duty ethic by which his property-conscious society is maintained: the gaining of an absolution involves the forging of a conscience (Fortune, 1935). And the same self-discipline which rewards a Javanese mystic staring fixedly into the flame of a lamp with what he takes to be an intimation of divinity drills him in that rigorous control of emotional expression which is necessary to a man who would follow a quietistic style of life (Geertz, 1960). Whether one sees the conception of a personal guardian spirit, a family tutelary or an immanent God as synoptic formulations of the character of reality or as templates for producing reality with such a character seems largely arbitrary, a matter of which aspect, the model *of* or model *for*, one wants for the moment to bring into focus. The concrete symbols involved—one or another mythological figure materializing in the wilderness, the skull of the deceased household head hanging censoriously in the rafters, or a disembodied "voice in the stillness" soundlessly chanting enigmatic classical poetry—point in either direction. They both express the world's climate and shape it.

.   .   .

So far as religious activities are concerned (and learning a myth by heart is as much a religious activity as detaching one's finger at the knuckle), two somewhat different sorts of disposition are induced by them: moods and motivations.

A motivation is a persisting tendency, a chronic inclination to perform certain sorts of act and experience certain sorts of feeling in certain sorts of situation, the "sorts" being commonly very heterogenous and rather ill-defined classes in all three cases:

> ...on hearing that a man is vain [i.e., motivated by vanity] we expect him to behave in certain ways, namely to talk a lot about himself, to cleave to the society of the eminent, to reject criticisms, to seek the footlights and to disengage himself from conversations about the merits of others. We expect him to indulge in roseate day dreams about his own successes, to avoid recalling past failures and to plan for his own advancement. To be vain is to tend to act in these and innumerable other kindred ways. Certainly we also expect the vain man to feel certain pangs and flutters in certain situations; we expect him to have an acute sinking feeling when an eminent person forgets his name, and to feel buoyant of heart and light of toe on hearing of the misfortunes of his rivals. But feelings of pique and buoyancy are not more directly indicative of vanity than are public acts of boasting or private acts of daydreaming... (Ryle, 1949, p. 86).

Similarly for any motivations. As a motive, "flamboyant courage" consists in such enduring propensities as to fast in the wilderness, to conduct solitary raids on enemy camps, and to thrill to the thought of counting coup. "Moral circumspection" consists in such ingrained tendencies as to honor onerous promises, to confess secret sins in the face of severe public disapproval, and to feel guilty when vague and generalized accusations are made at seances. And "dispassionate tranquility" consists in such persistent inclinations as to maintain one's poise come hell or high water, to experience distaste in the presence of even moderate emotional displays, and to indulge in contentless contemplations of featureless objects. Motives are thus neither acts (i.e., intentional behaviors) nor feelings, but liabilities to perform particular classes of act or have particular classes of feeling. And when we say that a man is religious, i.e., motivated by religion, this is at least part—though only part—of what we mean.

Another part of what we mean is that he has, when properly stimulated, a susceptibility to fall into certain moods, moods we sometimes lump together under such covering terms as "reverential," "solemn," or "worshipful." Such generalized rubrics actually conceal, however, the enormous empirical variousness of the dispositions involved, and, in fact, tend to assimilate them to the unusually grave tone of most of our own religious life. The moods that sacred symbols induce, at different times and in different places, range from exultation to melancholy, from self-confidence to self-pity, from an incorrigible playfulness to a bland listlessness—to say nothing of the erogenous power of so many of the world's myths and rituals. No more than there is a single sort of motivation one can call piety is there a single sort of mood one can call worshipful.

The major difference between moods and motivations is that where the latter are, so to speak, vectorial qualities, the former are merely scalar. Motives have a directional cast, they describe a certain overall course, gravitate toward certain, usually temporary, consummations. But moods vary only as to intensity: they go nowhere. They spring from certain circumstances but they are responsive to no ends. Like fogs, they just settle and lift; like scents, suffuse and evaporate. When present they are totalistic: if one is sad everything and everybody seems dreary; if one is gay, everything and everybody seems splendid. Thus, though a man can be vain, brave, willful and independent at the same time, he can't very well be playful and listless, or exultant and melancholy, at the same time (Ryle, 1949, p. 99). Further, where motives persist for more or less extended periods of time, moods merely recur with greater or lesser frequency, coming and going for what are often quite unfathomable reasons. But perhaps the most important difference, so far as we are concerned, between moods and motivations is that motivations are "made meaningful" with reference to the ends toward which they are conceived to conduce, whereas moods are "made meaningful" with reference to the conditions from which they are conceived to spring. We interpret motives in terms of their consummations, but we interpret moods in terms of their sources. We say that a person is industrious because he wishes to succeed, we say that a person is worried because he is conscious of the hanging threat of nuclear holocaust. And this is no less the case when the interpretations invoked are ultimate. Charity becomes Christian charity when it is enclosed in a conception of God's purposes; optimism is Christian optimism when it is grounded in a particular conception of God's nature. The assiduity of the Navaho finds its rationale in a belief that, since "reality" operates mechanically, it is coercible; their chronic fearfulness finds its rationale in a conviction that, however "reality" operates, it is both enormously powerful and terribly dangerous (Kluckhohn, 1949).

3. ...*by formulating conceptions of a general order of existence and* ...

That the symbols or symbol systems which induce and define dispositions we set off as religious and those which place those dispositions in a cosmic framework are the same symbols ought to occasion no surprise. For what else do we mean by saying that a particular mood of awe is religious and not secular except that it springs from entertaining a conception of all-pervading vitality like mana and not from a visit to the Grand Canyon? Or that a particular case of asceticism is an example of a religious motivation except that it is directed toward the achievement of an unconditioned end like nirvana and not a conditioned one like weight-reduction? If sacred symbols did not at one and the same time induce dispositions in human beings and formulate, however obliquely, inarticulately, or unsystematically, general ideas of order, then the empirical differentia of religious activity or religious experience would not exist. A man can indeed be said to be "religious" about golf, but not merely if he pursues it with passion and plays it on Sundays: he must also see it as symbolic of some transcendent truths. And the pubescent boy gazing soulfully into the eyes of the pubescent girl in a William Steig cartoon and murmuring, "There is something about you, Ethel, which gives me a sort of religious feeling," is, like most adolescents, confused. What any particular religion affirms about the fundamental nature of reality may be obscure, shallow, or, all too often, perverse, but it must, if it is not to consist of the mere collection of received practices and conventional sentiments we usually refer to as moralism, affirm something. If one were to essay a minimal definition of religion today it would perhaps not be Tylor's famous "belief in spiritual beings," to which Goody (1961), wearied of theoretical subtleties, has lately urged us to return, but rather what Salvador de Madariaga has called "the relatively modest dogma that God is not mad."

Usually, of course, religions affirm very much more than this: we believe, as James (1904, vol. 2, p. 299) remarked, all that we can and would believe everything if we only could. The thing we seem least able to tolerate is a threat to our powers of conception, a suggestion that our ability to create, grasp, and use symbols may fail us, for were this to happen we would be more helpless, as I have already pointed out, than the beavers. The extreme generality, diffuseness, and variability of man's innate (i.e., genetically programmed) response capacities means that without the assistance of cultural patterns he would be functionally incomplete, not merely a talented ape who had, like some under-privileged child, unfortunatley been prevented from realizing his full potentialities, but a kind of formless monster with neither sense of direction nor power of self-control, a chaos of spasmodic impulses and vague emotions (Geertz, 1962). Man depends upon symbols and symbol systems with a dependence so great as to be decisive for his creatural viability and, as a result, his sensitivity to even the remotest indication that they may prove unable to cope with one or another aspect of experience raises within him the gravest sort of anxiety:

[Man] can adapt himself somehow to anything his imagination can cope with; but he cannot deal with Chaos. Because his characteristic function and highest asset is conception, his greatest fright is to meet what he cannot construe—the "uncanny," as it is popularly called. It need not be a new object; we do meet new things, and "understand" them promptly, if tentatively, by the nearest analogy, when our minds are functioning freely; but under mental stress even perfectly familiar things may become suddenly disorganized and give us the horrors. Therefore our most important assets are always the symbols of our general *orientation* in nature, on the earth, in society, and in what we are doing: the symbols of our *Weltanschauüng* and *Lebensanschauüng*. Consequently, in a primitive society, a daily ritual is incorporated in common activities, in eating, washing, fire-making, etc., as well as in pure ceremonial; because the need of reasserting the tribal morale and recognizing its cosmic conditions is constantly felt. In Christian Europe the Church brought men daily (in some orders even hourly) to their knees, to enact if not to contemplate their assent to the ultimate concepts (Langer, 1960, p. 287, italics original).

There are at least three points where chaos—a tumult of events which lack not just interpretations but *interpretability*—threatens to break in upon man: at the limits of his analytic capacities, at the limits of his powers of endurance, and at the limits of his moral insight. Bafflement, suffering, and a sense of intractable ethical paradox are all, if they become intense enough or are sustained long enough, radical challenges to the proposition that life is comprehensible and that we can, by taking thought, orient ourselves effectively within it—challenges with which any religion, however "primitive," which hopes to persist must attempt somehow to cope.

Of the three issues, it is the first which has been least investigated by modern social anthropologists (though Evans-Pritchard's (1937) classic discussion of why granaries fall on some Azande and not on others, is a notable exception). Even to consider people's religious beliefs as attempts to bring anomalous events or experiences—death, dreams, mental fugues, volcanic eruptions, or marital infidelity—within the circle of the at least potentially explicable seems to smack of Tyloreanism or worse. But it does appear to be a fact that at least some men—in all probability, most men—are unable to leave unclarified problems of analysis merely unclarified, just to look at the stranger features of the world's landscape in dumb astonishment or bland apathy without trying to develop, however fantastic, inconsistent, or simpleminded, some notions as to how such features might be reconciled with the more ordinary deliverances of experience. Any chronic failure of one's explanatory apparatus, the complex of received culture patterns (common sense, science, philosophical speculation, myth) one has for mapping the empirical world, to explain things which cry out for explanation tends to lead to a deep disquiet—a tendency rather more widespread and a disquiet rather deeper than we have sometimes supposed since the pseudo-science view of religious belief was, quite rightfully, deposed. After all, even that high priest of heroic atheism, Lord Russell, once remarked that although the problem of the existence of God had never bothered him, the ambiguity of certain mathematical axioms had threatened to unhinge his mind. And

Einstein's profound dissatisfaction with quantum mechanics was based on a—surely religious—inability to believe that, as he put it, God plays dice with the universe.

But this quest for lucidity and the rush of metaphysical anxiety that occurs when empirical phenomena threaten to remain intransigently opaque is found on much humbler intellectual levels. Certainly, I was struck in my own work, much more than I had at all expected to be, by the degree to which my more animistically inclined informants behaved like true Tyloreans. They seemed to be constantly using their beliefs to "explain" phenomena, or, more accurately, to convince themselves that the phenomena were explainable within the accepted scheme of things, for they commonly had only a minimal attachment to the particular soul possession, emotional disequilibrium, taboo infringement, or bewitchment hypothesis they advanced and were all too ready to abandon it for some other, in the same genre, which struck them as more plausible given the facts of the case. What they were *not* ready to do was abandon it for no other hypothesis at all; to leave events to themselves.

And what is more, they adopted this nervous cognitive stance with respect to phenomena which had no immediate practical bearing on their own lives, or for that matter on anyone's. When a peculiarly shaped, rather large toadstool grew up in a carpenter's house in the short space of a few days (or, some said, a few hours), people came from miles around to see it, and everyone had some sort of explanation—some animist, some animatist, some not quite either—for it.... Toadstools play about the same role in Javanese life as they do in ours and in the ordinary course of things Javanese have about as much interest in them as we do. It was just that this one was "odd," "strange," "uncanny"—*aneh*. And the odd, strange, and uncanny simply must be accounted for—or, again, the conviction that it *could be accounted* for sustained. One does not shrug off a toadstool which grows five times as fast as a toadstool has any right to grow. In the broadest sense the "strange" toadstool did have implications, and critical ones, for those who heard about it. It threatened their most general ability to understand the world, raised the uncomfortable question of whether the beliefs which they held about nature were workable, the standards of truth they used valid.

•　　•　　•

The second experiential challenge in whose face the meaningfulness of a particular pattern of life threatens to dissolve into a chaos of thingless names and nameless things—the problem of suffering—has been rather more investigated, or at least described, mainly because of the great amount of attention given in works on tribal religion to what are perhaps its two main loci: illness and mourning. Yet for all the fascinated interest in the emotional aura that surrounds these extreme situations, there has been, with a few exceptions such as Lienhardt's recent (1961, pp. 151 ff.) discussion of Dinka divining, little conceptual advance over the sort of crude confidence-type theory set forth by Malinowski: viz., that religion helps one to endure "situations of emotional stress" by "open[ing] up escapes from such situations and such impasses as offer no empirical way out except by ritual and belief into the domain of the supernatural" (1948, p. 67). The inadequacy of this "theology of optimism," as Nadel (1957) rather drily called it, is, of course, radical. Over its career religion has probably disturbed men as much as it has cheered them; forced them into a head-on, unblinking confrontation of the fact that they are born to trouble as often as it has enabled them to avoid such a confrontation by projecting them into sort of infantile fairy-tale world where— Malinowski again (1948, p. 67)—"hope cannot fail nor desire deceive." With the possible exception of Christian Science, there are few if any religious traditions, "great" or "little," in which the proposition that life hurts is not strenuously affirmed and in some it is virtually glorified.

.   .   .

As a religious problem, the problem of suffering is, paradoxically, not how to avoid suffering but how to suffer, how to make of physical pain, personal loss, worldly defeat, or the helpless contemplation of others' agony something bearable, supportable—something, as we say, sufferable.... Where the more intellective aspects of what Weber called the Problem of Meaning are a matter affirming the ultimate explicability of experience, the more effective aspects are a matter of affirming its ultimate sufferableness. As religion on one side anchors the power of our symbolic resources for formulating analytic ideas in an authoritative conception of the overall shape of reality, so on another side it anchors the power of our, also symbolic, resources for express- ing emotions—moods, sentiments, passions, affection, feelings—in a similar conception of its pervasive tenor, its inherent tone and temper. For those able to embrace them, and for so long as they are able to embrace them, religious symbols provide a cosmic guarantee not only for their ability to comprehend the world, but also, comprehending it, to give a precision to their feeling, a definition to their emotions which enables them, morosely or joyfully, grimly or cavalierly, to endure it.

Consider in this light the well-known Navaho curing rites usually referred to as "sings" (Kluckholn and Leighton, 1946; Reichard, 1950). A sing—the Navaho have about sixty different ones for different purposes, but virtually all of them are dedicated to removing some sort of physical or mental illness— is a kind of religious psychodrama in which there are three main actors: the "singer" or curer, the patient, and, as a kind of antiphonal chorus, the patient's family and friends. The structure of all the sings, the drama's plot, is quite similar. There are three main acts: a purification of the patient and audience; a statement, by means of repetitive chants and ritual manipula- tions, of the wish to restore well-being ("harmony") in the patient; an identification of the patient with the Holy People and his consequent "cure." The purification rites involved forced sweating, induced vomiting, etc., to expel the sickness from the patient physically. The chants, which are num- berless, consist mainly of simple optative phrases ("may the patient be well,"

"I am getting better all over," etc.). And, finally, the identification of the patient with the Holy People, and thus with cosmic order generally, is accomplished through the agency of a sand painting depicting the Holy People in one or another appropriate mythic setting. The singer places the patient on the painting, touching the feet, hands, knees, shoulders, breast, back, and head of the divine figures and then the corresponding parts of the patient, performing thus what is essentially a communion rite between the patient and the Holy People, a bodily identification of the human and the divine (Reichard, 1950). This is the climax of the sing: the whole curing process may be likened, Reichard says, to a spiritual osmosis in which the illness in man and the power of the deity penetrate the ceremonial membrane in both directions, the former being neutralized by the latter. Sickness seeps out in the sweat, vomit, and other purification rites; health seeps in as the Navaho patient touches, through the medium of the singer, the sacred sand painting. Clearly, the symbolism of the sing focuses upon the problem of human suffering and attempts to cope with it by placing it in a meaningful context, providing a mode of action through which it can be expressed, being expressed, understood, and being understood, endured. The sustaining effect of the sing (and since the commonest disease is tuberculosis, it can in most cases be only sustaining), rests ultimately on its ability to give the stricken person a vocabulary in terms of which to grasp the nature of his distress and relate it to the wider world. Like a calvary, a recitation of Buddha's emergence from his father's palace or a performance of *Oedipus Tyrannos* in other religious traditions, a sing is mainly concerned with the presentation of a specific and concrete image of truly human, and so endurable, suffering powerful enough to resist the challenge of emotional meaninglessness raised by the existence of intense and unremovable brute pain.

The problem of suffering passes easily into the problem of evil, for if suffering is severe enough it usually, though not always, seems morally undeserved as well, at least to the sufferer. But they are not, however, exactly the same thing—a fact I think Weber, too influenced by the biases of a mono-theistic tradition in which, as the various aspects of human experience must be conceived to proceed from a single, voluntaristic source, man's pain reflects directly on God's goodness, did not fully recognize in his generalization of the dilemmas of Christian theodicy Eastward. For where the problem of suffering is concerned with threats to our ability to put our "un-disciplined squads of emotion" into some sort of soldierly order, the problem of evil is concerned with threats to our ability to make sound moral judgments. What is involved in the problem of evil is not the adequacy of our symbolic resources to govern our affective life, but the adequacy of those resources to provide a workable set of ethical criteria, normative guides to govern our action. The vexation here is the gap between things as they are and as they ought to be if our conceptions of right and wrong make sense, the gap between what we deem various individuals deserve and what we see that they get—a phenomenon summed up in that profound quatrain:

The rain falls on the just
And on the unjust fella;
But mainly upon the just,
Because the unjust has the just's umbrella.

Or if this seems too flippant an expression of an issue that, in somewhat different form, animates the Book of Job and the *Baghavad Gita*, the following classical Javanese poem, known, sung, and repeatedly quoted in Java by virtually everyone over the age of six, puts the point—the discrepancy between moral prescriptions and material rewards, the seeming inconsistency of "is" and "ought"—rather more elegantly:

We have lived to see a time without order
In which everyone is confused in his mind.
One cannot bear to join in the madness,
But if he does not do so
He will not share in the spoils,
And will starve as a result.
Yes, God; wrong is wrong:
Happy are those who forget,
Happier yet those who remember and have deep insight....

Thus the problem of evil, or perhaps one should say the problem *about* evil, is in essence the same sort of problem of or about bafflement and the problem of or about suffering. The strange opacity of certain empirical events, the dumb senselessness of intense or inexorable pain, and the enigmatic unaccountability of gross iniquity all raise the uncomfortable suspicion that perhaps the world, and hence man's life in the world, has no genuine order at all—no empirical regularity, no emotional form, no moral coherence. And the religious response to this suspicion is in each case the same: the formulation, by means of symbols, of an image of such a genuine order of the world which will account for, and even celebrate, the perceived ambiguities, puzzles, and paradoxes in human experience. The effort is not to deny the undeniable—that there are unexplained events, that life hurts, or that rain falls upon the just—but to deny that there are inexplicable events, that life is unendurable, and that justice is a mirage. The principles which constitute the moral order may indeed often elude men, as Lienhardt puts it, in the same way as fully satisfactory explanations of anomalous events or effective forms for the expression of feeling often elude them. What is important, to a religious man at least, is that this elusiveness be accounted for, that it be not the result of the fact that there are no such principles, explanations, or forms, that life is absurd and the attempt to make moral, intellectual or emotional sense out of experience is bootless. The Dinka can admit, in fact insist upon, the moral ambiguities and contradictions of life as they live it because these ambiguities and contradictions are seen not as ultimate, but as the "rational," "natural," "logical" (one may choose one's own adjective here, for none of them is truly adequate) outcome of the moral structure of reality which the myth of the withdrawn "Divinity" depicts, or as Lienhardt says, "images."

The Problem of Meaning in each of its intergrading aspects (how these aspects in fact intergrade in each particular case, what sort of interplay there is between the sense of analytic, emotional, and moral impotence, seems to me one of the outstanding, and except for Weber untouched, problems for comparative research in this whole field) is a matter of affirming, or at least recognizing, the inescapability of ignorance, pain, and injustice on the human plane while simultaneously denying that these irrationalities are characteristic of the world as a whole. And it is in terms of religious symbolism, a symbolism relating man's sphere of existence to a wider sphere within which it is conceived to rest, that both the affirmation and the denial are made.[1]

4. *. . . and clothing those conceptions with such an aura of factuality that . . .*

There arises here, however, a profounder question: how is it that this denial comes to be believed? how is it that the religious man moves from a troubled perception of experienced disorder to a more or less settled conviction of fundamental order? just what does "belief" mean in a religious context? Of all the problems surrounding attempts to conduct anthropological analysis of religion this is the one that has perhaps been most troublesome and therefore the most often avoided, usually by relegating it to psychology, that raffish outcast discipline to which social anthropologists are forever consigning phenomena they are unable to deal with within the framework of a denatured Durkheimianism. But the problem will not go away, it is not "merely" psychological (nothing social is), and no anthropological theory of religion which fails to attack it is worthy of the name. We have been trying to stage Hamlet without the Prince quite long enough.

It seems to me that it is best to begin any approach to this issue with frank recognition that religious belief involves not a Baconian induction from everyday experience—for then we should all be agnostics—but rather a prior acceptance of authority which transforms that experience. The existence of bafflement, pain, and moral paradox—of The Problem of Meaning—is one of the things that drive men toward belief in gods, devils, spirits, totemic principles, or the spiritual efficacy of cannibalism (an enfolding sense of beauty or a dazzling perception of power are others), but it is not the basis upon which those beliefs rest, but rather their most important field of application:

> We point to the state of the world as illustrative of doctrine, but never as evidence for it. So Belsen illustrates a world of original sin, but original sin is not an hypothesis to account for happenings like Belsen. We justify a particular religious belief by showing its place in the total religious conception; we justify a religious belief as a whole by referring to authority. We accept authority because we discover it at some point in the world at

which we worship, at which we accept the lordship of something not ourselves. We do not worship authority, but we accept authority as defining
the worshipful. So someone may discover the possibility of worship in the
life of the Reformed Churches and accept the Bible as authoritative; or in the
Roman Church and accept papal authority (MacIntyre, 1957, pp. 201–202).

This is, of course, a Christian statement of the matter; but it is not to be
despised on that account. In tribal religions authority lies in the persuasive
power of traditional imagery; in mystical ones in the apodictic force of
supersensible experience; in charismatic ones in the hypnotic attraction of an
extraordinary personality. But the priority of the acceptance of an authoritative
criterion in religious matters over the revelation which is conceived to flow
from that acceptance is not less complete than in scriptural or hieratic ones.
The basic axiom underlying what we may perhaps call "the religious perspective" is everywhere the same: he who would know must first believe.

But to speak of "the religious perspective" is, by implication, to speak of
one perspective among others. A perspective is a mode of seeing, in that
extended sense of "see" in which it means "discern," "apprehend," "understand," or "grasp." It is a particular way of looking at life, a particular
manner of construing the world, as when we speak of an historical perspective,
a scientific perspective, an aesthetic perspective, a common-sense perspective,
or even the bizarre perspective embodied in dreams and in hallucinations.[2]
The question then comes down to, first, what is "the religious perspective"
generically considered, as differentiated from other perspectives; and second,
how do men come to adopt it.

If we place the religious perspective against the background of three of
the other major perspectives in terms of which men construe the world—
the common-sensical, the scientific, and the aesthetic—its special character
emerges more sharply. What distinguishes common sense as a mode of
"seeing" is, as Schutz (1962) has pointed out, a simple acceptance of the
world, its objects, and its processes as being just what they seem to be—
what is sometimes called naïve realism—and the pragmatic motive, the
wish to act upon that world so as to bend it to one's practical purposes, to
master it, or so far as that proves impossible, to adjust to it. The world of
everyday life, itself, of course, a cultural product, for it is framed in terms of
the symbolic conceptions of "stubborn fact" handed down from generation
to generation, is the established scene and given object of our actions. Like
Mt. Everest it is just there and the thing to do with it, if one feels the
need to do anything with it at all, is to climb it. In the scientific perspective
it is precisely this givenness which disappears (Schutz, 1962). Deliberate
doubt and systematic inquiry, the suspension of the pragmatic motive in
favor of disinterested observation, the attempt to analyze the world in terms
of formal concepts whose relationship to the informal conceptions of common
sense become increasingly problematic—these are the hallmarks of the attempt
to grasp the world scientifically. And as for the aesthetic perspective, which
under the rubric of "the aesthetic attitude" has been perhaps most exquisitely

examined, it involves a different sort of suspension of naïve realism and practical interest, in that instead of questioning the credentials of everyday experience, that experience is merely ignored in favor of an eager dwelling upon appearances, an engrossment in surfaces, an absorption in things, as we say, "in themselves": "The function of artistic illusion is not 'make-believe'...but the very opposite, disengagement from belief—the contemplation of sensory qualities without their usual meanings of 'here's that chair,' 'That's my telephone,'...etc. The knowledge that what is before us has no practical significance in the world is what enables us to give attention to its appearance as such" (Langer, 1957, p. 49). And like the common-sensical and the scientific (or the historical, the philosophical, and the autistic), this perspective, this "way of seeing" is not the product of some mysterious Cartesian chemistry, but is induced, mediated, and in fact created by means of symbols. It is the artist's skill which can produce those curious quasi-objects—poems, dramas, sculptures, symphonies—which, dissociating themselves from the solid world of common sense, take on the special sort of eloquence only sheer appearances can achieve.

The religious perspective differs from the common-sensical in that, as already pointed out, it moves beyond the realities of everyday life to wider ones which correct and complete them, and its defining concern is not action upon those wider realities but acceptance of them, faith in them. It differs from the scientific perspective in that it questions the realities of everyday life not out of an institutionalized scepticism which dissolves the world's givenness into a swirl of probabilistic hypotheses, but in terms of what it takes to be wider, nonhypothetical truths. Rather than detachment, its watchword is commitment; rather than analysis, encounter. And it differs from art in that instead of effecting a disengagement from the whole question of factuality, deliberately manufacturing an air of semblance and illusion, it deepens the concern with fact and seeks to create an aura of utter actuality. It is this sense of the "really real" upon which the religious perspective rests and which the symbolic activities of religion as a cultural system are devoted to producing, intensifying, and, so far as possible, rendering inviolable by the discordant revelations of secular experience. It is, again, the imbuing of a certain specific complex of symbols—of the metaphysic they formulate and the style of life they recommend—with a persuasive authority which, from an analytic point of view is the essence of religious action.

Which brings us, at length, to ritual. For it is in ritual—i.e., consecrated behavior—that this conviction that religious conceptions are veridical and that religious directives are sound is somehow generated. It is in some sort of ceremonial form—even if that form be hardly more than the recitation of a myth, the consultation of an oracle, or the decoration of a grave—that the moods and motivations which sacred symbols induce in men and the general conceptions of the order of existence which they formulate for men meet and reinforce one another. In a ritual, the world as lived and the world as imagined, fused under the agency of a single set of symbolic forms, turn out to be the same world, producing thus that idiosyncratic transformation in one's sense of reality to which Santayana refers in my epigraph. Whatever role divine intervention may or may not play in the creation of faith—and it is not the business of the scientist to pronounce upon such matters one way or the other—it is, primarily at least, out of the context of concrete acts of religious observance that religious conviction emerges on the human plane.

However, though any religious ritual, no matter how apparently automatic or conventional (if it is truly automatic or merely conventional it is not religious), involves this symbolic fusion of ethos and world-view, it is mainly certain more elaborate and usually more public ones, ones in which a broad range of moods and motivations on the one hand and of metaphysical conceptions on the other are caught up, which shape the spiritual consciousness of a people....

> Whenever Madrasi Brahmans (and non-Brahmans, too, for that matter) wished to exhibit to me some feature of Hinduism, they always referred to, or invited me to see, a particular rite or ceremony in the life cycle, in a temple festival, or in the general sphere of religious and cultural performances. Reflecting on this in the course of my interviews and observations I found that the more abstract generalizations about Hinduism (my own as well as those I heard) could generally be checked, directly or indirectly, against these observable performances (Singer, 1958).

Of course, all cultural performances are not religious performances, and the line between those that are and artistic, or even political ones is often not so easy to draw in practice, for, like social forms, symbolic forms can serve multiple purposes. But the point is that, paraphrasing slightly, Indians— "and perhaps all peoples"—seem to think of their religion "as encapsulated in these discrete performances which they [can] exhibit to visitors and to themselves" (Singer, 1955). The mode of exhibition is however radically different for the two sorts of witness, a fact seemingly overlooked by those who would argue that "religion is a form of human art" (Firth, 1951, p. 250). Where for "visitors" religious performances can, in the nature of the case, only be presentations of a particular religious perspective, and thus aesthetically appreciated or scientifically dissected, for participants they are in addition enactments, materializations, realizations of it—not only models *of* what they believe, but also models *for* the believing of it. In these plastic dramas men attain their faith as they portray it.

· · ·

5. ...*that the moods and motivations seem uniquely realistic.*
But no one, not even a saint, lives in the world religious symbols formulate all of the time, and the majority of men live in it only at moments. The everyday world of common-sense objects and practical acts is, as Schutz (1962, pp. 226 ff.) says the paramount reality in human experience—paramount in

the sense that it is the world in which we are most solidly rooted, whose inherent actuality we can hardly question (however much we may question certain portions of it), and from whose pressures and requirements we can least escape. A man, even large groups of men, may be aesthetically insensitive, religiously unconcerned, and unequipped to pursue formal scientific analysis, but he cannot be completely lacking in common sense and survive. The dispositions which religious rituals induce thus have their most important impact—from a human point of view—outside the boundaries of the ritual itself as they reflect back to color the individual's conception of the established world of bare fact. The peculiar tone that marks the Plains vision quest, the Manus confession, or the Javanese mystical exercise pervades areas of the life of these peoples far beyond the immediately religious, impressing upon them a distinctive style in the sense both of a dominant mood and a characteristic movement. The interweaving of the malignant and the comic, which the Rangda-Barong combat depicts, animates a very wide range of everyday Balinese behavior, much of which, like the ritual itself, has an air of candid fear narrowly contained by obsessive playfulness. Religion is sociologically interesting not because, as vulgar positivism would have it (Leach, 1954, pp. 10 ff.), it describes the social order (which, in so far as it does, it does not only very obliquely but very incompletely), but because, like environment, political power, wealth, jural obligation, personal affection, and a sense of beauty, it shapes it.

.   .   .

It is this particularity of the impact of religious systems upon social systems (and upon personality systems) which renders general assessments of the value of religion in either moral or functional terms impossible. The sorts of moods and motivations which characterize a man who has just come from an Aztec human sacrifice are rather different from those of one who has just put off his Kachina mask. Even within the same society, what one "learns" about the essential pattern of life from a sorcery rite and from a commensal meal will have rather diverse effects on social and psychological functioning. One of the main methodological problems in writing about religion scientifically is to put aside at once the tone of the village atheist and that of the village preacher, as well as their more sophisticated equivalents, so that the social and psychological implications of particular religious beliefs can emerge in a clear and neutral light. And when that is done, overall questions about whether religion is "good" or "bad," "functional" or "dysfunctional," "ego strengthening" or "anxiety producing" disappear like the chimeras they are, and one is left with particular evaluations, assessments, and diagnoses in particular cases. There remain, of course, the hardly unimportant questions of whether this or that religious assertion is true, this or that religious experience genuine, or whether true religious assertions and genuine religious experiences are possible at all. But such questions cannot even be asked, much less answered, within the self-imposed limitations of the scientific perspective.

For an anthropologist, the importance of religion lies in its capacity to serve, for an individual or for a group, as a source of general, yet distinctive conceptions of the world, the self, and the relations between them, on the one hand—its model *of* aspect—and of rooted, no less distinctive "mental" dispositions—its model *for* aspect—on the other. From these cultural functions flow, in turn, its social and psychological ones.

Religious concepts spread beyond their specifically metaphysical contexts to provide a framework of general ideas in terms of which a wide range of experience—intellectual, emotional, moral—can be given meaningful form. The Christian sees the Nazi movement against the background of The Fall which, though it does not, in a causal sense, explain it, places it in a moral, a cognitive, even an affective sense. An Azande sees the collapse of a granary upon a friend or relative against the background of a concrete and rather special notion of witchcraft and thus avoids the philosophical dilemmas as well as the psychological stress of indeterminism. A Javanese finds in the borrowed and reworked concept of *rasa* ("sense-taste feeling-meaning") a means by which to "see" choreographic, gustatory, emotional, and political phenomena in a new light. A synopsis of cosmic order, a set of religious beliefs, is also a gloss upon the mundane world of social relationships and psychological events. It renders them graspable.

But more than gloss, such beliefs are also a template. They do not merely interpret social and psychological processes in cosmic terms—in which case they would be philosophical, not religious—but they shape them. In the doctrine of original sin is embedded also a recommended attitude toward life, a recurring mood, and a persisting set of motivations. The Zande learns from witchcraft conceptions not just to understand apparent "accidents" as not accidents at all, but to react to these spurious accidents with hatred for the agent who caused them and to proceed against him with appropriate resolution. *Rasa*, in addition to being a concept of truth, beauty, and goodness, is also a preferred mode of experiencing, a kind of affectless detachment, a variety of bland aloofness, an unshakeable calm. The moods and motivations a religious orientation produces cast a derivative, lunar light over the solid features of a people's secular life.

•　　•　　•

The anthropological study of religion is therefore a two-stage operation: first, an analysis of the system of meanings embodied in the symbols which make up the religion proper, and, second, the relating of these systems to social-structural and psychological processes. My dissatisfaction with so much of contemporary social anthropological work in religion is not that it concerns itself with the second stage, but that it neglects the first, and in so doing takes for granted what most needs to be elucidated. To discuss the role of ancestor worship in regulating political succession, of sacrificial feasts in defining kinship obligations, of spirit worship in scheduling agricultural practices, of divination in reinforcing social control, or of initiation rites in propelling personality maturation are in no sense unimportant endeavors.... But to attempt them with but the most general, common-sense view of what ancestor worship, animal sacrifice, spirit worship, divination, or initiation rites are as religious patterns seems to me not particularly promising. Only when we have a theoretical analysis of symbolic action comparable in sophistication to that we now have for social and psychological action, will we be able to cope effectively with those aspects of social and psychological life in which religion (or art, or science, or ideology) plays a determinant role.

NOTES

[1] This is *not*, however, to say that everyone in every society does this; for as the immortal Don Marquis once remarked, you don't have to have a soul unless you really want one. The oft-heard generalization (e.g., Kluckhohn, 1953) that religion is a human universal embodies a confusion between the probably true (though on present evidence unprovable) proposition that there is no human society in which cultural patterns that we can, under the present definition or one like it, call religious are totally lacking, and the surely untrue proposition that all men in all societies are, in any meaningful sense of the term, religious. But if the anthropological study of religious commitment is underdeveloped, the anthropological study of religious non-commitment is non-existent. The anthropology of religion will have come of age when some more subtle Malinowski writes a book called "Belief and Unbelief (or even "Faith and Hypocrisy") in a Savage Society."

[2] The term "attitude" as in "aesthetic attitude" (Bell, 1914) or "natural attitude" (Schutz, 1962; the phrase is originally Husserl's) is another, perhaps more common term for what I have here called "perspective." But I have avoided it because of its strong subjectivist connotations, its tendency to place the stress upon a supposed inner state of an actor rather than on a certain sort of relation— a symbolically mediated one—between an actor and a situation. This is not to say, of course, that a phenomenological analysis of religious experience, if cast in inter-subjective, non-transcendental, genuinely scientific terms (see Percy, 1958) is not essential to a full understanding of religious belief, but merely that is not the focus of my concern here. "Outlook," "frame of reference," "frame of mind," "orientation," "stance," "mental set," etc., are other terms sometimes employed, depending upon whether the analyst wishes to stress the social, psychological, or cultural aspects of the matter.

REFERENCES

CRAIK, K. 1952. *The Nature of Explanation.* Cambridge: Cambridge University Press.
EVANS-PRITCHARD, E. E. 1937. *Witchcraft, Oracles and Magic Among the Azande.* Oxford: Clarendon Press.

FIRTH, R. 1951. *Elements of Social Organization*. London: Watts; New York: Philosophical Library.

FORTUNE, R. F. 1935. *Manus Religion*. Philadelphia: American Philosophical Society.

VON FRISCH, K. 1962. Dialects in the Language of the Bees. *Scientific American*, August.

GEERTZ, C. 1958. Ethos, World-View and the Analysis of Sacred Symbols. *Antioch Review*, Winter (1957–1958): 421–437.

———— 1960. *The Religion of Java*. Glencoe, Ill.: Free Press.

———— 1962. The Growth of Culture and the Evolution of Mind. In J. Scher (ed.), *Theories of the Mind*. New York: Free Press, pp. 713–740.

———— 1964a. Ideology as a Cultural System. In D. Apter (ed.), *Ideology of Discontent*. New York: Free Press.

———— 1964b. 'Internal Conversion' in Contemporary Bali. In J. Bastin and R. Roolvink (eds.), *Malayan and Indonesian Studies*. Oxford: Oxford University Press, pp. 282–302.

GOODY, J. 1961. Religion and Ritual: The Definition Problem. *British Journal of Sociology* **12**: 143–164.

HOROWITZ, N. H. 1956. The Gene. *Scientific American*, February.

JAMES, W. 1904. *The Principles of Psychology*. New York: Holt, 2 vols.

JANOWITZ, M. 1963. Anthropology and the Social Sciences. *Current Anthropology* **4**: 139, 146–154.

KLUCKHOHN, C. 1949. The Philosophy of the Navaho Indians. In F. S. C. Northrop (ed.), *Ideological Differences and World Order*. New Haven: Yale University Press, pp. 356–384.

———— 1953. Universal Categories of Culture. In A. L. Kroeber (ed.), *Anthropology Today*. Chicago: University of Chicago Press, pp. 507–523.

KLUCKHOHN, C., and LEIGHTON, D. 1946. *The Navaho*. Cambridge, Mass.: Harvard University Press.

LANGER, S. 1953. *Feeling and Form*. New York: Scribner's.

———— 1960. *Philosophy in a New Key*. Fourth Edition. Cambridge, Mass.: Harvard University Press.

———— 1962. *Philosophical Sketches*. Baltimore: Johns Hopkins.

LEACH, E. R. 1954. *Political Systems of Highland Burma*. London: Bell; Cambridge, Mass.: Harvard University Press.

LÉVY-BRUHL, L. 1926. *How Natives Think*. New York: Knopf.

LIENHARDT, G. 1961. *Divinity and Experience*. Oxford: Clarendon Press.

LORENZ, K. 1952. *King Solomon's Ring*. London: Methuen.

LOWIE, R. H. 1924. *Primitive Religion*. New York: Boni and Liveright.

MACINTYRE, A. 1957. The Logical Status of Religious Belief. In A. MacIntyre (ed.), *Metaphysical Beliefs*. London: SCM Press, pp. 167–211.

MALINOWSKI, B. 1948. *Magic, Science and Religion*. Boston: Beacon Press.

NADEL, S. F. 1957. Malinowski on Magic and Religion. In R. Firth (ed.), *Man and Culture*. London: Routledge & Kegan Paul, pp. 189–208.

REICHARD, G. 1950. *Navaho Religion*. New York: Pantheon, 2 vols.

RYLE, G. 1949. *The Concept of Mind*. London: Hutchinson; New York: Barnes and Noble.

SANTAYANA, G. 1905–1906. *Reason in Religion*. Vol. 2 of *The Life of Reason, or The Phases of Human Progress*. London: Constable; New York: Scribner's.

SCHUTZ, A. 1962. *The Problem of Social Reality* (vol. I. of *Collected Papers*). The Hague: Martinus Nijhoff.

SINGER, M. 1955. The Cultural Pattern of Indian Civilization. *Far Eastern Quarterly* **15**: 23–36.

———— 1958. The Great Tradition in a Metropolitan Center: Madras. In M. Singer (ed.), *Traditional India*. Philadelphia: American Folklore Society, pp. 140–182.

✛•✛•✛•✛•✛•✛•✛•✛•✛•✛•✛•✛•✛•✛•✛

Religion as Autobiography and Story

MICHAEL NOVAK

A purely pragmatic civilization assigns me a social security number. Key decisions about my future are made by men who shuffle in their hands a set of papers on which, at various times, the standard measures of my performance have been recorded. They read brief recommendations about the way I appeared to virtual strangers at various times. I am known from outside, given a character, assigned a place and a role. Those others think they *know* me. More or less "objectively."

And often, when I try to be "objective" about myself I know myself rather in the way that they know me. I see myself through other people's eyes. But that objective portrait "out there" can be shattered so easily by one outrageous act in an otherwise droning life. "I never would have thought he was capable of. . . ." The images one has lived out until now are subject to change. Until provoked, perhaps, by a time of great danger and enormous social change, mysteries hidden deeply in the self await their liberation. What we have been we do not have to remain.

On the other hand, most personal growth is organic, continuous, gradual. Humans grow, like oaks, in silence and almost imperceptibly. We invent our identities and fashion our characters through hundreds of thousands of tiny gestures, intonations, acts. People often look alike, seem all the same, appear as if of equal substance; but then tragedy, calamity, or necessity strikes and thin surfaces are sheared away. We see, then, who stands on a base of thousands of repeated acts, fashioned hard, firm, unyielding, and who stands on the crumbling fungus of appearances. Langdon Gilkey's marvelous book, *Shantung Compound*,[1] shows how many Christians who had preached eloquently were stripped by the pressures of a Japanese concentration camp to their petty souls. When the test comes, as it inevitably comes for all, the chaff is beaten away, the cheap metals are melted off, and only hard grains of wheat, only the gold, still stand.

Religion, some think, is believing in doctrines, belonging to an organization, saving one's soul through an attitude (trust in God) or works. But there are countless ways of living out the same doctrines, many different ways of

From Michael Novak, "Religion as Autobiography," *Ascent of the Mountain, Flight of the Dove*, pp. 44–49, 50–52. Copyright 1971 by Michael Novak. Reprinted with the permission of Harper & Row, Publishers, Inc.

Michael Novak is consultant for the humanities at the Rockefeller Foundation.

"belonging," an endless number of ways of misperceiving one's own soul. That is why it seems better to imagine religion as the telling of a story with one's life. Willy-nilly, each person's life does tell a story. Often the stories are pointless, meander, seem to have no single thread or set of threads. "Purity of heart is to will one thing" (Kierkegaard).[2] Few persons tell one single story. Few lives are wholly integrated. In lives as in works of art there are few masterpieces. Most lives are somewhat stale, flat, dispersed, undirected.

Still, even dispersal is a story and an astute novelist might untangle its many threads. To trace the history of acts of will, the history of choices made (even those made not by choosing but by drifting), is to trace a voyage, a pilgrimage, a search in a labyrinth, perhaps an endless struggle like that of Sisyphus. No man or woman does everything at once, chooses infinitely, acts with infinite scope; men and women are finite. Their freedom is a selection among possibilities. Acting, they define a story.

In this weak sense, all men and women are religious. The completed lives of each trace out a story, whose implications reveal what they took the world in which they lived to be, who they thought they were, what in their actions they actually cared about. Action is a declaration of faith: one cannot act without implicitly imagining the shape of the world, the significance of one's own role, the place at which struggle is effectively joined. It is not true that faith, creed, convictions come first and then action. It is rather true that we are already acting long before we are clear about our ultimate convictions. More important still: our actions, reflected on, reveal what it is we really care about, more accurately than our words or aspirations about what we would like to care about. We do not know what our deepest views and root concerns may be until we see them bloom into action.

Action is the starting place of inquiry. Action reveals being. Action is our most reliable mode of philosophizing. In action we declare our cosmology, our politics, our convictions, our identity. Who am I? I am what I do.

The word "religious" is used, then, in two quite different senses. In its most neutral sense it simply means that a human life is a declaration of identity, significance, role, place: all action is the living out of a story in a cosmos. In this sense, whether they are aware of it or not, all men and women live out a commitment, a faith, a selection. In its second, more normative sense, religion is the awareness of the story dimension of life: it is an awe, reverence, wonder at the risk and terror of human freedom. It is an awakening from a merely routine, pragmatic round of actions and a sense of being responsible for one's own identity and for one's own involvement with the identities of others.

The two fundamental religious questions are: Who am I? and Who are we, we human beings under these stars? The person who treats his life as taken-for-granted, and unreflectively defines it wholly in terms of its instrumental functions (eating, sleeping, making friends and influencing people, storing up goods), is virtually nonreligious; his story lacks awareness of the choices he is in fact making. It is the sense of choice, of selection, of commitment, of contingent existence that gives rise to the primal religious sense.

There is, of course, a third and stronger sense for the word "religious." According to this sense, not only does a man or a woman in fact live out a story; not only is a man or a woman aware of the alternatives among which he or she is choosing; but also, a man or a woman adds a *religious interpretation* to what each and others are doing. Each interprets the operations each is performing (of wonder, inquiry, commitment, longing) as signs that each is in the presence of—in Dante's words—"the Love that moves the Sun and all the Stars." That is, they take humans in their striving and freedom as a clue to the central significance of the universe, interpreting it in the image of the human person. They address the moving power and presence of existence as "Thou." They see the world not in the metaphor of objectivity, mechanism, science, but in the metaphor of persons. Although the unseen, untouched, to which they address their "Thou" is, they know, unnamable (we cannot know him/it as we know other things we name), they may be willing to place the letters GOD where in normal speech they would speak of a person.

This third meaning of religion is often taken to be the basic, traditional, orthodox, and normative meaning. But it seems wiser to take the first meaning as our own basic term. *In fact*, humans live out a commitment, select their own identity. In religious studies, one ought to study all such possibilities, including the unreflective, self-satisfied, pragmatic one. There are people whose metaphysics are, in effect, the comfortable feeling they have just after a heavy lunch; they see no need to raise ontological questions. They live and they die; and they think persons who torment themselves about ultimate questions both waste their time and overlook the pleasantness of the present. To such people, Jesus and the prophets addressed some of their most moving discourses. Among such people, the Buddhist "way" begins. From one point of view, such persons live in a prereligious state; from another, they too are freely declaring their own identity.

In any case, each person can become aware of the story each is telling with his or her own life. Without such self-awareness, religious studies are pointless: like persons deliberately starving themselves at a banquet table. To enter upon religious studies perceptively is to make one's own story conscious to oneself.

Such questions as the following help to uncover one's own story: What are the experiences of my life which, when I look back upon them, most tell me who I am? This emphasis upon *experiences* is important. Often our experiences have been far richer than the images or concepts by which we earlier dealt with them. Their original fullness, charged with new, conflicting experiences, often lies buried in memory, awaiting our exploration. The search for self takes place in large part through memory.

What has been my history in the use of the word "God"? Our notions of self and of God are correlatives; and a surprisingly fruitful way to uncover some things about one's own identity is to explore one's resistances and attractions to the ways one has encountered the uses of the word "God."

To tell a story with one's life is simply to act. One may be oblivious to one's own story or quite aware of it. One may be, as it were, the author or the reader: creating it, shaping it, or, on the other hand, looking back afterward on what has been happening. Since we are far from wholly being masters of ourselves and our destiny, it is always true that the significance of the story we are trying to tell in large part escapes us. It may not be quite as we imagine it. The image of the story in our consciousness may not be very like what we are actually living out. The impact of our story on others, or its meaning in the context in which we live it, may not be as we imagine it. "There's a divinity that shapes our ends, Rough-hew them how we will" (*Hamlet*, V. 2).

What David Riesman has called "inner-directed" people tend to be quite stubborn and self-directing in the story they are trying to live out. "Other-directed" people tend to let the story be shaped by the audience.[3] It is quite American "to hang loose," "to play it by ear," "to wait and see what develops," "to take it easy," "to play it cool." In a highly organized society, where roles and stories are quite clearly tracked out, individuals in self-defense try to work out their lives in the interstices. It is risky to have too strong-minded a story of one's own; irresistible forces collide with immovable objects. The result is an extraordinary amount of drift, lack of self-direction, waiting for things to happen. Americans do not so much tell stories with their lives as expect to be amazed by the unsolicited things that happen to them. A mobile society fills the vacuum where self-direction used to be.

.   .   .

How does one acquire a story? The culture in which one is born already has an image of time, of the self, of heroism, of ambition, of fulfillment.[4] It burns its heroes and archetypes deeply into one's psyche. The tendencies and fears of one's parents, the figures one hears described in church, the living force of teachers and uncles and grandparents and neighbors, the example of companions along the way, the tales read in books or visualized in legend, cinema, the arts: all such influences impress one's imagination with possible courses of action, possible styles of life. One economic class visualizes certain possibilities and certain styles, another visualizes another. The Catholic way is not identical with the Methodist, Lutheran, or Presbyterian way. The Jewish sensibility and imagination project a unique way of life. The Buddhist does not imagine the basic story of the noble man in the same terms—or in the same context—as the Christian. The American style differs from the Italian style. In a word, cultural stories as well as personal stories are in question.

A lower-middle-class male in the United States, for example, whose father is a construction worker, mailman, gas station attendant, owner of a small business—a man who probably did not go to college and is a Veteran of Foreign Wars—was probably brought up to live out some variant of the following story. Life is hard, and its few rewards go to those who achieve public respectability, who work hard, and who are willing to sacrifice themselves for the community—to work to put themselves through school or to help support their family, to give up two to four years of their youth to demanding military service and perhaps the risk of losing their life, and to have nightmares about a future of failure and lack of status and security. It is, perhaps, to labor under a name that is not Anglo-Saxon but "foreign," and to feel the suspicion and distrust of those who speak more smoothly and who seem to know what to do on any social occasion. It is to be less than certain of oneself when dealing in ideas, historical parallels, information about other cultures. It is to imagine culture, education, and morality as a matter of absorption, docility, and conformity rather than as a matter of alienation and dissent. It is to suppose that radical social change is not possible in this life, and that God is the God of good order, the God of stability, the God of peace. Life is lived mainly for eternity, not for evanescent, passing political changes. By and large, authorities know best. One is endlessly cynical about the persons who fill public office. But the office deserves respect, as if it were from God himself. The story of the good man is the story of affirmation, docility, cooperation with authority and custom, good will, and optimism—not the story of dissent, disobedience, change. . . .

In a word, the woman who wishes to understand what stories she is living out does well to ask herself what it means to be brought up as an American, of a given social class, ethnic background, religious or secular tradition. All such cultural forces generate their own way of structuring human life. All have their own set of stories which they invite their young to live out, some stories for men only, some for women.

In a pluralistic culture, in which many stories are simultaneously and powerfully presented to the young, a certain confusion, malaise, and loss of confidence often result. No one story commands allegiance. Action, therefore, lacking a story to give it significance, seems pointless. Why bother to do anything at all? What is worth trying to become? The young often begin to sleep a lot.

Not to have any story to live out is to experience nothingness: the primal formlessness of human life below the threshold of narrative structuring. Why become anything at all? Does anything make any difference? Why not simply die? . . . Or drift: which is a death-in-life.

NOTES

[1] New York: Harper & Row, 1966.

[2] *Purity of Heart* (New York: Harper Torchbooks, 1966).

[3] With NATHAN GLAZER and REUEL DENNY, *The Lonely Crowd* (Garden City, N.Y.: Doubleday Anchor Books, 1953), abridged by the authors.

[4] See, e.g., H. RICHARD NIEBUHR, *The Responsible Self: An Essay in Christian Moral Philosophy* (New York: Harper & Row, 1963), especially pp. 48–54 and 152–153; also ERICH AUERBACH, *Mimesis: The Representation of Reality in Western Literature*, trans. Willard Trask (Garden City, N.Y.: Doubleday Anchor Books, 1959), especially Ch. 1.

⊹⋅⊹⋅⊹⋅⊹⋅⊹⋅⊹⋅⊹⋅⊹⋅⊹⋅⊹⋅⊹⋅⊹⋅⊹⋅⊹⋅⊹⋅

Ritual Among Track Athletes

REID COLE

Even in this scientific age when man likes to think he lives by reason, he faces the world with the help of symbols—I shall call the ones I describe superstitions—on which he may not fully reflect but which help him feel safe and secure in an unpredictable and sometimes hostile world.

As an athlete I am particularly aware of the little idiosyncrasies of the athlete prior to competition. Each athlete goes through his own personalized warmup ritual.

"Basically, then, myth and ritual reduce anxiety, or the anticipation of disaster."[1] In the highly competitive world of track and field when any number of unexpected results could occur, each event is a very stressful situation for the competing individual. It is very seldom that an athlete does not become highly anxious (although this anxiety can be used for the athlete's benefit precisely with the help of the warmup ritual).

In preparation for this paper I interviewed twelve of my teammates to get an idea of the many warmup ritual techniques. My sampling included both American and foreign athletes (one Peruvian, four Swedes, one Canadian, six Americans, including two blacks and one chicano).

Hargrove says of ritual, "All societies appear to have some forms of repeated symbolic behavior that is tied by explanatory verbalization to their basic way of understanding human existence."[2] Although, at first glance, this quote seems to deal with more important basic aspects of life, it really does explain the behavior of the athlete. Our lives are, after all, made up of everyday, seemingly trivial situations. It seems to me that athletic competition is a more unusually symbolic representation of the strivings of every man. Participating in a track meet, for example, is like living in a miniature life. All the human emotions—joy and sorrow, vanity, greed, jealousy and fear—are in play and are magnified out of their usual daily proportions. The human need to win or succeed, and therefore be happy and satisfied with one's self, is so important that men will resort to all sorts of measures to insure that goal.

For the most part the people I interviewed were cooperative and willing to reveal their own special formula for success; still I sense that every one of them held back certain ritualistic behavior which he probably felt was too superstitious and perhaps foolish to reveal. (I had previously observed certain repetitive compulsive acts by certain individuals and when I pressed them

---

Reid Cole, a member of the University of New Mexico class of 1973, was an all-American half-miler during his junior and senior years.

they reluctantly admitted that these things were part of their ritual. I am quite sure that there were many other behaviors that I did not notice.)

I found that some athletes begin their ritual preparations days ahead of the scheduled competition, so I concentrated not only on activity immediately prior to the event itself but also on long-range warm-up starting as much as a week ahead of time.

One of my main interests was the part that God played in the athlete's ritual. I found a marked contrast between the American and European athletes' relationship to God. Not one European that I talked with prayed to a Supreme Being before or after competition, while an overwhelming majority (all but one) of the Americans admitted to praying for strength before the race or for solace or in gratitude after the race. (They said they only asked for strength to finish the race and not to win the race.)

The use of various mechanisms as ritual is very obvious in the athletic world. For example, there is a member of a track team—I will call him W— who frequently employs a reaction ritual. "In those areas of life where it is most difficult to predict what is going to happen next or what can be done about it, we can in reaction so rigidly structure our behavior that every detail is predictable."[3] When W feels particularly unsure of himself, when he knows that he is probably going to lose, he begins to boast that he has the race sewed up. All of the other members on the track team know that this is ridiculous, and I think that even W secretly knows it is impossible for him to win. I think he needs this defense mechanism, this self-assurance to bolster his shaky confidence. This behavior is an integral part of W's ritual as well. Another example of reaction ritual can be seen in the "psych techniques" of the black sprinters. A black sprinter running against someone he fears or respects will affect confidence—singing as he sets his blocks, jumping the gun to make opponents nervous, strutting self-assuredly past an opponent with a disdainful stare—getting across the subtle message "I'm gonna kick your ass" (when he probably secretly fears it's his ass that's going to get the kicking).

Another ritualized mechanism often used is introjection, "accomplished through identification with mythic heroes, sometimes to the extent of providing ritual opportunities to reenact their deeds and postures."[4] I myself, for example, have admired, almost worshipped Jim Ryun (world record holder in the mile and the 880) since my high school days. I've read books on his life and running techniques and have incorporated his techniques into my own ritual. As my hero, he was more a source of inspiration than actual information, however. Even now when he is no longer a celebrity on TV and in magazines, but a person with whom I have run in meets, I still look up to him. A reversal of this situation exists with one of my teammates who is younger and so far less successful in meets than I am. During the premeet warmup, G follows me around imitating my every action. Ironically he does not particularly care for me off the track, so I suppose you could say I am more a source of information than inspiration for him.

The shoe industry takes full advantage of this ritual mechanism, introjection. Every year they give away thousands of pairs of shoes to track stars, all-Americans, and Olympians. Young inspired runners, knowing that their heroes achieve success wearing "x-brand" shoes, for example, rush out and spend huge amounts of money on that brand. The shoe industry has profited well from its initial investment.

Hargrove, citing Homans, lists seven basic elements of ritual.[5] These can be easily seen in the track warmup ritual.

"1. Primary anxiety—a recognition of one's inability to achieve certain ends through ordinary knowledge and skills." Even if an athlete has worked out hard for eight to nine months in preparation for the outdoor track season and is in top condition, and if he has the *physical* potential to win every race, unless he is emotionally and mentally prepared through the security that his ritual can provide, it is possible he could lose every race. It has been said that the mental part of track is 90 percent of success or failure and the seemingly important physical is worth a mere 10 percent (although being in top physical condition is a major part of that mental confidence).

"2. Primary ritual—the performance of actions which, though they have no direct effect in achieving the end, do relieve the anxiety." It is amazing to realize how silly and superstitious most of the people I talked to (including myself) are about little things that are probably irrelevant to the outcome of an event. One person, for example, refuses to wear shoes that aren't of the lace type. Another insists on wearing shoes that he wore when he won the week before; still another never wears shoes that he wore in practice (I suppose this change makes him feel confident and special or official, in contrast to an ordinary day). There are many idiosyncrasies, that are not only unbeneficial but are actually harmful, such as eating whole sugar right before running. Some think it gives them quick energy when actually it just sits in their stomachs and will produce acute side aches. Even after being told the dangers, they still continue this practice.

"3. Secondary anxiety—the fear that primary ritual was not done correctly, nor the tradition properly followed." There is a great reluctance on the athlete's part to omit any part of his ritual or to make any new additions. For example, most athletes practice sexual restraint the night before a track meet. If an athlete breaks this rule, he is apt to worry that his performance will not be up to par. The worry, not the sex, will probably be the cause of any failure. Another thing most athletes try to do is get a good night's sleep (or not oversleep, depending on the particular ritual of the athlete). If by some accident the specified number of hours of sleep was not obtained, the athlete will probably feel tired and run-down and generally "psyched out." Also, adding any new part of the warmup ritual is a very careful and selective process. I, for example, have just learned a new "scientific" method of warmup before a race. I know it works; it has worked for me. But I still fall back on the old tried and true traditions that have always worked in the past.

"4. Secondary ritual—ceremonies of purification or expiation to compensate for possible errors in primary ritual." Although the ideal is to follow a ritual to the letter, if deviations occur, compensations must be made. If, for example, an athlete did not get the right amount of sleep, he will be more careful with himself, doing less warmup jogging or stretching to preserve his strength. Or if he has eaten too late (usually tries to eat four hours before the meet), he will try to compensate by walking around more to try to digest the food faster.

"5. Rationalization—reasons given for the specific form of primary and secondary ritual." Even though a great deal of the ritual is based on superstition, talking with an athlete, one realizes that they do not find their ritual irrational at all. For example, a teammate feels that eggs are bad for him before a race, and I feel, equally as strongly, that they are good for me. We obviously base our beliefs on our own past experiences rather than any scientific evidence about the effect of eggs on the runner. I do not suppose any of us would openly admit that we base our precious rituals on anything irrational. We have to believe our methods really work.

"6. Symbolization—reference to the connection between the rituals and primary myths of the society." American society has built up its own cultural myth of the all-American boy, and these traditions have been socialized into us more than we know. The Protestant Ethic, the belief that hard work will achieve success, is acted out in the athlete's ritual. Dedication is thought to be a major ingredient in any successful track career. Therefore most American athletes do not drink or smoke. Our European teammates, however, see nothing wrong in drinking during the week or even smoking (field event men), as long as neither is done in excess. Another belief that is peculiarly American is that long hair is a handicap to the dedicated runner (although many Americans probably feel any athlete who has long hair is not dedicated anyway).

"7. Function—incorporating all these consequences of myth and ritual we have been discussing." The final result of all of these practices is a complex symbolic way of dealing with the highly anxious competitive situation. Even though the athlete may not even be aware of parts of his ritual, or why he does the things he is aware of, the ritual still makes him feel more confident and secure for his moment of truth.

Not until I started this essay did I begin to realize the important part ritual plays in preparing for a competitive event (which is odd, because I follow this ritual, almost without thinking, every day of my life). This dedication (and almost mindless adherence) to a routine touches almost every phase of an athlete's life. In fact, the rituals I have described come together to form a whole symbolic world that becomes the real world of the track athlete.

NOTES

[1] BARBARA W. HARGROVE, *Reformation of the Holy: A Sociology of Religion* (Philadelphia: F. A. Davis, 1971), p. 31.

[2] Ibid., p. 29.

[3] Ibid., p. 30.

[4] Ibid.

[5] The seven functions cited in the remainder of this essay are listed in Hargrove, pp. 32–33.

TOWARD A NEW SOCIOLOGY OF RELIGION

RICHARD K. FENN

To what extent does religion in the most advanced societies have major functions for the *total* social system? The way most contemporary sociologists would probably answer the question is summed up in Levy's statement that "religion in the most general sense is never separated from government" (1966: 616). But Levy also admits that this question of functional inter-dependence has not yet received the attention it deserves, in part, perhaps, because it is so complex that it requires expertise both in the history of religions and in the social sciences (1966: 610). Clearly, then, the problem of the interdependence between religion and whole societies is one of the major pieces of unfinished investigation in the sociology of religion. The way to begin this investigation is to examine the assumptions which underlie some of the current thinking in the field.

One assumption which appears in sociological analyses of religion maintains that religion supports the cultural integration of whole societies. However valid this assumption may have been in less differentiated societies, it can be argued that conditions of advanced differentiation make it unlikely, if not impossible, for cultural integration to develop around any set of religious symbols. The "end of ideology" thesis means just this: "partial ideologies" may develop around separate sets of interests in advanced societies, but a "total ideology" cannot now develop which could mobilize the passion and the intelligence of an entire population (Bell, 1962: 405).

The possibility, then, that *religious symbols* can still provide the basis for cultural integration is diminished by several factors, each of which reflects differentiation at one level or another of modern societies. Religious values seem to have little *demonstrable* relationship to what people actually do in work and politics. The President of the U.S. may as well be a Quaker as a Catholic; a computer programmer may as well be a Zen Buddhist as a Protestant. In either case political or occupational performance cannot be de-duced from the religious values of the actor. Looking at differentiation *within* the culture, we find individuals exposed through multiple memberships to alternatives of religious belief and practice; religious pluralism acts in such a way as to make it impossible for any set of religious symbols to acquire

From *Journal for the Scientific Study of Religion*, 11, no. 1 (March 1972): 16–32. Reprinted with the permission of the publisher and the author.

Richard K. Fenn is a member of the Sociology Department at the University of Maine at Orono a monopoly of authority within the culture (Berger, 1967). These are conditions, moreover, which have been found in Festinger's experimental work to be *least* favorable to the development of a uniformity of opinion (Festinger, 1950).

The notion that a return to a normative order based on religious beliefs and values is still possible even in advanced societies seems to depend on a second assumption: that a "cybernetic hierarchy" exists which keeps religious symbols in creative tension with ongoing social change. An equally strong case can be made, however, that a point of no return has been reached in which religious change may occur quite independently of changes in the rest of the social system. Change in religious symbolization, that is, may develop without any impact on other areas of the society. Conversely, the fact that occupational, educational, and political systems in advanced society have achieved considerable independence from direct religious control may well reduce to near zero the level of interdependence between social factors and religious change. It may therefore be quite appropriate to expect even a widespread charismatic development in religion without assuming that it will have any implications whatsoever for the normative order of the *whole* society.

This is not to say that religion will have no functions in advanced societies. On the contrary, religion may serve for a while longer to define ethnic or traditional boundaries or to legitimate the demands of various groups for local control over educational and political institutions. And it seems entirely likely that religion will serve expressive functions for individuals and groups. Such nonrational aspects of individual behavior as play, or the exploration of human relationships, or activities intended to relieve boredom may find expression in religious symbols. Nor is it to say that churchmen and theologians will not continue to anticipate a renewed cultural integration under the aegis of religious symbols. It is to argue, however, that the conditions for renewed cultural integration under religious auspices are not perceptible at the present.

A third assumption to be examined is that societies require a religious basis for cultural integration if they are to survive. This assumption may well be justified in the case of societies which have difficulty in motivating and training an adequate work force; it may also be justified in the case of societies which are unable to satisfy popular demands for participation and consumption. It can be argued, however, that the U.S., at least, does not have these problems, but rather their opposites. Automation gives to modern societies the task of "cooling out" portions of the population that are superfluous to the work force; and modern societies generally can rely on the techniques of adult socialization rather than on religious training to prepare individuals for participation in the occupational system. Finally, legitimacy in these most advanced societies depends on the capacity to meet most popular demands for participation in the polity and for high levels of consumption rather than on the manipulation of religious symbols. Cultural integration on the level of religious beliefs and values, then, is under these conditions no longer either possible or even necessary for the maintenance of motivation and order.

. . .

Although the religious situation is therefore enormously complex, and the crystal ball of prediction somewhat cloudy, it is reasonable to predict that religion in the future will increasingly develop along lines that are independent of any individual's or group's position in the social system. We need to go beyond the level of arguing that religion either enables an individual to legitimate his privileges or gives him psychic compensation for his losses. To put it another way: the individual who does not invest his work or his citizenship with personal or moral significance is not only "alienated" but also well adapted to the conditions of role-differentiation and mobility. He effectively compartmentalizes the sacred from the secular aspects of his role-set and demands from the world of work and politics only the effective delivery of goods and services. Under these conditions certain types of sectarian religion appear unlikely. One would expect not the "revolutionary" or "conversionist" forms of sectarian religion (to use Wilson's typology, 1969: 224–225), but rather expect spiritualism and scientology, or churchly religion devoted to personal growth and interpersonal experience, to predominate eventually over various forms of religious protest. And the constituency for these types of religiosity need not come primarily from the deprived or from the disenchanted, but only from those who wish to engage in nonrational behavior, in action which is its own justification rather than a means to another end.

In short, if religion continues to have functions in modern society, it will be necessary to specify their scope with considerable precision. Are these functions relevant to the whole society or only to particular groups or strata? And is it not possible that religion is being shoved to the periphery of the social system, where it enables personalities to maintain their boundaries with society, and where it expresses primarily the unsocialized aspects of the personality and the nonrational interests of the individual?

The remainder of the discussion will attempt to answer the hypothetical questions raised above concerning the functional interdependence of religion with total societies. The major assumption, viz. that a religious foundation to the normative order of modern societies is both possible and necessary will be assessed for its goodness of fit to the conditions of modernized societies. It will be necessary to defer a second set of questions, which inquire into the actual functions of religion for particular individuals or strata, to a later context, although some propositions regarding them will be suggested at the conclusion of this discussion.

The answers to these questions depend in part on the assumptions which we hold regarding the functional interdependence of religion with modern societies. The remainder of this paper, then, will explore in more detail the argument outlined above, viz. that differentiation in modern societies makes it impossible—and unnecessary—for religion to provide the basis for cultural integration.

THE POSSIBILITY OF CULTURAL INTEGRATION

It may be helpful to clarify at this point what is meant by cultural integration. If the basic elements of any culture are beliefs, values, and norms, cultures which are highly integrated would be those in which there is uniformity of agreement in the population about these elements. Societies may therefore be ranked along a continuum from the most to the least integrated. At one end of the spectrum are those societies which have the highest degree of uniformity regarding the population's beliefs, values, and the norms for behavior. Conversely, at the other end of the spectrum, are those societies which have the least uniformity regarding these cultural elements. If societies which have little or no consensus regarding beliefs, values, and norms are relatively stable, it is reasonable to assume that they are highly regulated. On the other hand, it is not necessary to assume that societies with high levels of cultural integration are also orderly and stable.

Cultural integration may be further analyzed in terms of the intensity and the scope with which the various beliefs, values, and norms are held by members of the population. The dimension of intensity has to do with the salience of particular beliefs and values for the decisions made by individuals in the routine performance of their various roles. The dimension of scope refers to the relevance of cultural elements to the entire set of roles held by an individual.

. . . It appears to be characteristic of modern societies to transform questions of ultimate concern or of political commitment into questions of proper management and administration. The "quality of life" in modern societies, at the very least a crucial political issue in the 1970's, is likely to be defined in terms of the standard of living and of the effectiveness of law enforcement: in terms of facts which can be verified and performances which can be predicted. Health care, to take a less obvious example, may increasingly be discussed less in value-laden terms, such as the "sacred" doctor-patient relationship, than in terms of the effective delivery of medical services to the entire population.

The relevance of major American values to the organized work and politics of the society is at the very best problematical. Critics of the mass society tend to agree with critics of traditional religiosity that there is little "goodness to fit" between many of our values and the actual social organization of an advanced industrialized and urban society (Mills, 1959: 299 ff.; Cox, 1965). Parsons himself calls attention to the fact that one cannot deduce the actual obligations of a role from the values which cluster around it, or indeed actual behavior from the norms of a particular role. Personal characteristics and situational pressures take precedence over the generalized prescriptions and values of the culture in the performance of actual tasks (Parsons, 1968). In the same vein, Levy argues that there is in modern societies a wide gap between myth and reality, the ideal and the actual (1966: 22–30). One has only to think of such incongruities as the relationship between the values of a Protestant work ethic and the realities of population expansion and automation, or the relationship between traditional values surrounding the kinship system or the neighborhood and the realities of geographic and social mobility, to appreciate the argument that many of the most strongly held values in American society are irrelevant to the major political or productive tasks of the society. Under these conditions, then, pressures toward cultural uniformity will weaken and the level of possible integration diminish accordingly.

. . . In modernized societies with increasing degrees of equality, however, with institutionalized pluralism and multiple group memberships, pressures toward uniformity, if they are present at all, are likely to be limited to achieving agreement on the facts relevant to political or to economic decision-making. The critical question for modern societies, then, is the rate at which it can meet the demands of its citizens for equality. Too slow a rate creates social protests which challenge the legitimacy of the society. The attempts to support that legitimacy through restoring cultural uniformity (i.e., a moral or normative order) generate further resistance from groups seeking to defend their ideal as well as their material interests. . . .

THE NECESSITY FOR CULTURAL INTEGRATION

One way to conceptualize the necessity for cultural integration is to return to the problem of order. Does order in a society depend on normative order, i.e., on a set of norms which is supported by an integrated and widely accepted system of beliefs and values? To put it another way: can centralized administration, intelligence agencies, and police forces maintain order effectively in the long run without the socialization process which depends on religious, educational and therapeutic institutions? While this is clearly too complex a question to be disposed of in a few paragraphs, it is nevertheless possible to suggest ways in which the question can be answered.

The question, in fact, has two parts. The first has to do with the integrating function of cultural symbols, while the second concerns the level of equity in the society. The integrating function of cultural symbols refers particularly to the effect of cultural elements on the motivations and commitments of individual workers and citizens. What is it that enables people to get up in the morning and go to work without intolerable levels of strain in their personalities? To put it more positively, what is it that enables individuals to invest their personalities in their work and to view their occupation as being worthwhile? In terms of the political subsystem of the society, one may ask what it is that attracts and holds the loyalty and commitment of citizens to the institutions of government. This, of course, is the problem of legitimacy. In Parsonian imagery, a society depends on underlying, or latent, commitments which can be guaranteed only if the society is well regulated and has a moral order with religious beliefs and values guaranteeing the trustworthiness and desirability of the social system.

The second question, that of the level of equity in the social system, is too complex to be considered in this discussion. The problem is one of specifying the effect of cultural disintegration on the maintenance of social order under the conditions of greater or lesser equality among social groups. Eisenstadt (1964), for instance, argues that the mobilization of many elements of a society into the body politic can create severe disorder if there is no over-arching cultural system which integrates the diverse groups into a single moral community. It is not clear, however, whether the disruptive effects of inadequate cultural integration depends on the claims of various groups for more socioeconomic as well as political equality. Glazer (1969) has noted, furthermore, that the demand of certain ethnic groups for local control of political and educational institutions has little to do with the relative affluence or deprivation of these groups. Given the theoretical and methodological un-certainties of this problem, then, it is wiser to defer a treatment of this aspect of the problem to another context.

There are trends in the more advanced societies which suggest that their requirements for production and administration may increasingly be satisfied with proportionately fewer members of the population in the labor force....

A society in which many jobs are nonessential, and in which almost as many persons either ignore or leave the occupational system as enter it, is clearly moving toward a dual system in which many persons are unrelated to or at best tenuously placed within the labor force. In modern societies there is evidently more and more work to be done, but there are more than enough individuals to do it.

Finally, it is necessary to revise the estimate to which motivational commit-ment on the part of individuals is needed in societies which enjoy both affluence and a complex division of labor. One effect of the process of auto-mation is to lower the proportion of the civilian population which it is neces-sary to mobilize into the labor force. With cultural pluralism and the passage of modern societies into automation and affluence there is at least the possi-bility of a system with chronically low levels of occupational commitment. Indeed, it is when unusually large numbers of individuals insist on partici-pating in the labor force or in the decision-making process that tensions are likely to ensue. A decrease in the levels of motivational commitment may, therefore, well be a positive source of order in modern social systems.

LEGITIMACY

It follows from these preliminary changes in basic assumptions that in the most modernized societies strains may increasingly be met without in-voking the most general cultural symbols available to the society. The question of legitimacy tends to be solved on a lower level of generality.

Conflicts in modern societies are more likely to be discussed in terms of priorities for public policy than in terms of the basic values of the society itself. Debate over national goals is reduced to questions of timing, of priorities within an area of apparently common agreement. Similarly, the legitimacy of existing social arrangements will increasingly depend not on traditional notions of what is right, but on their effectiveness in meeting basic human needs. The demands of the political and economic marketplace, as determined by public opinion polls and patterns of consumption, are the basis on which leaders and managers will make their case for the legitimacy of their position. Whether these "needs" are regarded as genuinely basic or as being the artificial creation of the technology of marketing is a question requiring separate treatment. In any case, the holders of power will base their claims for legitimation on their effectiveness in meeting the conscious needs of the public(s). Finally, to lessen strains in certain segments of the society by introducing new policies and programs, politicians and managers may appeal for legitimacy to their conformity with proper procedures for deciding upon and effecting such changes, rather than to a more general or traditional court of appeal. It is possible, for instance, for an entrepreneurial society to transform itself into a form of state-directed capitalism if the proper electoral and legislative procedures are followed along the way.

Neither religious nor moral values, but duly established priorities, effectiveness, and propriety become the primary sources of legitimacy. As none of these refer to general ideological or evaluational elements in the traditional religious or civic culture, there is clearly no need to invoke a concept of cybernetic hierarchy to explain the process by which legitimacy is maintained. Even modern societies, of course, require that tensions be released and that the social order be seen as at least provisionally satisfying. Despite this perennial requirement, however, it does not seem unreasonable to assume that such societies can dispense with cultural integration.

To begin with, the very fact of differentiation in the culture and in the institutions of modern societies creates a potential for the release of tensions which far exceeds that of less differentiated societies. On the one hand, the taste for cultural variety is far more easily satisfied under the conditions of pluralism than under those of a more coherent normative order; on the other, aspirations for recognition and status which are frustrated in one area may be satisfied elsewhere in another institution or hierarchy of prestige. Pluralism, with its attendant relativity in values and increase in individual discretion, is itself a mechanism for the release of tensions in modern societies.

If under modern conditions a society which is integrated by means of a moral order is no longer necessary, attempts to restore a normative order tend to have disruptive consequences. A large measure of the conflict in the United States, for instance, is generated by those individuals and groups who still expect occupation and citizenship to be congruent with a set of generalized values. Parsons, for instance, notes that it is the fundamentalists and the "value absolutists" who generate most of the protest in advanced societies (1968). Perhaps one should add to these categories the most idealistic, especially among the younger groups in the population. Each, to be sure, is distrustful of the other's values, but all are aligned in protest against a social order in which personal values have been replaced by the requirements of efficiency, the rule of the experts, and the "cash nexus" which, according to Marx, alone hold together industrial society. Black protest, too, has used as its motto Fanon's manifesto against modernization and looks toward the reunification of what Western society has "torn asunder," i.e., to a repeal of the process of rationalization and differentiation (Carmichael and Hamilton, 1967: xi). The nostalgia for a society in which legitimacy is conferred by the moral order on both work and citizenship indeed creates severe strains in modern societies.

TOWARD A NEW SOCIOLOGY OF RELIGION

In these concluding comments it will be helpful to contrast the argument of this paper with Robert Bellah's suggestions as to the future direction of research and theory in the sociology of religion (1970: 3–19). The contrast will focus upon the basic points at which the present argument departs from current sociological theory and interpretation.

Bellah argues that religion is "the most general mechanism for integrating meaning and motivation in action systems" (1970: 12). In his view, social change and stability depend on a cybernetic process in which energy and information interact to produce decisions as to the direction of the system and its immediate adaptation to its environment. Religious symbols, for instance, provide direction and meaning to the motivations which are structured in social systems. The religious symbols may vary, of course, in the degree to which they permit control and flexibility, adaptation and rigidity. The literature on the Protestant Ethic provides comparative data from several societies as to the flexibility and stability which Protestantism, as compared with other religious ideologies, has permitted in the modernizing societies of the East and West.

This paper, however, assumes that the process of differentiation is so far advanced at least in the most modern societies that the cybernetic process no longer *necessarily* includes the levels of religious meaning. This is not to say that societies are not systems of action in which information interacts with energy to produce a moving equilibrium. It is to say, however, that the information in the system need no longer be assumed to include the most general levels of symbolism, viz. the religious. This is the point, for instance, behind the brief discussion above of changes in the type of legitimation characteristic of modern societies.

·   ·   ·

While it is possible to agree with Bellah that all societies have the problem of structuring the motivations of individuals, it has been argued here that the process of automation in modern societies will increasingly diminish the severity of this problem so far as recruitment for civic and productive roles is concerned. Modern societies, that is, will be able to afford higher levels of motivational *non*commitment and may even seek to raise the level of *non*-commitment in order to "cool out" overmobilized segments of the population.

This leaves quite open, however, the question of the personal needs which religion will continue to fulfill. Modern bureaucracies are generally not de-signed for intimate personal relationships or for altruistic actions; they continue to exist by the exercise of power, by establishing priorities that satisfy the demands of the market, by efficiency, and by conforming to proper procedures. This is no less true of universities and colleges than it is of insurance companies and the medical profession. Whether the source of protest against bureaucratic or technological rationality is among the youth who attend colleges and universities, or among churchmen with an ideo-logical commitment to a moral community, it is doubtful whether any hope for a "greening" of modernized societies can be more than a fantasy. In short, more introversionist and quietist types of sectarian religions are well adapted to survival under the conditions of differentiation precisely because they free the individual from expectations that cannot be fulfilled under the conditions of advanced differentiation.

It is true, of course, that one characteristic of the sectarian orientation in the past has been the individual's conviction that the larger society does not reflect or embody the individual's own primary set of values. As such the society is not perceived by the sectarian actor as an appropriate object for his motivational commitment. His civic or occupational work-role, then, is tangential to the core of his personality and to his basic convictions. To this extent, of course, the sectarian orientation is an alienated one and has at times been marked by active or passive hostility to the larger society. In modernized social systems, however, the introversionist or quietist type of orientation is peculiarly well adapted to the managerial form of politics and to the organization of work on the basis of technology. The sectarian, in contrast to the churchman, does not ask more from the society than it can give. He is either indifferent to his civic and occupational roles or evaluates them positively because they require little affective or evaluational involve-ment on his part. Because they remain discrete areas that do not impinge on the deeper dimensions of his personal and social life, he is able to find meaning and satisfaction in the "free" areas of leisure time and primary relationships.

Bellah argues in several contexts for a view of man which takes into account the perennial return of the nonrational in his personal and social life. The Enlightenment view of man as "cool," self-confident, "secular," and engaged only in a series of *quid pro quo* exchanges with other individuals, can hardly do justice to the spontaneous generation of symbols which embrace the whole of life and which have the potentiality for new syntheses of meaning and motivation (1970: 237 ff.). Bellah rightly chastises the sociology of religion for its naive, rationalist assumptions about the diminishing role of religion in modern societies. One can hardly quarrel with his demand that social science replenish its own inadequate views of social reality from the traditional concern of Weber and Durkheim with the nonrational as well as from the resources of religious symbolism itself. In view of his criticisms, then, it is all the more important to specify precisely the modifications of functionalist interpretation which would follow from greater attention to the nonrational, nonutilitarian aspects of religious behavior.

One consequence of a shift in sociological assumptions away from the functionalist standpoint will be a break in the circular reasoning of much recent sociological interpretation of religion. On the one hand, the attempt is often made to "explain" religious behavior as serving to relieve a variety of deprivations. On the other hand, where no deprivations may be apparent, one sociological "out" has been to argue that religion gives the comfortable a good conscience about their good fortune. By the functionalist definition, then, religion is either compensatory or legitimating; it seldom is self-validating, in the sense of being nonutilitarian, an end in itself. While it is not necessary to abandon the long-standing recognition that ulterior motives affect religiosity, a shift in basic assumptions may help to overcome the intellectual aridity of much interpretation by making greater allowance for nonrational religious activity: activity which *is* an end in itself, and which is precisely what it appears to be, i.e., a search for "truth" or "transcendence."

The sociological interpretation of religion which is advocated in this paper therefore resists the tendency to designate a wide variety of phenomena as "functional alternatives" to religion. The difficulty, perhaps, in speaking of "functional alternatives" to traditional religion lies in the lack of specification of which functions are being served, and for which units in the social system. It is therefore more accurate to acknowledge that, while the culture now has a number of symbolic systems which can be used to integrate individual biographies, or legitimate the claims of certain strata and institutions, these systems are inadequate to transform secular societies into a coherent normative order.

These very ideologies and elements of mass culture, which on traditional assumptions appear to be "functional alternatives" to religion, can be interpreted quite differently, however, in line with the general argument of this paper.

If it is increasingly the case that no total ideology can overcome the differentiation of modern societies sufficiently to substitute for traditional forms of religion, it is misleading at best to state that partial ideologies and folk heroes are serving the *same* functions religion has served in the past, *at least insofar as the total society is concerned.* Whatever the functions may be which ideologies and elements of popular culture may serve for certain strata or for particular individuals, it is not possible (and, I have argued, not necessary) for these cultural elements to legitimate and integrate the whole society into a single normative order.

The same line of reasoning may be applied to the argument that high science and aesthetics as well as mass entertainment are functional alternatives to religion. That is, while these elements in the culture may indeed substitute for the traditional symbols of religion in providing meaning and direction to individual biographies, it is entirely doubtful that science, aesthetics, or the personalities and symbols of mass entertainment can either singly or together serve to integrate the activities and aspirations of a whole society around a coherent set of values and goals. On the contrary, they are themselves indicative of the pluralism which makes the integration of modern societies into moral communities a present and future impossibility.

Secularization therefore does not drive religion from modern society, but rather fosters a type of religion which has no major functions for the *entire* society. Whatever their relevance to particular individuals and groups, introversionist or quietist sects (to use Wilson's typology, 1969: 225), or movements devoted to spiritualism or problems of personal growth and familial harmony, offer little that is relevant to the legitimation and integration of a complex social system. The affinity between secular societies and certain types of sectarian religiosity, then, derives from the tendency of both to foster the disengagement of the individual's deepest motivations and highest values from the areas of political and economic action. This disengagement is the natural outcome of the process of differentiation and of the rational organization of work and administration, which makes the political and economic sectors of society irrelevant to the pursuit of salvation.

REFERENCES

ALLARDT, ERIK. 1964. "A theory on solidarity and legitimacy conflict," *Transactions of the Westermarck Society,* 10, 78–96.

BELLAH, ROBERT N. 1970. *Beyond Belief.* New York: Harper and Row.

BERGER, PETER L., and THOMAS LUCKMANN. 1967. *The Social Construction of Reality.* New York: Doubleday.

CARMICHAEL, STOKELY, and CHARLES V. HAMILTON. 1967. *Black Power.* New York: Vintage Books.

DURKHEIM, EMILE. 1957. *The Elementary Forms of the Religious Life.* New York: Macmillan (originally published in 1912).

EISENSTADT, S. N. 1964. "Social change, differentiation, and evolution," *American Sociological Review,* 29 (June): 375–386.

ERIKSON, ERIK. 1958. *Young Man Luther.* New York: Norton.

—— 1968. *Identity, Youth and Crisis,* New York: Norton.

FANON, FRANTZ. 1963. *The Wretched of the Earth.* New York: Grove Press.

FESTINGER, LEON. 1950. "Informal social communications," *Psychological Review,* 57, 271–282.

GLAZER, NATHAN. 1969. "For white and black, community control is the issue," *The New York Times Magazine,* April 27.

GLOCK, CHARLES Y., and RODNEY STARK. 1965. *Religion and Society in Tension.* Chicago: Rand McNally.

LENSKI, GERHARD. 1961. *The Religious Factor.* New York: Doubleday.

LEVY, MARION J., JR. 1966. *Modernization and the Structure of Societies.* Princeton, N.J.: Princeton University Press.

LITTLE, DAVID. 1969. *Religion, Order, and Law.* New York: Harper & Row.

MERTON, ROBERT K. 1957. *Social Theory and Social Structure.* Glencoe, Ill.: Free Press (revised edition).

NIEBUHR, H. RICHARD. 1954. *The Social Sources of Denominationalism.* New York: Shoestring Press (first published in 1929).

PARSONS, TALCOTT. 1964. *Societies: Evolutionary and Comparative Perspectives.* Englewood Cliffs, N.J.: Prentice-Hall.

————. 1968. "On the concept of value-commitments," *Sociological Inquiry,* 3 (Spring).

SLATER, PHILIP. 1966. *Microcosm: Structural, Psychological, and Religious Evolution in Groups.* New York: Wiley.

WILLIAMS, ROBIN M., JR. 1951. *American Society.* New York: Knopf.

WILSON, BRYAN R. 1969. *Religion in Secular Society.* Baltimore: Penguin Books.

YINGER, J. MILTON. 1970. *The Scientific Study of Religion.* New York: Macmillan.

SELECTION C

+-+-+-+-+-+-+-+-+-+-+-+-+-+-+-+-+-+-+

The New American

GEORGE MCGOVERN

The English author Hilaire Belloc was once told by the chairman of a public meeting that he could address the audience on any subject except religion and politics.

"Whereupon," said Belloc, "having been prevented from discussing either of the subjects that most concerned mankind, I turned on my heel and departed."

If one believes that avoiding controversy is essential to the good life, he will tend to support the chairman's ruling. But if he believes that each individual has some responsibility for the spiritual and political health of the community, he will endorse Belloc's position.

I have no doubt that the Christian bears a special responsibility for both the spiritual vitality and the political tone of his society. It is unthinkable for him to be indifferent to such important issues as education, social justice, public health, the conservation of resources, and peace or war. Indeed, the preamble of the Constitution places on each citizen the responsibility "to establish justice, insure domestic tranquility, provide for the common defense, promote the general welfare, and secure the blessings of liberty...."

Those great issues of citizenship were spelled out by men who drew deeply on their religious heritage, and at bottom such matters involve ethical and spiritual judgments. This is not to say that every Christian should be a candidate for public office, although that is a calling many Christians have heard in the past and need to hear in the future. What is required of all Christians, however, is an obligation to think soberly and exercise judgment about public issues, candidates, and programs as effectively as possible. This means not only voting but also influencing the quality and the direction of our political process.

The Christian has much to contribute by mixing in politics. Where there is a tendency toward narrow, partisan expediency, he can help keep the eyes of the community focused on the larger problems of our society.

When appeals to passion and prejudice are rife, he can counter with the voice of reason.

Where there is bitterness or violence, he can exercise the restraining influence of charity and good humor.

Reprinted with the permission of the author and of *Theology Today*, 26, no. 4 (January 1970).

George McGovern is United States Senator from South Dakota.

Where there is a laxity or indifference in the face of dishonesty, he can bring to bear the demands of a Christian conscience.

At a time when nuclear energy has ended whatever claim warfare might once have offered as a means of settling international disputes, the Christian can help reassert the claims of brotherhood and the family of man.

And at a time when our values and institutions are subject to convulsive questioning and ferment, the Christian has a special responsibility in refocusing our moral sensitivities. He must relate the Christian traditions of love, tolerance, and purpose to the tensions and divisions of today.

It is my growing conviction that out of the probing and unrest, a new American is struggling to be born—an American who will draw heavily on the richness of his past but who will also reach out to the new dimensions of today's world, an American who can draw heavily on the spiritual eloquence and moral traditions of the Christian vision. . . .

◦•◦•◦•◦•◦•◦•◦•◦•◦•◦•◦•◦•◦•◦

Superstition, Ecstasy, and Tribal Consciousness

ANDREW M. GREELEY

A witty divinity school faculty member (suspected by many to be some relation to the *Christian Century's* Pen-ultimate) commented recently that the secular city was born in Selma and died in Watts. He meant that the secularist optimism of the radical theologians could not survive the breakup of the Civil Rights movement and the emergence of the violent form of black nationalism. It is also rather doubtful if the secular city model could have survived very long in any case, because although this concept leaned heavily on sociological categories, its proponents were not willing to face the full implications of either social theory or social research. The secular man may indeed exist, particularly on some of the university campuses, or in the skyscrapers of Manhattan Island, but there is no reason to think that he is any more common than he has been in the past, or that he represents the wave of the future.

This is not to say that sociologists themselves have not, on occasion, embraced a fairly simple-minded model of the "desacralization" of man or the "decline of religion." European Catholic sociologists, in particular, are quite fond of speaking of urbanization and secularization, and Bryan R. Wilson's book is certainly the most naive exposition of the secularization hypothesis for which one could wish (*Religion in Secular Society: A Sociological Comment.* London, Watts, 1966).

But one need only re-read the theoretical works of Parsons, Geertz, or Luckmann, to say nothing of Shils' article on ritual,[1] and the relevant passages about religion in Durkheim and Weber to realize that on theoretical grounds the case against the secularization hypothesis is quite powerful. Furthermore, empirical research in the United States has not been able to pick up any significant indicators of an increase in secularization of the American population.[2] Also, the work of European sociologists like Martin raises serious questions as to how de-religionized English and Continental populations really are, and how religious they ever were in the past. For example, the survey of the Diocese of St. David in Wales in the early eighteenth century shows that it was a fairly de-christianized locale even during that period, and

From *Social Research*, 37, no. 2 (Summer 1970): 203–210. Reprinted with the permission of the publisher.

Rev. Andrew M. Greeley is a senior staff member of the National Opinion Research Center in Chicago.

the French religious geographers can trace low levels of religious participation in France back to the middle ages. Secularization is more a function of the social and economic history of an area or a country than of modernization.

Peter Berger has argued on theoretical grounds that the "plausibility structure" of a believer is threatened when he finds himself in a religiously pluralistic society.[3] However, in fact, it seems that religious denominations are strongest precisely in those societies which are most likely to be marked by denominational pluralism. This leads one to suspect that when the plausibility structure is threatened, man's social psychological reaction is to become more aggressively committed to it, especially if that structure is also the basis for important means of self-identification and social location.

It is, then, in my judgment inaccurate to assume that some of the more recent and bizarre manifestations of religion and the sacred represent a "re-sacralization." Society was never really "de-sacralized," in the first place. What we are witnessing, I think, is rather the expansion of Thomas Luckmann's "marketplace of interpretive schemes." New forms of the sacred are becoming available in that marketplace, though at least some of them are in fact very old. These new forms are entering the marketplace precisely for the reason that, like any other marketplace, this one expands the range of commodities offered, provided there is an increased demand for them. The political and social crises of the 1960's, the apparent failure of the liberals' scientific dream, the alienation from traditional faith, both religious and secular, of the younger generation—all of these have raised a demand for new interpretive schemes and new religious communities that can provide meaning and belonging for human life.

We shall speak of three of these "new Gods" (two of which are also very old): superstition, ecstasy, and "groupism."

The outburst of bizarre forms of the sacred on college campuses during the last two years is an extraordinarily fascinating phenomenon. Professor Huston Smith indicated this trend almost two years ago when he described an experience with a seminar containing some of the best students at the Massachusetts Institute of Technology:

> ...I cannot recall the exact progression of topics, but it went something like this: Beginning with Asian philosophy, it moved on to meditation, then yoga, then Zen, then Tibet, then successively to the *Bardo Thodol*, tantra, the kundalini, the chakras, the *I Ching*, karati and aikido, the yang-yin macrobiotic (brown rice) diet, Gurdjieff, Maher Baba, astrology, astral bodies, auras, UFO's, Tarot cards, parapsychology, witchcraft, and magic. And, underlying everything, of course, the psychedelic drugs. Nor were the students dallying with these subjects. They were *on* the drugs; they were eating brown rice; they were meditating hours on end; they were making their decisions by *I Ching* divination, which one student designated the most important discovery of his life; they were constructing complicated electronic experiments to prove that their thoughts, via psychokinesis, could affect matter directly.

And they weren't plebeians. Intellectually they were aristocrats with the highest average math scores in the land, Ivy League verbal scores, and two to three years of saturation in MIT science.[4]

．　　　．　　　．

Young people who engage in such behavior are quite frank about why they do so. They are looking for "experience"; they are looking for something to which to belong; and they are looking, as one young man put it, "for someone in the universe that cares about me." There is something of the "put-on," and not a little of the comic in such behavior, but also a hesitant attempt to find, as another student put it, "something or someone on which even the IBM 360 must depend." And he added, "Whether I am drafted, whether I go to Vietnam, whether I am killed there or not, all depend on arbitrary decisions by non-human forces. I would like to believe that there is something more than arbitrariness at work."

The tribal Gods are being worshipped once again, in substantial part as a protest against the hyper-rationalist society and the failures of that society. There are few better ways of rejecting science than turning to astrology; few more effective ways of snubbing the computer than relying on Tarot cards; and few better ways of coping with rationalist "liberal" college professors than putting hexes on them.

The second old God is called ecstasy. Whether it be in drugs, rock music, psychedelic art, contemplation, hippie communes, or prolonged periods of fasting, the new initiates are seeking an experience that will "snatch" them out of the ordinary; they are trying to establish some sort of communion with the basic and primordial forces of the universe, even if they have to "blow their minds" to do so. The *representations collectives* of the summer rock festivals are clearly attempts at group ecstasy. In the immortal words of Timothy Leary, one tunes out in order that one may turn on. Ecstasy, even drug-induced ecstasy or ecstasy induced by musical forms, is of course not a new phenomenon in human experience. Indeed, one can probably find direct connections between some elements of rock music and the ecstatic music of African religious ceremonies. Nor is the establishment of communities which self-consciously seek ecstatic experience for their membership a new phenomenon. The only really astonishing thing about the cult of ecstasy is that it seems to be most vigorous precisely among those young people who are the sons and daughters of proud, arrogant, secular men who no longer need the sacred or the ecstatic.

The third new God—"groupism"—is a little harder to define in terms of religious traditions. The desire for open and honest discourse among human beings has been part of many religious beliefs of the past, but that "open" and "honest" relationships become themselves a religion is, it appears, something new. Nevertheless, the immense popularity of T-groups, encounter groups, marathon groups (clothed or unclothed), affinity groups, communes, educational villages, and other kinds of neo-tribalism, are sufficient indication that in the post-Freudian world there are many people who desperately, and at times pathologically, want to find meaning in group interaction.

Evidence that any of these kinds of group experiences produce solid emotional growth is, at best, very inconclusive, but they are a hell of a lot of fun. In fact, many of the claims made for such experiences (that they expand consciousness, provide new insights, enlarge one's life, bring one into a whole "new reality of behavior") are not dissimilar from the enthusiastic defenses of marijuana and LSD by people who are engaged in the particular cults that make use of them. The group dynamics phenomenon seems to be, at least for many of its devotees, merely a somewhat different form of search for the transcendent. One might even go so far as to say that it is a ritualistic form, because there are certain highly specific phases that devotees of sensitivity encounters are supposed to go through as part of their experience. The leader or trainer is the high priest of his group or congregation; their words and behavior are a ritualistic dance, which increasingly includes the very strong sexual overtones that have characterized most ritualistic dances.

These three new religions, two of which are certainly also very old, overlap one another. The neo-sacralists use sensitivity language, and the mystics and ecstatics form communes and read horoscopes. But there do seem to be certain distinctive elements in each. The neo-sacralists are explicitly concerned with a transcendent power. The ecstatics want to experience transcendence, but elaborate few theories to explain it. And the "groupists" seek transcendence in human interaction.

Whatever the differences are among these three new Gods, there are plenty of common characteristics. They are non-rational, if not explicitly anti-rational. Whatever theories are propounded are simple and elementary; theology and philosophy (as opposed to complex magic) are definitely rejected. One can only find transcendence by breaking out of the bonds of the rationalist world; if necessary, even by "blowing one's mind." On any continuum of Apollonian versus Dionysian religious behavior, the new religions are about as far toward the Dionysian end as they could possibly be.

There are, secondly, Pelagians. Human nature is basically good, at least if it can break away from the trammels of the "square" world. When one is "oneself," one can do no wrong. As long as one does "one's own thing," one is on the side of virtue (unless, of course, "one's own thing" happens to be recruiting for the CIA or Dow Chemical). While the members of the new religions are only too eager to denounce the sins of the square world, they are convinced that the squares would themselves become virtuous if they shed their "hang-ups," "turned on," and "did their thing." Indeed, the Pelagianism of the new religions is fantastically naive; the cynical exploitation of the Haight-Ashbury district and the regressive parent and sibling fixations of the hippie communes have done little to shake their Pelagian faith. The new religions continue to "feel" good, no matter what goes wrong.

Furthermore, the new religions are *salvationist*: that is to say, they preach a way of salvation and preach it with the serene confidence that is only allowed to those who know that they have already been saved. . . .

The new faiths are *millennialistic*. They can, if given half a chance, create a new world, a world in which everyone is free to "do his own thing," to be "upfront" in his relationships with his fellows, to be honest, open, and authentic; to "swing," to "turn on," and "be with it." Such a millennialistic community, with rock music beating in the background and marijuana smoke drifting over the intense T-group sessions, may seem like a nightmare to those of us who are rationalists or liberals. But then, most millennial communities in ages past looked more like hell than heaven to those who were not part of them.

The new faiths are *charismatic* both because their leaders, whether they are called "trainers," "gurus," or "chief wizards," are highly charismatic individuals, and because, implicitly at least, all the members are presumed to have a charisma within them that enables them to "tell it like it is," and to "do their own thing." . . .

Finally, the new religions are *liturgical* in the sense that ritual, vestments, sacred instruments, and sacred places and times are of extreme importance, partly because they represent a break with the rationalized, bureaucratized, computerized society which respects none of these values, and partly because liturgy is seen as an avenue to transcendence. Liturgy may be the very simple low-Church ritual Roman Catholic mass celebrated by the priest in his shirt sleeves before a sensitivity session, or the orgy of the Woodstock Rock Festival; liturgies these both are, and would be seen as such by any objective anthropologist curious enough to get himself involved in either such event.

. . .

There are those who argue that this resurgence of nonrational religion is but a temporary phenomenon that will prevail no longer than the secular city has. Maybe they are right, though one can only observe that the new faiths now seem quite powerful. They are, to a greater or lesser extent, the result of the disillusionment with the bourgeois, secular, liberal, democratic, scientific society, and the failure of that society during the 1960's to produce peace in the world, justice for blacks, meaningful challenge on the college campus, and authentic friendship among human beings. If the liberal society can recoup its losses, the new faiths may recede, but at the present time such an event does not seem likely. Whether a new form of rationalist faith, conceding far more to human emotions, sentiments and yearnings for the transcendent than the formal liberal faith, will appear in the immediate future must remain problematic. While the tribal religions certainly will never capture a very substantial segment of the population, they are likely to remain with us for some time. Presumably sociologists, or at least anthropologists, will want to study this phenomenon. Some may even join it.

NOTES

1 EDWARD SHILS, "Ritual and Crisis," in *The Religious Situation 1968,* ed. Donald R. Cutler (Boston: Beacon, 1968).

2 ANDREW M. GREELEY, *Religion in the Year 2000* (New York: Sheed and Ward, 1968); Seymour Martin Lipset, *The First New Nation* (New York: Basic Books, 1963).

3 PETER BERGER, *A Rumor of Angels* (New York: Doubleday, 1969).

4 HUSTON SMITH, "Secularization and the Sacred," in *The Religious Situation 1968,* ed. Donald R. Cutler (Boston: Beacon, 1968), pp. 594–595.

THE INVISIBLE RELIGION

THOMAS LUCKMANN

The social form of religion emerging in modern industrial societies is characterized by the direct accessibility of an assortment of religious representations to potential consumers. The sacred cosmos is mediated neither through a specialized domain of religious institutions nor through other primary public institutions. It is the direct accessibility of the sacred cosmos, more precisely, of an assortment of religious themes, which makes religion today essentially a phenomenon of the "private sphere." The emerging social form of religion thus differs significantly from older social forms of religion which were characterized either by the diffusion of the sacred cosmos through the institutional structure of society or through institutional specialization of religion.

The statement that the sacred cosmos is directly accessible to potential consumers needs to be explicated. It implies that the sacred cosmos is not mediated by primary public institutions and that, correspondingly, no obligatory model of religion is available. It does not imply, of course, that religious themes are not socially mediated in some form. Religious themes originate in experiences in the "private sphere." They rest primarily on emotions and sentiments and are sufficiently unstable to make articulation difficult. They are highly "subjective"; that is, they are not defined in an obligatory fashion by primary institutions. They can be—and are—taken up, however, by what may be called secondary institutions which expressly cater to the "private" needs of "autonomous" consumers. These institutions attempt to articulate the themes arising in the "private sphere" and retransmit the packaged results to potential consumers. Syndicated advice columns, "inspirational" literature ranging from tracts on positive thinking to *Playboy* magazine, *Reader's Digest* versions of popular psychology, the lyrics of popular hits, and so forth, articulate what are, in effect, elements of models of "ultimate" significance. The models are, of course, nonobligatory and must compete on what is, basically, an open market. The manufacture, the packaging and the sale of models of "ultimate" significance are, therefore, determined by consumer preference, and the manufacturer must remain sensitive to the needs

Thomas Luckmann is a member of the faculty of sociology at the University of Frankfurt, Germany.

and requirements of "autonomous" individuals and their existence in the "private sphere."[1]

·   ·   ·

The fact that the sacred cosmos rests primarily on the "private sphere" and the secondary institutions catering to the latter, combined with the thematic heterogeneity of the sacred cosmos, has important consequences for the nature of individual religiosity in modern society. In the absence of an "official" model the individual may select from a variety of themes of "ultimate" significance. The selection is based on consumer preference, which is determined by the social biography of the individual, and similar social biographies will result in similar choices. Given the assortment of religious representations available to potential consumers and given the absence of an "official" model it is possible, in principle, that the "autonomous" individual will not only select certain themes but will construct with them a well-articulated private *system* of "ultimate" significance. To the extent that some themes in the assortment of "ultimate" meanings are coalesced into something like a coherent model (such as "positive Christianity" and psychoanalysis), some individuals may internalize such models en bloc. Unless we postulate a high degree of reflection and conscious deliberation, however, it is more likely that individuals will legitimate the situation-bound (primarily emotional and affective) priorities arising in their "private spheres" by deriving, *ad hoc*, more or less appropriate rhetorical elements from the sacred cosmos. The assumption seems justified, therefore, that the *prevalent* individual systems of "ultimate" significance will consist of a loose and rather unstable hierarchy of opinions legitimating the affectively determined priorities of "private" life.

Individual religiosity in modern society receives no massive support and confirmation from the primary public institutions. Overarching subjective structures of meaning are almost completely detached from the functionally rational norms of these institutions. In the absence of external support, subjectively constructed and eclectic systems of "ultimate" significance will have a somewhat precarious reality for the individual.[2] Also, they will be less stable—or rigid—than the more homogeneous patterns of individual religiosity that characterize societies in which "everybody" internalizes an "official" model and in which the internalized model is socially reinforced throughout an individual's biography. In sum, while the systems of "ultimate" significance in modern society are characterized by considerable variability in content, they are structurally similar. They are *relatively* flexible as well as unstable.

While individual religiosity fails to receive the massive support and confirmation from primary public institutions, it comes to depend upon the more ephemeral support of other "autonomous" individuals. In other words, individual religiosity is socially supported by other persons who, for reasons discussed above, are found primarily in the "private sphere." In the "private sphere" the partial sharing, and even joint construction, of systems of "ultimate" significance is possible without conflict with the functionally rational norms of the primary institutions. The so-called nuclear family prevalent in industrial societies performs an important role in providing a structural basis for the "private" production of (rather fleeting) systems of "ultimate" significance. This holds especially for the middle-class family ideal of "partnership marriage" of which it is typically expected that it provide "fulfillment" for the marriage partners.[3] If the situation is viewed in this perspective there is nothing surprising about the upsurge of "familism" in industrial societies, unexpected as this fact would have been for the social scientists of the nineteenth century. On the other hand the relatively low average stability of the family as an institution becomes readily intelligible if one allows for the extraordinarily heavy social–psychological burden that is placed upon the family by such expectations.[4]

Support for subjective systems of "ultimate" significance may also come from persons outside the family. Friends, neighbors, members of cliques formed at work and around hobbies may come to serve as "significant others" who share in the construction and stabilization of "private" universes of "ultimate" significance.[5] If such universes coalesce to some degree, the groups supporting them may assume almost sectarian characteristics and develop what we earlier called secondary institutions. This, to list only the most unlikely example, seems to be the case even with such "ultimately" significant hobbies as wife-swapping.[6] Nevertheless, it is safe to assume that the family remains the most important catalyst of "private" universes of significance.

NOTES

[1] Cf. PETER BERGER and THOMAS LUCKMANN, "Sociology of Religion and Sociology of Knowledge," in *Sociology and Social Research*, 47 no. 4 (1963).

[2] Cf. FRIEDRICH TENBRUCK, "Die Kirchengemeinde in der entkirchlichten Gesellschaft," in *Soziologie der Kirchengemeinde*, ed. Dietrich Goldschmidt, Franz Greiner, and Helmut Schelsky (Stuttgart: Enke, 1959).

[3] Cf. PETER BERGER and HANSFRIED KELLNER, "Marriage and the Construction of Reality," *Diogène*, 46, no. 2 (1964): 3–32.

[4] Cf. HANSFRIED KELLNER, *Dimensions of the Individual's Conception of Social Reality Arising Within Marriage*, unpublished Ph.D. dissertation, Graduate Faculty, New School for Social Research, 1966.

[5] DAVID RIESMAN's analysis of "other direction" is highly pertinent here. He provides a general perspective in which the importance of "significant others" in providing support for the individual can be understood as a consequence of the fact that clear-cut socialization profiles are not available in a relatively mobile urban-industrial society. Cf. DAVID RIESMAN with NATHAN GLAZER and REUEL DENNEY, *The Lonely Crowd* (New Haven, Yale University Press, 1950).

[6] Cf. THOMAS J. W. WILSON with EVERETT MEYERS, *Wife Swapping: A Complete Eight Year Survey of Morals in America* (New York, 1965).

PLAUSIBILITY STRUCTURES

PETER BERGER

One of the fundamental propositions of the sociology of knowledge is that the plausibility, in the sense of what people actually find credible, of views of reality depends upon the social support these receive. Put more simply, we obtain our notions about the world originally from other human beings, and these notions continue to be plausible to us in a very large measure because others continue to affirm them. There are some exceptions to this—notions that derive directly and instantaneously from our own sense experience—but even these can be integrated into meaningful views of reality only by virtue of social processes. It is, of course, possible to go against the social consensus that surrounds us, but there are powerful pressures (which manifest themselves as psychological pressures within our own consciousness) to conform to the views and beliefs of our fellow men. It is in conversation, in the broadest sense of the word, that we build up and keep going our view of the world. It follows that this view will depend upon the continuity and consistency of such conversation, and that it will change as we change conversation partners.

We all exist within a variety of social networks or conversational fabrics, which are related in often complex and sometimes contradictory ways with our various conceptions of the universe. When we get to the more sophisticated of these conceptions, there are likely to be organized practices designed to still doubts and prevent lapses of conviction. These practices are called therapies. There are also likely to be more or less systematized explanations, justifications, and theories in support of the conceptions in question. These sociologists have called legitimations....

Thus each conception of the world of whatever character or content can be analyzed in terms of its plausibility structure, because it is only as the individual remains within this structure that the conception of the world in question will remain plausible to him. The strength of this plausibility, ranging from unquestioned certitude through firm probability to mere opinion, will be directly dependent upon the strength of the supporting structure. This dynamics pertains irrespective of whether, by some outside observer's criteria of validity, the notions thus made plausible are true or false. The dynamics

Peter Berger is a member of the Sociology Department at Rutgers University.

most definitely pertains to any religious affirmations about the world because these affirmations are, by their very nature, incapable of being supported by our own sense experience and therefore heavily dependent upon social support.

Each plausibility structure can be further analyzed in terms of its constituent elements—the specific human beings that "inhabit" it, the conversational network by which these "inhabitants" keep the reality in question going, the therapeutic practices and rituals, and the legitimations that go with them. For example, the maintenance of the Catholic faith in the consciousness of the individual requires that he maintain his relationship to the plausibility structure of Catholicism. This is, above all, a community of Catholics in his social milieu who continually support this faith. It will be useful if those who are of the greatest emotional significance to the individual (the ones whom George Herbert Mead called significant others) belong to this supportive community—it does not matter much if, say, the individual's dentist is a non-Catholic, but his wife and his closest personal friends had better be. Within this supportive community there will then be an ongoing conversation that, explicitly and implicitly, keeps a Catholic world going. Explicitly, there is affirmation, confirmation, reiteration of Catholic notions about reality. But there is also an implicit Catholicism in such a community. After all, in everyday life it is just as important that some things can silently be taken for granted as that some things are reaffirmed in so many words. Indeed, the most fundamental assumptions about the world are commonly affirmed by implication—they are so "obvious" that there is no need to put them into words. Our individual, then, operates within what may be called a specifically Catholic conversational apparatus, which, in innumerable ways, each day confirms the Catholic world that he coinhabits with his significant others.... The details of all this vary in different circumstances, especially as between a situation in which the plausibility structure is more or less coextensive with the individual's over-all social experience (that is, where Catholics constitute the majority) and a situation in which the plausibility structure exists as a deviant enclave within the individual's larger society (that is, where Catholics are a cognitive minority). But the essential point is that the plausibility of Catholicism hinges upon the availability of these social processes.

❖·❖·❖·❖·❖·❖·❖·❖·❖·❖·❖·❖·❖·❖·❖·❖

Yoga Made Plausible: A Personal Account

PAUL N. CARNES, JR.

Berger's thesis about plausibility structure to me was very interesting and thought-provoking. If we think about what we regard as real, we can easily see that much of it is dependent on some kind of social support. If a particular social base disappears, then rather than go out on our own and find our own unique new reality, we are very likely (and in Berger's view we must) find another social base that will define the world for us and involve us in a new community of believers.

On many points from my own experience, I would agree with Berger. On some I would not. I use some examples from my own past which I think in many respects demonstrate Berger's plausibility structure in action.

For a while a few years ago I was deeply into the drug culture. My attachment to it was strong, for I was just recovering from disillusionment with the radical social protest thing. By this time I was seeing revolution as just a violent ego trip. But getting back to drugs, I began to want explanations for the spheres of reality I was experiencing during drug trips. When I came to the university, I was still trying to figure out this reality and find some group that would help me do this. Then one day I looked out my window to see a class sitting on the field in front of the dorm. I went down to see what it was about. It turned out to be a class in yoga. It looked like an interesting trip so I tried it.

As I got more into the yoga philosophy and Eastern doctrines I found that they seemed to explain much. They explained not only drug-induced consciousness but life as a whole. Pain and suffering, death, work, everything was given a place in a larger system. My disillusionment with politics was confirmed as correct, because the physical world was essentially an illusion. Now I had an excuse for nonaction. The law of karma and other Indian doctrine took away my guilt about dropping out.

Looking back, I can see how I was steadily encouraged to become more and more yogic. It seemed so gradual. First I began to attend classes regularly. Here we did exercises and got a steady dose of yogic philosophy. They work it well. While you are in a mellow frame of mind (candles lit, incense burning, darkness, and you're relaxed from the exercises and eating some fruit), the leader raps to you. You suddenly realize that you are thinking like he is, but you don't know exactly why.

Paul N. Carnes, Jr., is a member of the University of New Mexico, class of 1972. He is currently attending the University of Kentucky Graduate School of Library Science.

For the really dedicated there are classes other days, too. But for these you have to go down to the Ashram (the place where the leader lives along with other real devotees). This greatly aids them in converting you. The Ashram is isolated. Gradually you come earlier and leave later until eventually you are spending a lot more time there. Then you occasionally eat with them. If you stay with it as I did, you eventually move into the Ashram to live. Once you do this and are fully into the fold, the plausibility structures become very visible and ever present. Rituals keep you with the group. Everyone rises at the same time—4:30 A.M. Then all take a cold shower, exercise for an hour, then chant for an additional hour. Then everyone eats together. Unless you have an outside job or classes to attend, you work with the others around the Ashram. They even give the work a special name—Karma Yoga—so that you feel somehow more holy for having done it. After lunch, more work or perhaps reading. All the books, of course, are "religious," which tends to reinforce you in your beliefs and keep doubts at bay. Evening classes are again filled with ritual. Finally, periodic discussions during the day with members and with the leader help to increase your faith that what you are doing is ultimately the best thing—the true path.

The whole attempt, then, is to structure your days in such a way that you can have no free time in which to do something "wrong." You are presented with a routine which, if followed, is guaranteed to lead you to liberation (no questions about it; just ask the leader; just read this book; and so on). All over the building are pictures of holy men, yogis from India, and saints. Nothing mundane is present. You're in the world of the sacred—completely.

Periodically feasts and celebrations are held either at the Ashram or in the mountains. At these reaffirmations of the group, outsiders may be invited. This helps members in that they can feel "superior" ("I'm glad I'm not like that") and can enhance their sense of belonging by helping others see through the veil of maya, or illusion, and place themselves on the path to enlightenment. When newcomers attend classes, the same pattern can be seen. You talk only of the good points of being a yogi: good food, feel high all the time, and living your life for God. Neglected are the bummers—getting up early, cold showers, hard work, no meat or drugs.

Eventually you are given a chance to lead some of the classes. This is a definite sign that you have arrived and tends to cement you more tightly into the group.

Everything will be fine—but only if you can maintain the game. But with me, doubts began to creep in. The thing that probably started me on the road to deconversion was old friends. I had not totally isolated myself (as would have been ideal). I went out with old friends to the mountains, to parties. This brings on a crisis. They're all doing one thing and you for some reason can't. You refuse to get stoned; they ask why. You give the established reasons. O.K. Inside, though, you'd really like to, but it would bring down everything you believe in (your plausibility structure is pretty vulnerable). All you can do is hope that when you become higher (attain a new level of consciousness), you won't feel any desire to partake of such amusements.

As Berger puts it, the supportive therapies go to work when the leader finds out you have doubts. He tells you how remaining on the path would guarantee you freedom from the cycle of rebirth. You don't want to blow it, so you go on your way determined to suffer inconvenience now so that you'll be free from dying and being reborn. A fellow devotee got bummed out when she was continuously asked to do the dishes. When she complained, the leader told her "do it for God." This was the classic answer. Since God was everything, how could you refuse? The leader was closer to God than you were, anyway.

But my friends finally got to me. The clincher came when one of them said to me casually, "That's great if you really dig it, but I'd rather get high, sleep till noon, and eat steak." I got this flash that said, so would I. I suddenly realized I had a choice in how I lived so I moved out the next day and returned to the "normal world." From then on, I tried to construct my own individual reality. I tried to take whatever I felt to be truth wherever I found it. I began to find no one plausibility structure satisfactory. Each plausibility structure seems to put you in a game and every game is limited. To step out of the game (all games) is hard. I guess Berger would say it's impossible. But I think you have to try to hit some middle ground between letting the group make your world and being a total loner.

On Commitment

WALTER KAUFMANN

Some who love Big Brother claim that, deep down, everybody loves Big Brother; only some of us fail to realize it. To be more precise: some modern theologians argue that everybody is committed, whether he knows it or not. Some put the point this way: the question is merely who our gods are, for everybody has some gods. Others claim that all men have some ultimate concern or something that is holy to them, and the question is only whether the object of this concern is really ultimate or rather idolatrous. Some admit that most men have many ultimate concerns and are really "polytheists"; others insist that true ultimacy involves monotheism, and that as long as we are dealing with many concerns none can be really ultimate.

All these ways of speaking are metaphorical, evocative, and exceedingly unclear. Not only frivolous people lack any ultimate concern and are in an important sense uncommitted but the same is true of millions of very serious college students who wonder what they should do with themselves after graduation. There is nothing to which they greatly desire to give themselves, nothing that matters deeply to them. They are not shallow; they are not playboys; they enjoyed many of their courses and appreciate the opportunity to discuss their problems with sympathetic professors. They do not say: nothing matters to me. What they do say is: no one or two things matter more to me than anything else. These young men and women constitute the uncommitted generation; and it seems better to recognize this difference than to gloss it over by claiming that everybody has his own ultimate concern.

In any case, what is an "ultimate concern"? What is mine? What is my "God"—if these theologians are right and everybody ultimately has his "God"? I am not non-committal, not adrift, not hard put to find some project to devote myself to. I feel no inclination to pose as a cynic, saying: nothing is holy to *me*. But what, specifically, *is* holy to me?

The fashionable assumption that what is holy to a man is what he is ultimately concerned with is extremely dubious. When we say that something is holy to a person, we often mean that he won't stand for any humorous remarks about it, that the object is taboo for him in some sense. But such a taboo does not necessarily indicate any ultimate concern, perhaps only an underdeveloped sense of humor.

Walter Kaufmann is a member of the Philosophy Department at Princeton University.

The dedications of at least some of my books, including this one, point to deep concerns, but hardly to "gods" or to any one "ultimate" concern. Some sense of responsibility to the six million Jews killed in my lifetime, especially to some whom I loved and who loved me, and to millions of others, Jew and Gentile, killed in our time and in past centuries, is certainly among my deepest feelings. Still, that is hardly my ultimate concern. Neither is this book, though I am deeply involved in that. Nor is it at all plausible to say that these are symbols for something more ultimate.

Perhaps I come closest to discovering my ultimate concerns when I ask what I consider the cardinal virtues. I shall try to answer that question in the "Morality" chapter of this book. But here, too, it is exceedingly difficult to know just what virtues one considers most important. And if one selects several, does that make one a polytheist?

The point at stake here is not autobiographical. I merely want to bring out how unhelpful and misleading many fashionable statements about commitment are. And instead of confining myself to semantic considerations, I have tried to take these statements as seriously as possible, seeing what they might mean if one applied them to oneself.

Much of the talk in this vein that one hears from theologians can hardly be taken seriously. It is said that man must have a god, or that man always worships either God or an idol, and that man cannot find true existence in the worship of an idol. One asks oneself whether Shakespeare, Goethe, or Van Gogh worshiped God or—hateful thought—unlike our theologians, never did find "true existence." Surely, some great artists are believers, and some are not; there is no party line among great artists in this matter; and it is futile to argue who did, and who did not achieve "true existence."

One question, however, is worth pressing. Who really has a single ultimate concern? If that phrase has any definite meaning, it would seem to imply a willingness to sacrifice all other concerns to one's sole ultimate concern. Having only one ultimate concern might well be the recipe for fanaticism. It is the mark of a humane person that he has several ultimate concerns that check and balance each other.

To have many commitments might seem to be the formula of an arid and scattered life, spread thin, lacking depth; but it is hard to generalize about that. Goethe had a staggering number of commitments—and a singularly rich and fruitful life, with no lack of passion or profundity. But one can safely generalize that those who, spurning more than one concern, insist on a single commitment either abandon humanity for fanaticism or, more often, engage in loose talk.

CHAPTER 2

❖•❖•❖•❖•❖•❖•❖•❖•❖•❖ •❖•❖•❖•❖•❖•❖•❖

Cultural Integration
and the Role of Religion

Chapter 1 looked at religion as provider of a symbolic interpretative framework for coming to terms with the stark realities of bafflement, suffering,
and moral dilemma. Religion creates a sacred world and sustains it principally
through ritual celebration, which in turn acts to enhance a sense of oneness
with others in the community.

This latter function of enhancing group solidarity stems, of course, from
Emile Durkheim's discussion of religion's tendency to sacralize the norms
and values of the established society. But religion may also be a vehicle of
protest against accepted values and developing policies of the dominant
society. This last function is called prophetic. It is worth noting that the same
religious institution, or its spokesmen, can be both "sacralizing" and prophetic
regarding a society's values and norms. Thus, the political and economic
institutions may be praised for implementing a religiously rooted ideal, for
example, equality of opportunity for all men, yet criticized for failure to
uphold other values such as the freedom of the individual—either generically
or in some specific context.

Robert Bellah's widely discussed essay, "Civil Religion in America," points
to a series of interrelated religious themes visible throughout American
history. These themes may be couched in the familiar phrases of the Judaeo-
Christian tradition, but together they constitute a kind of national faith
distinct from the religion of the churches and synagogues. These themes may

be employed both sacrally and prophetically. Thus the American Revolution was viewed as an exodus from Europe and the beginning of "a new Israel." The Civil War and Lincoln's death added themes of death, sacrifice, and rebirth (a kind of prophetic calling to national rededication). The Presidency of John F. Kennedy brought with it "the problem of responsible action in a revolutionary world," an opposition to tyranny, poverty, disease, and war wherever they may be found.

Bellah's essay has seemed to some a potentially dangerous and historically inaccurate glorification of the nation-state. In a later commentary, however, Bellah responded:

> I think it should be clear from the text that I conceive of the central tradition of the American civil religion not as a form of national self-worship but as the subordination of the nation to ethical principles that transcend it and in terms of which it should be judged. I am convinced that every nation and every people come to some form of religious self-understanding whether the critics like it or not. Rather than simply denounce what seems in any case inevitable, it seems more responsible to seek within the civil religious tradition for those critical principles which undercut the ever-present danger of national self-idolization.[1]

Selections G and H offer the student examples of religion as sacralizing as well as a satirical critique of this function. (Religion as prophetic is well illustrated in Chapter 10, "Religion and Current Social Protest.") Billy Graham's ringing blend of patriotism and religion is, of course, shared by millions of Americans. Cornish Rogers, on the other hand, strikes a decidedly sour note. Religion, politics, and sports—notably football—combine to form a special version of civil religion. Its theme: ". . . the winner is somehow more virtuous than the loser or at least more pleasing to the gods."

That practice of one's religion, particularly Christianity, is the "way to success" in the world of politics and business (with St. Paul set forth as a model "supersalesman") is another version of civil religion aptly portrayed in Selection I from *Newsweek* magazine.

NOTES

[1] ROBERT N. BELLAH, "Civil Religion in America," *Beyond Belief: Essays on Religion in a Post-Traditional World* (New York: Harper & Row, 1970), p. 168, footnote.

CIVIL RELIGION IN AMERICA

ROBERT N. BELLAH

While some have argued that Christianity is the national faith, and others that church and synagogue celebrate only the generalized religion of "the American Way of Life," few have realized that there actually exists alongside of and rather clearly differentiated from the churches an elaborate and well-institutionalized civil religion in America. This article argues not only that there is such a thing, but also that this religion—or perhaps better, this religious dimension—has its own seriousness and integrity and requires the same care in understanding that any other religion does.[1]

THE KENNEDY INAUGURAL

Kennedy's inaugural address of 20 January 1961 serves as an example and a clue with which to introduce this complex subject. That address began:

> We observe today not a victory of party but a celebration of freedom—symbolizing an end as well as a beginning—signifying renewal as well as change. For I have sworn before you and Almighty God the same solemn oath our forebears prescribed nearly a century and three quarters ago.
>
> The world is very different now. For man holds in his mortal hands the power to abolish all forms of human poverty and to abolish all forms of human life. And yet the same revolutionary beliefs for which our forebears fought are still at issue around the globe—the belief that the rights of man come not from the generosity of the state but from the hand of God.

And it concluded:

> Finally, whether you are citizens of America or of the world, ask of us the same high standards of strength and sacrifice that we shall ask of you. With a good conscience our only sure reward, with history the final judge of our deeds, let us go forth to lead the land we love, asking His blessing and His help, but knowing here on earth God's work must truly be our own.

These are the three places in this brief address in which Kennedy mentioned the name of God. If we could understand why he mentioned God, the way in which he did it, and what he meant to say in those three references, we

From *Daedalus* (Winter 1967): 1–21. Reprinted with the permission of the publisher.

Robert N. Bellah is a member of the Sociology Department at the University of California at Berkeley.

would understand much about American civil religion. But this is not a simple or obvious task, and American students of religion would probably differ widely in their interpretation of these passages.

Let us consider first the placing of the three references. They occur in the two opening paragraphs and in the closing paragraph, thus providing a sort of frame for the more concrete remarks that form the middle part of the speech. Looking beyond this particular speech, we would find that similar references to God are almost invariably to be found in the pronouncements of American presidents on solemn occasions, though usually not in the working messages that the president sends to Congress on various concrete issues. How, then, are we to interpret this placing of references to God?

It might be argued that the passages quoted reveal the essentially irrelevant role of religion in the very secular society that is America. The placing of the references in this speech as well as in public life generally indicates that religion has "only a ceremonial significance"; it gets only a sentimental nod which serves largely to placate the more unenlightened members of the community, before a discussion of the really serious business with which religion has nothing whatever to do. A cynical observer might even say that an American president has to mention God or risk losing votes. A semblance of piety is merely one of the unwritten qualifications for the office, a bit more traditional than but not essentially different from the present-day requirement of a pleasing television personality.

But we know enough about the function of ceremonial and ritual in various societies to make us suspicious of dismissing something as unimportant because it is "only a ritual." What people say on solemn occasions need not be taken at face value, but it is often indicative of deep-seated values and commitments that are not made explicit in the course of everyday life. Following this line of argument, it is worth considering whether the very special placing of the references to God in Kennedy's address may not reveal something rather important and serious about religion in American life.

It might be countered that the very way in which Kennedy made his references reveals the essentially vestigial place of religion today. He did not refer to any religion in particular. He did not refer to Jesus Christ, or to Moses, or to the Christian church; certainly he did not refer to the Catholic Church. In fact, his only reference was to the concept of God, a word which almost all Americans can accept but which means so many different things to so many different people that it is almost an empty sign. Is this not just another indication that in America religion is considered vaguely to be a good thing, but that people care so little about it that it has lost any content whatever? Isn't Eisenhower reported to have said, "Our government makes no sense unless it is founded in a deeply felt religious faith—and I don't care what it is,"[2] and isn't that a complete negation of any real religion?

These questions are worth pursuing because they raise the issue of how civil religion relates to the political society, on the one hand, and to private religious organization, on the other. President Kennedy was a Christian, more specifically a Catholic Christian. Thus, his general references to God do not mean that he lacked a specific religious commitment. But why, then, did he not include some remark to the effect that Christ is the Lord of the world or some indication of respect for the Catholic Church? He did not because these are matters of his own private religious belief and of his relation to his own particular church; they are not matters relevant in any direct way to the conduct of his public office. Others with different religious views and commitments to different churches or denominations are equally qualified participants in the political process. The principle of separation of church and state guarantees the freedom of religious belief and association, but at the same time clearly segregates the religious sphere, which is considered to be essentially private, from the political one.

Considering the separation of church and state, how is a president justified in using the word *God* at all? The answer is that the separation of church and state has not denied the political realm a religious dimension. Although matters of personal religious belief, worship, and association are considered to be strictly private affairs, there are, at the same time, certain common elements of religious orientation that the great majority of Americans share. These have played a crucial role in the development of American institutions and still provide a religious dimension for the whole fabric of American life, including the political sphere. This public religious dimension is expressed in a set of beliefs, symbols, and rituals that I am calling the American civil religion. The inauguration of a president is an important ceremonial event in this religion. It reaffirms, among other things, the religious legitimation of the highest political authority.

Let us look more closely at what Kennedy actually said. First he said, "I have sworn before you and Almighty God the same solemn oath our forebears prescribed nearly a century and three quarters ago." The oath is the oath of office, including the acceptance of the obligation to uphold the Constitution. He swears it before the people (you) and God. Beyond the Constitution, then, the president's obligation extends not only to the people but to God. In American political theory, sovereignty rests, of course, with the people, but implicitly, and often explicitly, the ultimate sovereignty has been attributed to God. This is the meaning of the motto, "In God we trust," as well as the inclusion of the phrase "under God" in the pledge to the flag. What difference does it make that sovereignty belongs to God? Though the will of the people as expressed in majority vote is carefully institutionalized as the operative source of political authority, it is deprived of an ultimate significance. The will of the people is not itself the criterion of right and wrong. There is a higher criterion in terms of which this will can be judged; it is possible that the people may be wrong. The president's obligation extends to the higher criterion.

When Kennedy says that "the rights of man come not from the generosity of the state but from the hand of God," he is stressing this point again. It does not matter whether the state is the expression of the will of an autocratic monarch or of the "people"; the rights of man are more basic than any political structure and provide a point of revolutionary leverage from which any state structure may be radically altered. That is the basis for his reassertion of the revolutionary significance of America.

But the religious dimension in political life as recognized by Kennedy not only provides a grounding for the rights of man which makes any form of political absolutism illegitimate, it also provides a transcendent goal for the political process. This is implied in his final words that "here on earth God's work must truly be our own." What he means here is, I think, more clearly spelled out in a previous paragraph, the wording of which, incidentally, has a distinctly Biblical ring:

> Now the trumpet summons us again—not as a call to bear arms, though arms we need—not as a call to battle, though embattled we are—but a call to bear the burden of a long twilight struggle, year in and year out, "rejoicing in hope, patient in tribulation"—a struggle against the common enemies of man: tyranny, poverty, disease and war itself.

The whole address can be understood as only the most recent statement of a theme that lies very deep in the American tradition, namely the obligation, both collective and individual, to carry out God's will on earth. This was the motivating spirit of those who founded America, and it has been present in every generation since. Just below the surface throughout Kennedy's inaugural address, it becomes explicit in the closing statement that God's work must be our own. That this very activist and non-contemplative conception of the fundamental religious obligation, which has been historically associated with the Protestant position, should be enunciated so clearly in the first major statement of the first Catholic president seems to underline how deeply established it is in the American outlook. Let us now consider the form and history of the civil religious tradition in which Kennedy was speaking.

THE IDEA OF CIVIL RELIGION

The phrase *civil religion* is, of course, Rousseau's. In Chapter 8, Book 4, of *The Social Contract*, he outlines the simple dogmas of the civil religion: the existence of God, the life to come, the reward of virtue and the punishment of vice, and the exclusion of religious intolerance. All other religious opinions are outside the cognizance of the state and may be freely held by citizens. While the phrase *civil religion* was not used, to the best of my knowledge, by the founding fathers, and I am certainly not arguing for the particular influence of Rousseau, it is clear that similar ideas, as part of the cultural climate of the late-eighteenth century, were to be found among the Americans. For example, Franklin writes in his autobiography:

> I never was without some religious principles. I never doubted, for instance, the existence of the Deity; that he made the world and govern'd it by his

Providence; that the most acceptable service of God was the doing of good to men; that our souls are immortal; and that all crime will be punished, and virtue rewarded either here or hereafter. These I esteemed the essentials of every religion; and, being to be found in all the religions we had in our country, I respected them all, tho' with different degrees of respect, as I found them more or less mix'd with other articles, which, without any tendency to inspire, promote or confirm morality, serv'd principally to divide us, and make us unfriendly to one another.

It is easy to dispose of this sort of position as essentially utilitarian in relation to religion. In Washington's Farewell Address (though the words may be Hamilton's) the utilitarian aspect is quite explicit:

Of all the dispositions and habits which lead to political prosperity, Religion and Morality are indispensable supports. In vain would that man claim the tribute of Patriotism, who should labour to subvert these great Pillars of human happiness, these firmest props of the duties of men and citizens. The mere politician, equally with the pious man ought to respect and cherish them. A volume could not trace all their connections with private and public felicity. Let it simply be asked where is the security for property, for reputation, for life, if the sense of religious obligation *desert* the oaths, which are the instruments of investigation in Courts of Justice? And let us with caution indulge the supposition, that morality can be maintained without religion. Whatever may be conceded to the influence of refined education on minds of peculiar structure, reason and experience both forbid us to expect that National morality can prevail in exclusion of religious principle.

But there is every reason to believe that religion, particularly the idea of God, played a constitutive role in the thought of the early American statesmen.

Kennedy's inaugural pointed to the religious aspect of the Declaration of Independence, and it might be well to look at that document a bit more closely. There are four references to God. The first speaks of the "Laws of Nature and of Nature's God" which entitle any people to be independent. The second is the famous statement that all men "are endowed by their Creator with certain inalienable Rights." Here Jefferson is locating the fundamental legitimacy of the new nation in a conception of "higher law" that is itself based on both classical natural law and Biblical religion. The third is an appeal to "the Supreme Judge of the world for the rectitude of our intentions," and the last indicates "a firm reliance on the protection of divine Providence." In these last two references, a Biblical God of history who stands in judgment over the world is indicated.

The intimate relation of these religious notions with the self-conception of the new republic is indicated by the frequency of their appearance in early official documents. For example, we find in Washington's first inaugural address of 30 April 1789:

It would be peculiarly improper to omit in this first official act my fervent supplications to that Almighty Being who rules over the universe, who presides in the councils of nations, and whose providential aids can supply every defect, that His benediction may consecrate to the liberties and happiness of the people of the United States a Government instituted by themselves for these essential purposes, and may enable every instrument employed in its administration to execute with success the functions allotted to his charge.

No people can be bound to acknowledge and adore the Invisible Hand which conducts the affairs of man more than those of the United States. Every step by which we have advanced to the character of an independent nation seems to have been distinguished by some token of providential agency....

The propitious smiles of Heaven can never be expected on a nation that disregards the eternal rules of order and right which Heaven itself has ordained.... The preservation of the sacred fire of liberty and the destiny of the republican model of government are justly considered, perhaps, as *deeply*, as *finally*, staked on the experiment intrusted to the hands of the American people.

Nor did these religious sentiments remain merely the personal expression of the president. At the request of both Houses of Congress, Washington proclaimed on October 3 of that same first year as president that November 26 should be "a day of public thanksgiving and prayer," the first Thanksgiving Day under the Constitution.

The words and acts of the founding fathers, especially the first few presidents, shaped the form and tone of the civil religion as it has been maintained ever since. Though much is selectively derived from Christianity, this religion is clearly not itself Christianity. For one thing, neither Washington nor Adams nor Jefferson mentions Christ in his inaugural address; nor do any of the subsequent presidents, although not one of them fails to mention God.[3] The God of the civil religion is not only rather "unitarian," he is also on the austere side, much more related to order, law, and right than to salvation and love. Even though he is somewhat deist in cast, he is by no means simply a watchmaker God. He is actively interested and involved in history, with a special concern for America. Here the analogy has much less to do with natural law than with ancient Israel; the equation of America with Israel in the idea of the "American Israel" is not infrequent.[4] What was implicit in the words of Washington already quoted becomes explicit in Jefferson's second inaugural when he said: "I shall need, too, the favor of that Being in whose hands we are, who led our fathers, as Israel of old, from their native land and planted them in a country flowing with all the necessaries and comforts of life." Europe is Egypt; America, the promised land. God has led his people to establish a new sort of social order that shall be a light unto all the nations.[5]

This theme, too, has been a continuous one in the civil religion. We have already alluded to it in the case of the Kennedy inaugural. We find it again in President Johnson's inaugural address:

They came here—the exile and the stranger, brave but frightened—to find a place where a man could be his own man. They made a covenant with this land. Conceived in justice, written in liberty, bound in union, it was meant one day to inspire the hopes of all mankind; and it binds us still. If we keep its terms, we shall flourish.

What we have, then, from the earliest years of the republic is a collection of beliefs, symbols, and rituals with respect to sacred things and institutionalized in a collectivity. This religion—there seems no other word for it—while not antithetical to and indeed sharing much in common with Christianity, was neither sectarian nor in any specific sense Christian. At a time when the society was overwhelmingly Christian, it seems unlikely that this lack of Christian reference was meant to spare the feelings of the tiny non-Christian minority. Rather, the civil religion expressed what those who set the precedents felt was appropriate under the circumstances. It reflected their private as well as public views. Nor was the civil religion simply "religion in general." While generality was undoubtedly seen as a virtue by some, as in the quotation from Franklin above, the civil religion was specific enough when it came to the topic of America. Precisely because of this specificity, the civil religion was saved from empty formalism and served as a genuine vehicle of national religious self-understanding.

But the civil religion was not, in the minds of Franklin, Washington, Jefferson, or other leaders, with the exception of a few radicals like Tom Paine, ever felt to be a substitute for Christianity. There was an implicit but quite clear division of function between the civil religion and Christianity. Under the doctrine of religious liberty, an exceptionally wide sphere of personal piety and voluntary social action was left to the churches. But the churches were neither to control the state nor to be controlled by it. The national magistrate, whatever his private religious views, operates under the rubrics of the civil religion as long as he is in his official capacity, as we have already seen in the case of Kennedy. This accommodation was undoubtedly the product of a particular historical moment and of a cultural background dominated by Protestantism of several varieties and by the Enlightenment, but it has survived despite subsequent changes in the cultural and religious climate.

CIVIL WAR AND CIVIL RELIGION

Until the Civil War, the American civil religion focused above all on the event of the Revolution, which was seen as the final act of the Exodus from the old lands across the waters. The Declaration of Independence and the Constitution were the sacred scriptures and Washington the divinely appointed Moses who led his people out of the hands of tyranny. The Civil War, which Sidney Mead calls "the center of American history,"[6] was the second great event that involved the national self-understanding so deeply as to require expression in the civil religion. In 1835, Tocqueville wrote that the American republic had never really been tried, that victory in the Revolutionary War was more the result of British pre-occupation elsewhere and the presence of a powerful ally than of any great military success of the Americans. But in 1861 the time of testing had indeed come. Not only did the Civil War have the tragic intensity of fratricidal strife, but it was one of the bloodiest wars of the nineteenth century; the loss of life was far greater than any previously suffered by Americans.

The Civil War raised the deepest questions of national meaning. The man who not only formulated but in his own person embodied its meaning for Americans was Abraham Lincoln. For him the issue was not in the first instance slavery but "whether that nation, or any nation so conceived, and so dedicated, can long endure." He had said in Independence Hall in Philadelphia on 22 February 1861:

> All the political sentiments I entertain have been drawn, so far as I have been able to draw them, from the sentiments which originated in and were given to the world from this Hall. I have never had a feeling, politically, that did not spring from the sentiments embodied in the Declaration of Independence.[7]

The phrases of Jefferson constantly echo in Lincoln's speeches. His task was, first of all, to save the Union—not for America alone but for the meaning of America to the whole world so unforgettably etched in the last phrase of the Gettysburg Address.

But inevitably the issue of slavery as the deeper cause of the conflict had to be faced. In the second inaugural, Lincoln related slavery and the war in an ultimate perspective:

> If we shall suppose that American slavery is one of those offenses which, in the providence of God, must needs come, but which, having continued through His appointed time, He now wills to remove, and that He gives to both North and South this terrible war as the woe due to those by whom the offense came, shall we discern therein any departure from those divine attributes which the believers in a living God always ascribe to Him? Fondly do we hope, fervently do we pray, that this mighty scourge of war may speedily pass away. Yet, if God wills that it continue until all the wealth piled by the bondsman's two hundred and fifty years of unrequited toil shall be sunk, and until every drop of blood drawn with the lash shall be paid by another drawn with the sword, as was said three thousand years ago, so still it must be said "the judgements of the Lord are true and righteous altogether."

But he closes on a note if not of redemption then of reconciliation—With malice toward none, with charity for all. . . ."

With the Civil War, a new theme of death, sacrifice, and rebirth enters the civil religion. It is symbolized in the life and death of Lincoln. Nowhere is it stated more vividly than in the Gettysburg Address, itself part of the Lincolnian "New Testament" among the civil scriptures. Robert Lowell has recently pointed out the "insistent use of birth images" in this speech explicitly devoted to "these honored dead": "brought forth," "conceived," "created," "a new birth of freedom." He goes on to say:

The Gettysburg Address is a symbolic and sacramental act. Its verbal quality is resonance combined with a logical, matter of fact, prosaic brevity. . . . In his words, Lincoln symbolically died, just as the Union soldiers really died— and as he himself was soon really to die. By his words, he gave the field of battle a symbolic significance that it had lacked. For us and our country, he left Jefferson's ideals of freedom and equality joined to the Christian sacrificial act of death and rebirth. I believe this is a meaning that goes beyond sect or religion and beyond peace and war, and is now part of our lives as a challenge, obstacle and hope.[8]

Lowell is certainly right in pointing out the Christian quality of the symbolism here, but he is also right in quickly disavowing any sectarian implication. The earlier symbolism of the civil religion had been Hebraic without being in any specific sense Jewish. The Gettysburg symbolism (". . . those who here gave their lives, that that nation might live") is Christian without having anything to do with the Christian church.

The symbolic equation of Lincoln with Jesus was made relatively early. Herndon, who had been Lincoln's law partner, wrote:

For fifty years God rolled Abraham Lincoln through his fiery furnace. He did it to try Abraham and to purify him for his purposes. This made Mr. Lincoln humble, tender, forebearing, sympathetic to suffering, kind, sensitive, tolerant; broadening, deepening and widening his whole nature; making him the noblest and loveliest character since Jesus Christ. . . . I believe that Lincoln was God's chosen one.[9]

With the Christian archetype in the background, Lincoln, "our martyred president," was linked to the war dead, those who "gave the last full measure of devotion." The theme of sacrifice was indelibly written into the civil religion.

The new symbolism soon found both physical and ritualistic expression. The great number of the war dead required the establishment of a number of national cemeteries. Of these, the Gettysburg National Cemetery, which Lincoln's famous address served to dedicate, has been overshadowed only by the Arlington National Cemetery. Begun somewhat vindictively on the Lee estate across the river from Washington, partly with the end that the Lee family could never reclaim it,[10] it has subsequently become the most hallowed monument of the civil religion. Not only was a section set aside for the Confederate dead, but it has received the dead of each succeeding American war. It is the site of the one important new symbol to come out of World War I, the Tomb of the Unknown Soldier; more recently it has become the site of the tomb of another martyred president and its symbolic eternal flame.

Memorial Day, which grew out of the Civil War, gave ritual expression to the themes we have been discussing. As Lloyd Warner has so brilliantly analyzed it, the Memorial Day observance, especially in the towns and smaller cities of America, is a major event for the whole community involving a rededication to the martyred dead, to the spirit of sacrifice, and to the American vision.[11] Just as Thanksgiving Day, which incidentally was securely institutionalized as an annual national holiday only under the presidency of Lincoln, serves to integrate the family into the civil religion, so Memorial Day has acted to integrate the local community into the national cult. Together with the less overtly religious Fourth of July and the more minor celebrations of Veterans Day and the birthdays of Washington and Lincoln, these two holidays provide an annual ritual calendar for the civil religion. The public-school system serves as a particularly important context for the cultic celebration of the civil rituals.

In reifying and giving a name to something that, though pervasive enough when you look at it, has gone on only semiconsciously, there is risk of severely distorting the data. But the reification and the naming have already begun. The religious critics of "religion in general," or of the "religion of the 'American Way of Life,' " or of "American Shinto" have really been talking about the civil religion. As usual in religious polemic, they take as criteria the best in their own religious tradition and as typical the worst in the tradition of the civil religion. Against these critics, I would argue that the civil religion at its best is a genuine apprehension of universal and transcendent religious reality as seen in or, one could almost say, as revealed through the experience of the American people. Like all religions, it has suffered various deformations and demonic distortions. At its best, it has neither been so general that it has lacked incisive relevance to the American scene nor so particular that it has placed American society above universal human values. I am not at all convinced that the leaders of the churches have consistently represented a higher level of religious insight than the spokesmen of the civil religion. Reinhold Niebuhr has this to say of Lincoln, who never joined a church and who certainly represents civil religion at its best:

> An analysis of the religion of Abraham Lincoln in the context of the traditional religion of his time and place and of its polemical use on the slavery issue, which corrupted religious life in the days before and during the Civil War, must lead to the conclusion that Lincoln's religious convictions were superior in depth and purity to those, not only of the political leaders of his day, but of the religious leaders of the era.[12]

Perhaps the real animus of the religious critics has been not so much against the civil religion in itself but against its pervasive and dominating influence within the sphere of church religion. As S. M. Lipset has recently shown, American religion at least since the early-nineteenth century has been predominantly activist, moralistic, and social rather than contemplative, theological, or innerly spiritual.[13] Tocqueville spoke of American church religion as "a political institution which powerfully contributes to the maintenance of a democratic republic among the Americans"[14] by supplying a strong moral consensus amidst continuous political change. Henry Bargy in 1902 spoke of American church religion as "la poésie du civisme."[15]

It is certainly true that the relation between religion and politics in America has been singularly smooth. This is in large part due to the dominant tradition. As Tocqueville wrote:

The greatest part of British America was peopled by men who, after having shaken off the authority of the Pope, acknowledged no other religious supremacy: they brought with them into the New World a form of Christianity which I cannot better describe than by styling it a democratic and republican religion.[16]

The churches opposed neither the Revolution nor the establishment of democratic institutions. Even when some of them opposed the full institutionalization of religious liberty, they accepted the final outcome with good grace and without nostalgia for an *ancien régime*. The American civil religion was never anticlerical or militantly secular. On the contrary, it borrowed selectively from the religious tradition in such a way that the average American saw no conflict between the two. In this way, the civil religion was able to build up without any bitter struggle with the church powerful symbols of national solidarity and to mobilize deep levels of personal motivation for the attainment of national goals.

Such an achievement is by no means to be taken for granted. It would seem that the problem of a civil religion is quite general in modern societies and that the way it is solved or not solved will have repercussions in many spheres. One needs only to think of France to see how differently things can go. The French Revolution was anticlerical to the core and attempted to set up an anti-Christian civil religion. Throughout modern French history, the chasm between traditional Catholic symbols and the symbolism of 1789 has been immense.

American civil religion is still very much alive. Just three years ago we participated in a vivid re-enactment of the sacrifice theme in connection with the funeral of our assassinated president. The American Israel theme is clearly behind both Kennedy's New Frontier and Johnson's Great Society. Let me give just one recent illustration of how the civil religion serves to mobilize support for the attainment of national goals. On 15 March 1965 President Johnson went before Congress to ask for a strong voting-rights bill. Early in the speech he said:

Rarely are we met with the challenge, not to our growth or abundance, or our welfare or our security—but rather to the values and the purposes and the meaning of our beloved nation.

The issue of equal rights for American Negroes is such an issue. And should we defeat every enemy, and should we double our wealth and conquer the stars and still be unequal to this issue, then we will have failed as a people and as a nation.

For with a country as with a person, "What is a man profited, if he shall gain the whole world, and lose his own soul?"

And in conclusion he said:

Above the pyramid on the great seal of the United States it says in Latin, "God has favored our undertaking."

God will not favor everything that we do. It is rather our duty to divine his will. I cannot help but believe that He truly understands and that He really favors the undertaking that we begin here tonight.[17]

The civil religion has not always been invoked in favor of worthy causes. On the domestic scene, an American-Legion type of ideology that fuses God, country, and flag has been used to attack nonconformist and liberal ideas and groups of all kinds. Still, it has been difficult to use the words of Jefferson and Lincoln to support special interests and undermine personal freedom. The defenders of slavery before the Civil War came to reject the thinking of the Declaration of Independence. Some of the most consistent of them turned against not only Jeffersonian democracy but Reformation religion; they dreamed of a South dominated by medieval chivalry and divine-right monarchy.[18] For all the overt religiosity of the radical right today, their relation to the civil religious consensus is tenuous, as when the John Birch Society attacks the central American symbol of Democracy itself.

With respect to America's role in the world, the dangers of distortion are greater and the built-in safeguards of the tradition weaker. The theme of the American Israel was used, almost from the beginning, as a justification for the shameful treatment of the Indians so characteristic of our history. It can be overtly or implicitly linked to the idea of manifest destiny which has been used to legitimate several adventures in imperialism since the early-nineteenth century. Never has the danger been greater than today. The issue is not so much one of imperial expansion, of which we are accused, as of the tendency to assimilate all governments or parties in the world which support our immediate policies or call upon our help by invoking the notion of free institutions and democratic values. Those nations that are for the moment "on our side" become "the free world." A repressive and unstable military dictatorship in South Viet-Nam becomes "the free people of South Viet-Nam and their government." It is then part of the role of America as the New Jerusalem and "the last best hope on earth" to defend such governments with treasure and eventually with blood. When our soldiers are actually dying, it becomes possible to consecrate the struggle further by invoking the great theme of sacrifice. For the majority of the American people who are unable to judge whether the people in South Viet-Nam (or wherever) are "free like us," such arguments are convincing. Fortunately President Johnson has been less ready to assert that "God has favored our undertaking" in the case of Viet-Nam than with respect to civil rights. But others are not so hesitant. The civil religion has exercised long-term pressure for the humane solution of our greatest domestic problem, the treatment of the Negro American. It remains to be seen how relevant it can become for our role in the world at large, and whether we can effectually stand for "the revolutionary beliefs for which our forebears fought," in John F. Kennedy's words.

The civil religion is obviously involved in the most pressing moral and political issues of the day. But it is also caught in another kind of crisis, theoretical and theological, of which it is at the moment largely unaware. "God" has clearly been a central symbol in the civil religion from the beginning and remains so today. This symbol is just as central to the civil religion as it is to Judaism or Christianity. In the late-eighteenth century this posed no problem; even Tom Paine, contrary to his detractors, was not an atheist. From left to right and regardless of church or sect, all could accept the idea of God. But today, as even *Time* has recognized, the meaning of the word *God* is by no means so clear or so obvious. There is no formal creed in the civil religion. We have had a Catholic president; it is conceivable that we could have a Jewish one. But could we have an agnostic president? Could a man with conscientious scruples about using the word *God* the way Kennedy and Johnson have used it be elected chief magistrate of our country? If the whole God symbolism requires reformulation, there will be obvious consequences for the civil religion, consequences perhaps of liberal alienation and of fundamentalist ossification that have not so far been prominent in this realm. The civil religion has been a point of articulation between the profoundest commitments of the Western religious and philosophical tradition and the common beliefs of ordinary Americans. It is not too soon to consider how the deepening theological crisis may affect the future of this articulation.

THE THIRD TIME OF TRIAL

In conclusion it may be worthwhile to relate the civil religion to the most serious situation that we as Americans now face, what I call the third time of trial. The first time of trial had to do with the question of independence, whether we should or could run our own affairs in our own way. The second time of trial was over the issue of slavery, which in turn was only the most salient aspect of the more general problem of the full institutionalization of democracy within our country. This second problem we are still far from solving though we have some notable successes to our credit. But we have been overtaken by a third great problem which has led to a third great crisis, in the midst of which we stand. This is the problem of responsible action in a revolutionary world, a world seeking to attain many of the things, material and spiritual, that we have already attained. Americans have, from the beginning, been aware of the responsibility and the significance our republican experiment has for the whole world. The first internal political polarization in the new nation had to do with our attitude toward the French Revolution. But we were small and weak then, and "foreign entanglements" seemed to threaten our very survival. During the last century, our relevance for the world was not forgotten, but our role was seen as purely exemplary. Our democratic republic rebuked tyranny by merely existing. Just after World War I we were on the brink of taking a different role in the world, but once again we turned our back.

Since World War II the old pattern has become impossible. Every president since Roosevelt has been groping toward a new pattern of action in the world, one that would be consonant with our power and our responsibilities. For Truman and for the period dominated by John Foster Dulles that pattern was seen to be the great Manichaean confrontation of East and West, the confrontation of democracy and "the false philosophy of Communism" that provided the structure of Truman's inaugural address. But with the last years of Eisenhower and with the successive two presidents, the pattern began to shift. The great problems came to be seen as caused not solely by the evil intent of any one group of men, but as stemming from much more complex and multiple sources. For Kennedy, it was not so much a struggle against particular men as against "the common enemies of man: tyranny, poverty, disease and war itself."

But in the midst of this trend toward a less primitive conception of ourselves and our world, we have somehow, without anyone really intending it, stumbled into a military confrontation where we have come to feel that our honor is at stake. We have in a moment of uncertainty been tempted to rely on our overwhelming physical power rather than on our intelligence, and we have, in part, succumbed to this temptation. Bewildered and unnerved when our terrible power fails to bring immediate success, we are at the edge of a chasm the depth of which no man knows.

I cannot help but think of Robinson Jeffers, whose poetry seems more apt now than when it was written, when he said:

Unhappy country, what wings you have! ...
Weep (it is frequent in human affairs), weep for
  the terrible magnificence of the means,
The ridiculous incompetence of the reasons, the
  bloody and shabby
Pathos of the result.

But as so often before in similar times, we have a man of prophetic stature, without the bitterness or misanthropy of Jeffers, who, as Lincoln before him, calls this nation to its judgment:

When a nation is very powerful but lacking in self-confidence, it is likely to behave in a manner that is dangerous both to itself and to others.

Gradually but unmistakably, America is succumbing to that arrogance of power which has afflicted, weakened and in some cases destroyed great nations in the past.

If the war goes on and expands, if that fatal process continues to accelerate until America becomes what it is not now and never has been, a seeker after unlimited power and empire, then Vietnam will have had a mighty and tragic fallout indeed.

I do not believe that will happen. I am very apprehensive but I still remain hopeful, and even confident, that America, with its humane and democratic traditions, will find the wisdom to match its power.[19]

Without an awareness that our nation stands under higher judgment, the tradition of the civil religion would be dangerous indeed. Fortunately, the prophetic voices have never been lacking. Our present situation brings to mind the Mexican-American war that Lincoln, among so many others, opposed. The spirit of civil disobedience that is alive today in the civil rights movement and the opposition to the Viet-Nam war was already clearly outlined by Henry David Thoreau when he wrote, "If the law is of such a nature that it requires you to be an agent of injustice to another, then I say, break the law." Thoreau's words, "I would remind my countrymen that they are men first, and Americans at a late and convenient hour,"[20] provide an essential standard for any adequate thought and action in our third time of trial. As Americans, we have been well favored in the world, but it is as men that we will be judged.

Out of the first and second times of trial have come, as we have seen, the major symbols of the American civil religion. There seems little doubt that a successful negotiation of this third time of trial—the attainment of some kind of viable and coherent world order—would precipitate a major new set of symbolic forms. So far the flickering flame of the United Nations burns too low to be the focus of a cult, but the emergence of a genuine transnational sovereignty would certainly change this. It would necessitate the incorporation of vital international symbolism into our civil religion, or, perhaps a better way of putting it, it would result in American civil religion becoming simply one part of a new civil religion of the world. It is useless to speculate on the form such a civil religion might take, though it obviously would draw on religious traditions beyond the sphere of Biblical religion alone. Fortunately, since the American civil religion is not the worship of the American nation but an understanding of the American experience in the light of ultimate and universal reality, the reorganization entailed by such a new situation need not disrupt the American civil religion's continuity. A world civil religion could be accepted as a fulfillment and not a denial of American civil religion. Indeed, such an outcome has been the eschatological hope of American civil religion from the beginning. To deny such an outcome would be to deny the meaning of America itself.

Behind the civil religion at every point lie Biblical archetypes: Exodus, Chosen People, Promised Land, New Jerusalem, Sacrificial Death and Rebirth. But it is also genuinely American and genuinely new. It has its own prophets and its own martyrs, its own sacred events and sacred places, its own solemn rituals and symbols. It is concerned that America be a society as perfectly in accord with the will of God as men can make it, and a light to all the nations.

It has often been used and is being used today as a cloak for petty interests and ugly passions. It is in need—as is any living faith—of continual reformation, of being measured by universal standards. But it is not evident that it is incapable of growth and new insight.

It does not make any decision for us. It does not remove us from moral ambiguity, from being, in Lincoln's fine phrase, an "almost chosen people." But it is a heritage of moral and religious experience from which we still have much to learn as we formulate the decisions that lie ahead.

NOTES

[1] Why something so obvious should have escaped serious analytical attention is in itself an interesting problem. Part of the reason is probably the controversial nature of the subject. From the earliest years of the nineteenth century, conservative religious and political groups have argued that Christianity is, in fact, the national religion. Some of them have from time to time and as recently as the 1950's proposed constitutional amendments that would explicitly recognize the sovereignty of Christ. In defending the doctrine of separation of church and state, opponents of such groups have denied that the national polity has, intrinsically, anything to do with religion at all. The moderates on this issue have insisted that the American state has taken a permissive and indeed supportive attitude toward religious groups (tax exemption, et cetera), thus favoring religion but still missing the positive institutionalization with which I am concerned. But part of the reason this issue has been left in obscurity is certainly due to the peculiarly Western concept of "religion" as denoting a single type of collectivity of which an individual can be a member of one and only one at a time. The Durkheimian notion that every group has a religious dimension, which would be seen as obvious in southern or eastern Asia, is foreign to us. This obscures the recognition of such dimensions in our society.

[2] Quoted in Will Herberg, *Protestant-Catholic-Jew* (New York, 1955), p. 97.

[3] God is mentioned or referred to in all inaugural addresses but Washington's second, which is a very brief (two paragraphs) and perfunctory acknowledgment. It is not without interest that the actual word *God* does not appear until Monroe's second inaugural, 5 March 1821. In his first inaugural, Washington refers to God as "that Almighty Being who rules the universe," "Great Author of every public and private good," "Invisible Hand," and "benign Parent of the Human Race." John Adams refers to God as "Providence," "Being who is supreme over all," "Patron of Order," "Foundation of Justice," and "Protector in all ages of the world of virtuous liberty." Jefferson speaks of "that Infinite Power which rules the destinies of the universe," and "that Being in whose hands we are." Madison speaks of "that Almighty Being whose power regulates the destiny of nations," and "Heaven." Monroe uses "Providence" and "the Almighty" in his first inaugural and finally "Almighty God" in his second. See *Inaugural Addresses of the Presidents of the United States from George Washington 1789 to Harry S Truman 1949*, 82nd Congress, 2d Session, House Document No. 540, 1952.

[4] For example, Abiel Abbot, pastor of the First Church in Haverhill, Massachusetts, delivered a Thanksgiving sermon in 1799, *Traits of Resemblance in the People of the United States of America to Ancient Israel*, in which he said, "It has been often remarked that the people of the United States come nearer to a parallel with Ancient Israel, than any other nation upon the globe. Hence

'Our American Israel' is a term frequently used; and common consent allows it apt and proper." Cited in Hans Kohn, *The Idea of Nationalism* (New York, 1961), p. 665.

[5] That the Mosaic analogy was present in the minds of leaders at the very moment of the birth of the republic is indicated in the designs proposed by Franklin and Jefferson for a seal of the United States of America. Together with Adams, they formed a committee of three delegated by the Continental Congress on July 4, 1776, to draw up the new device. "Franklin proposed as the device Moses lifting up his wand and dividing the Red Sea while Pharaoh was overwhelmed by its waters, with the motto 'Rebellion to tyrants is obedience to God.' Jefferson proposed the children of Israel in the wilderness 'led by a cloud by day and a pillar of fire at night.'" Anson Phelps Stokes, *Church and State in the United States,* Vol. 1 (New York, 1950), pp. 467–468.

[6] Sidney Mead, *The Lively Experiment* (New York, 1963), p. 12.

[7] Quoted by Arthur Lehman Goodhart in Allan Nevins (ed.), *Lincoln and the Gettysburg Address* (Urbana, Ill., 1964), p. 39.

[8] Ibid., "On the Gettysburg Address," pp. 88–89.

[9] Quoted in Sherwood Eddy, *The Kingdom of God and the American Dream* (New York, 1941), p. 162.

[10] Karl Decker and Angus McSween, *Historic Arlington* (Washington, D.C., 1892), pp. 60–67.

[11] How extensive the activity associated with Memorial Day can be is indicated by Warner: "The sacred symbolic behavior of Memorial Day, in which scores of the town's organizations are involved, is ordinarily divided into four periods. During the year separate rituals are held by many of the associations for their dead, and many of these activities are connected with later Memorial Day events. In the second phase, preparations are made during the last three or four weeks for the ceremony itself, and some of the associations perform public rituals. The third phase consists of scores of rituals held in all the cemeteries, churches, and halls of the associations. These rituals consist of speeches and highly ritualized behavior. They last for two days and are climaxed by the fourth and last phase, in which all the separate celebrants gather in the center of the business district on the afternoon of Memorial Day. The separate organizations, with their members in uniform or with fitting insignia, march through the town, visit the shrines and monuments of the hero dead, and, finally enter the cemetery. Here dozens of ceremonies are held, most of them highly symbolic and formalized." During these various ceremonies Lincoln is continually referred to and the Gettysburg Address recited many times. W. Lloyd Warner, *American Life* (Chicago, 1962), pp. 8–9.

[12] Reinhold Niebuhr, "The Religion of Abraham Lincoln," in Nevins (ed.), *op. cit.,* p. 72. William J. Wolfe of the Episcopal Theological School in Cambridge, Massachusetts, has written: "Lincoln is one of the greatest theologians of America—not in the technical meaning of producing a system of doctrine, certainly not as the defender of some one denomination, but in the sense of seeing the hand of God intimately in the affairs of nations. Just so the prophets of Israel criticized the events of their day from the perspective of the God who is concerned for history and who reveals His will within it. Lincoln now stands among God's latter-day prophets." *The Religion of Abraham Lincoln* (New York, 1963), p. 24.

[13] Seymour Martin Lipset, "Religion and American Values," Chapter 4, *The First New Nation* (New York, 1964).

[14] Alexis de Tocqueville, *Democracy in America*, Vol. 1 (New York, 1954), p. 310.

[15] Henry Bargy, *La Religion dans la Société aux États-Unis* (Paris, 1902), p. 31.

[16] Tocqueville, *op. cit.*, p. 311. Later he says, "In the United States even the religion of most of the citizens is republican, since it submits the truths of the other world to private judgment, as in politics the care of their temporal interests is abandoned to the good sense of the people. Thus every man is allowed freely to take that road which he thinks will lead him to heaven, just as the law permits every citizen to have the right of choosing his own government" (p. 436).

[17] U.S., *Congressional Record*, House, 15 March 1965, pp. 4924, 4926.

[18] See Louis Hartz, "The Feudal Dream of the South," Part 4, *The Liberal Tradition in America* (New York, 1955).

[19] Speech of Senator J. William Fulbright of 28 April 1968, as reported in *The New York Times*, 29 April 1966.

[20] Quoted in Yehoshua Arieli, *Individualism and Nationalism in American Ideology* (Cambridge, Mass., 1964), p. 274.

✦✦✦✦✦✦✦✦✦✦✦✦✦✦✦✦✦✦

The Unfinished Dream

BILLY GRAHAM

The Bible says in First Peter 2:17: "Honor all men. Fear God. Honor the king." And the king referred to was the Roman emperor. Since our nation is a republic and not a monarchy, this Scripture could read, "Honor the nation."

Today, in the capital of the United States, thousands of us have come together to honor America on her 194th birthday.

We stand here today within the shadow of three great monuments.

That great shaft over there honors George Washington, who led the revolution that obtained our freedom.

Not far away is the memorial to Thomas Jefferson, father of the Declaration of Independence, which proclaimed the rights of free men and began the greatest experiment in freedom the world has ever known.

Behind us is the memorial honoring Abraham Lincoln, who helped preserve the unity of this country by his courage, faith, and perseverance—and who gave black men hope that they, too, would become first-class citizens.

We can listen to no better voices than these men who gave us the dream that has become America. These men represent thousands who worked, prayed, suffered, and died to give us this nation.

We are not here today only to honor America; we are come as citizens to renew our dedication and allegiance to the principles and institutions that made her great. Lately our institutions have been under attack: the Supreme Court, the Congress, the presidency, the flag, the home, the educational system, and even the church—but we are here to say with loud voices that in spite of their faults and failures we believe in these institutions!

Let the world know today that the vast majority of us still proudly sing: "My country, 'tis of thee, sweet land of liberty." America needs to sing again! America needs to celebrate again! America needs to wave the flag again! This flag belongs to all Americans—black and white, rich and poor, liberal and conservative, Republican and Democrat.

I think there is too much discouragement, despair, and negativism in the nation today. On every hand critics tell us what is wrong with America, where we have failed, and why we are hated. We have listened and watched

Address delivered at the Honor America Day religious service held in Washington, D.C., July 4, 1970. Copyright 1970 by *Christianity Today*. Reprinted with permission.

The Rev. Billy Graham is one of America's best-known evangelists.

while a relatively small extremist element, both to the left and to the right in our society, has knocked our courts, desecrated our flag, disrupted our educational system, laughed at our religious heritage, and threatened to burn down our cities—and is now threatening to assassinate our leaders.

The overwhelming majority of concerned Americans—white and black, hawks and doves, parents and students, Republicans and Democrats—who hate violence have stood by and viewed all of this with mounting alarm and concern. Today we call upon all Americans to stop this polarization before it is too late—and let's proudly gather around the flag and all that it stands for.

Many people have asked me why I, as a citizen of heaven and a Christian minister, join in honoring any secular state. Jesus said, "Render unto Caesar the things that are Caesar's." The Apostle Paul proudly boasted of being a Roman citizen. The Bible says "Honor the nation." As a Christian, or as a Jew, or as an atheist, each of us has a responsibility to an America that has always stood for liberty, protection, and opportunity.

There are many reasons why we honor America today.

First, we honor America because she has opened her heart and her doors to the distressed and the persecuted of the world. Millions have crossed our threshold into the fresh air of freedom. I believe that the Bible teaches that God blesses a nation which carries out the words of Jesus, "For I was hungered, and ye gave me meat: I was thirsty, and ye gave me drink: I was a stranger, and ye took me in."

Secondly, we honor America because she has been the most generous nation in history. We have shared our wealth and faith with a world in need. When a disaster occurs any place in the world, America is there with help. In famine, in earthquakes, in floods, in stresses of every kind, we pour out millions of dollars every year, even if we have to borrow the money and go in debt.

Thirdly, we honor America because she has never hidden her problems and debts. With our freedom of the press and open communications system, we don't sweep our sins under the rug. If poverty exists, if racial tension exists, if riots occur, the whole world knows about it. Instead of an Iron Curtain we have a picture window. "The whole world watches"—sometimes critically and sometimes with admiration, but nobody can accuse America of trying to hide her problems.

Fourthly, we honor America because she is honestly recognizing and is courageously trying to solve her social problems. In order to fulfill the ultimate problem, much remains to be done—but even our critics abroad are saying, "America is trying." The men who penned the Declaration of Independence were moved by a magnificent dream. This dream amazed the world 194 years ago. And this dream is rooted in a book we call the Bible. It proclaims freedoms that most people of the world thought were impossible. We are still striving to achieve for all men equally those freedoms bought at such a high price. From the beginning, the dream of freedom and equal opportunity has been a beacon to oppressed peoples all over the world.

Let those who claim they want to improve the nation by destroying it join all of us in a new unity and a new dedication by peaceful means to make these dreams come true.

Fifthly, we honor America because she defends the right of her citizens to dissent. Dissent is impossible in many countries of the world, whereas constructive dissent is the hallmark of our freedom in America. But when dissent takes violent forms and has no moral purpose, it is no longer dissent but anarchy. We will listen respectfully to those who dissent in accordance with constitutional principles, but we strongly reject violence and the erosion of any of our liberties under the guise of a dissent that promises everything but delivers only chaos. As General Eisenhower once wrote: "We must never confuse honest dissent with disloyal subversion."

Sixthly, we honor America because there is woven into the warp and woof of our nation faith in God. The ethical and moral principles of the Judeo-Christian faith and the God of that tradition are found throughout the Declaration of Independence. Most presidents of the United States have declared their faith in God and have encouraged us to read the Bible. I am encouraged to believe that Americans at this hour are striving to retain their spiritual identity despite the inroads of materialism and the rising tide of permissiveness.

On the front page of a Chicago newspaper some time ago there appeared a picture of Betsy Ross sewing the first American flag. Over the picture was the caption, "Time to check our stitches." Let's check the stitches of racism that still persist in our country. Let's check the stitches of poverty that bind some of our countrymen. Let's check the stitches of foreign policy to be sure that our objectives and goals are in keeping with the American dream. Let's check the stitches of pollution brought on by technology. Let's check the stitches of a moral permissiveness that could lead us to decadence. Let's even check the stitches of freedom to see if our freedom in America has become license. A liberal British writer recently said, "You Americans have become too free until you are no longer free."

.   .   .

I'm asking all Americans today, especially our young people, to pursue this vision under God, to work for freedom and for peace. It will not be easy. The journey will be hard. The day will be long. And the obstacles will be many.

But I remember today a word spoken by Sir Winston Churchill, whose courage and faith and persistence carried his nation through the darkest days of World War II. The headmaster of Harrow, the famous prep school that Churchill had attended as a boy, asked Mr. Churchill to address the students. The headmaster told the young people to bring their pencils and their notebooks to record what Britain's greatest man of the century would say. The moment they waited for came. The old man stood to his feet and spoke these words: "Never give in! Never give in! Never! Never!"

I say to you today, "Pursue the vision, reach the goal, fulfill the American dream—and as you move to do it, never give in! Never give in! Never! Never! Never! Never!"

✛✛✛✛✛✛✛✛✛✛✛✛✛✛✛✛✛

Sports, Religion and Politics:
The Renewal of an Alliance

CORNISH ROGERS

"My wife said you'd do it, and sure enough you did," remarked a member of my congregation after services one fall Sunday morning several years ago. What had I done? I asked, and he explained: "As we were driving to church today, I asked my wife who won the UCLA–USC basketball game last night, since I hadn't had a chance to read the morning papers. She didn't know either but predicted that we'd soon find out when we heard your sermon." After a slight pause, he added, smiling: "As you know, Reverend, you are forever using illustrations from recent athletic events."

No one in America who is interested in both sports and religion can overlook the unmistakable link between them—and that link is by no means limited to the fact that the lessons of sports lend themselves readily to analogies concerning godly living. Whether athletic events involve interschool rivalry or competition between the teams of two cities, the spectators tacitly infer that the contest represents the symbolic acting-out of a larger cosmic drama, and that the winner is somehow more virtuous than the loser, or at least more pleasing to the gods. The winning team's victory is appropriated by those the team represents; the entire supporting crowd can shout with conviction, "We're number one!" The cathartic effect of victory, be is propitiatory or celebrative, is felt not only by the participants but also by those on whose behalf they compete.

THE ANCIENT TIES

It is clear, then, that the more closely we analyze the mystique of sports, psychologically and functionally, the more we tend to use religious language to describe it. And no wonder: from its beginnings, athletics was regarded as a religious cult and as a preparation for life. According to Rabbi Rudolph Brasch, "Its roots were in man's desire to gain victory over foes seen and unseen, to influence the forces of nature, and to promote fertility among his crops and cattle."

The word "sport" itself is an abbreviation, the shortened form of *disport*—

Mr. Rogers is an associate editor of *The Christian Century* magazine, and an ordained minister in the United Methodist Church.

an amusement or diversion. It is a derivative of the Latin *des-porto*, which literally means "carry away." But though the enjoyment of sports has often diverted people from day-to-day cares and anxieties and carried them away to a world of excitement and thrills, sports began as a necessity for primal man's survival. In addition to fulfilling his innate desire for competition, sports enabled primitive man to develop the muscular strength and alertness to defend himself against human, animal and other natural foes.

But primitive man perceived his greatest enemies not as natural but as supernatural. The Zuni Indians in New Mexico played games which they believed would magically bring rain to their drought-filled land and thus enable their crops to grow. Wrestling bouts in southern Nigeria were designed to encourage the growth of crops by sympathetic magic. Many games were held in the winter in order to hasten the return of spring and to ensure a fruitful season. And during the fall, at the end of the harvest season, an Eskimo tribe played a cup-and-ball game to "catch the sun" and thus delay its departure. "Playing the game," says Rabbi Brasch, was man's way to assure the "revival of nature and the victory of vegetation."

The association of sports with religion during the classical period is exemplified by the Olympic games, played in honor of Zeus, and the Pythian games, which were related to the oracles of Apollo and his shrine at Delphi. Such competitions were intended not only to honor the gods but also to celebrate peace and were in fact regarded as exercises in holiness. E. Norman Gardiner, in his book *Athletics of the Ancient World*, indicates that some of the events were funeral games conducted in honor of some soldier slain in battle. (And even the apostle Paul, though he rejected the pagan religious implications of the games, employed athletic metaphors in speaking of the faith—the early Christian wrestled with the powers of darkness, fought the good fight, and finished the race.)

THE SPORTS MYSTIQUE AND POLITICS

That politics should intrude into the relationship between sports and religion is readily understandable when it is remembered that many ancient rulers (like some present ones) also served as heads of the state religious establishment and in some cases were themselves considered at least semidivine. Thus sports have become a valuable political device for political leaders to use in consolidating—and even sacralizing—their power. When Richard Nixon awarded the University of Nebraska football team the title as national champions, he was courting for himself the mystique of a "divine king." And in this presidential year, he is not alone: a few weeks ago during the Florida primary race John Lindsay threw out the first baseball in a New York Yankees preseason game. No doubt other presidential aspirants will seek in some way to appropriate the sports mystique in the coming months.

Each of the serious candidates knows that, by whatever name it is called, America's "civil religion" is a vital force to be reckoned with. They recognize that Richard Nixon, by holding "nondenominational" Sunday services in the White House, has tried to co-opt for himself the symbolic embodiment of the undefined but pervasive religious consciousness that has characterized our public life since the founding of the nation. He has sought to make more explicit the "American Shinto" by giving it a more pronounced shape and by according it an honored place in his presidency. Billy Graham, the foremost apostle of American evangelical nondenominationalism, has been installed as high priest. Recently one U.S. denominational leader, taking note of this trend, complained that there seems to be a stronger movement toward nondenominational religion than toward ecumenical religion.

RELIGION IN THE FOOTBALL STADIUM

In a manner comparable to the classical period of the Olympic games, the public festivals of America's civil religion are often held in the midst of massive sporting events. Anyone who watched televised football games last fall and winter can attest to the "religious" nature of the spectacle.

Several of last winter's games were dedicated to the late coach of the Green Bay Packers, Vince Lombardi, who seems to have earned a place in the panoply of the saints in American civil religion for his fierce discipline and his straightforward philosophy of play: "Winning is the only thing."

Football's halftime ceremonies often deal with patriotic themes. Through ingenious patterns on the playing field marching bands and prancing semi-nude girls form massive representations of the American flag. Meanwhile, overhead, U.S. air force planes fly intricate, close formations. Over the loud-speaker come appeals for the freeing of U.S. prisoners of war in Vietnam, and moments of silence are observed for those slain in the war. On occasion the restless television camera spies the President himself, enjoying the proceedings from a box seat.

The games are usually opened with prayer by a clergyman (it doesn't seem to matter whether the invoker is Protestant, Catholic or Jew), who offers prayer before the hushed thousands in the stadium, shamelessly linking God, country and good sportsmanship in his intercessions. The players as well as the spectators stand in respectful and reverent silence, though occasionally the television camera pans to a distracted athlete tugging at a private part of his anatomy or to a player chatting amiably with a colleague or vigorously chewing gum. To be sure, before leaving the dressing room, most teams have already had their "devotions," led by one of the players, probably a member of the Fellowship of Christian Athletes.

It is perhaps because religious fervor is such a powerful physical stimulant that American athletics has developed its own religion. The essence of that religion is embodied in the Fellowship of Christian Athletes, a nationwide network of active and former college and professional athletes who meet together to witness to their faith—usually a personal pietistic, triumphalist faith—and to provide worship leadership to all professional teams, especially on Sunday mornings when the teams are on the road. Aggressively non-denominational, the group seeks to instill in young people a sense of the relationship between competitive sports and the struggle to maintain a Christian life. Its members preach that disciplines developed in sports provide a solid foundation for successful and holy living; they testify that their Christian faith has stood them in good stead on the athletic field.

Several leaders of the Fellowship of Christian Athletes have gone on to become public relations directors for commercial enterprises; some of the more able have landed political patronage jobs in conservative administrations for which they direct "physical fitness" programs. But the athletes of the fellowship make their most significant contribution in personifying what it means to be dedicated and successful adherents of American civil religion. And buttressed by the examples of those paragons, sports are rapidly becoming the dominant ritualistic expression of the reification of established religion in America.

•‡•‡•‡•‡•‡•‡•‡•‡•‡•‡•‡•‡•‡•‡•‡•‡•

Breakfast with God
Newsweek MAGAZINE

Every Tuesday morning at 8, a score of Chicago's most prominent business and professional leaders gathers in the handsome lounge of the First Federal Savings and Loan Association for a lean breakfast of coffee and rolls—plus a generous portion of spontaneous prayer. Each week in a dozen Atlanta restaurants, the eggs and buttery grits come first—followed by prayers. And last month in a Detroit church more than 100 businessmen turned out at the "ungodly" hour of 6:30 A.M. to break bread and hear a General Motors marketing executive describe St. Paul as "the most dynamic, dedicated supersalesman of all."

The settings and the menus may vary, but in most major American cities, midweek prayer breakfasts are fast replacing Sunday evening chicken suppers as the preferred form of Christian fellowship—especially for busy executives who want to make room for God in their profit pictures. "We pray for peace, and sometimes for the POW's, and sometimes to do the right thing," says Elliot Frank, a retired Chicago banker who eats with the elite at First Federal, "because the right thing is usually the profitable thing, too. We want God to show us the right way to success."

No one seems to look harder for heavenly guidance, however, than the government officials who have turned Washington, D.C., into the prayer-breakfast capital of the U.S.—and possibly the world. In Washington there are weekly breakfasts for senators, congressmen, wives of congressmen, Senate restaurant waitresses, Indians, blacks and military men. The premiere attraction, of course, is the annual National Prayer Breakfast, which earlier this month drew more than 3,000 faithful to the Washington Hilton Hotel to hear testimonies by President Nixon and eight other government leaders. Afterward, more than 500 guests, many of them members of local prayer groups, remained for seminars on how to spread the prayer-breakfast movement.

Historians of the movement believe it began 37 years ago in Seattle when an itinerant preacher from Norway named Abraham Vereide brought a group of local businessmen together to pray over the problems of their depression-ridden city. But it wasn't until the late President Dwight D. Eisenhower established the first Presidential prayer breakfast in 1953 that the idea caught fire among governors, mayors, local chambers of commerce

From *Newsweek*, February 19, 1973, p. 90. Copyright 1973 by *Newsweek*, Inc. Reprinted with permission.

and trade associations. Last November in Honolulu, more than 8,000 real estate dealers showed up to hear Billy Graham speak at the largest prayer breakfast on record—and incidentally to commandeer nearly all the available coffee urns on the island. The man who arranged that event, millionaire Miami realtor L. Allen Morris, also helped organize the first Orange Bowl football game prayer breakfast this year and has spoken at chapel services for four professional football teams.

Planning: In a movement this big, spontaneity gives way to organization. The largest planning group, Washington-based Fellowship House, spends $100,000 annually trying to make certain that prayer breakfasts serve God rather than man. It isn't always easy. "I was in the mass production of prayer breakfasts," says one Fellowship staffer who organized 104 such Washington sessions. "And we found people who exploited the meetings for personal gain."

Although most men in the movement are probably sincere, some members question whether the prayers served up at breakfast are directed to the proper deity. In a handbook for organizers of prayer breakfasts, realtor Morris urges groups to thank the God who gave us the "blessings of living in America, of free enterprise." At the recent National Prayer Breakfast, Sen. Mark Hatfield of Oregon criticized prayer based on such spiritual exclusivity. "Events such as this prayer breakfast contain the real danger of misplaced allegiance, if not downright idolatry," he warned from a head table that included the President and evangelist Graham. "If we as leaders appeal to the God of an American civil religion, our faith is in a small and exclusive deity." No one in the audience was heard to say "Amen."

PART TWO

Religious Organization

CHAPTER 3

❖•❖•❖•❖•❖•❖•❖•❖•❖•❖•❖•❖•❖•❖•❖

"Mainstream" Protestantism:
The Denominations

The Constitution of the United States makes it very clear that no one religion shall be official for the nation. Most often quoted is the First Amendment: "Congress shall make no law respecting an establishment of religion or prohibiting the free exercise thereof." But this is simply a general statement, phrased as a principle, of a firm viewpoint expressed ten years previously in Article VI of the Constitution itself: "No religious test shall ever be required as a qualification to any office or public trust under the United States." These statements guarantee a clean separation between church and state and were intended to ensure the freedom of each institution in its respective spheres of authority. It had not always been so. Though American history texts emphasize the early colonies as havens for the religiously persecuted of England and western Europe, the Puritan Church in New England and the Episcopal Church established from New York southward attempted to limit the freedom of the many nonconformist sects that came to express their beliefs in the colonies. By the time of the Revolution, however, both strongholds—Puritan and Episcopal—had been seriously weakened. Liberal ideas antithetical to orthodox Calvinism were firmly entrenched in the thinking of Massachusetts delegates to the Constitutional Convention; in Virginia, the other state sharing prominence in both the Revolution and the framing of the new federal government, "three-quarters of the Episcopal clergy . . . had gone back to England, and the church was left shorn of its leadership."[1] Thus neither Church was in a position to press for national establishment; the latter was neither desired nor politically feasible.

As for other religious groups—Baptists, Quakers, Catholics, among others—none desired (in fact, they were wholly opposed to) any church establishment. Guaranteed freedom of worship, given their histories of protracted struggles against the former ecclesiastical establishments, was the most they wanted. The framers of the Constitution, then, reflected both the growing liberal—even indifferent-toward-religion—temper of the times as well as good political sense in providing for the separation of church and state. The individual states, of course, were left free to regulate their own church-state relationships. In New England, supportive arrangements such as applying tax monies to clergy (generally Congregational) salaries obtained until the early 1930s.

The ensuing historical picture is extremely complex and will not be pursued in detail here. The interested student is referred to the references cited below.[2] American Protestantism's animus against Roman Catholicism, which deepened as streams of Catholic immigration widened following the Civil War, has been well chronicled (many observers felt this animus died only with the election of John F. Kennedy to the presidency).

Both Protestant and Catholic churchmen, however, found themselves faced in the closing decades of the nineteenth century with the rapid growth of *urban* America and the apparently inevitable problems we have come to identify with city life. Among Protestants, differing theological outlooks dictated a variety of responses. The mainline Protestant response was generally conservative, viewing the Church's role in terms of missionary outreach and organized charity. To create a new society men would first have to be born anew as individuals. Nondenominational city missions sprang up in New York, Philadelphia, and Boston, offering food and shelter and attempting to reclaim drunkards and criminals as well as care for the young through such organizations as the YMCA and later the YWCA. Roman Catholic counterparts quickly developed, such as the lay missionary movement known as the Society of St. Vincent de Paul. Perhaps best known of the philanthropic organizations has been the Salvation Army whose Slum Brigades were familiar sights in the overcrowded tenement neighborhoods of our large cities.

Of special note is the Social Gospel Movement. Josiah Strong and Washington Gladden, together with Walter Rauschenbusch, were ministers who challenged the whole laissez-faire philosophy buttressing the social and economic world of the late nineteenth and early twentieth centuries. "The power of Christian love" should lead to cooperation between capital and labor, including giving workers a share in business profits. Municipal ownership and trade-unionism were other programs advocated by Social Gospel adherents, many of whom frankly believed the teaching of Christ indicated some kind of socialism in order to achieve a just social order.

It should be noted that many early American sociologists were profoundly influenced by this movement and conceived sociology as a discipline appropriately focusing on the analysis and solution of social (that is, urban) problems of the day. The movement eventually advocated, in the opening decades of this century, such now-accepted policies as child labor laws, worker protection statutes, old-age benefits, shorter working hours, and higher wages. The "prosperity decade" of the 1920s took a great deal of impetus from the movement, however, and the New Deal era of the 1930s saw many of its proposals enacted into federal legislation. An important historical consequence of both conservative and Social Gospel involvement in urban social problems was a trend toward interdenominational unity and cooperation. Federations of churches developed on both national and state levels. These bureaucracies have continued to flourish and have provided skilled leadership and impetus to programs of social reform shared across denominational lines. Another consequence was a growing liberalism that placed more emphasis on common denominational boundaries and a refusal to confine Christianity to individual salvation and righteousness only.

The initial reading in Part Two, from Martin Marty's *Righteous Empire*, sketches developments in American Protestantism in the post-World War II decades. Note the recurring polarities, in the distinct cultural milieus of the 1950s and 1960s, of religion as individual reform and salvation (with the early Billy Graham "premillennialism" as a context) against religion as movement for social and institutional change (the "secular city" motif of the mid-1960s). Marty also speaks of "two clusters of interpreters" of that faith which can be called generically Protestant: the *transformers* who preach of God's kingdom in terms of programs designed to transform institutions and the *rescuers* bent on saving individuals who, in turn, may decide to help save others in the society. Both these traditions have responsive publics. "Neither has been successful at displacing the other, and perhaps neither ever shall be." Subsequent readings and selections in Part Three on the prophetic role of religion will further illustrate these two interpretative "ideal types."

Reading 6, from Jeffrey Hadden's *The Gathering Storm in the Churches*, demonstrates the role of denominational membership in the belief system of church members. This selection has the advantage of including some salient findings of the large-scale survey conducted by Glock and Stark in the early 1960s. Consensus of belief is strongest in the more doctrinally conservative denominations such as the Southern Baptists, the sects, and the Missouri Synod Lutherans. The more liberal bodies exhibit a wider range of beliefs. Yet, as Hadden points out, *within* denominations, even within some local congregations, there is a remarkable degree of disagreement regarding what is to be believed. For Hadden this is a striking finding. The implication, as he stresses, is not only a lack of clear consensus concerning belief but also the absence of clear authority that might *resolve* the incertitude. For the liberal bodies the crisis is particularly acute. Adoption of a "new reformation" theology is accompanied by patterns of nonparticipation in church activities, including the crucial one of financial support. The more conservative churches, however, are flourishing institutionally. Fifty-nine percent of the Southern Baptists report giving $7.50 per week to the church; Congregationalists, presumably more wealthy, can claim only 15 percent contributing this amount weekly. Orthodoxy is associated with institutional commitment.

Selection J from Kelley's *Why Conservative Churches Are Growing*, presents evidence showing the phenomenal growth of theologically conservative churches. They supply, he maintains, an essential "need" discussed in the opening chapter: bestowing of meaning at a time when liberal churches seem to have downplayed this function in favor of social action. The ensuing selection from evangelist Don Wilkerson's *The Gutter and the Ghetto* illustrates this function of meaning-provision in the context of those seeking escape from drug addiction. It also demonstrates that the "rescuers" continue to make their presence felt where individual needs are most acute.

NOTES

[1] WILLARD L. SPERRY, *Religion in America* (New York: Macmillan, 1946), p. 51.

[2] See MARTIN E. MARTY, *Righteous Empire: The Protestant Experience in America* (New York: Dial, 1970); SIDNEY E. AHLSTROM, *A Religious History of the American People* (New Haven: Yale University Press, 1972); and RAY ALLEN BILLINGTON, *The Protestant Crusade, 1800–1860: A Study of the Origins of American Nativism* (Chicago: Quadrangle, 1964).

THE REVIVAL AND THE REVOLUTION

MARTIN E. MARTY

In her study of a world unsure of authority, Hannah Arendt describes a sense of the loss of the groundwork of the world, a world which shifts, changes, and transforms itself "with ever-increasing rapidity from one shape into another, as though we were living and struggling with a Protean universe where everything at any moment can become almost anything else." Worldly permanence and reliability were gone, she argued in *Between Past and Future*. She might as well have been speaking of Protestant religious life in America and, indeed, she did include religion in the field of lost authority and sudden change.

In the 1950s American Protestants participated in a general revival of interest in religion. In the 1960s they were part of what was called a revolution in religion. Energies devoted to building up one day were directed to tearing down the next. Devotion to religious institutions in one decade became massive assault on religious institutionalism in the next. People who said "Never!" in one decade became agents of change in the next. Analysts vacillated in their interpretations of American life as being religious, or secular, and religious again. The same culture could produce contradictory signs which were interpreted in a wildly disparate fashion "at any moment."

An understanding of Protestantism after two centuries of national life begins with a recovery of the sense of renewal and revival that marked the decade and more after World War II. While many Protestant energies were going into ecumenical endeavor, inter-faith relations, and the attempt to come to terms with pluralism, others were devoted to restoring Protestant institutions. One way to do this was to fill them with people, to house them well, to have them regularly supported, and to seek their good name. After the American religious depression of the 1930s and the preoccupations of World War II, it became clear that by around 1950 many Americans were in the settling-down mood. They needed a means of justifying their complacencies, soothing their anxieties, pronouncing benedictions on their way of life, and organizing the reality around them. Millions turned to religion, and Protestantism profited from the return to religion.

Martin E. Marty is an associate editor of *The Christian Century* and a member of the faculty of The University of Chicago Divinity School.

All the old tendencies of Protestantism came to the surface again, but by far the best known and in its own way most curious was the celebrity status extended one mass evangelist, Billy Graham. A study of his career suggests some of the directions Protestantism was taking. Not for almost half a century, since the prime of Billy Sunday, had Americans all come to know and recognize one outstanding evangelist. Not for almost a century, since Dwight L. Moody, had they turned for an interpretation of history of a premillennialist. Graham was one, explicitly and overtly, if not with full consistency. His not always sympathetic biographer, William G. McLoughlin, Jr., at the height of the Graham crusades in 1960, gathered some of Graham's premillennial expressions. Premillennialism, it will be recalled, is a pessimistic view of human history. It was well expressed in Moody's statement, "I look upon this world as a wrecked vessel. God has given me a lifeboat and said to me, 'Moody, save all you can.'" Graham spoke in similar terms.

Premillennialism, a view that would have been heretical to colonial and early national period evangelicals, says in effect that the churches cannot do much about the nagging issues of their day. The only substantial change in history will occur with the Second Coming of Christ, after which apocalyptic change a millennium, or thousand-year reign of peace and justice, will come about. Most premillennialists used the signs of their own time to interpret the imminence of the millennium. Graham was no exception, and in his prime Communism and Russia abroad and immorality at home provided the basic metaphors and illustrations.

In McLoughlin's little treasure, Graham is heard as follows: "I sincerely believe, if I can study the Scriptures aright and read current events and keep up with my current reading, that we are living in the latter days. I sincerely believe that the coming of the Lord draweth nigh." Ever after William Miller in 1843, premillennialists had been wary of predicting the day. But in 1950 Graham indulged in the temptation. "I believe the judgment hand of God is about to fall upon you tonight...We may have another year, maybe two years ... [then] ... I believe it's all going to be over ... I said in Los Angeles one year ago that we had five years. People laughed; some sneered. I'd like to revise that statement and say that we may have two years. Two years and it's all going to be over."

The Middle East, to a biblical literalist, had to be the beginning of the scene. "The Bible teaches us that history began in the Middle East ... and the Bible teaches us that it will end in the Middle East." Russia was both the great enemy of the Kingdom and the agent of apocalypse. And America was to hold the fort until the Second Coming. Here Graham picked up the mainline evangelical note: "I believe that America is truly the last bulwark of Christian civilization," he said in 1952. In spite of "corruption, crime, and moral decay," which he chronicled in detail, "we were created for a spiritual mission among the nations." But "until this nation humbles itself and prays and...receives Christ as Savior, there is no hope for preserving the American way of life." In classic revivalist tones he reminded that if one was converted, "when you make your decision, it is America through you making its decision."

.   .   .

The acceptance of Billy Graham demonstrated how theologically inclusive and ethically disinterested the revival of the 1950s had become. The churches in that decade were not notable for their devotion to the cause of racial justice. The Supreme Court had to take the initiative on that front in 1954 and the Protestant churches were everywhere regarded as latecomers. The issues of world population, hunger, poverty, and disease were minor emphases in a decade of sermons devoted to Billy Graham's *Peace with God*, Rabbi Joshua Loth Liebman's *Peace of Mind*, Bishop Fulton Sheen's *Peace of Soul,* or Graham's fellow Protestant and other best-known symbol of the revival, Norman Vincent Peale's *Power of Positive Thinking*. All advocated a kind of escape from the world, even as they implied that serene souls would help transform it. Graham's pessimism was easily overlooked in his alliance with these optimists. What gave him internal power was that his self-confessed secret may have been important to his fellow neo-evangelicals, but was conveniently overlooked by the culture which made him a celebrity.

.   .   .

Everywhere the indicators that America was enjoying a return to a generalized religion were recognized. As standards for church membership went down, membership rose and Protestantism benefited from its climb. In 1920, 43 percent of the people were on the rolls; in 1930, 47 percent; in 1940 this had grown only to 49 percent but in 1950 57 percent were members, and by 1956 this had grown to 62 percent. Eventually the crest was reached at 63 percent or 64 percent, and almost 50 percent of the American people claimed to have attended church in any week.

The Gallup polls in the 1950s indicated the degree of interest in morality and religion, and the Ben Gaffin survey for *Catholic Digest* revealed that Protestants in 1952 were content with historic doctrines or symbols of faith. One billion dollars was spent annually on church building. Motion pictures made heroes of men like Senate Chaplain Peter Marshall.

This generalized religion adapted the Protestant doctrine of God and marketed him as a convenient and benign figure, a "man upstairs." The formulator of the new faith on the highest level was the newly converted Presbyterian, President Dwight Eisenhower, who picked up the old theocratic and imperial language. God supported the American crusade. "America is the mightiest power which God has yet seen fit to put upon his footstool." "America is great because she is good." And in the midst of new material affluence, "Happily our people have always reserved their first allegiance to the kingdom of the spirit." Protestant distinctiveness was disappearing, and

Professor Arthur Mann could note that to nationalists "American Catholicism, American Protestantism, and American Judaism appear like parallel shoots on a common stock."

.   .   .

The revival was self-defeating, and produced a surfeit. People tried *Positive Thinking* and still Russia would not go away. The Second Coming did not occur, even though the Graham rallies came to be racially integrated. Suddenly after 1957 or 1958, and certainly by 1960, a dramatic cultural shift had occurred.

People were reacting to organization men and suburbia and peace of mind. The Russians had lofted Sputnik, and the Space Age placed a new premium on mass higher education. Words like "third world" and "Sputnik" and "cybernetics" came into common currency. The movement for racial integration was sweeping the churches, and the American conscience began to be awakened. In southeast Asia a war in Vietnam was increasingly involving American material, technical aid, and was eventually to see a commitment of American soldiers. Latin America verged on revolution, and Cuba went Communist. A different religious impulse and a different religious interpretation became necessary. What resulted was sometimes described as a revolution in religion.

A symbol for the shift: in the 1950s metropolitan newspaper editors enlarged the religion page in Saturday newspapers. They gave more space to announcements of sermons and parish fashion shows, cornerstone-layings and smorgasbords. In the 1960s, they reduced these pages and placed religion back on the front page. Protestantism shared in this relocation of religion. The old explanations no longer seemed to explain, and the old forms no longer seemed to sustain. Young people often lost curiosity about denominations, parishes, Sunday Schools, foreign missions, and even the ecumenical movement. They were obsessed with themes of race and peace, university life, "soul," and spiritual values.

The peace movement was often frustrated after President Lyndon B. Johnson committed land troops to Vietman and the war there was seen to be morally and militarily pointless and plotless. After 1965 Protestant leadership was in the front rank of opposition to the war and to the military draft, several years before the majority of the American people indicated their distaste for the war to inquiring pollsters. And many Protestants who began resisting the war on non-violent bases now turned to the support of violence in the racial revolution and in the "third world"—and sometimes against universities or "the military-industrial complex" at home. Once again, everything could turn into something else very suddenly.

What was consistent in the mainline Protestant leadership's response to the issues after the religious revival was this: they would not retreat back into self-serving institutionalism. They were committed to seeing the churches, with what power remained among them, as agents of change in the world.

The conservatives who resisted them regularly accused them of having chosen to meddle in politics. The World Council of Churches held a study conference at Geneva, Switzerland in the summer of 1966 and subsequently at Detroit, in a localized version. Reaction to these conferences, filled as they were with representatives and advocates of "third world revolution," included anger and backlash. The result was a growing gulf between the pulpit and the pew.

"Between pulpit and pew." That was the conventional way of pointing to the tension, though it would be more accurate to say that a certain kind of clergy-lay coalition teamed up against another kind of clergy-lay team. Once again, the century-old developing schism in Protestantism's parties was being widened. To the radicals, conservatism was not as neutral as it claimed to be. To claim to be neutral meant that one's votes were being counted on the side of the status quo: in support of the Vietnamese War, slum housing, school segregation despite laws to the contrary, and of American support of rightist regimes in Latin America. To the conservatives, radicals were compromising the gospel by tying it to questionable public causes and losing the confidence of people by their frequent changes.

What was occurring was still another variation on the ever-changing attempt of American Protestants to come to terms with their environment. The church's early adjustments to modernity's charter, an innovation which conservatives made seem to be ancient, was being torn up. That charter had decreed that the churches would be favored so long as they endorsed the approved American way of life and stayed with private affairs. Public Protestantism wanted to return to a pattern of many more centuries' standing, in which the people of God concerned themselves with all the areas of life, no matter what the risk. This attempt placed its leadership in a situation of unpopularity with "the powers that be" and in tension with much of their own clienteles.

To the observer of Protestant history it must often have seemed as if one half of Protestantism had more in common with certain "outsiders" than it did with the other half of Protestantism. The neo-evangelicals were closer to secular Social Darwinists on almost all their attitudes to the world than they were to the social gospel leaders, who seemed to be closer to the socialists. The evangelical critics of the social involvement of the church in the 1960s, often seemed to be closer to the American Medical Association, the National Association of Manufacturers, and sometimes to the White Citizens' Councils than they were to other Protestants like ecumenist Eugene Carson Blake or Harvey Cox. In many senses the schism was that deep.

Yet Protestantism somehow cohered. Through all the travails of change, the trend was toward more interdenominational unity, not less; there were few substantial schisms. No large group broke off an existing denomination. Few new seminaries were started to fight the vast majority of existing ones, almost all of whom were committed to change. Conservative journals like *Christianity Today* could be started to give a voice to neo-evangelicalism, but these efforts of conservatives did not seem to pull people away from the liberal or radical camps. In each denomination "concerned laymen" rose to support a tie between Christianity and latter-day laissez-faire stances, but seldom did they unseat the leadership which was more moderate on such issues.

The Protestant community, then, remained strong even if by the time of the approaching American bicentennial few in it plausibly spoke in imperial terms. Born in a secular age (in the time of the "Enlightenment"), Protestant America seemed to have resources for living again with secularity. Born suspicious of religious institutions, Protestants somehow seemed to weather the worst of anti-institutionalism. Despite revolutionary changes in institutions, there were few immediate drastic declines as a result of backlash or weariness, and membership, attendance, building, giving, and the seeking of churchly vocations seemed to be relatively stable in the 1960s, though few would predict the consequences of a vastly altered youth culture toward the end of the decade.

Whatever happens in the future, it would seem as if two factors should be present for some time to come. They are a Protestant deposit in the culture and a two-party approach to that deposit.

In his study *Thought and Change*, British philosopher Ernest Gellner compared Western Judaic-Christian societies to the Marxism in Russian society. He pictured that the religion or philosophy with which a society interprets itself at a time of fundamental change will tend to remain as a constituent element for some time to come. Since industrialization has been the most inclusive event of modern times, accompanied as it was by political revolution, the societies who experienced political-industrial revolution will revert repeatedly and even constantly to the set of ideas that helped carry them "over the hump of transition."

The world changes, however. America cannot crawl back into the thought world of the Enlightenment or of the Protestantism that fused with it to help produce the national ethos. Instead, it is constantly reshaping the images and ideas of that historic moment of fusion. In Gellner's picture, Jewish–Christian religious phenomena are part of our landscape just as glacial moraine is a semi-permanent part of the landscape where a glacier has been. The Protestant deposit may not be the working, living faith of later Americans. Citizens may devote and, indeed, they have devoted themselves to variations on this faith, including belief in nationalism, the self-made man, the work-ethic, success, or sex—or a combination of all of these. But they found it difficult to do so without some reference to the original symbols. In the American case, these included words derived from Protestantism, Puritanism, and Evangelicalism.

As so often was the case, the change was made under transformed theological symbolism, and professional theologians took up their task this time with vigor. At the base of their interpretation was an updated version of postmillennial thought. Few used the biblical symbol of the millennium, but many returned to the talk about the Kingdom of God. In the most successful and style-setting book to come out of Protestantism, Professor Harvey Cox spoke of *The Secular City*, the modern metropolis or technopolis as the workshop of God, the milieu for his Church and his avant-garde people.

The new writings of Cox, England's Bishop John Robinson (whose *Honest to God* was also an American best-seller) and a number of other new theologians breathed a spirit of optimism. The Second Vatican Council under Pope John was an endorsement of church unity strivings, and Protestants would never again be so lonely in their attempts to build the Kingdom. Through a score of books with the word "secular" in the title, a number of theologians spoke again of the potential in the world around them. They embraced the empirical method, celebrated the pragmatic style, and urged people not to be too concerned with otherworldliness or metaphysics. The new model Protestant was to be a cool, problem-solving, social activist who celebrated life in the world and was not too concerned about sanctuaries or the "noise of solemn assemblies."

.   .   .

Just as suddenly as the new progressivism appeared, it was threatened by cultural change and subjected to corrections and revisons from within. At the turning point, in late 1965 and early 1966, a number of Protestant thinkers tried to work out a complete transformation of the most cherished symbols and spoke of "the death of God." It was widely surmised that they had probably diagnosed the issues properly. Men today were regarding metaphysics the way they regarded alchemy. They found it difficult to see how God made a difference in human affairs. Sensitive people were reacting to the cheap usage of the term "God" in the years of the religious revival. The theater of the absurd was portraying a universe in which the old questions about the doctrine of God did not even come up. Yet Jesus was a figure who could impart meaning and freedom to life, so one could become a "Christian atheist."

While the diagnosis may have been correct, the name given not the disease but the cure—the celebration of "the death of God"—was rejected. The theological community found the metaphor largely unsatisfying. But more devastating was a change in the culture itself. In 1965, after Protestant participation in pro-integration marches at Washington, D.C., and Selma, Alabama, and after some civil rights legislation, the community of Watts in Los Angeles burned. The dream of racial integration, having been widely accepted but hardly acted upon, was repudiated by articulate young blacks. The Black Power movement swept the churches. As black militants became increasingly assertive in the churches, many Protestant thinkers who had once advocated integration of races now followed the mood and urged separation, so long as blacks wanted it—often claiming that that was what God had had in mind all along.

In a complex society, certain people are recognized as the translators or transformers of symbols. In American religion, the presidents of the United States, poets and prophets, evangelists and theologians, preachers and pamphleteers have played that role from time to time. It was their task to assure the nation that the moves it was making were in line with the original covenants, covenants which made the old social contracts possible. At the same time, they served as jeremiahs or judges whenever it seemed as if people moved too far beyond the confines of the covenant. They called people back.

.   .   .

Resort to the old covenants in American Protestantism gradually came to be in the hands of two clusters of interpreters. Both groups could with some reason claim elements of the old covenant, for the original charters were themselves ambiguous. Jonathan Edwards stood at the head of the postmillennial tradition: "The latter-day glory, is probably to begin in America." The millennium was attainable here; in the *History of the Work of Redemption* he saw that the thousand years of good would come *before* the Judgment of Men. Dwight L. Moody picked up the loose strands of premillennial theory and reversed the process. The Edwardseans, with countless variations, have been the more optimistic transformers of society, without neglecting the individual. The Moodyites have been the more pessimistic, concentrating on rescuing the individual and then turning him loose, if he will, to help save other persons in the society.

The transformers have usually been out of step with the powers that be, defining themselves as innovators, inconveniencers, agents of change. Their rhetoric made them sound more happy with the world as being God's workshop, his secular city, the scene of his kingdom. But their programs were upsetting to people who had put the world together a certain way. The rescuers have usually been adopted by representatives of the approved world, supported by manufacturers and fêted by presidents. Their language made them sound more discontented with the world as being beyond God's power— until he ushers in a new age with Christ's Second Coming. They may have seemed strident about the signs of the times and angry about the vices of individuals. But their postponements of reform were comforting to people who would stay in control short of a millennium in which many of them only half believed.

So long as the American republic contains people who will be responsive to both sets of symbols, it is probable that there will be two kinds of Protestantism. Neither has been successful at displacing the other, and perhaps neither ever shall be. Both of them have too much tradition going for them. In each generation, both have been blessed with ingenious and dedicated men who could translate their symbols one more time.

✛

✛·✛·✛

THE RELIGIOUS BELIEFS OF PROTESTANT LAITY

JEFFREY K. HADDEN

The study by Glock and Stark of Christian laity was mentioned in the introductory chapter and again in this chapter in making some comparisons between clergy and laity.[1] This is an important study and merits a closer look.

The Glock and Stark study involved a random sample of some three thousand church members residing in the four metropolitan counties of the San Francisco Bay Area.[2] While the initial published reports on this study were primarily concerned with differences in beliefs *among* denominations, an examination of the data reveals that sharp differences exist *within* denominations as well. Table 1 reproduces just a few of the responses to Glock and Stark's multifaceted exploration of religious belief. The questions included here cover a wide range of doctrines, including belief in God, the divinity of Christ, miracles, and life after death.

A word of explanation is necessary regarding the interpretation of the responses in Table 1. On the first three statements, respondents were asked "Which of the following statements comes closest to expressing what you believe about (God, Jesus, miracles)?" The responses presented represent the orthodox or literalist position. The other response alternatives involve varying degrees of doubt to rejection of belief in the Christian doctrine. For example, on the question regarding belief in God, the responses range from unfaltering acknowledgment of the existence of God ("I know God really exists and I have no doubt about it") to rejection of the existence of God ("I don't believe in God"). The final statement in the table is taken from a check list of specific doctrines in which respondents were asked to respond on a four-point continuum as follows: "completely true," "probably true," "probably not true," and "definitely not true."

Table 1 dramatically demonstrates the diversity of belief patterns across denominations. The pattern is highly similar to the one we have already observed for clergy. The additional denominations included in the Glock and Stark study provide a perspective for placing the six denominations included in the clergy study. Congregationalists are consistently the most liberal group,

From Jeffrey K. Hadden, *The Gathering Storm in the Churches*. Copyright © 1969 by Jeffrey K. Hadden. Reprinted with the permission of Doubleday & Company, Inc.

Jeffrey K. Hadden is a member of the Department of Sociology and Anthropology at the University of Virginia.

TABLE I

Laity Also Show Wide Range of Beliefs on Religious Doctrines

	CONGREGATIONAL	METHODIST	EPISCOPALIAN	PRESBYTERIAN	DISCIPLES OF CHRIST	AMERICAN LUTHERAN	AMERICAN BAPTIST	MISSOURI SYNOD LUTHERAN	SOUTHERN BAPTIST	SECTS	TOTAL PROTESTANT	CATHOLICS
Belief in God "I know God really exists and I have no doubts about it."	41	60	63	76	75	73	78	81	99	96	71	81
Belief in Divinity of Jesus "Jesus is the Divine Son of God and I have no doubts about it."	50	54	59	74	72	74	76	93	99	97	69	86
Miracles "Miracles actually happened just as the Bible says they did."	28	37	41	62	58	69	62	89	92	92	57	74
Life Beyond Death "There is a life beyond death." (% who answered "completely true.")	36	49	53	64	69	70	72	84	97	94	69	75

Source: Charles Y. Glock and Rodney Stark, *Religion and Society in Tension* (Chicago: Rand McNally, 1965), Chapter 5, "The New Denominationalism," Tables 1, 2, 4, and 5.

and the Southern Baptists and sects are consistently the most conservative groups on religious beliefs.

In the laity study only among Southern Baptists and sectarian groups is there a consensus of belief on these doctrinal issues. Missouri Synod Lutherans are also highly orthodox, but a minority at least have doubts about orthodox doctrine. No other denomination even approaches consensus on doctrine, either in terms of accepting or rejecting the orthodox position. Congregationalists are the least willing to accept orthodox doctrine. But even among Congregationalists there is a significant minority who do adhere to a literalist position.

Denominationalism is clearly a powerful force in influencing what people believe about Christian doctrine. But perhaps even more important is the fact that within denominations and even within individual congregations there is a significant degree of dissensus. This diversity of belief can perhaps best be seen by examining the responses of Christian laity in a single congregation. The data come from a large Lutheran church (Lutheran Church in America) located in a Minneapolis suburb. A total of 1628 laymen of Faith Lutheran Church, representing approximately 80 per cent of the adult congregation, completed questionnaires in the fall of 1966 which explored the nature of their religious beliefs.[3] The Faith Lutheran study included one hundred statements which were designed to explore the nature of religious belief. Members were asked to respond to the belief statements in the same manner as the clergy study—a six-point continuum ranging from "strongly agree" to "strongly disagree." We need not present a detailed analysis of their religious beliefs here, but a few selected issues will serve to demonstrate the varieties of belief that exist even within a single congregation of a conservative denomination.[4]

Eighty-seven per cent of the Faith Lutheran respondents agreed with the statement "I believe in a Supreme Being who sees and knows everything." An additional 8 per cent indicated that they probably agree with the statement. The response to this question, thus, is similar to national polls which ask, "Do you believe in God?" But while the Faith Lutheran members affirm the existence of God, they are widely divided on their views of what God is like and the extent to which God is revealed in the Christian religion. Only half (49 per cent) of the respondents positively affirmed the statement "Only in Christianity is the one true God revealed." In a similar vein, 44 per cent said, "It is not important what religion one believes in, because all religions worship the same God even though they speak of the divine differently." In short, roughly half of the members of this congregation take a very broad view of their religious faith and do not exclude the possibility that other religious faiths constitute an equally legitimate source of knowledge of the deity. For the other half, Christianity constitutes a unique faith through which God's truth has been revealed. The significance of this divergence cannot be easily dismissed, for it suggests that the saliency with which any specific doctrine is held will vary considerably. Keep in mind also that the Lutherans are among the most conservative groups. If these issues are not salient for Lutherans, we can hardly expect them to be so for more liberal traditions.

This becomes clear when we examine their responses to questions about the doctrine of salvation. What does salvation mean? What meaning does the traditional doctrine of eternal life have for contemporary Christians? What happens to man when his physical body dies? Examination of five different statements dealing with the doctrine of salvation reveals that the issue is a perplexing one for the Faith Lutheran congregation. Only slightly more than half (52 per cent) of the members are able to affirm with certainty that "There is a divine judgment after death where some will be rewarded and others punished." But even this affirmation must reflect a certain amount of tenuousness since slightly less than half (46 per cent) feel that "Every man has an immortal soul that lives on after death." Approximately half of the members, thus, believe in some kind of immortal soul which is subject to judgment and half the members express varying degrees of doubt or disbelief in this doctrine.

Just what this immortal soul is like, however, is unclear. Some possible clarification may be added by the statement "I expect to have a bodily existence after death in which I will be recognizable to myself and others." Eighteen per cent agreed with this proposition and another 18 per cent indicated that they probably agreed. When asked if they thought heaven and hell were geographical places, 84 per cent said they were not. At the same time, only about a third (36 per cent) were able to affirm the modernist view that "Salvation in the Christian sense refers to the possibility of living a fully human life." Yet, 53 per cent agree and 22 per cent probably agree that "Salvation means winning heaven and escaping hell."

The doctrine of salvation, thus, is at best a perplexing one for Faith Lutheran laity. They approach consensus only in rejecting heaven and hell as geographical places. In spite of rejecting heaven and hell as geographical places, a third express some anticipation of a corporate existence somewhere "out there." Another third see salvation in terms of deeper meaning in this life. Still another group (again approximately one third) seem to suggest by their responses that salvation is not a very salient issue, having rejected both tradition and symbolic conceptions of salvation.

Although this same dissensus is apparent in almost every theological issue raised in the study of the Faith Lutheran congregation, we need not belabor this point with a detailed description. The central theme of the Glock and Stark data, our clergy data, and the Faith Lutheran data is the same: *Christians join together in a common expression of faith when in reality there is no shared consensus regarding the nature of that faith.*

Observing this wide range of adherence to Christian doctrine is one matter. Interpreting the significance of the findings is another. Clearly these findings cannot be divorced from a theological perspective. We know that theology has been undergoing a very radical reinterpretation for many years. The central doctrinal issues of yesterday are, for many Christians, no longer the most critical issues today. But to dismiss the responses to the doctrinal issues raised here as irrelevant or meaningless because they do not tap the frontiers of theological thought is to miss the significance of what the data tell us. While the doctrinal issues raised may not be critical to some, it is quite apparent that they are terribly important to others. And herein lies the dilemma of contemporary Protestantism: *There is no consensus as to what is believed, as to what is central and what is peripheral, nor is there any clear authority to resolve the uncertainty.*

The question of authority looms very large. As a doctrine of infallible truth, Christianity possesses enormous authority. It is a belief system which professes to hold the essence of truth about the nature and meaning of life, a system which offers rewards for those who believe and practice this doctrine of truth and punishes those who reject it. But when the foundations of this belief system are no longer certain, what happens to its authority? Without certainty of belief, is it possible for the institution to exercise the kind of authority which will keep its membership firmly committed to the institution and its programs?

The Gallup Poll data presented in Chapter I suggest an answer to this question. The Gallup data show that church attendance is highest in the theologically conservative denominations and lowest in those denominations where rejection of orthodox theology is the greatest. As doubt about the validity of Christian beliefs emerges, commitment to ritual participation in religious institutions declines. In other words, with doubt comes a rejection of the church's authority to demand regular participation in the life of the church.

This is, perhaps, reading too much into the Gallup Poll figures, but a second volume recently published by Stark and Glock[5] lends overwhelming evidence to support this thesis. Stark and Glock examine the relationship between denominationalism and involvement in a wide range of ritual activities, including church attendance, membership in church organizations, time spent in religious activities, listening and watching religious programs in the mass media, financial contributions to the church, perceived importance of church membership, and private ritual including prayer, reading the Bible and devotional literature, and table grace. On every single indicator of ritual involvement, the theologically liberal denominations scored lower than the conservative denominations. Stark and Glock conclude that "a general corrosion of commitment presently accompanies the acceptance of a modernized, liberal theology."[6]

The authors elaborate their conclusion as follows: . . . the majority of members of liberal bodies are dormant Christians. They have adopted the theology of the new reformation, but at the same time they have stopped attending church, stopped participating in church activities, stopped contributing funds, stopped praying, and are uninformed about religion. Furthermore, only a minority of members of the liberal bodies feel that their religious perspective provides them with the answers to the meaning and purpose of life, while the overwhelming majority of conservatives feel theirs does supply the answers. Finally, the liberal congregations resemble theater audiences, their members are mainly strangers to each other, while conservative congregations resemble primary groups, united by bonds of personal friendships.[7]

Perhaps most revealing in terms of the implications for the sustained institutional life of the church are figures on financial contributions. Fifty-nine per cent of the Southern Baptists reported that they gave $7.50 a week or more to the church, compared with only 15 per cent of the Congregationalists who reported giving that much. These figures become even more dramatic if one considers the fact that Congregationalists have a higher income level than Southern Baptists. None of the Southern Baptists, compared with 23 per cent of the Congregationalists, in the Stark and Glock study had an income of $16,000 a year or greater. Yet 32 per cent of the Southern Baptists, compared with only 1 per cent of the Congregationalists, reported contributions of $15 a week or more. In brief, those who believe in the literal teachings of scripture are much more deeply involved in every phase of church life, including financial support. Moreover, Stark and Glock find a general shift in membership away from conservative toward liberal church bodies.

The implications of these data will be explored more fully in a later chapter, but it should be clear that commitment to and recognition of the authority of the church is very much dependent on the degree to which one accepts the orthodox teachings of the Christian faith. Furthermore, there is considerable evidence of movement away from these orthodox teachings, among both clergy and laity.

SUMMARY

The results of two major surveys, my study of clergy and the Glock and Stark study of laity, reveal that Protestantism is divided within and among denominations on the most basic issues of theological doctrine. The clergy data suggest that there may be a more basic core of humanistic concerns which unite Christians. The Stark and Glock data introduce a more complex dimension which indicates that laity commitment to the institutional life of the church is in large part a function of their adherence to orthodox Christian doctrine. The full implications of these findings, however, are not clear. Of critical importance is the relationship between religious beliefs and beliefs about social issues. Do the religiously orthodox express greater or less concern about social issues, or do the two realms of belief operate independently of each other? Chapter III addresses itself to this question.

NOTES

[1] CHARLES Y. GLOCK and RODNEY STARK, "The New Denominationalism," *Religion and Society in Tension* (Chicago: Rand McNally, 1965).

[2] A national sample by the same scholars reveals that the basic conclusions from the Bay Area study are generalizable to the nation. See RODNEY STARK and CHARLES Y. GLOCK, *American Piety: The Nature of Religious Commitment* (Berkeley: University of California Press, 1968).

[3] "Faith Lutheran" is a pseudonym to preserve the anonymity of the congregation.

[4] A detailed report of this study is currently being prepared by the author of this volume.

[5] STARK and GLOCK, *American Piety*, op. cit.

[6] Ibid., p. 213.

[7] Ibid., p. 221.

·▸·◂·▸·◂·▸·◂·▸·◂·▸·◂·▸·◂·▸·◂·▸·◂·▸·◂··

Why Conservative Churches Are Growing

DEAN M. KELLEY

Those who plead obsolescence as an explanation for organizational deterioration must rely rather heavily upon a similar state of affairs afflicting other structures similarly engaged. It is awkward indeed if the competition is thriving, growing, proliferating in what is supposed to be a uniformly hostile climate. Such a state of affairs casts doubt upon the whole notion that the trouble is in the times and not in the particular organization. Yet this is precisely the situation among the churches: *not all religious bodies are declining*. While most of the mainline Protestant denominations are trying to survive what they hope will be but a temporary adversity, other denominations are overflowing with vitality, such as the Southern Baptist Convention, the Assemblies of God, the Churches of God, the Pentecostal and Holiness groups, the Evangelicals, the Mormons (Church of Jesus Christ of Latter-Day Saints), Jehovah's Witnesses, Seventh-day Adventists, Black Muslims, and many smaller groups hardly even visible to the large denominations. Their statistics show a startling contrast to those in the preceding chapter.

Figure 1 shows a comparison of growth rates between two long-time rivals, the Southern Baptist Convention and the Methodist Church. In 1967, the former overtook the latter and has continued to increase at a rate of 2.26% per year, while the latter has begun to diminish, despite its merger with the Evangelical United Brethren Church in 1968. But even with the addition of 737,000 former EUB members, the United Methodist Church is not as large as the Southern Baptist Convention, which (unlike the United Methodist Church) is still increasing.

The foreign missionary personnel of the Southern Baptist Convention more than doubled, from 1,186 in 1958 to 2,494 in 1971, while the United Methodist overseas task force decreased from 1,453 to 1,175 in the same period.[1]

Figure 2 is a reminder of the membership trends of the other large Protestant denominations mentioned in the preceding chapter. The three Lutheran churches are shown separately. It is evident that of the six shown only the Lutheran Church–Missouri Synod is still increasing, and this at a decreasing rate, no longer matching the rate of U.S. population increase.

Dean M. Kelley, a United Methodist minister, is Director for Civil and Religious Liberty, National Council of Churches.

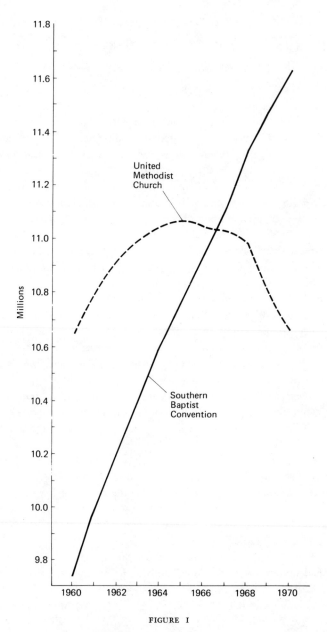

FIGURE I

FIGURE I

Membership comparison: 1960–1970.

Figure 3 includes the membership rates for five rapidly growing churches of 250,000–400,000 members: the Seventh-day Adventists (3.2% increase per year), the Church of the Nazarene (2.6% increase), the Jehovah's Witnesses (5% increase per year), the Salvation Army (average 2.9% increase per year) and the Christian Reformed Church (2.2% per year). They are designated

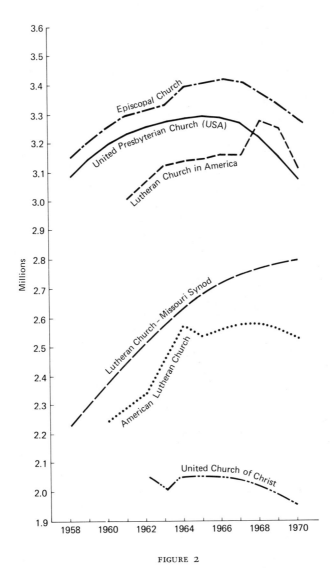

FIGURE 2

Membership comparison: 1958–1970.

as rapidly growing because their growth rates exceed the rate of population growth.

·   ·   ·

Since the incentives held out by the liberal churches—fellowship, entertainment, knowledge (about personality and adjustment, planned parenthood, woman's liberation, home management, and so on), respectability, etc.—are offered by many other (nonreligious) groups, those churches place themselves in competition for adherents with organizations which may have more com-

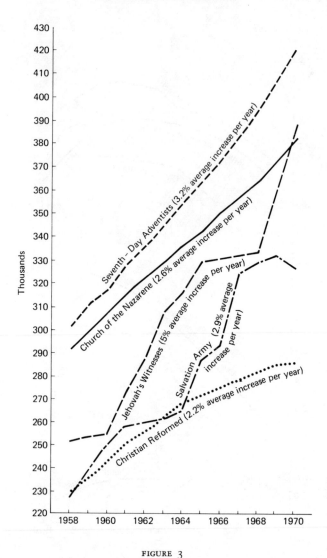

FIGURE 3

Membership comparison: 1958–1970.

pelling forms of the same attractions. An example LaNoue gives is civil rights: persons wanting to work for civil rights will find a more specialized and effective vehicle in the NAACP or the Urban League or other groups devoted to that cause than in even the most activist churches. If that is the incentive that satisfies them, they may be drawn to churches which are engaged in that sort of activity. But if and when the church turns its attention to another issue, they will readily abandon it for an organization that still pursues civil rights.

Conservative churches, on the other hand, offer an incentive (or commodity?) that is not as widely available—salvation—and offer it persistently. Thus they are spared competition from more highly specialized secular organizations; their only competition is from other conservative churches, which is more limited and easier to handle (they are fighting on their own turf, as it were). Persons forced to limit their nonoccupational interests, activities, and expenditures will tend to eliminate those that are marginal in favor of those whose incentives are intensive and unique. . . .

The new religious groupings (I shall not refer to them as movements until they begin to *move* with the coherence, force, and directionality described in the last chapter) all too often show a lack of confidence in the efficacy of the stock-in-trade of religion, which is meaning. Many a grouplet in the churches which has gathered itself around the banner of civil rights, or the war on poverty, or community organization, or preserving the biosphere, seems to feel that the best contribution churchmen can make to the cause is one indistinguishable from what a secular group might make. That is known in some circles as being relevant to the felt needs of the world; but some of the needs the world feels may not be its real and underlying needs. Religious groups should not abdicate their unique and essential contribution to healing the world's wounds: *meaning*.

. . . [R]eligious organizations have a contribution to make to the human predicament that is different from the technological interventions of secular groups. The distinctively religious contribution is to give *meaning* to the situation: purpose, promise, and possibility. That does not mean that meaning should displace technological remedies—men still need food, shelter, clothing, jobs, education, medical care—or even view them as inferior to meaning. And if society or its secular agencies cannot provide the needed technological remedies, religious organizations may need to do so, but with the recognition that such stopgap measures are a distraction and diversion from their distinctive and indispensable service: making sense of the life of man.

But this service does not seem to be enough for some religious leaders— "they want to dash in 'where the action is' and help do whatever needs doing: 'Here, fellows, let me hand out those blankets!' They sometimes seem a little impatient and embarrassed to be standing around with nothing to offer but words when everyone else is busy dispensing layettes, birth-control pills or surplus foodstuffs. . . . They want to 'get into the act too' in some more immediately productive way. Yet they may thereby be neglecting or withholding the very ingredient without which the rest will not hold together!"[2]

●   ●   ●

Contrary to the impression given by many contemporary churches, the true business of the genuinely *religious* organization is not baby-sitting or entertainment, not social work or social action, not even what passes for religious education or theology, unless these activities are the means for acting out or otherwise communicating the *meaning* of life which the religious group wants to proclaim.

This is not necessarily a reactionary role for religion; it can be very radical. But it should not be misunderstood. It does *not* mean that the church's business is saving souls rather than social action. Either of these can be the means to, or effect of, proclaiming the meaning of life; both can be a substitute for, or diversion from, that proclamation. Neither does it mean that the religious group's business is "spiritual" or "sacred," and that it should leave material, temporal, secular affairs to those who—allegedly—understand them better. This is a common confusion between treatment and subject matter.

The subject matter of religion is *the entire life of man and whatever affects him*. But the distinctively religious treatment of that subject matter is not technological so much as *meaning-oriented—how can the life of man be understood, its meaning perceived, developed, celebrated, and enhanced?* This treatment may well have its technological implications and consequences—it may even be couched, if nothing better offers, in the not-very-evocative terms of technology—but it is not finally aimed at technological considerations. One religious group may preach the necessity of contraception and another opposition to it; both are talking about a technological mechanism for controlling population, but each is doing so as an implication and illustration of what it believes about the meaning of human life and how that meaning is best honored and enhanced. If its message is understood only in the technological dimension, then the religious group has grievously failed in its *religious* mission, which is in the dimenson of meaning.

That is precisely where many churches fail today. One young lady of my acquaintance, who was an organizer for Saul Alinsky for a while and has since completed law school in order to struggle in the courts for social change, has little use for the churches, not because they are not radical enough, but because they are not religious enough! "When my friends want to talk about the meaning of life," she complains, "about whether to bring children into the world, we have to gather in one of our homes for a kaffee-klatch rather than at the church; the church isn't really struggling with those questions in any way that would help us."

．　　　．　　　．

But today many churches seem to avoid serious discussions of the meaning of life, perhaps because many of the members would rather not get involved in any examination of the answers they have precariously accepted or avoided, and don't know quite *how* to talk about what really matters to them. The churches cannot fulfill their proper function until they find and effectuate ways for their members to talk about the meaning of life, to explore it in a climate of mutual confidence and support, to try out together how to celebrate, embody, and proclaim the "explanations" they believe make life worth living. Such ways of struggling with the conundrum of human existence are being worked out in some of the new religious groupings—even as they are preserved in some of the old—where the religious group refuses to be diverted from its distinctive mission in the realm of meaning.

NOTES

[1] "The Missionary Retreat," *Christianity Today*, Nov. 19, 1971, pp. 26, 27.

[2] "The Church and the Anti-Poverty Program," *Christian Century*, June 8, 1966, p. 741.

❖•❖•❖•❖•❖•❖•❖•❖•❖•❖•❖•❖•❖•❖•

Who Are These People?

DON WILKERSON

"When I had my first taste of heroin, I loved it. By the time I had reached 17, I was a nervous wreck, self-conscious and full of complexes. I was always depressed and life was hell on earth to me.

"After a while, the price of stuff went up and I got strung out. I stopped working and learned to steal. I would boost steaks: I could make it out of a super market with four or five nice sirloins under my belt. Sometimes I'd get busted and either go to jail or catch a beating from the manager. At first I hated to steal, but before long I couldn't pass a super market without a strong desire to go in and see what I could sneak out the door with. I didn't like hurting other people, but if it came to a choice between my getting high or someone getting hurt, well, it would be all right once I got high.

"Then I met the girl who is now my wife. Mary was also on junk. Our first night together, Mary wondered if two people who really loved each other could stop using drugs. For the first time in many years, I loved someone more than I loved satisfying my need for dope.

. . .

"One night while waiting for Mary on 96th Street and Broadway, I was scooped up for consenting to obtain narcotics. I was back in a cell in the Tombs, making it my fifteenth trip there. Usually when I would sit in my cell, I would say a prayer that went something like this: 'God, get me out of here and I'll never get in trouble again.' This time I felt moved to pray, but it was a different prayer. I thought, 'God, it seems like things are going from bad to worse, but for some reason, I feel that you have been doing something in my life and I'm leaving the future up to you.' For the first time in my life, I prayed expecting God to do something for me.

"A few days later, my case was thrown out and Mary and I had just smashed a store window so that we could get merchandise to sell and have enough money for heroin. While we were standing on 96th Street waiting for a connection to show up, I started to think about a drug addict friend of mine who had stopped fooling around with junk. He had told me about

---

From Don Wilkerson, *The Gutter and the Ghetto*. Copyright 1969, Word Books, Publishers.

Don Wilkerson is the Director of Teen Challenge Center in Brooklyn, New York.

a church in The Bronx where he and many other boys had been freed from the drug habit.

"I reminded Mary about our friend and asked her if she would go with me to the church. She thought I suddenly had gone crazy. But Mary gave in and up we went. At the Damascus Church we met drug addicts who were staying clean. One of them took us in a corner and told us the power of God was keeping him clean. He told us a lot of other things, but we didn't understand. What we did understand was that he was clean. There was no room for us at Damascus, so they gave us the name of Teen Challenge.

"When we came to Teen Challenge, we were skinny and dirty. Little by little, we took our faith out of the things of this world and put our faith in Jesus Christ. He did nothing but reward us. Even before, we knew our Lord as our own Savior, He blessed us. He gave us a peace and calm right from the beginning and each day did a work in our lives.

"Mary is now so calm and happy that people who remember her past now gape when they see her. Christ has removed the dependent, clinging love we had for each other and replaced it with a real love for each other and for those around us and for Him. He has given us everything we have and now we try to give everything we have to His service."

To this Mary adds these closing comments:

"Salvation was very hard for me to accept in the beginning. I wanted to earn it, to do something for it. God did a miracle here, because I was raised on religion by nuns in Mother Cabrini's Convent, and as a result my heart was very hard towards the gospel. I knew all about Jesus, but I didn't know Jesus, as I do now, as my personal Savior and personal friend. What a difference. You can know all there is to know about someone without ever knowing him personally. As I sat under the gospel and the teaching of the Bible at Teen Challenge, though, something wonderful happened: my heart opened to the full knowledge that salvation was a free gift of God and that all I had to do was to accept it. I accepted it, and my joy has been unspeakable.

"Two weeks after entering Teen Challenge, Bunny and I were given a beautiful Christian wedding. Now we are studying to be missionaries. There are those who have never even heard of Jesus once. We want to tell them. Someone came and told us."

These are some of the people who come to us. In their own way, they each frantically searched for happiness and a purpose for living. Their quest brought them to a reliance upon Benzedrene, cough syrup, marijuana, money, Zen Buddhism, hippie living, involvement in school and church activities, promiscuous sex, heroin, physical love, and hospital cures. Not a single one of those remedies did any good. All of these people—men and women, rich and poor, Negro, Puerto Rican and white—found what they were looking for only when they turned to Jesus Christ.

. . .

We have had almost-dead people come to us and have watched them return to society with something worth living for. Having seen lives transformed in this way, we press on in the hope that all drug addicts and all troubled men will find similar joy through Christ Jesus. I have yet to meet anyone—school teacher, bank president, truck driver, housewife, student—who has found complete happiness and satisfaction without having found Christ.

. . .

There is a need for our ministry right where it is. I think that one of the best reasons any of our converts ever gave for coming to Teen Challenge was, as he put it, "because I've felt the power of the devil all my life and I *knew* there had to be another power on the other side." If we were not on that "other side," a lot of people would be looking in vain.

Another addict told me, "Your Christianity is all right for kids and old ladies, but it won't work out here in the gutter and the ghetto." Well, Christianity has worked because we have brought it to precisely those two places: the gutter and the ghetto. We have stooped down to the gutter and we have labored in the ghetto. And we have looked at the wretched people there, lifting them up, showing them Christ, and praying with them for a new life, one with meaning and love. The first time you reach down to the gutter and put your hands on a crusty alcoholic or dope addict who is caked with filth, the first time you bend down and your nostrils are filled with the stench that has been his for so long, the first time you are not certain whether the body you are lifting is dead or alive—that's when you realize there isn't a thing that *you* can do for him and that you must commit this man to God in prayer. To see such a man as this months later as he walks out of Teen Challenge with Bible in hand makes me pause to thank God for what He has wrought.

CHAPTER 4

The Sectarian Religious Bodies

The church-sect distinction has generated more discussion and caused more ink to be spilled than perhaps any conceptual framework in the sociology of religion. As "ideal-types" in the tradition of Max Weber, church and sect possess polar characteristics. These are well summed up by sociologists Demerath and Hammond:

> The ideal-typical "church" and "sect" differ in both internal and external characteristics. Externally the church seeks to make its peace with the secular society surrounding it, whereas the sect is either aloof or hostile. Internally, the church has many of the earmarks of a bureaucracy with professionalized leadership, high valuation of ritual, and an impersonal evangelizing strategy that welcomes persons wherever and whatever they may be. The sect, on the other hand, is more of an amateurish social movement with lay, charismatic leadership, an emphasis upon perfervid spontaneity, and a sense of religious exclusiveness as reflected in high membership standards.[1]

The distinction has also been used to devise ways of looking at the *process* by which religious groups grow and evolve. In this light, new religious movements begin as cults and proceed to succeeding stages of sect, denomination, and finally church, each stage reflecting more accommodation to and "being comfortable with" the larger secular society.

British sociologist Bryan Wilson has written extensively about religious sects. In defining the sect, he remarks:

> The sect then has a strong sense of self-identity: who is admitted becomes "one of us." And this "us" is set over against all others, the more compellingly

so because sects lay claim to special and usually exclusive access to supernatural truths. The sect is a body which claims complete and conscious
allegiance of its members, that should transcend where it does not eclipse all
other allegiances, whether to state, tribe, class or kin-group.[2]

Sects admit of many classifications. Wilson bases his own classification on
the variety of sectarian patterns of seeking salvation from an "evil" world
and its institutions. Sects may be conversionist, revolutionist, introversionist,
manipulationist, thaumaturgical (healing), reformist, or utopian.

Mormonism presents us with an excellent example of a sect becoming a
church. Yet as Thomas O'Dea points out in this chapter's opening reading,
Mormonism avoided stagnation as it grew; it did not become a denomination
or a church (sociologically speaking) but instead retained many sectlike
characteristics (Wilson refers to Mormonism as a "many-sided sect"[3]). O'Dea
illustrates how a sociologist examines received categories, noting their definitions and examining their applicability to a concrete social phenomenon—
in this case, the Mormon Church. He concludes that the categories do not
fit well and cannot be used to predict development; in fact, he stresses that
sociological analysis alone is inadequate to account for "the emergence of
one type of social structure as against another." Unique interaction of particular historical factors must be considered and blended with sociological
theory to account for what the researcher observes.

Not all sectarian groups accommodate to the larger society. Revolutionist
sects such as the Jehovah's Witnesses are a case in point. The Witnesses,
says Joseph Zygmunt (Reading 8), have succeeded in maintaining, even
intensifying, their rigorous opposition to the world, while surmounting a
series of crises resulting from unfulfilled prophecies of the destruction of
the world. By cultivating social exclusivity among their members, discrediting
secular authority, and stigmatizing the present world as satanically dominated,
the Witnesses have in effect imposed a powerful symbolic construction on
the "everyday" empirical world. This symbolic creation has enabled them
to interpret events consistently as manifestations of the inexorable working
out of the "Divine Plan" as the Witnesses profess it. The study illuminates
Clifford Geertz's definition of religion as creating a set of symbols—here a
pervasive world outlook—in terms of which everyday events make sense,
in terms of which the everyday world is "read." Organizational developments
accompanying the sect's growth did not "bend" it to compromise with the
world. Instead they served to give renewed strength to its sectlike qualities:
launching recruitment campaigns, renewing and adjusting its prophetic
stance (that is, abandoning date-centered pronouncements concerning the end
of the world). As Zygmunt remarks, "While undergoing ideological and
structural changes, the sect has not only retained its millenarian character but
has managed to adapt its millenarian style to the requirements of long-
term organizational survival."

Christian Science is represented in "Coping with Cumbersome Demands of

Contemporary Living." As a "manipulationist" sect, Christian Science sees salvation "largely...as the ability to realize the good things of the world, and particularly long life, health, happiness and a sense of superiority or even triumph."[4] Its adherents can deal with current world and personal crises by realizing that these are "at root suggestions of illusory material consciousness, not actual conditions." Manipulationist sects may be particularly appealing in historical periods characterized by disillusion with political and cultural programs of change. The individual is asked to look within himself for the resources to cope with a confusing and intractable world.

Psychiatrist Robert Coles's sensitive recording of religious sentiments of more recent (late 1960s) migrants to Chicago speaks vividly of both supportive and interpretative roles of conversionist (holiness) sectarian faith. Religion becomes an intimate element in interpreting a new and alienating environment.

NOTES

[1] DEMERATH and HAMMOND, op. cit., p. 157.

[2] BRYAN WILSON, *Religious Sects: A Sociological Study* (World University Library) (New York: McGraw-Hill, 1970), p. 26.

[3] Ibid., p. 197.

[4] Ibid., p. 141.

MORMONISM AND THE AVOIDANCE
OF SECTARIAN STAGNATION

THOMAS F. O'DEA

One of the many churches founded in the region south of the Great Lakes in the first half of the nineteenth century, the Church of Jesus Christ of Latter-day Saints, or the Mormon Church, alone avoided the stagnant backwaters of sectarianism. Founded in New York State in 1830 by a small group of men, it has today more than a million members in the United States and in its mission countries of Europe and the South Seas. It is the only religious body to have a clear majority of the population in a single state (Utah), and it has been the central and strategic group in the settlement of the intermountain West. Of its numerous dissident bodies, five survive, the largest of which has 100,000 members; the smallest, 24. The former, the Reorganized Church of Jesus Christ of Latter-day Saints, is an important denomination in parts of the Middle West.[1] From its founding the Mormon Church has set out to establish the Kingdom of God on earth and had created—once in Ohio, twice in Missouri, and once in Illinois—settlements in which this ideal was to be realized, only to see them consumed by external conflict and internal dissent. Finally, in 1847, the Mormons, harassed and persecuted, dispossessed of all but faith, leadership, and superb organization crossed the plains and settled in the Utah desert. There, relying on these spiritual and sociological assets, they established a regional culture area bearing the pronounced imprint of their peculiar values and outlook.

This chapter attempts to answer two questions: (1) What enabled the Mormon Church to avoid sectarianism? (2) If the Mormon Church did not become a sect, is it, then, an ecclesiastical body or "church" in the sense in which that term has been understood in the sociology of religion since Ernst Troeltsch?[2] In answering these two questions, two others—of more general interest—suggest themselves; the first of interest to sociological theory, the second to the growing concern with interdisciplinary research: (3) Is the accepted dichotomy, church or sect, conceptually adequate to handle the empirical data in the sociology of religion? (4) Can sociological analysis

From Thomas F. O'Dea, "Mormonism and the Avoidance of Sectarian Stagnation: A Study of Church, Sect, and Incipient Nationality," *Sociology and the Study of Religion*. Copyright © 1970 by Basic Books, Inc., Publishers, New York.

Thomas F. O'Dea is a member of the Departments of Sociology and of Religious Studies at the University of California at Santa Barbara.

alone adequately explain the emergence of one type of social structure as against another?

Presented here are the findings of a larger study of Mormon values and Mormon social institutions[3]—a study which involved an analysis of Mormon theology and religious teaching, the development of Mormon social institutions—ecclesiastical, political, economic, and educational—and a community study based on participant observation in a rural village, the characteristic product of Mormon efforts at settlement in the West.[4]

CHURCH AND SECT

Ernst Troeltsch and Max Weber define a sect as a body of believers based on contracted or freely elected membership in contrast to the institutional ecclesiastical body or church in which membership is ascribed. "Born into" and "freely chosen" signify the vital distinction. Park and Burgess, Simmel and von Wiese, and, following them, Becker elaborate this definition.[5] For them a church or *ecclesia* is characterized by the following: (1) membership on the basis of birth; (2) administration of the means of grace and its sociological and theological concomitants—hierarchy and dogma; (3) inclusiveness of social structure, often coinciding with ethnic or geographical boundaries; (4) orientation to the conversion of all; and (5) a tendency to compromise with and adjust to the world. The sect, on the contrary, is characterized by (1) separatism and defiance of or withdrawal from the demands of the secular sphere, preferring isolation to compromise; (2) exclusiveness, expressed in attitude and social structure; (3) emphasis on conversion prior to membership; and (4) voluntary election or joining.

The sect is often persecuted and is always ascetic. It usually rejects hierarchy and endeavors to implement the "priesthood of believers" in an egalitarian if narrow social organization. As H. Richard Niebuhr has observed, sectarianism, strictly defined, cannot outlast the founding generation[6] and, as Liston Pope has shown, often does not last it out.[7] The birth of children to the freely electing sectaries and the worldly success which so often crowns sectarian frugality and industry result in that adjustment to the world which Weber has called "the routinization of charisma." To cover this phenomenon, von Wiese and Becker introduce a third type, as does Niebuhr—the denomination. "Denominations are simply sects in an advanced stage of development and of adjustment to each other and the secular world."[8]

There have been attempts—often highly suggestive—to characterize the sectarian personality.[9] Von Wiese and Becker introduce a fourth type—the cult in which religion is private and personal; and Wach introduces another— the independent group. This latter is a semiecclesiastical body which starts out resembling a sect and through slow transformation and organizational differentiation becomes much more like a church. Wach's chief example is the Mormon Church. This classification is perceptive, but arguments will be given below to show that it is inadequate.

Wach also points out the impossibility of applying any of the above-mentioned criteria with rigor. Accepting the importance of sociological criteria and of theological and philosophical doctrines in differentiating sects from other religious bodies, he concludes that the characteristic attitude is most pertinent—an attitude which claims to be "renewing the original spirit of the absolute or relative beginnings" of a religious movement.[10] In what follows the criteria of von Wiese and Becker and of Wach are applied to Mormonism.

THE AVOIDANCE OF SECTARIANISM

The Mormon Church claimed to be a divine restoration of the Apostolic Church after centuries of apostasy. The mark of the new dispensation was contemporary revelation. Through the prophet Joseph Smith, the Lord was believed to have called the elect. The result was the church which was founded in western New York, at the time a near frontier and the scene of a great religious enthusiasm.[11] To its converts it offered security—a resolution of the outer conflict and inner turmoil of denominational confusion and one which claimed the sanction of divine revelation. Convinced of a covenant to build the Kingdom of God on earth, the Latter-day Saints attempted to establish their settlements on the basis of the Law of Consecration, or United Order of Enoch, a plan announced by the prophet-founder which reconciled Christian socialism with private initiative and management.[12] This law was withdrawn in 1838 after some seven years of experiment marked by contentions and jealousies, and tithing was substituted for it.

The Mormon Church placed great emphasis on the restoration of Hebrew ideals and on the revival of Old Testament practices and institutions. The Saints were, they believed, a modern Israel: called by God, party to the covenant, and about to be gathered unto Zion. Polygamy was but one, although the most notorious, example of such revivals. In restoration and peculiarity, two important aspects of the Mormon gospel, the attitudes of renewal and exclusiveness characteristic of sects, were palpably present.

While commitment to building the Kingdom was sectarian insofar as it required withdrawal from the world and refusal to accommodate to the routine demands of secular life, it certainly had other possible implications. The idea of a Christian commonwealth was capable of quite nonsectarian interpretation. Moreover, the withdrawal from "Babylon" did not involve a repudiation of worldly pursuits, for in the City of God, the New Jerusalem, business, family life, government, and even armed defense would be acceptable and accepted. Nature was not seen as corrupted, and the vitiating effect of original sin on preternatural virtue was denied—a most unsectarian doctrine. Work and recreation were both accepted and sanctified. Against the sectarian notions of renewal and exclusiveness must be placed the nonsectarian possibilities of building a Christian society and the doctrine of human goodness—of total "undepravity."

Yet other groups had set out to build the Kingdom, and whatever nonsectarian possibilities lie hidden in the idea of a Christian commonwealth were never made apparent. How many sects built isolated little communities where prosperity followed upon the sectarian ascetic of work and thrift? Such settlements often reached a membership of a thousand and then stopped growing. Others experienced "swarming"; that is, excess numbers, usually in excess of a thousand, migrated and established a new settlement emulating the mother community but independent of its authority. This was the common sectarian fate. How were the Mormons to avoid it and realize the nonsectarian possibilities of their vision?

The Kirtland attempt to build the Kingdom failed because of internal dissent, external opposition, and economic distress—the last the most important. The Saints then migrated to Missouri and there at two points— Jackson County and Far West—endeavored to construct the New Jerusalem. Their strange doctrines claiming contemporary converse with God, their frugality and industry and consequent prosperity, their talk of making the region a "promised land," and their northern manners accentuated by rumors of abolition sentiments aroused the animosity of their neighbors. Consequently, they were driven from the land, and, crossing the Mississippi, the only eastward move in their long wanderings, they entered Illinois, where they built another city. Nauvoo, on the east bank of the river, saw the arrival of converts in great numbers, the first fruits of the European harvest. But there, too, hostility followed the Saints, and rumors that the leaders were practicing polygamy—rumors that turned out to be true—and a more defiant attitude from the Mormon leadership increased gentile antagonism. In 1844 Joseph Smith was murdered at Carthage jail, and in the next three years the Saints were driven from Nauvoo. In 1847, after a period of disorganization and hardship, they migrated to Utah under the leadership of Brigham Young.

In the West the church gained the respite needed for its internal recovery and at the same time the relative isolation required for establishing a civilization whose institutions would be informed by Mormon conceptions and Mormon values. In the 1880's and 1890's, however, the Mormon–gentile conflict broke out anew with considerable acuteness, the issues now being polygamy and the admission of Utah to the Union. After harsh federal legislation and prosecution of Mormon leaders, the church abandoned polygamy and accommodated itself to the demands of the larger American community into which it was reintegrated. Yet relative isolation had done its work: Utah and the surrounding region remained a Mormon culture area, although the implicit claim to it as an exclusive homeland was given up. Moreover, Mormon peculiarity and self-consciousness remained.

In this early period of Mormon history many marks of sectarianism were present: not only the attitude of renewal and exclusiveness but voluntary election as the basis of membership, withdrawal from the secular community, asceticism which placed a high value on hard work, persecution which increased in-group cohesion, and the conception of the priesthood of believers.

The last doctrine, however, was not interpreted in terms of an egalitarian congregationalism. Rather it found expression in a hierarchical priesthood organization, authoritarian in structure and function. As the church grew, as its early charismatic leadership became more institutionalized in the leading offices, and as it had to stand against external threats, the early congregationalism gave way more and more to authoritarian rule.

What factors militated against the development of a typical sect in this situation? Two have already been mentioned: (1) *the nonsectarian possibilities of building the Kingdom which could require so much subtle accommodation and* (2) *the doctrine of natural goodness, by way of which nineteenth-century American optimism entered Mormon religious consciousness to blend there with the chiliastic expectations of a restorationist movement.* Yet the former alone could not effect the avoidance of sectarianism, as the record of many other groups makes clear; nor could the latter; although, when combined with other factors effective in the concrete situation, both could affect the issue in a powerful and pervasive manner. These two factors combined with the following eight to effect the issue:

3. *Universal missionary understanding of the notion of "gathering the elect."* The Mormon notion of peculiarity was exclusive, but it was not necessarily sectarian in the strictest sense. It was rather committed to missionary work: to calling the elect from the world. This was of great consequence when taken together with several other factors, despite its being a rather sectarian idea of missionary work.

4. *The temporal appropriateness of the doctrine in the late 1830's.* A generation before, the "gathering of the elect" might have been understood in terms of calling the elect from the neighboring counties. But in the second decade of the nineteenth century, American Protestantism had discovered a bigger world. The Mormons came upon the scene in time to inherit the newer and broader definition. The universal understanding of calling the elect, combined with the new worldwide definition of the mission field, worked against a sectarian issue.

5. *The success of missionary work.* The ability of the Mormon gospel to bring meaning and hope to many, in America and in Europe, especially England and Scandinavia, resulted in thousands of conversions. With increased numbers, the notion of the holy city which the Saints were called to build now took on dimensions hardly compatible with sectarianism. Nauvoo had a population of 20,000 when Chicago had 5,000.

6. *The withdrawal of the Law of Consecration.* Had the Law of Consecration worked, the Mormons might have built another one of the successful communitarian settlements of which our history has seen so many. The failure of the Law, on the other hand, deprived them of a blueprint, rigid conformity to which could have been interpreted as the only permissible economic ethic, thereby lending a sectarian narrowness to their activities and inhibiting growth. Moreover, the Law was withdrawn by Joseph Smith in a revelation which still held up its ideals as the will of God. As a result,

the flexibility of charismatic leadership was transmitted to the institutionalized church in economic matters, and its spirit vivified economic experiment for the next century, while a killing economic literalism was successfully eschewed. This is all the more striking, since in scriptural interpretation Mormons have generally been literalists.

7. *The failures and consequent necessity of starting again.* The need to start over again four times in sixteen years also contributed to flexibility, preventing a set routine from developing which could then have been imposed on new problems, thereby limiting growth and contributing to a sectarian atmosphere and structure. Combined with the withdrawal of the Law of Consecration, this made a dogmatism of minutiae impossible.

8. *The expulsion from the Middle West.* The Middle West, the continent's most attractive ecological area, was destined to draw large numbers of non-Mormon settlers. In such a situation it would have been quite impossible for the Mormon Church to maintain any hegemony, spiritual, political, or economic. Instead, it would in all likelihood have become one of a number of denominations accommodating to each other and to the secular world and thus would be reintegrated into the general American community with which it shared many common roots as another small and unimportant Protestant group.

9. *The choice and the existence of a large, unattractive expanse of land in the West.* The Mormon leadership deliberately chose an unattractive region to gain the necessary respite that isolation would give and resisted the seductions of more pleasant prospects. The existence of this arid region was something over which they had no control. It was unquestionably a prerequisite for the future form of their community. The result was the opening up of a huge area waiting to be converted from desert, supporting a scant nomadic population, to a Mormon culture area based on irrigation farming. This also gave the necessary time in isolation for Mormon social institutions to emerge and to "set."

10. *The authoritarian structure of the church and the central government which it made possible.* The existence of a charismatic leader in the early stages of Mormon Church history whose right to rule was believed to be based on divine election and the consequent authoritarian and hierarchical structure of church government permitted scattered settlement in the West under central direction. Such authoritarian characteristics were strengthened by the external conditions of conflict and hardship. Centrifugal tendencies in the West were restrained when not completely inhibited. The priesthood structure and the routinization of prophetic rule might in other circumstances have been completely compatible with sectarianism; yet in the western settlement they combined with open and relatively empty and isolated land, and missionary success and consequent emigration, to make large-scale settlement possible under central government. This combination ruled out the last chance of sectarianism.

These last eight factors, then, combined to militate against a sectarian issue to the Mormon experiment and to bring into existence the Mormon Church of the present day. Instead of becoming a sect, the church became the core of a large culture area. In these eight factors and their combination we have the answer to our first question.

NEITHER CHURCH NOR SECT

The Mormon Church is excluded by definition from the category of church or *ecclesia*, unless it has become one in the course of its development. Similarly with regard to the category of denomination: since we have defined denominations as "routinized sects," Mormonism, having avoided sectarianism, at the same time avoided denominationalism. However, to be of genuine interest, these two statements must be true in more than a formal sense: they must be more than mere analytical inferences from definitions. The question is, then: Has the Mormon Church become an ecclesiastical body in the course of its evolution?

Despite the avoidance of typical sectarian structure and isolation, the Mormon Church has displayed and retained many sectarian characteristics. Most important are: (1) a sense of peculiarity, of election, and of covenant, which is reinforced by explicit theological doctrine; (2) a tendency to withdrawal from the gentile world (this is now most frequently expressed in admonition and symbolic practices; yet it found large-scale expression in the Church Welfare Plan with which the Mormon Church sought to meet the Great Depression as a separate body capable of considerable autarchy); (3) a commitment to "warning the world" and "gathering the elect," the implications of which have been more routine and less dramatic since the accommodation which followed the defeat of the church on the polygamy issue; and (4) chiliastic expectations, still important not only among rural groups but in the writings of some leaders of the church.

While the Mormons have never identified group membership with peculiarity of dress as sectarists have frequently, the strict interpretation of Joseph Smith's no-liquor, no-tobacco counsel serves an analogous function today and has become the focus of the expression of exclusivist sentiments. Moreover, although persecution has stopped, the memory of it preserves ingroup solidarity and strengthens loyalty.

Yet despite the *notae* of the sect, the basic fact in Mormon history since 1890 has been the accommodation of the church to the demands of the larger gentile community. The abandonment of polygamy—that camel at which many strained but which became so identified with loyalty that all were willing to suffer in its defense—was the surrender of what had become the typical Mormon institution. Economic experimentation—the communism of the United Order, for example—became less characteristic of Mormon activities, and, in general, the secular demands of Babylon displaced the earlier enthusiasm for the New Jerusalem. Even the successes of earlier fervor strengthened the trend to accommodation. Having become the dominant group over a large culture area, the Mormon Church experienced the conservatism of the successful, which was not likely to upset a working equilibrium. The involvement of church leadership in established political, economic, and educational institutions, the education of children, the comparatively long-established hierarchy and dogma—all display ecclesiastical features of Mormon organization. The demand for conversion and the aversion to the ecclesiastical practice of infant baptism were soon institutionally compromised in the baptism of the eight-year-old children of Mormon families.

This combination of sectarian characteristics with structure, policy, and circumstances similar to many *ecclesias* suggests that the Mormon Church is a mixture of the pure categories outlined in our typology. Joachim Wach, recognizing this problem—specifically about the Mormons and generally in such typologies—has characterized the Mormon Church as an independent group with semi-ecclesiastical organization.[13] It is, for Wach, neither church nor sect; it is an independent group through whose organization its members have access to the necessary means of salvation.

In terms of theology and group structure there is considerable justification for Wach's classification. Yet, in larger terms, there is more to be said. The Mormon restoration was not only a Christian renewal; it was a Hebrew revival. Mormondom conceived itself as a modern Israel. This alone is not uncommon in Christian experience, and we are likely to take it for granted. Yet in the Mormon case, contemporary conditions of life were to give the revival of Hebrew ideals a more genuine content than would have been possible in smaller groups in less demanding circumstances. The acceptance of a model is always important in the patterning of subsequent behavior, and in the Mormon case the model of the chosen people could not but affect Mormon belief and behavior: polygamy is but the most notorious example.

Guided by this model, the Saints withdrew from the modern Babylon to build the modern Zion. Owing to circumstances over which they had little control, they found themselves wandering in the wilderness. They had sought but part of the Israelitish parallel; circumstances had provided the rest. For sixteen years they were driven about, attempting four times to build their city. Their size, the extent and duration of their suffering, and the way in which defeat several times crowned the most palpable successes combined to transform the bread and water of sectarian affliction into the real presence of national potentiality. Common effort in success and in failure, common suffering from elemental and human adversaries, even common struggle with arms against common enemies—all these lent to the symbolic emulation of ancient Israel an existential reality which devoted sectaries in more (or less) fortunate circumstances could hardly surmise. Mormonism lived its Exodus and Chronicles, not once but many times. It had its Moses and its Joshua. Circumstances had given it a stage on which its re-enactment of biblical history was neither farce nor symbolic pageant.

Throughout this intense group experience—an experience which produced a genuine folk tradition in a decade and a half—Mormon family life and Mormon economic and political activity continued. During this time the Mormons courted and married, begat children and reared them, and established ties of consanguinity and affinity—made more numerous and complex by polygamy—which reinforced and impenetrated those of membership in the church. Economic activity, both co-operative and private, and political necessities established further bonds. Moreover, in the years of wandering the Saints spent their lives in largely Mormon surroundings. This was even more true in the years that followed 1847, when geographical reinforced social isolation.

Fellowship in the Gospel became—and remains today—supported by and imbedded in a matrix of kinship. The circumstance of enforced nomadism and of successive resettlement, brought about by no design of the Saints and yet in close emulation of their Hebraic model, was experienced in a manner that would guarantee its transmission as informal family history as well as the more formally taught church history. In each attempt at settlement a group increasingly conscious of itself as a chosen vessel established its holy city—its spiritual and temporal homeland—only to be driven out under circumstances that strengthened in-group loyalty and increased self-consciousness. In Utah a homeland was finally found where "the desert would blossom as the rose," and all previous Mormon history was reinterpreted as precursory of this final fruition in "the place which God for us prepared." The death of Joseph on the eastern side of the Mississippi was the final act of the first stage, as was that of Moses on the borders of the land of Canaan. It was the first stage in the development of incipient nationhood. The members of the Church of Jesus Christ of Latter-day Saints had become—to use the significant term often used most casually by the Mormons themselves—the "Mormon people." Moreover, the Mormon people had found a homeland. The ties of religious faith were reinforced by those of blood and marriage, of common group memories often involving suffering and heroism, of common economic and cultural aspirations—and now by a region whose very physiognomy would become symbolic of another and perhaps greater group achievement, the successful settlement in the desert.

The Mormons were not completely unaware of what they had become. It is true that their American patriotism, which was an article of faith with them, inhibited any movement for national independence, and they tended to see their own religious homeland as part of a secular manifest destiny. Yet the latter was certainly subordinate to a religious conception of Zion in the mountaintops. In 1850 the Mormons established the state of Deseret— much larger than present-day Utah—and applied for admission to the Union. The covenant people would become an American state rather than an independent nation. In Nauvoo they had been virtually a state within a state through grant of a special charter from the Illinois legislature, and all previous attempts to build the city were characterized by considerable autonomy. The Civil War had not yet settled certain limitations of autonomy, nor had postwar developments in politics, economics, and technology made autonomy seem so far-fetched as one might imagine in today's conditions. Moreover, it must be recalled that, in moments of passion in the Mormon–gentile conflict, separatism and secession were openly considered and that armed, if inconclusive, conflict with federal forces did take place.

The Mormons had gone from near sect to near nation. The Zionism of the nineteenth-century Mormons stopped short of the national fulfillment of the Jewish Zionism of the twentieth century. Yet the Saints had in large part realized the implications of the model which had guided them in such auspicious circumstances. If their own patriotism combined with their defeat in the Mormon–gentile conflict to inhibit the full fruition of national sovereignty, Mormondom, nevertheless, became a subculture with its own peculiar conceptions and values, its own self-consciousness, and its own culture area. The Mormons, in a word, had become a people, with their own sub-culture within the larger American culture and their own homeland as part of the American homeland.

CONCLUSION

We have now answered the first two questions. A peculiar concatenation of ten factors—ideal, matters of conceptions and values; historical, matters of unique concomitance or convergence in time; and structural, matters of social structure—combine to explain how the Mormon Church escaped sec-tarianism. In avoiding the fate of an isolated sect which had been the nemesis of so many other restorationist religious groupings, it did not become either a denomination or a church in the sense of the accepted definitions, although it displayed characteristics of both. Rather, the emulation of the Old Testa-ment Hebrews in the unsettled conditions of the nineteenth-century Middle and Far West resulted in the emergence of a Mormon people—a phenomenon not unlike the emergence of nations and empires from religious groups in the past or in our own day. The development of nationhood, such as we have seen in contemporary Jewish Zionism, or in the fulfillment of the aspirations of Indian Islam, was inhibited by American patriotic convictions on the part of the Latter-day Saints themselves and by the integrating power of the larger American community; yet the flare-up of separatist sentiment in the heat of conflict suggests the possibilities of development, had circum-stances been different.

What of the third and fourth questions asked above?

The dichotomy of church and sect and their derivatives—independent group and denomination—do not exhaust the possibilities which are offered by empirical research in the sociology of religion. The development of a people with a peculiar culture and with developed self-consciousness as well as a native region identified with themselves and their group "myth" is another possibility as was realized in the history of Mormonism.[14]

The final question is whether sociological analysis alone can adequately explain the emergence of one type of social structure as against another. Ten factors have been given as preventing the Mormon Church from becoming a sect despite a theological and sociological tendency in the sectarian direction. Eight of these have been presented as particularly effective. It should be noted that, of these, all but the third and tenth factors are matters of historical contingency. That is, in the cases of factors 4 through 7 unique convergence of specific events must be considered in any adequate explanation. These matters could hardly have been predicted from, or be explained in terms of, a purely sociological frame of reference. It would seem that sociology in the uncontrolled field situation—and most significant problems are still in that category—must not attempt to solve its problems in terms of abstract schemata which do not take account of historical contingency and which abstract from time. From another point of view it may be said that intellectual analysis of the content of conceptions and values often gives a much richer understanding and a much safer lead concerning their implications for social action than do categorizations in terms of highly abstract schemata. Yet this difficulty seems less formidable than the historical. The inability of sociological analysis alone to predict or explain the emergence of one type of social structure as against another must be granted, at least in the present example.

This concession has great significance for sociology, whether in the planning of research or in the training of specialists. It proves again the importance of interdisciplinary co-operation. This may be either what Linton used to call several disciplines under one skull or collaboration between social scientists and scholars across departmental lines. In larger research it must certainly mean the latter.

NOTES

[1] ELMER T. CLARK, *The Small Sects in America* (New York: 1937). Clark gives the following dissidents besides the Reorganized Church: Bickertonites, Hedrickites, Strangites, and Cutlerites. None of these groups had over 1,500 members; the Cutlerites had about two dozen and practiced community of property.

[2] See JOACHIM WACH, *The Sociology of Religion* (Chicago: 1944), pp. 195 ff.

[3] This research was done as part of the Values Study Project of the Laboratory of Social Relations of Harvard University and was supported financially and otherwise by the project. It will be published in the forthcoming monograph by the writer entitled "Mormon Values: The Significance of a Religious Outlook for Social Action," published (Chicago: 1957) as *The Mormons*.

[4] See LOWRY NELSON, *The Mormon Village* (Salt Lake City: 1953).

[5] ROBERT PARK and ERNEST W. BURGESS. *Introduction to the Science of Sociology* (Chicago: 1921), pp. 50, 202, 203, 611–612, 657, 870–874; HOWARD BECKER, *Systematic Sociology: On the Basis of the "Beziehungslehre und Gebildelehr" of Leopold von Wiese: Adapted and Amplified* (New York: 1932), pp. 624–628.

[6] H. RICHARD NIEBUHR, *The Social Sources of Denominationalism* (New York: 1929), pp. 17 ff.

[7] LISTON POPE, *Millhands and Preachers: A Study of Gastonia* (New Haven: 1942).

[8] BECKER, *op. cit.*

[9] See JOHN L. GILLIN, "A Contribution to the Sociology of Sects," *American Journal of Sociology*, XVI (1910): 236 ff.; ROBERT P. CASEY, "Transient Cults," *Psychiatry*, IV (1941): 525 ff.; and ELLSWORTH FARIS, "The Sect," in *The Nature of Human Nature* (New York: 1937), Chapter V.

[10] WACH, *op. cit.*, pp. 194–196. For an excellent discussion of the church–sect problem, see *ibid.*, pp. 195–205, and especially his later "Church, Denomination, and Sect," Chapter IX in *Types of Religious Experience* (Chicago: 1951), pp. 187–208.

[11] WHITNEY CROSS, *The Burned-over District* (Ithaca: 1950).

[12] See Doctrine and Covenants 42:30–36; also 51:1–16; 70:3, 9; 104; 82; and 92. This is a standard scriptural work of the Mormon Church and contains the revelations of Joseph Smith. See also LEONARD ARRINGTON, "Early Mormon Communitarianism," *Western Humanities Review*, VII, No. 4 (Autumn 1953): 341–369; and also ARTHUR E. BESTOR, JR., *Backwoods Utopias: The Sectarian and Owenite Phases of Communitarian Socialism in America: 1663–1829* (Philadelphia: 1950).

[13] WACH, *The Sociology of Religion*, pp. 194–197.

[14] After I had worked through my data to the conclusion that Mormonism developed into something like an incipient nationality I found the following paragraph in PARK and BURGESS, *op. cit.*, pp. 872–873: "Once the sect has achieved territorial isolation and territorial solidarity, so that it is the dominant power within the region that it occupies, it is able to control the civil organization, establish schools and a press, and so put the impress of a peculiar culture upon all the civil and political institutions that it controls. In this case it tends to assume the form of a state, and become a nationality. Something approaching this was achieved by the Mormons in Utah." Although Park did nothing more with the idea, its statement here leaves little to be desired in clarity—a strong argument in favor of more familiarity with the masters of American sociology.

PROPHETIC FAILURE AND CHILIASTIC IDENTITY: THE CASE OF ·JEHOVAH'S WITNESSES[1]

JOSEPH F. ZYGMUNT

Chiliastic movements bid for sociological attention because of the rather distinctive manner in which they express their alienation from the world, justify their rejection of it, and propound their programs of social salvation. Their belief systems represent a curious blend of escapist and quasi-revolutionary orientations, well conveyed in their central convictions: that the prevailing social order is doomed to more or less imminent destruction; that it will be replaced by an ideal system from which all evil will be banished; and that this cataclysmic change will be effected, not by human effort, but by some supernatural agency. Although the eschatological doctrines developed by chiliastic groups vary greatly in their particulars, they tend to induce characteristic social-psychological orientations which unite believers into solidary collectivities and often inspire them to engage in unconventional actions (Case, 1918; Cohn, 1957; Hobsbawm, 1959; Kromminga, 1945; Talmon, 1965; Thrupp, 1962). At the same time, the chiliastic mood and outlook also render such movements vulnerable to organizational crises. These are likely to be especially acute when specific prophecies have been publicly announced and have been phrased in a manner open to disconfirmation. Even in the absence of such specific prophetic failures, the prolonged sustenance of chiliastic fervor is likely to be problematic, and the typically foreshortened time perspectives of such movements may discourage or retard the development of organizational provisions for self-perpetuation.

How chiliastic movements adapt themselves to such exigencies has begun to be explored (Festinger, Riecken, and Schachter, 1956; Hardyck and Braden, 1962; Lofland, 1966). Attention has been focused mainly upon short-term adjustments to specific prophetic failures, with relatively little inquiry into long-term modes of adaptation occasioned by recurrent prophetic failures or by extended delays in prophetic fulfillment. While the historical record does suggest that many such movements turn out to be short-lived because of their incapacity to meet the hazards to which they are peculiarly vulnerable, it also

Reprinted from *American Journal of Sociology*, 75, no. 6 (May 1970): 926–948, with the permission of the author and The University of Chicago Press. Copyright © 1970 by The University of Chicago Press.

Joseph F. Zygmunt is a member of the Sociology Department at the University of Connecticut.

shows that some have managed to surmount them and, indeed, to "institutionalize" their millenarian outlooks.

The present paper deals with one such sectarian movement, Jehovah's Witnesses. During its career of almost a century, this group has assimilated a series of specific prophetic failures, sustained its millennial hopes through decades of "watchful waiting," and resisted secularization with considerable success (Czatt, 1933; Salzman, 1951; Sprague, 1942; Stroup, 1945; Zygmunt, 1953, 1967). From a small cluster of adherents in Allegheny, Pennsylvania, it has expanded to about a third of a million members in the United States and over a million throughout the world (Watchtower Bible and Tract Society, 1966a, pp. 36–43). This paper presents an analysis of the impact of the group's chiliastic commitments upon its career. Inquiry is focused upon the ways in which the sect has adapted its collective identity to sustain these commitments, especially in the face of recurrent prophetic failures and of prolonged delays in the coming of "Armageddon." In this focus, the group provides a striking illustration of the process of "self-fulfilling prophecy," operating at the symbolic-interactional level as an agency not only of collective identity confirmation, but also of collective identity change.[2]

·   ·   ·

TIME PERSPECTIVE

One feature of the movement's belief system which strongly influenced its development was the time perspective derived from its millenarian views. In attempting to round out its identity, the group formulated a body of historical doctrine, including a mythical self-history, which provided a comprehensive symbolic linkage with the past (Russell, 1886, vol. 1; 1891, vol. 3). Such symbolic reconstructions of the past, like the group's constructions of the present, however, were designed to fortify the movement's expectations of things to come. In its basic contours, the group's collective identity was thus really anticipatory in character, anchored mainly in its image of the future.

·   ·   ·

Although the sect had come to espouse millenarian views virtually from its inception in the early 1870s, for several years it ventured no predictions as to when the Second Coming and associated events would occur (Russell, 1874). Little more than an independent local congregation at this time, it was predominantly gnostic rather than conversionist in character (Wilson, 1959). Crucial in transforming it into the launching ground for a translocal movement were some contacts between the group's founder, Charles Taze Russell, and certain Adventist preachers.[3] The latter, previously involved in the Millerite movement of the 1840s, were now trying to revive some of its prophecies in revised form, expecting Christ to return in the flesh in 1873–74. In an attempt to meet the prophetic failure that followed, some of them advanced the view that Christ had indeed come as predicted, but in the unexpected form of a spirit being. It was not until 1876, however, that Russell adopted their belief that the Second Coming had already occurred and that the gathering of the little flock preliminary to the final climax was already in progress. According to certain biblical calculations, this harvest was to extend only to 1878, at which time the gathered saints were to be translated into spirit form. It was the belated injection chiliasm of this short-term, date-focused variety that supplied the note of urgency required to launch a broader evangelistic enterprise. This strain of chiliasm, however, also predisposed the group to experience a succession of prophetic failures which were to disturb it periodically during the next fifty years.

The first of these failures in 1878 did not appreciably alter the short-term, date-focused orientation of the movement. A biblical basis for extending the harvest to another proximate date, 1881, was very shortly discovered, and the movement continued its preoccupation with evangelistic ventures, devoting relatively little attention to organizing its following (*Watchtower*, February 1881).

The second prophetic failure in 1881 precipitated a more serious crisis which required a longer period to assimilate. For several years, the group maintained its general posture of watchful waiting for the belated translation to occur. While its chronological doctrine did identify the year 1914 as marking the final end of the "time of trouble," at this point the group found it inconceivable that its earthly departure might be delayed that long (*Watchtower*, October–November 1881; October 1883).

The attitude of tense expectancy was gradually relaxed, and before long the sect began to recast its perspective upon the future. One of the first evidences of reorientation emerged in 1884, when the group applied for a formal charter of incorporation from the state of Pennsylvania. The harvest which had previously been defined as ending in 1881 was eventually redefined to extend to 1914 (*Watchtower*, October 1884). This shift from short-term to long-term chiliasm was to have important bearings upon the movement's subsequent development. Although the sect still conceived of itself as a temporary enterprise, its terminus was now thirty years away, beyond the life-span of many members. Heretofore operating on a short-run basis, the movement was now obliged to face the problems of self-perpetuation more squarely. At the same time, in expanding the boundaries of its own future, it provided itself with respite from the crises of prophetic failure.

It was during the next three decades that the movement underwent its first major cycle of institutionalization. The tasks of organization and control began to receive belated attention, resulting in the crystallization of a more formal structure. The sect's doctrinal, cultic, and ethical systems were elaborated and integrated. The identity design previously sketched became more firmly established.

While these institutional forms strengthened the movement's capacity to endure, its commitment to the date-focused form of chiliasm continued to be a source of instability. As 1914 approached, excitement over the prospective "change" mounted and preparations for it began to be made (*Watchtower*, December 1, 1912; November 15, 1913; January 1, 1914). Decades of preaching had by now committed the movement publicly to its prophecies in a firm and extensive way. The third prophetic failure in 1914 accordingly proved to be a major crisis; yet the movement had by now developed the organizational resources needed to meet the new crisis with minimal disruption. Not only did it cling to its chiliastic hopes, it now regressed to its earlier short-term orientation (*Watchtower*, November 1, 1914). A revised set of prophecies were issued, focusing upon 1918 as the new terminus (*Watchtower*, September 1, 1916). After the fourth failure, another round of prophetic revision ensued, focusing upon 1925 (Rutherford, 1920). With this fifth failure, the further issuance of dated prophecies was suspended, the movement's millenarian stance assuming a diffusely imminent form detached from any specific point in time (*Watchtower*, March 1, 1925).

The abandonment of date-centered chiliasm, which had prevailed in the movement for half a century and had occasioned its five major prophetic failures, was not the only feature of the group's long-term adaptation. Additional adjustments are discernible in the more specific ways in which the movement sought to meet its prophetic failures and the cumulative impact of these efforts upon its identity and mission.

RESPONSES TO PROPHETIC FAILURE

The fact that the group's early identity had come to be anchored in specific chiliastic commitments made prophetic fulfillment a vital identity-confirming need and prophetic failure a source of serious identity problems. Potentially, such failures precipitated crises of faith in the broader belief system on the basis of which the prophecies had been ventured. They also occasioned crises of mission, since the movement conceived of its evangelistic operations as temporally limited, its mandate for harvesting saints expiring when the specified prophetic dates were reached. Prophetic failures, furthermore, damaged the movement's public image as well as its self-conception as a divinely directed group.

The sect's responses to the prophetic failures conformed to the following general pattern:[4]

1. The initial reaction was usually a composite of disappointment, puzzlement, and chagrin. This describes the reactions of the leaders as well as of the rank and file.

2. As a secondary adjustment to its dejection and confusion, the group usually regressed for a time to its earlier orientation, maintaining an attitude of watchful waiting for its predictions to materialize. During this interval, the group was likely to adhere to the view that its prior evangelistic mission had been completed, that the harvest had indeed "closed" on the dates previously announced. Proselytism usually declined for a time but did not cease

altogether, its continuation being justified as an "educational" rather than a "recruitment" operation. Such incipient redefinitions of group mission were likely to be temporary, however. This was also the phase during which the doctrinal bases for the previously issued prophecies were reexamined and conjectures entertained as to why the events expected might have been "delayed."

3. Sooner or later, the group achieved a fuller resolution of its quandary. The symbolic strategies through which this was accomplished were substantially the same in all five instances of prophetic failure. The group first asserted the claim that its previously advanced prophecies had been, in fact, partially fulfilled, or that some event of prophetic significance had actually transpired on the dates in question. The conviction that the Plan of God was, indeed, unfolding in the general way indicated by the belief system was thus sustained. The "events" selected to give substance to this claim were supernatural and hence not open to disconfirmation. Thus, in its efforts to convert the prophetic failure of 1878 into a partial "success," the group asserted, retrospectively, that the year marked the point at which the "nominal Christian churches were cast off from God's favor" (*Watchtower*, February 1881). The year 1881 was said to mark the time when "death became a blessing," in the sense that any saint who happened to die would henceforth be instantaneously changed into a spirit being at the moment of expiration (*Watchtower*, December 1881). The year 1914 allegedly signified the "end of the Time of the Gentiles," when God's benevolent disposition toward the Christian nations was withdrawn (*Watchtower*, November 1, 1914). The year 1918 was retrospectively defined as the time when Christ "entered the temple for the purpose of judgment" (Rutherford, 1920). A further elaboration of the prophetic significance of the latter year was issued on the eve of the prophetic failure of 1925: the year 1918 marked the time when the heavenly portion of the Kingdom was established and when a "New Nation" was born (*Watchtower*, March 1, 1925). Each of the prophetic failures was thus redefined in retrospect in a manner which provided nonempirical confirmation for the group's chiliastic outlook.

4. The supplementary strategy used to revitalize the group's millennial hopes was the projection of unfulfilled portions of prior prophecies into the future through the issuance of redated predictions. As indicated previously, this strategy was used in combination with the strategy of retrospective reinterpretation to meet the first four prophetic failures. A variant of it was used to meet the fifth—the issuance of undated prophecies covering still-unrealized expectations. In addition to renewing the group's chiliastic orientation, this supplementary strategy helped to resolve the crisis in group mission by extending the mandate to proselytize.

5. Beyond the two basic strategies outlined above, the movement employed a variety of other devices to sustain its chiliastic outlook. These have been used not only in conjunction with specific prophetic failures but also more generally to confirm the group's faith in its image of the future. The most frequently used device has been the selective interpretation of emerging his-

torical events as confirming signs of the approaching end (see Russell, 1886, vol. 1; Rutherford, 1920). The group's negative and pessimistic world view sensitized it to perceive virtually every major and minor social disturbance and natural catastrophe as an indicator of the impending collapse of the earthly system. The varied forms of unrest, generated in a society undergoing rapid industrialization, urbanization, secularization, and other changes, were exploited to affirm the hopeless bankruptcy of the prevailing social system and its disastrous downward spiral. The expressions of vexation, alarm, and impending doom voiced by various outside commentators on the passing scene were similarly drawn upon as validating evidence. A related device has been the effort to interpret the experiences and achievements of the movement itself as confirming signs of the approaching climax and as validation of the sect's conception of itself as an agency of prophetic fulfillment (see Watchtower Bible and Tract Society, 1959).

Although these several strategies proved to be very helpful in coping with prophetic failures, they also served to introduce some important changes in the movement's general orientation and sectarian style. In these changes are discernible some additional features of the movement's long-term adaptation to the hazards and dilemmas of being a chiliastic group.

IDENTITY CHANGES

In pursuing the strategy of claiming that some supernatural event of prophetic significance had transpired on the dates previously announced, the group was, in effect, recasting its definition of the present in terms of its symbolic model of the unfolding historical process, thus preparing the context for changes in its own identity. The retrospective claim that 1878 marked the time when "nominal Christian churches were cast off from God's favor," for example, had the effect of stiffening the sect's posture toward other religious organizations. While the movement had from the outset been critical of many features of orthodox theology, its early attitude toward fellow Protestants had been rather benign. As noted previously, Protestant churchgoers were regarded as the most promising candidates for membership in the spiritual elite which was to rule the world. Withdrawal from established churches, though implicitly favored, was at this time not explicitly demanded. After 1878, however, the movement rapidly took on the characteristics of a "come-outer" group, even offering its converts specially prepared "withdrawal letters" to be sent to their former congregations, explaining their reasons for quitting "Babylon."

.   .   .

The claims advanced later that in 1918 Christ had "entered his temple for the purpose of judgment," that he had assumed his "right to rule," had cast Satan down to Earth, and had, in effect, inaugurated the heavenly portion of the Kingdom, supplied additional grounds for a fundamental change in group identity and mission. In 1925, a short time before the translation was expected, a new revelation was announced regarding the fuller significance of the year 1918: it heralded "the birth of a New Nation." In that year Christ inaugurated a supernatural "government," with himself as "King." Having cast Satan and his hordes from the Earth as well in the Battle of Armageddon, the government's hegemony would be extended over the whole world. While this New Nation was, at the moment, mainly an extramundane establishment, members of the movement were its loyal earthly citizens and "ambassadors." While awaiting their own "crowning," they were to prepare the way for the new government's assumption of universal authority (*Watchtower*, March 1, 1925).

Besides helping to assimilate prior prophetic failures more fully, the 1925 announcement served to offset the prospective failure which faced the movement at this time. It was, in fact, accompanied by the suspension of future date setting, thus eliminating this long-standing source of instability. Cosmic history had moved into its very last stage; the Kingdom had *begun* to be established. The Battle of Armageddon, through which the Kingdom would assume control over the Earth, still lay in the future, but "no man knew the time nor the hour" of its coming.

From this time onward, the image of the New Nation became the main symbolic anchorage for the movement's self-conception. The sect was no longer to conceive of itself merely as the agency for completing the ranks of the 144,000 who were to rule with Christ. This mission had been completed. God had ordained, however, that the "anointed remnant" still on earth were to play an important role in preparing the way for the Kingdom's fuller triumph. A twofold mission was derived from this view: (1) to recruit and train a "Great Company" of righteously disposed people who, in the safety of the "Lord's Organization," would be "carried through Armageddon" and would be privileged to live in the earthly Kingdom as perfect physical creatures; and (2) to expose the machinations of Satan in trying to obstruct the Kingdom's earthly establishment (Rutherford, 1928, 1932).

Evangelistic activity came to be recognized around these two goals. Although the Great Company recruiting ground was, at first, identified with the movement's earlier reference group, it underwent extension to include non-Protestants, non-whites, and those without church affiliation.[5] As an earthly enterprise, the movement no longer conceived of itself as temporary nor inherently limited in ultimate size. Having a role now not only in the heavenly phase of the Kingdom but in the earthly phase as well, its own earthly future was endless and its expected ultimate size infinitely larger than 144,000. While the status of new converts remained ambiguous for several years, by the middle thirties a distinction between two categories of members had emerged: the "Anointed class" (those who joined before the "special harvest call" had ceased and who were destined to become a part of Christ's heavenly government) and the "Jonadab class" (those who joined more recently in response to the "general call" and who were destined to inherit the New

Earth as perfect physical creatures) (Rutherford, 1932; *Watchtower*, August 1 and 15, 1935).

Even more striking changes occurred in the course of the movement's efforts to discharge its second mission of "exposure." A doctrine of Satanic conspiracy was developed, emphasizing the "unholy alliance" between the "commercial, political, and religious powers" to "exploit the common people" and to oppose Jehovah and his Kingdom. Through identification with the figure of Satan, recently "cast down to Earth," the major institutional spheres thus came to be defined as havens of wickedness, as sources of injustice and oppression, and accordingly as appropriate objects not only of avoidance but of vigorous verbal assault. In the late twenties a doctrinal revision was introduced regarding the meaning of the "Higher Powers" to which the Bible urged subjection (*Watchtower*, June 1, 1929). It was now declared that the phrase did not refer to secular authorities but rather to "Jehovah God and Christ Jesus." This was part of the context in which the group shortly became involved in flag-salute controversies with authorities throughout the country (Manwaring, 1962).

The focus of the movement's chiliasm changed from awaiting its collective escape from earth to waiting for the impending destruction of the present order in the Battle of Armageddon. The image of Armageddon as a class war was changed to that of a war between "Satan's Organization" and the "Lord's Organization" for hegemony over the earth. The sect continued to adhere to the belief that it would not be a direct combatant in the war, but the anticipatory image of the Battle nevertheless exerted influence upon the movement's operations. The group's evangelistic programs became progressively radical in content and more aggressive in execution.[6] The present was perceived as the preliminary "staging" phase of the Great Battle, during which people were being given an opportunity to "choose sides." The conviction of the Battle's imminence was kept alive, but the chiliastic zeal thus generated was channelized mainly into militant evangelistic forays against Satan's Organization. A concerted drive was now made to enlist every member in these assaults. Evangelism came to be linked to a broader range of supernatural issues, such as the "vindication of Jehovah's name." The enlarged identity salience of preaching was well expressed in the change of the sect's name in 1931 from Bible Students to Jehovah's Witnesses (Watchtower Bible and Tract Society, 1931).

In reorganizing the movement's identity around militant preaching and in defining the latter as battling against Satan and witnessing for Jehovah, the major source of identity validation was shifted from prophetic fulfillment to evangelization per se. In its identity-affirming aspects, evangelistic success was to be measured not only in terms of the numbers of converts won, but also in terms of the volume, extensiveness, and vigor of the preaching effort, and even the negative reactions it evoked. This shift also entailed changes in such supplementary sources of internal identity support as the previously institutionalized cult of character development, which had played an important role in sustaining the group's earlier pietistic identity. The latter type of rather introverted cultivation of the fruits of the Spirit had little place in the new identity design and, in fact, came to be eliminated (*Watchtower*, November 1, 1933).

The movement's steady drift in an aggressively antiworldly direction after 1925 was reinforced by the correspondingly aggressive reactions of other groups to its militant and often offensive campaigns. Organized opposition against the movement increased steadily, reaching serious proportions by the early forties. During the year 1940 alone more than 335 cases of mob violence against the group were reported in 44 states (American Civil Liberties Union, 1941, p. 3). Arrests of group members became widespread. The sect responded with renewed displays of militancy, challenging arrests through vigorous court action and developing tactical innovations to circumvent obstructions to its activities. In all of this, group leaders made adroit use of conflict incidents to bolster the movement's solidarity and to confirm its new identity. Chiliastic sentiment received reinforcement from the same source, particularly in the form of a deepening conviction that Armageddon was nearing.

While functional in affirming the sect's new image of itself and in sustaining its chiliasm, the pattern of militant evangelism turned out to be rather costly. The increasingly serious waves of persecution taxed the movement's resources, resulted in damage to its public image, and retarded its rate of growth. It became clear that still another round of adaptation was called for before the movement achieved stability. This has, in fact, been happening since the middle and late forties.

RECENT ADAPTATIONS[7]

Proselytism has remained the central preoccupation of the group, but the avowed purposes of preaching have undergone some redefinition, with consequent changes in its content and techniques. Thus, there has been a deemphasis of one aspect of the sect's previous mission, that of "declaring Jehovah's judgment" upon the Satanically dominated world. Recent definitions of the group's mission have dwelt upon its more positive educational and salvational aspects. Evangelism has thus become, in large part, a "warning and rescue" operation, with "deliverance" as one of its major themes (Watchtower Bible and Tract Society, 1961). The view of the prevailing order as doomed continues to be held as strongly as ever; but the vituperative attempts at institutional discreditation have been markedly toned down. Members have been urged to exercise "theocratic tact" in their preaching, to avoid direct attacks on other religious groups, and to refrain from making other remarks which might be construed as offensive.

. . .

The movement might be described, then, as currently passing through another cycle of change in its sectarian style. It is becoming less antiworldly and more transworldly in its outlook. While its millennial dream still looks to the future for completion, it is cast in terms of earthly renewal rather than earthly escape. In this connection it is interesting to note that questions of an ethical nature have come to receive increasing attention within recent years and that disfellowshipments on moral grounds have become more frequent.[8] This is not to suggest that the group is espousing the view that the Kingdom will be established on earth through the group's own spiritual perfection or its moral uplift of humanity. The triumph of God's Kingdom under Christ is no moral allegory but is rather still conceived of as a supernaturally engineered revolution, concrete rather than abstract, cataclysmic rather than peaceful, imminent rather than remote. The sect's refocused chiliasm has been maintained with the aid of the various symbolic techniques previously developed. The resultant feeling in the sect today is not simply that the end has been delayed these many years but rather that the world has been moving steadily closer to it.

Interestingly, after refraining from dated prophesying since 1925, the group has recently begun to revitalize its chiliasm by pinning it once again to a more or less definite time. The year 1975, believed to mark the end of the sixth millennium since Adam's creation and the beginning of the seventh, is presently being discussed as a turning point of prophetic significance. This seventh millennium in world history, it is believed, will coincide with Christ's thousand-year reign over the earth, and is expected to usher in the long-awaited "worldwide jubilee" (Watchtower Bible and Tract Society, 1966b). While return to this old strategy would seem to expose the sect once again to prophetic failure, the risks are balanced by the potent ideological reinforcement accruing from this forthright renewal of faith, which thirty-five years of diffuse watchful waiting seem to have made necessary. Considering the movement's long-term development, the risks of another serious prophetic failure actually appear to be minimal. The new prophecy is being phrased in a manner that lends itself to "confirmation" by the old device of claiming partial supernatural fulfillment, and the group has given itself a thousand years for the remainder of its millennial dream to be realized. If, however, in 1975 the group does advance the claim that the millennial reign of Christ over the earth has indeed begun, some new developments in its collective identity may be forthcoming.

CONCLUSIONS

Contemporary sociologists of religion have questioned the generalizations ventured by earlier theorists regarding the organizational changes which sectarian movements typically undergo in the course of their institutionalization over time (Pfautz, 1955; Wilson, 1959, 1961; Yinger, 1946, 1957).[9] The career of the Witness movement supports this line of theoretical criticism.

Considering the organizational hazards to which millenarian groups would seem to be peculiarly vulnerable, the success of the Witnesses in sustaining their chiliastic fervor over more than nine decades is an instructive example of the capacity of sectarian groups to adapt to crises, to perpetuate themselves, and to grow without appreciable capitulation to the "world" in the realm of values. The present case, in fact, indicates that a sectarian group may undergo an intensification of its rigor and militance over time. More interesting still is the demonstration that a sectarian movement may develop successively different collective identities, expressing qualitatively distinctive styles of "antiworldliness," while maintaining its organizational continuity (see Wilson, 1959).

The major key to the group's success in keeping its millennial hopes alive and in resisting secularization has been its development of an essentially self-confirming and socially isolating symbolic-interactional system which has sustained its basic convictions and reduced its stakes in the present world. Significant portions of the group's symbolic system were designed to define the supernatural realm and did so in a manner that subordinated the "reality status" of the empirical world per se. The supernatural world was assigned psychological priority as an object of concern and as a source of meaning. Empirical events were perceived as occurring within this broader nonempirical context, and an understanding of their "true" significance required viewing them within the frame of reference supplied by the group's symbolic system. The logic of demonstration used to validate reality constructions was quite different from that normally employed by "common sense" or "science" (see Geertz, 1957, 1965; Schutz, 1955).

The millenarian complex to which the movement developed an early commitment was premised on a teleological, indeed a predestinarian, theory of the historical process. Human history was believed to follow an essentially predetermined course, in conformity with the Divine Plan. The sect's prophetic declarations were public affirmations of faith in the inexorable outworkings of this Plan. . . . The sect's belief system led it to develop a decidedly negative and pessimistic world view which discouraged involvement in social projects of a melioristic sort. The prevailing social order was regarded as irreparably evil and beyond reform. Human salvation was to come, not through moral uplift or gradual institutional renovation, but rather through cataclysmic, supernaturally mediated revolution. The movement's negative world view and its cataclysmic theory of salvation fostered an estrangement from external reference groups which might have induced outlooks and concerns favorable to secularization. The sect's conception of itself as an exclusive, divinely chosen elite, whose status was not dependent upon external social validation, served as a psychological insulating device. The provision of non-worldly standards and modes of identity validation helped to maintain the group's separateness from the world. The development of a supportive ethical system which encouraged minimal or marginal secular participation and discouraged upward mobility was an additional obstacle to secularization.

The evangelistic campaigns and programs of the movement, a central feature of its organizational life, were likewise of extraordinary significance in occasioning frequent public declarations of faith and defenses of its foundations, which deepened the believer's commitments to the sect. Insofar as it was successful, proselytism broadened the consensual base supporting the belief system. Insofar as it failed, it confirmed the group's conviction that only a select few were spiritually equipped to discern the truth. Insofar as it provoked opposition, it reinforced the group's alienation from the world and confirmed its self-image as a band of moral heroes, who, in Christlike fashion, were persevering through suffering to implement the purposes of Jehovah.

. . .

While undergoing ideological and structural changes, the sect has not only retained its millenarian character but has managed to adapt its millenarian style to the requirements of long-term organizational survival. The expectation of miraculous escape from earth, an early source of prophetic failure and disappointment, has been abandoned; the previously limited conception of the group's earthly future has been extended; its original image of itself as a little flock of preordained size has been enlarged; its recruiting ground has been expanded; its proselytization has been maintained at a high level and intensified. Date setting, which had precipitated prophetic failures in the past, was eventually suspended. Its current revival, in connection with a loosely phrased, not easily disconfirmable set of prophecies, embracing an epoch of a thousand years, is not likely to be disorganizing, but seems rather to be having a revitalizing effect. The sect has, thus far, refrained from advancing the claim which has often marked the transformation of millenarian sects into "denominations" and "churches"; namely, that the Kingdom of God has already been established on earth. In long-term perspective, the sect approximates Zald and Ash's (1966) characterization of the "perfectly stable" movement organization, as "one which over time always seemed to be getting closer to its goal without quite attaining it."

NOTES

[1] This paper is based, in part, upon documentary evidence presented more fully in the author's Ph.D. dissertation (ZYGMUNT, 1967) and in a forthcoming book on the development of the Witness movement.

[2] The analytical perspective of the present study has been drawn from a variety of sources, especially the following: BLUMER (1946); FESTINGER et al. (1956); GEERTZ (1965); LOFLAND (1966); MEAD (1934); MERTON (1957); PARSONS (1951); SCHUTZ (1955); THOMAS (1929); WILSON (1959, 1961).

[3] The early issues of the sect's journal, *Zion's Watch Tower and Herald of Christ's Presence*, contain accounts of some of these contacts (see especially the issues dated October–November 1881; April 1890; April 25, 1894; July 15, 1906).

[4] Data regarding the sect's adjustments to these prophetic failures were gleaned

mainly from an intensive study of documentary sources, especially the group's principal journal, the *Watchtower*.

[5] See the yearbooks published by the Watchtower Society for the period 1926–1932.

[6] For examples, see RUTHERFORD (1928, 1937).

[7] This portion of the analysis is based upon participant observation, intensive interviews with sect members, as well as an examination of the group's literature.

[8] For an example of this renewed moral emphasis, see Watchtower Bible and Tract Society (1967, pp. 170–186).

[9] For a broader critique of the standard Weber-Michels model of institutionalization as applied to secular social movement organizations as well, see Zald and Ash (1966).

REFERENCES

American Civil Liberties Union. 1941. *The Persecution of Jehovah's Witnesses.* New York: American Civil Liberties Union.

BLUMER, HERBERT. 1946. "Collective Behavior." In *New Outline of the Principles of Sociology,* edited by A. M. Lee. New York: Barnes and Noble.

CASE, SHIRLEY J. 1918. *The Millennial Hope.* Chicago: University of Chicago Press.

COHN, NORMAN. 1957. *The Pursuit of the Millennium.* London: Secker & Warburg.

CZATT, MILTON S. 1933. *The International Bible Students, Jehovah's Witnesses.* Scottsdale, Pa.: Mennonite Press.

DURKHEIM, ÉMILE. 1947. *The Elementary Forms of Religious Life.* Translated by J. W. Swain. Glencoe, Ill.: Free Press.

FESTINGER, LEON, H. W. RIECKEN, and S. SCHACHTER. 1956. *When Prophecy Fails.* Minneapolis: University of Minnesota Press.

GEERTZ, CLIFFORD. 1957. "Ethos, World-View and the Analysis of Sacred Symbols." *Antioch Review* 17 (Winter): 421–437.

——— 1965. "Religion as a Cultural System." In *Reader in Comparative Religion,* edited by William A. Lessa and Evon Z. Vogt. New York: Harper & Row.

GERSTNER, JOHN H. 1963. *The Theology of the Major Sects.* Grand Rapids, Mich.: Baker House.

HARDYCK, J. A., and M. BRADEN. 1962. "Prophecy Fails Again: A Report of a Failure to Replicate." *Journal of Abnormal and Social Psychology* 65:136–141.

HOBSBAWM, ERIC J. 1959. *Primitive Rebels.* Manchester: Manchester University Press.

KLUCKHOHN, CLYDE. 1951. "Values and Value Orientations in the Theory of Action." In *Toward a General Theory of Action,* edited by Talcott Parsons and E. A. Shils. Cambridge, Mass.: Harvard University Press.

KROMMINGA, D. H. 1945. *The Millennium in the Church.* Grand Rapids, Mich.: Eerdmans.

LOFLAND, JOHN. 1966. *Doomsday Cult.* Englewood Cliffs, N.J.: Prentice-Hall.

MACMILLAN, A. H. 1957. *Faith on the March.* Englewood Cliffs, N.J.: Prentice-Hall.

MANWARING, DAVID R. 1962. *Render unto Caesar: The Flag-Salute Controversy.* Chicago: University of Chicago Press.

MEAD, GEORGE H. 1934. *Mind, Self, and Society.* Chicago: University of Chicago Press.

MERTON, ROBERT K. 1957. *Social Theory and Social Structure.* Glencoe, Ill.: Free Press.

NIEBUHR, H. R. 1920. *The Social Sources of Denominationalism*. New York: Holt, Rinehart, and Winston.

PARSONS, TALCOTT. 1951. *The Social System*. Glencoe, Ill.: Free Press.

PFAUTZ, H. W. 1955. "The Sociology of Secularization." *American Journal of Sociology* 61 (September): 121–128.

PIKE, ROYSTON. 1954. *Jehovah's Witnesses*. London: Watts.

POPE, LISTON. 1942. *Millhands and Preachers*. New Haven, Conn.: Yale University Press.

RUSSELL, CHARLES TAZE. 1874. *The Object and Manner of the Lord's Return*. Allegheny, Pa.: Published by author.

—— 1886–1904. *Studies in the Scriptures*. Vols. 1–6. New York: Watchtower Bible and Tract Society.

RUTHERFORD, JOSEPH FRANKLIN. 1920. *Millions Now Living Will Never Die*. New York: Watchtower Bible and Tract Society.

—— 1928. *Government*. New York: Watchtower Bible and Tract Society.

—— 1932. *Vindication*. New York: Watchtower Bible and Tract Society.

—— 1937. *Enemies*. New York: Watchtower Bible and Tract Society.

SALZMAN, DONALD M. 1951. "A Study of the Isolation and Immunization of Individuals from the Larger Society in Which They Are Living." Master's thesis, University of Chicago.

SCHUTZ, ALFRED. 1955. "Symbol, Reality and Society." In *Symbols and Society*, edited by Lyman Bryson et al. New York: Conference on Science, Philosophy and Religion.

SIMMONS, J. L. 1964. "On Maintaining Deviant Belief Systems: A Case Study." *Social Problems* 11: 250–256.

SPRAGUE, THEODORE W. 1942. "Some Problems in the Integration of Social Groups with Special Reference to Jehovah's Witnesses." Doctoral dissertation, Harvard University.

STROUP, HERBERT H. 1945. *The Jehovah's Witnesses*. New York: Columbia University Press.

TALMON, YONINA. 1965. "Pursuit of the Millennium: The Relation between Religious and Social Change." In *Reader in Comparative Religion*, edited by William A. Lessa and Evon Z. Vogt. New York: Harper & Row.

THOMAS, W. I. 1929. "The Behavior Pattern and the Situation." In *Personality and the Social Group*, edited by E. W. Burgess. Chicago: University of Chicago Press.

THRUPP, SYLVIA L., ed. 1962. *Millennial Dreams in Action*. Comparative Studies in Society and History, suppl. 2. The Hague: Mouton.

Watchtower Bible and Tract Society. 1879–. *The Watchtower*. Bimonthly journal. New York: Watchtower Bible and Tract Society.

—— 1931. *1932 Yearbook of the International Bible Students Association*. New York: Watchtower Bible and Tract Society.

—— 1941. *1942 Yearbook of Jehovah's Witnesses*. New York: Watchtower Bible and Tract Society.

—— 1959. *Jehovah's Witnesses in the Divine Purpose*. New York: Watchtower Bible and Tract Society.

—— 1961. *Let Your Name Be Sanctified*. New York: Watchtower Bible and Tract Society.

—— 1966a. *1967 Yearbook of Jehovah's Witnesses*. New York: Watchtower Bible and Tract Society.

——— 1966*b*. *Life Everlasting in Freedom of the Sons of God*. New York: Watchtower Bible and Tract Society.

——— 1967. *Your Word Is a Lamp to My Foot*. New York: Watchtower Bible and Tract Society.

WHALEN, WILLIAM J. 1962. *Armageddon around the Corner*. New York: John Day.

WILSON, BRYAN. 1959. "An Analysis of Sect Development." *American Sociological Review* 24:3–15.

——— 1961. *Sects and Society*. Berkeley: University of California Press.

WORSLEY, PETER. 1957. *The Trumpet Shall Sound*. London: Macgibbon & Kee.

YINGER, J. M. 1946. *Religion in the Struggle for Power*. Durham, N.C.: Duke University Press.

——— 1957. *Religion, Society, and the Individual*. New York: Macmillan.

ZALD, MAYER N., and ROBERTA ASH. 1966. "Social Movement Organizations: Growth, Decay and Change." *Social Forces* 44: 327–341.

ZYGMUNT, JOSEPH F. 1953. "Social Estrangement and the Recruitment Process in a Chiliastic Sectarian Movement." Master's thesis, University of Chicago.

——— 1967. "Jehovah's Witnesses: A Study of Symbolic and Structural Elements in the Development and Institutionalization of a Sectarian Movement." Doctoral dissertation, University of Chicago.

❖❖❖❖❖❖❖❖❖❖❖❖❖❖❖❖

Coping with Cumbersome Demands of
Contemporary Living

GEOFFREY J. BARRATT

Christian Science is not a hideaway for escaping into. It's a base from which we can cope with the insistent demands of contemporary living. Rapid advances in the fields of electronics and engineering, the fast growth of cities, changes in population patterns, a faster pace in business—these seem to have launched a cluster of challenges to simple, quiet private living and spiritual development.

Such challenges were unknown a few decades ago. Now many people are troubled with new anxieties, while spiritually inclined people sometimes feel under a huge threat from materialism. In Christian Science we can find a workable means of coping with today's apparent menaces and pressures.

Without question, contemporary demands must be met; and what better way to meet them than with the spiritually scientific insights of the Christian metaphysician? The pressures of today's living bugle advance, not retreat, to us. They should stimulate us to regular, perceptive study of Christian Science, purer living, a greater exercise of our God-bestowed intelligence. These assure us the spiritual poise needed today.

A consciousness of something wrong in our community or in the larger world is a nudge to clarify our sense of the world, to translate material appearances into spiritual realities.

Pictures of current world dramas are projected into our living rooms via television, and if we are not watchful, they may be projected into our thought and linger there worryingly, long after we have switched off the television set. But we don't need to shrink from watching television or reading about current affairs. On the contrary, if we are to be active and effective contributors to the healing of mankind's problems, this watching and reading may be a necessary preliminary. It helps us learn the world's language so we can better communicate with it. Sharply aware of the world's difficulties, we know how to apply specific healing work.

Moreover, actively looking for evidences of the Christ, Truth, at work on today's human stage can be highly encouraging. We may find more instances than we anticipate. Wherever human thought is being uplifted and pacified,

Geoffrey Barratt, a Christian Science practitioner and teacher, is Associate Editor of *The Christian Science Journal*.

there is the Christ. Wherever men are being truly unified—where there are devoted educators lessening ignorance, where there are those trying to live better lives, wherever there is true beauty and art, wherever a film maker or writer or composer is working to ennoble us or to expose evil and promote good—there the Christ is impinging on human thought.

As for the rest—the apparent evidences of mortal, material thinking at work—we can take our spiritual initiative to its challenges. But we shouldn't let a catalog of problems accumulate in our thought before we begin to play our part in healing them spiritually through prayer. If we do so, we may start to feel helpless.

We can only be wearied by the demands of today if we take them on as personal responsibilities. They are occasions for vigorously knowing the truth of harmonious spiritual being as God unfolds it to us through the Christ. Though they are masked as worrying and depressing conditions, we shouldn't be taken in by the disguise. Contemporary demands are contemporary opportunities to exercise our spiritual clarity and conviction.

Do we seem overburdened by mankind's affairs? Then let's recall that "the basic error is mortal mind,"[1] as Mrs. Eddy says in *Science and Health*. Many things that seem wrong—tense international relations, trouble in the national government or in industry, friction with the neighbors—are at root suggestions of illusory material consciousness, not actual conditions. We can cope with them on this basis.

In essence, all problems are one problem: the illegitimate claim that there is life, substance, and intelligence in matter. As we cope with that foundational claim, under the direction of Christian Science, we are helping to erode the base of every problem. When the fundamental spiritual verities of Science are in the forefront of our thought, we're praying without ceasing, and we're healing momently, even though not always with conscious effort.

Christ, Truth, which reveals and sustains the divine oneness, or unity, of all real being, is never outnumbered by a multiplicity of problems. To rejoice in this scientific fact is to accept the legacy of Jesus, the Master: "These things have I spoken unto you, that my joy might remain in you, and that your joy might be full."[2]

Initiative lies with our spiritual energy, leaving the materiality presented by the world, the abrasions of present-day life, without initiative. We shouldn't give prestige to materialism, imbuing it with influence, authority, and attractiveness. Its only inherent characteristics are nothingness and impotence. Mrs. Eddy reminds us, "Jesus taught us to walk *over*, not *into* or *with*, the currents of matter, or mortal mind."[3]

Almost all of us are faced with everyday obligations. Perhaps many of us would prefer to be giving our lives to leisure or quiet study—and to contacts with others who think just as we do, who sympathize with our values and outlook—rather than to be coping with those distracting obligations.

The kind of life in which quiet contemplation is a major element is accessible to few (and probably of real value only to few). But adequate spirituality enables the rest of us to cope with more clamorous careers without compromising our spiritual awareness. We have trouble in maintaining our stability, it seems, only when we let material demands outstrip our spiritual development. Christ Jesus included both the silence of the mountains and the jangle of the marketplace in his earthly experience; he was not afraid of the worldliness of the market or the synagogue, because the measure of his spirituality was always in excess of the demands.

We retain our initiative and control in a demanding situation when we assert emphatically that good is natural, right is natural, mastery over material sense is natural, peace is natural. But if we try to *make* our light shine, we may feel strained and artificial. We do better to *let* our light shine. The real, spiritual man is the perfect reflection of Soul. Spiritual radiance is as much intrinsic to him as beauty and glory are intrinsic to the lilies of the field mentioned by the Master.[4]

Letting ourselves be transparencies for spiritual light helps those around us who may be sharing a crisis or emergency with us and depending on us for direction. It is Truth, Good, which we let shine through our consciousness, doing the work and the directing. Understanding this eases the strains of personal responsibility.

No amount of use can weary or consume this radiance. A lighthouse would not be progressively exhausted if more and more ships in its vicinity should take their bearings from its beam.

Recognizing a need for prayerful metaphysical work in a particular situation, we should not feel daunted by the prospect—fearful that we don't have the necessary time or understanding to give a thorough, successful treatment. There has never been a claim of discord beyond the power of Truth to resolve. And Truth is not tired by remaining absolutely All. It is this allness which outshines and cancels out error. Just as the ocean is equally capable of supporting a plastic beach ball or a supertanker, so divine Truth can cope equally with problems that seem to be of tanker dimensions and with those that seem to be of beach ball size.

Sometimes we may be troubled by what we analyze as a clash between the divine realities we're grasping and our insistent and continuous human obligations. How can we be spiritually minded when we have so many earthly things to do? So many decisions to make, so many bills to pay, so many appointments to keep, so many community projects to take part in?

Of course, we may be giving too much time to the things of the world in relation to the time we're giving to absorbed study and solitary prayer, and it may be wise to trim our involvements. Often, though, we need to be clearer that our human obligations are not simply clashing with the divine; on the contrary, we can expect our higher, Christly sense of being to take care of our lower, human sense of things.

The divine ideas we entertain through Christian Science don't fight the human duties of our everyday lives but care for them, direct them intelligently, reduce the labor and effort they require, purify them. The divine Truth applied understandingly cares for the human rather than jarringly conflicts with it. When approached scientifically, heavy worldly demands can enhance our poise rather than confuse us.

Science and Health tells us, "Undisturbed amid the jarring testimony of the material senses, Science, still enthroned, is unfolding to mortals the immutable, harmonious, divine Principle—is unfolding Life and the universe, ever present and eternal."[5]

The sometimes noisy demands of contemporary living can be coped with confidently through the spiritual methods opened up by Christian Science. The real demand is that we cultivate spiritual sense to the degree that we subordinate material sense and overrule it.

NOTES

[1] Mary Baker Eddy, *Science and Health* (Boston: Christian Science Publishing Society, 1875), p. 405.

[2] John 15:11.

[3] Mary Baker Eddy, *Unity of Good* (Boston: Christian Science Publishing Society, 1887), p. 11.

[4] See Matthew 6:28, 29.

[5] *Science and Health, op. cit.,* p. 306.

✛✛✛✛✛✛✛✛✛✛✛✛✛✛✛✛✛✛

The Lord in Our Cities

ROBERT COLES

Here briefly, soon enough gone, we who are fairly well off and consider ourselves well educated ask why and what. Why are we here? What is "life" all about? Here out of nowhere, soon aware that awareness lasts only so long and can mean only so much, some of us pray for answers to questions like those—and occasionally feel the glimmer of an answer or two. The answer often enough has to do with a sense of destination. And how much we want it, need it in our proud, self-conscious, cleverly humble, thoughtlessly arrogant and presumptuous minds: the conviction we are on a journey that matters, the sense that we have something ahead of us, a place waiting.

Like us, men and women who are poor and desperate and at best barely literate also hunger for a permanent home, a somewhere in which an arrival is never to be followed by a departure, "a guaranteed setup" is the way I heard it put by one of West Virginia's mountaineers now become a citizen of Chicago. He called upon a familiar and congenial "frame of reference," and in so doing he could give his head and his heart and his voice and his arms and his hands all the rein and sway he wanted and needed: "Before I came here to the city, I prayed; let me tell you, I did. I prayed and I prayed until I was so tired I thought God would just enter my head, all prayed-out like it was, and say something like, 'Listen, Mr. Allen, the way to go is that way, and when you get there, it'll be all right, so don't you worry yourself one bit more.' But I know my religion. I know God hasn't gone and wasted His time by putting us here just so He can always be whispering little hints into our ears and telling us all the answers before the game is over. You have to close your eyes sometimes. You have to trust in what's ahead. He did, on the Cross He did. His eyes were lowered, you know. I told my wife all the way up to Chicago that I'd rather not look too hard, I'd just rather not. I'd rather keep my eye on the road, so we'll be spared death; to look, to see what it's like as we got near to the city—well, that wasn't for me. I might have turned around. I might have lost my nerve and got to thinking like the devil wants you to—and according to the devil there's no Heaven, there's no rest in store for us, there's no guaranteed setup, even if God tries to build one for you. I might have stopped the car and sat there and shook and shook, while she was crying the way she always does, Clara—soft it is, and she lets the tears

---

From Robert Coles, *Children of Crisis*, Vol. III: *The South Goes North*. Reprinted by permission of Little, Brown and Company.

Robert Coles is a research psychiatrist and author.

go all the way down, and they fall off her face, or some of them find a way of getting onto her neck, and she doesn't seem to mind."

.   .   .

Maybe the man's wife can say what they both have in mind. Maybe she can find the words, the Clara he mentions all the time as the one with the "good sense and courage" to make him leave: "I never know what to say. I'm no good at saying anything. But I know one thing: it's good to be here in the city, as bad as it is here. And I believe God was the one who told us, finally, that we had to go. He came to us, God did, and He told us that He'd done it before, asked people to move across rivers and deserts. It used to be I could hear God in church, don't ask me how. Sometimes I'd hear Him in the woods; I'd hear His voice in the wind, or I'd hear His voice go washing down the side of the hill, bubbling and gurgling along, right inside the creek. I told the minister that, and he smiled, and he said that of course it will happen, because that's what God did it for, provided us with all of Nature's things, so we could have them, and sometimes we could listen to Him through them. Here in the city there's not much of Nature, only us folks, a lot of people. I see people everywhere, and in church it's so crowded. I'm not in West Virginia any more—but I still can hear Him, only it'll be the knock of our radiator or the street traffic that sets me to thinking about Him. I've wondered since we came to the city if Jesus hasn't actually come down here to stay with us. I mean, there are so many people in Chicago, I would think He'd be able to hide among us all, and that way get to know a lot about His poor flock down here.

CHAPTER 5

∗∙∗∙∗∙∗∙∗∙∗∙∗∙∗∙∗∙∗∙∗∙∗∙∗∙∗∙∗∙∗∙∗∙∗

American Catholicism:
A Church in Crisis

"The church of immigrants"—so have historians frequently described Roman Catholicism in the United States. Just as importantly, "the end of the immigrant era" appears to characterize the Church since the end of World War II. Both eras must be understood in order to grasp the vast changes, even upheavals, currently being experienced by Roman Catholicism—a theme amply suggested in the titles of the readings for this chapter.

Roman Catholics made up scarcely 1 percent of the population at the time of the signing of the Constitution, and although Catholics suffered under a number of social and legal restrictions, they were regarded as loyal Americans and patriots. All this began to change with the inpouring of Irish and, later, German Catholic immigrants in the 1820s. Nativism and its political expression in the antiforeigner, anti-Catholic Know-Nothing Party labeled Catholics as unwanted visitors loyal principally to a foreign power, the Papacy. Catholics in New York and Philadelphia were attacked by mobs, convents were burned, priests were tarred and feathered. During the great immigration following the Civil War, which saw the arrival of millions of Catholics from southern and eastern Europe, anti-Catholicism again arose, crystallizing in the American Protective Association in the late 1880s and the Ku Klux Klan in the years immediately preceding and following World War I.

Roman Catholic leaders, particularly bishops, reacted to this atmosphere in one of two ways: The "Americanizers" among them (a minority) emphasized American freedom and democracy as a climate in which Roman

Catholicism could flourish. Catholicism should therefore adapt to American organizational styles, including more democratic governance of parishes and dioceses. These bishops, along with many others less liberal, were quick to endorse the nascent American trade union movement in the face of Vatican pressures to condemn the new movement as inimical to the faith of Catholic workingmen.

But the predominant view was defensive. Catholics were to be protected from a hostile Protestantism; they were to be warned against cooperating with non-Catholics in political and social ventures. Andrew Greeley has spelled out the consequences of this attitude in terms of Church policies adopted and maintained well into this century.

> Separate school systems, separate charitable organizations, strong social controls, anti-intellectualism, fear of close contact with Protestants, belligerent defense of one's own rights, suspicion of attempts at intercreedal activity, strong loyalty to Rome, vigorous emphasis on sexual morality, and close alliance with international Catholicism—these were the characteristics of immigrant Catholicism. The Church was a garrison at war, and there was precious little room for individual freedom, much less dissent within the garrison, or communication with the enemy on the other side of the garrison walls. The parish Church and its vast array of social and religious activities became the bulwark of Catholicism in the United States. Its pastor was the unquestioned lord spiritual of the neighborhood and, together with the precinct captain, also the lord temporal . . . the necessity of presenting a united front to the nativist world outside was questioned by very few Catholics.[1]

In a sense, the fears of the hierarchy were partially unjustified, for the very virulence of nativist hatreds fused ethnicity and Catholicism together in the immigrants' consciousness and fostered such self-definitions as Irish Catholic, Italian Catholic, Polish Catholic, and German Catholic. Although countless numbers left the Church, the vast majority remained and exhibited loyalty in the most unmistakable way possible: unprecedented financial support of their churches and their schools, convents, rectories, and charitable institutions.

The close of World War II saw the beginning of Roman Catholic advance in the educational and occupational worlds of American society. These assimilative trends, resulting in a new breed of younger clergy and laity, would probably have resulted eventually in challenges to the "old style" of authoritarian governance and religious training even without the dramatic occurrence of the Second Vatican Council. That the Second Vatican Council touched off changes in the Catholic Church is probably the understatement of the past ten years. The readings attempt, in diverse ways, to interpret these changes and spell out their implications for the Church and its role in America.

The first reading, from Daniel Bell's "Religion in the Sixties," documents the "rebellion against authority" in the Church. As a sociologist, Bell is alert to the predictable outbreaks of charismatic leadership in times of upheaval. The Berrigan brothers provide an apt illustration of this thesis and further call into question by their acts and writings the credibility of the "institutional

Church" as representative of the "Gospel of Christ" and the nature of the "call" to the ministry of priesthood itself. The reading deeply probes the implications for continuing exercise of traditional authority in the Church.

Schneider and Zurcher examine the authority crisis as mirrored in a group of Catholic priests who requested the resignation of their archbishop. The authors suggest that the "psychotherapeutic ethic" that the priests seemed to espouse may come into conflict with the bureaucratic requirements of a "universal" church. This dissident ideology is also heard, of course, in other groups similarly confronted with institutions seen as authoritarian, for example, protesting college students versus "the administration."

Monsignor J. Murray Elwood, a campus chaplain, reflects thoughtfully upon another kind of dissenter—the young Catholic drop-out. A "new Catholicism" may be in the making, but in the meantime younger Catholics exposed to contemporary life styles and ethical patterns find these incompatible with the Catholic world in which they were raised.

Priest-sociologist Andrew Greeley, perhaps the best known social analyst of American Catholicism, teams with William C. McCready to sketch another bleak picture of eroding Catholic practice and moral stance. In terms of attitudes on premarital sexual behavior and on abortion, younger Catholics in particular seem to be moving away from Catholic tradition and coming to resemble their Protestant and Jewish contemporaries. The authors berate American Catholic leadership, clerical and lay, for failing to offer creative guidance when "the meaning system is gone or at least going." Their insistence that Catholicism once more provide *meaning* as an essential religious function repeats almost verbatim the analysis of Dean Kelley in Selection J., "Why Conservative Churches Are Growing."

The breakup of a long and authoritative tradition need not bring personal chaos, however. Sister Elaine Prevallet restates changes cited by previous authors but interprets them as a welcome challenge to appropriate personally the meaning of one's faith, because external guidelines are no longer reliable. Her essay demonstrates the symbolic vitality of long-established religious traditions, for in the process of encountering and needing to come to terms with vast cultural and historical changes, these traditions achieve considerable flexibility in the interpretation of doctrine and ethics. Such flexibility results in expanded meaning of these symbols and permits the kind of gradual, and at times painful, reappropriation illustrated in this personal reflection.

NOTES

[1] ANDREW M. GREELEY, op. cit., pp. 189–190.

RELIGION IN THE SIXTIES

DANIEL BELL

[The] institutional crisis, particularly its effect on the clergy, was evident most dramatically in the 1960s in the Catholic Church if only because the Church had, longer than any other institution, maintained a posture of unquestioned authority in matters of dogma and on practices of faith and morals. The Catholic Church, going back more recently to 1870, when the doctrine of papal infallibility in faith and morals was established, had consistently presented itself as a basically finished, perfect institution that clearly distinguishes truth from error and imposes its distinctions with the authority derived from its settlement on the Petrine rock. In a world of change, the Church presented a doctrinal tradition of dogmatic immutability and unquestioned continuity. Catholics were able, as Eugene Bianchi put it, "to mark off rather clearly in creed, code and cult the lines of demarcation between the 'one true church' and other groups."[1]

The Second Vatican Council called by Pope John XXIII, coming almost a hundred years after the Vatican Council which had condemned liberalism and modernism, initiated an extraordinary redefinition of the Church in its role as teacher and arbiter of morals, in its liturgy, and in the structure of internal authority.[2] Vatican II had been preceded by a theological questioning of the Church's role, unprecedented since the time of Dollinger and Lord Acton. It is striking that while Protestantism in the 1960s produced no new theologians of stature, Catholic writers such as Hans Küng and Karl Rahner brought new force into theological discussion. What they sought to introduce was history and eschatology, and with it a sense of conditional doctrine and hope. For Küng, the Church is a historical instrument, therefore morally imperfect, and a collective learning community renewed by the Spirit through continuing historical experiences. For Rahner, God is the "absolute future" of mankind, and therefore a constant source of hope. Thus, against the essential quietism of the Church's role, based on its conception of the preservation of the essential dogmas of the past, the new orientation was towards change and immanence.

While Vatican II never went so far as to adopt these views, it did legitimate the debate. And while Pope Paul VI has sought to swing the balance back to

From *Social Research*, 38, no. 3 (Autumn 1971): 447–497. Reprinted with the permission of the publisher.

Daniel Bell is a member of the Sociology Department at Harvard University.

a more traditionalist view, the challenges cannot be stamped out as were the challenges of a hundred years ago. Significant changes were made in the liturgy. The national vernacular was substituted for Latin, and the Mass was simplified. In many instances, the role of the priest is now simply that of a leader of the services. In new liturgical experiments, vestments are abandoned, services are held in homes or other places away from the church, and efforts are made to approach the spirit of the original Christian communions. In a crucial sense, devotion and worship, which have been the central experiences of communicants, are no longer traditionally organized but have been set free on a participative and "democratic" basis. The effect has been to reduce the sense of mystery and distance which the Church service, with its genuflections and sacerdotal rituals, had emphasized.

On the level of formal authority, a concept of collegiality was introduced at Vatican II. Under this scheme, the pope would consult and share polity formulation with the bishops, the bishops with the priests, the priests with the laity, and the religious superiors with the membership of the order. As Father Joseph Fichter writes:

> In political terms, this implies a shift in the power centers from the Vatican Curia to the Episcopal Synod, from the diocesan chancery to the clergy senate. It does not mean popular democracy, but, to the extent that collegiality is seriously implemented ... it would tend to move the Catholic church from a strongly authoritarian structure to a semblance of representative or participatory democracy.[3]

The paradox of the post-conciliar Church—a paradox which Tocqueville pointed out about the nature of revolution—is that as the authority grows progressively weaker, the protest against it intensifies. Persons who were acquiescent under the rigid pre-conciliar regime now declare authority repressive even though the new system is more liberal.

The rebellion against authority in the Church is of two kinds. The one, with deepest implication for the nature of belief, is the denial of mystical authority. Mystical authority—the belief in a direct and special ordination by God conferred through sacramental means—in the past endowed popes and bishops and priests with that aura of sanctification which enabled the Church to direct the faithful on all questions of faith and morals and, given its authority, often on such temporal matters as politics as well. The second rebellion is against bureaucratic authority, the arbitrary power of bishops and chancery officials to rule the parishes and direct the priests.[4]

The first rebellion takes the sharp form of questioning papal infallibility—the doctrine that when the pope speaks extraordinarily and officially as vicar of Christ he does not and cannot err—and the sacramental authority of the clergy.[5] The second denies the structure of the bishopric as an organizational form.

But if the old structure of authority is shaken, whose voice is authentic? For some persons in the Church, the answer is the *periti*, the theologian-intellectuals who in the past have served as textual advisors for the bishops. In Vatican II, the leadership for change had come largely from the *periti*, mainly some celebrated progressive theologians from Northern Europe, while the great majority of the prelates were simply unprepared, intellectually, to confront the issues. As Professor Hitchcock writes:

> For many thoughtful persons...the experience of the Council has raised an important question—if the reforms in the Church were conceived, formulated, lobbied through, interpreted and supervised by experts, and if many bishops apparently can neither understand nor sympathize with these reforms, does not real leadership in the Church belong precisely to these experts rather than to the established hierarchy? Intentionally or otherwise, many theologians are now placed in positions of rivalry with the bishops. Progressives now assume that the "mind of the Church" is to be found more adequately expressed in the writings of certain theologians than in papal encyclicals or episcopal letters.[6]

The more radical view—a small minority, probably on theological issues—is that authority will derive from the communion, "the people of God," guided solely by the Spirit, or even each person himself who feels a voice speaking to him. And these feelings have led to the creation of "underground churches" where the effort is made to celebrate the sacraments in more primordial form in keeping with the original gospels.

But inevitably, in times of upheaval, a different kind of authority, predictable by now in its form, arises—the appearance of charismatic figures who, in the nature of the case, have special moral and personal qualities which dramatize, in their persons and actions, the troubled questioning of the times.

Charismatic authority, by its nature, is antinomian. But when this theological antinomianism becomes fused with political rebellion, inevitably the most central postulates of obedience and moral order quickly are called into question by a set of actions which challenge the foundations of all traditional and legal authority. This has been the case with the two Catholic figures who, at the end of the decade, had come to personify a new kind of Catholic radicalism—Fathers Daniel and Philip Berrigan.

Daniel and Philip Berrigan came to national attention on May 17, 1968 when, dressed in clerical garb, they and five other persons walked into the selective service headquarters in Catonsville, Maryland, a suburb of Baltimore, took the files of the local draft board, doused them with homemade napalm, and burned them. Shortly after, similar actions took place in Milwaukee, Chicago, San Francisco, New York, Washington, D. C. (against the Dow Chemical Co.), Indianapolis, Minneapolis–St. Paul and Boston. In these actions, as Catholic priests and nuns joined Catholic laymen, it was evident that a strong Catholic Left had emerged in the United States.

Indicted for the Catonsville action, the Berrigans went underground. Philip Berrigan, a member of the Josephite order, was arrested shortly after. Daniel Berrigan, his brother, a Jesuit, remained underground for four months, surfacing occasionally like the Scarlet Pimpernel to make dramatic appearances at Catholic meetings and student gatherings, until he was tracked down by the F.B.I. and apprehended. In early 1971 Philip Berrigan, then in Federal prison, was charged, with several others, with conspiring to kidnap President Nixon's national security advisor Henry Kissinger and to blow up several Federal buildings, as a means of stepping up resistance to the war. Thus national attention was focused on the "commandos of the new guerrilla Christianity," the "shock troops of the Catholic Peace Movement," the "Church's most militant and prolific writers on pacifism and civil rights."[7]

In a church which had been distinguished notably for political conservatism, and whose symbolic support for the Vietnam war was manifested by the yearly presence of Cardinal Spellman, the leader of the Church, in Vietnam during Christmas, the radical activities of the Berrigans were especially dramatic. What was even more notable was the fact that, while in 1965 the Berrigans were the only Catholic priests in the United States to sign a "declaration of conscience" pledging total non-cooperation with the government (the declaration had been initiated, following the commencement of round-the-clock bombing of North Vietnam, by Benjamin Spock and had been signed by Martin Luther King, Bayard Rustin, Lewis Mumford and hundreds of others), by 1971 the National Federation of Priests' Council, which represents a majority of American priests, had voted resolutions of solidarity with the Berrigans and praised the "non-violent witness of persons in the peace movement," calling it "a true form of the prophetic ministry."

But it is more than the political attitude of the Berrigans which is important for understanding the cultural forces at work in the Catholic Church in the decade. What is more important in the longer run is their attitude to the Church and theology itself. Of the two men, Philip Berrigan has been, chiefly, the activist. A large brawny figure, with few pretensions to theological complexities, Philip Berrigan came to his radicalism by identification with the plight of the black man. In his view, as Mrs. Gray writes, "the blacks are not children to be guided by the whites. They are rather the race of superior wisdom, gentleness and maturity, the prophetic people purified and matured by suffering who could bring adulthood to the white man" (p. 80). And it was his participation in the civil-rights movement which brought him into political radicalism.

But it is Daniel Berrigan, cast in the romantic mould of the poet-intellectual turned man of action, who is the avatar for the young. His influence among young Catholic priests is enormous. The "Jesuits' golden boy," as Mrs. Gray has called him, Daniel Berrigan had in twelve years published eight volumes of verse and prose, winning the Lamont Poetry Award in 1957. He had been a professor at Le Moyne University in Syracuse, associate editor of *Jesuit Missons*, a liberal monthly in New York, and Catholic chaplain at Cornell University in the days of student turbulence there. An essay (written in 1961) which described his ordination and his dreams of the Church but ended with the sharp comment that the "priesthood was a pallid vacuumatic enclosure, a sheepfold for sheep" had "become a favorite pamphlet of the

Jesuit seminarians' underground." After Vatican II "Daniel's essay became a Jesuit classic. It was printed by the thousands, distributed to numerous Catholic bookshops, assigned to novices' reading lists" (p. 67). When in the winter of 1965–1966 Daniel Berrigan was "exiled" to Mexico, at the instigation of Cardinal Spellman, a group called the "Committee for Daniel Berrigan" took a full-page advertisement in the *New York Times* demanding his return. It was signed by some ten thousand priests, nuns, seminarians and Catholic laymen.

But Daniel Berrigan is not only "the most controversial and idolized Jesuit of his generation" (p. 95), he is a hero to the influential literary establishment which is centered around the *New York Review of Books* and the world of New York radical chic as well. His book, *Flight to Hanoi*, follows the pattern of similar works by Mary McCarthy and Susan Sontag. While underground, Daniel Berrigan had long talks about morals and politics with psychiatrist Robert Coles which were featured in two issues of the *New York Review of Books*. His play, *The Trial of the Catonsville Nine*, has been a Broadway success. A book, written while underground, *The Dark Night of Resistance*, was published in spring 1971.

The charisma of Daniel Berrigan lies in his personality and the cultural roots that he taps. His appeal is that he is hip and humble. He dresses habitually in a black turtleneck, an old ski jacket and a beret in that "elegant emulation of the French worker-priests which has been his style for years" (p. 52). He sports a "medieval Joan of Arc haircut scraggled in jagged peaks across his forehead," giving him a gaunt, spiritual look. On his chest he wears a silver amulet, or a peace medallion, or some other stylish decoration (the "talisman of the week") (pp. 136, 166). His talk is mod slang, such as "Shalom, Man," as a style of greeting, or his description of his Cornell group as a "very bizzazz outfit." A Berrigan liturgy consists of long readings from Pablo Neruda, W. H. Auden and T. S. Eliot. "Like all glamorous Jesuits [he] mingles with the powerful. . . . He fraternized with the Kennedys, whom he considered 'excellent world servants.' He celebrated liturgies in Sargent Shriver's living room which participants described as 'fit to knock out your right eye' " (p. 96).

And yet, in their theology, their beliefs are simple and literal. "The Berrigans' radicalism," writes Mrs. Gray, "did not grow out of any philosophical theorizing but out of a disturbingly literal reading of the Gospels. . . . With a simplism that is sometimes maddening, they view the problems of racism, of war and of most human suffering as created by a system of unequally distributed wealth, by human beings' greed for private property" (p. 79).

If there is a philosophy, it is a philosophy of *kenosis*, the theology of poverty which grew up in the French avant garde in the forties. The Berrigans are men sworn to poverty by their religious orders "and a conversion to poverty is perhaps the only conversion which they desire to impose on mankind." Kenosis theology—the word means "emptying out" in Greek—is anti-institutional. It asks the Church to strip itself of its material wealth and power, to return to early styles of liturgy and communion, to reinstate the primordial community of the church as a set of cenacles outside the State, and to abolish the distinction between priest and layman.

For the Berrigans this means, too, a return to the early styles of Christian martyrdom.

> The Berrigans, like all revolutionaries and most martyrs, have little faith in the redeeming power of time. Their theology is Apocalyptic. It sees the day of judgment as thrusting itself continually into the present.... Like the early Christians on whom they model their vocations, the Berrigans see the Second Coming—either man's perfectability or his destruction—as imminent in their own lifetimes.... "Redeem the times," Daniel was to write the night before Catonsville, "the times are inexpressibly evil..." (p. 117).

It is in these sentiments, with their echoes of the Anabaptists who lived `in the "absolute presentness of time," that one finds the beliefs of the Berrigans merging with a disturbing antinomianism which has been so persistent in the culture of the modern era.

All these doubts and perplexities in the Catholic Church about the nature of the ministry have brought into question the nature of "the call" itself. Some priests have argued that the whole concept of a separate religious life is outmoded and that priestly work should be fused with other vocations; others feel that the religious life should retreat to the sacristy and sanctuary.[8] A double change of role has been taking place. For many priests, there has been a shift of emphasis from the large secondary association—the diocese for secular priests or the province for members of religious orders—to the small primary group—the task force in the form of the Christian *koinonia*— where they work. Religious sisters who formerly lived in large communities began to rent apartments where three to five can live together. Diocesan priests joined in teams to conduct new kinds of parish activities. And unprecedented numbers left convents, orders, and dioceses completely for more direct secular and political involvements.

Behind these impulses is an anti-institutional stand which rejects the bureaucratic structure of the Church and the authority of the bishops. The anti-institutional tendency among the young religious has its counterpart in a "new morality" among the Catholic laity. Traditional morality, combining faith and reason, was derived from natural law and interpreted casuistically by the Fathers of the Church. But this legalism has come into conflict with the demand of the lay member to decide moral questions—birth control, going to Sunday Mass, or violating the Index—on a personal basis.

Nowhere has this change been more dramatic than in the role of confession and penance. Since the thirteenth century, the Catholic Church has required that serious, or mortal, sins be confessed to a priest on an individual basis. Through the confession the individual is expected to be on guard against sinful acts, particularly those of a sexual nature. Catholics are expected to receive the sacrament at least once a year, though many devout believers go to confession monthly and even weekly. Now the "quantification" of sinful acts and the anonymous priestly absolution have ceased to be a central concern of the contemporary "theology of penance." Catholic churches are now beginning to hold communal penitential services. The priest no longer acts as judge. In the collective penitential rites, the emphasis shifts to group reading of scripture rather than personal confession of sin.[9]

Not only has there been a change in the attitude toward confession, but two studies by the American bishops of the Roman Catholic Church found that a majority of the country's priests reject the Church's teaching against artificial birth control and believe that priests should be free to marry. The studies, undertaken by Father Andrew Greeley, a sociologist at the National Opinion Research Center at the University of Chicago, found a "drastic difference" of opinion between the bishops and the priests on sexual morality. On the issue of celibacy "more than half the priests" are somewhat in favor of a change while the bishops remained strongly opposed. (Among priests between the ages of 26 and 35, the number favoring optional celibacy was 84 percent.) And more than half favored birth control.

But the deepest problem, and the most common complaint was "the way authority is exercised in the Church." The study concluded that the conservatism of the bishops on matters of doctrine, church government, and sexual morality had contributed to a "dangerous gap" between them and the priests, a gap which was not merely a "disagreement between those who have power and those who do not," but a sign of "fundamental ideological differences about the nature of the church and the religion."[10]

In this respect, the upheaval in American Catholicism is part of the larger cultural change in the American moral temper. The "new morality," with its emphasis on subjectivity, on personal decision, on situational ethics, while still far from influencing the overwhelming number of "middle Americans" in the society, has played an important role in unsettling the young, thoughtful, active, educated elites who give the culture its tone.

NOTES

[1] "John XXIII, Vatican II and American Catholicism," *The Annals*, January 1970, p. 31. I am indebted to Mr. Bianchi for many formulations in this section, though I have modified some of them in the light of other discussions cited.

[2] For a discussion of Vatican II, see XAVIER RYNNE (pseud.), *The Second Session: The Debates and Decrees of Vatican Council II* (New York, 1964).

[3] JOSEPH H. FICHTER, "Catholic Church Professionals," *The Annals*, January 1970, p. 80.

[4] For a judicious discussion of these issues, see JAMES HITCHCOCK, "The State of Authority in the Church," *Cross Currents*, Fall 1970.

[5] See, for example, HANS KÜNG, *Infallible? An Inquiry* (New York, 1971).

[6] HITCHCOCK, op. cit., pp. 373-374.

[7] The characterizations are by FRANCINE DU PLESSIX GRAY, the biographer of the Berrigans, in her profiles in *The New Yorker*, expanded and reprinted in *Divine*

Disobedience (Vintage edition, 1971). Since the factual references to the Berrigans are taken from Mrs. Gray's book, further page citations to quoted matter will be made in parentheses in the text. For the characterizations above, see pp. 41, 90.

[8] These views are debated by IVAN ILLICH, "The Vanishing Clergyman," *The Critic*, June–July 1967, and JOSEPH H. FICHTER, "The Myth of the Hyphenated Clergy," *The Critic*, December 1968–January 1969.

[9] See, for example, the *New York Times*, April 17, 1970:

> USE OF CONFESSIONAL IS DROPPING
>
> Like the Latin mass and fish on Friday, the regular visit to the confession box may be on its way to obsolescence in the Catholic Church.
>
> The number of individual confessions has dropped sharply in recent years. The Rev. John J. Bumstead of St. Catherine of Siena Parish in Riverside, Conn., for instance, said that "Saturday confessions are off by 50 to 60 per cent."
>
> Laymen and priests interviewed said that one reason for both the decline in individual confession and the growth of communal penitential rites was a decreasing sense of urgency about mortal sin.

[10] The study, with excerpts from the conclusions, is reported in the *New York Times*, April 15, 1971.

TOWARD UNDERSTANDING
THE CATHOLIC CRISIS:
OBSERVATIONS ON DISSIDENT
PRIESTS IN TEXAS

LOUIS SCHNEIDER   LOUIS ZURCHER

INTRODUCTION

One of the significant recent conflicts between Roman Catholic priests and their church superiors in the United States was launched in the San Antonio, Texas diocese late in 1968. The present study of the "dissident" priests involved in that conflict was designed to elicit their sentiments about the archbishop whose resignation they called for to ascertain some significant features of their social group-anchoring and their self-images. Interviews were used mainly to elicit the sentiments and, to obtain other relevant data, use was made of the Twenty Statements Test (TST), to be explained below. The study was conducted with an eye to its larger suggestions for Catholicism and for the more comprehensive society. We conceive that the Catholic crisis is a complex phenomenon, understanding of which will have to be derived from a variety of methods. One special approach, combining interview with paper-and-pencil test procedures, is here exemplified. Its results are best set out by a presentation of background; of problems centering on liberalism and authoritarianism; of some points regarding self-anchoring and self-evaluation; of several additional issues readily suggested by the material that will have been reviewed.

BACKGROUND

On 16 September 1968, fifty-one priests of the San Antonio, Texas archdiocese signed a letter that called for the resignation of the then 77-year-old Archbishop Robert E. Lucey. On 24 October this letter was made public, and great interest was aroused in the Lucey "affair," which over months was given considerable space by newspapers such as the *San Antonio Express*, the *Houston Chronicle*, and the *Alamo Messenger* (the official Catholic newspaper of the archdiocese).

From *Journal for the Scientific Study of Religion* 9, no. 3 (Fall 1970): 197–207. Reprinted with the permission of the publisher and the authors.

Louis Schneider and Louis Zurcher are members of the Sociology Department at the University of Texas at Austin.

In a new letter of 30 October, supportive of the first one, seventeen more priests joined their names to those of the original fifty-one, for a total of sixty-eight dissidents, as they soon came to be known.

The archbishop was respected by many of his priests for his past liberal leadership in social and economic matters. For example, he had ordered all Catholic schools in his archdiocese to integrate in 1953, well before the critically important May 1954 decision of the Supreme Court. Even in the letter of 16 September, Robert Lucey was described as "a champion of the Church's social teachings, speaking out fearlessly and often in prophetic lone-liness against the social and economic injustices about us." It was also clear from intensive interviews with thirty of the dissidents that a number of the younger priests of San Antonio and its environs had once been deeply affected by the archbishop's liberalism, which had in its time served them, in their own view, as model and as inspiration. True, to these same men, it had lately begun to appear that the archbishop's lead in social and economic justice was faltering: he was not going far enough; he was overcautious; he was too constrained by powerful conservative forces. Several of the men interviewed thought it tragic and ironic that the archbishop should have set in motion liberal orientations which now came back to him in intensified form, even embarrassing and disconcerting him.

There was in the interviews a more than incidental note of criticism of the archbishop on the ground that he knew little of the present-day Mexican-American community. Many insisted that he virtually never came to visit the numerous Mexican-American parishes and would be thoroughly un-comfortable with the people in them if he did. Here we come upon a change in tone. The archbishop was criticized to some extent because of dissatisfaction with his *present* performance in social and economic matters. Even this criticism, important as it was, hedged to an extent.

But once the matter of being "uncomfortable with people" is reached, criticism quickly extends to the entirety of the archbishop's relations to others, and strong reservations are expressed about him as a man seen as virtually tyrannical in his exercise of authority. It was frequently said that he was "all right" on social matters *outside* the church but not *inside* the church; any such thing as an organization of priests, for example, actually met with his thorough disapproval. Unions and the like were acceptable outside an ecclesiastical framework, but within the church: due docility; and one priest commented: "What he really means is not docility but servility." There can be no doubt that a very considerable number of the thirty dissidents interviewed at length felt their integrity and essential manhood threatened by what they perceived as unwarranted high-handedness by the archbishop and disregard of priests' personal needs and feelings. The letter of 16 September, addressed to the Pope, Cardinals Cicognani and Confalonieri, the President of the National Conference of Catholic Bishops, and the Apostolic Delegate to the United States, asserted that "we are not merely reciting a litany of woes but describing a pattern of aloofness, repression and paternalism."

On the one side, then, an aging archbishop (although no one denied him excellent retention of his physical and mental faculties) with a long past record of liberalism in socio-economic matters but probably not overpatient with signs of hesitation or reluctance in obeying his behest.[1] And on the other side, first fifty-one and then sixty-eight men, nearly all of whom were inclined to regard the archbishop as an impossible authoritarian and some of whom were disposed even to depreciate his liberalism, either out of sheer dislike of what they saw as his authoritarianism or for his alleged recent caution on social issues.

The sixty-eight dissenters were predominantly diocesan or regular priests owing their first loyalty to the archbishop, with a sprinkling of religious priests owing primary loyalty to their orders (such as the Franciscans or the Redemptorist Fathers). The entire archdiocese had about 448 priests at the time of the dissidence, these being secular (or regular) and religious in about equal numbers and serving a community of just over half a million Roman Catholics. In a statement of 24 October 1968, the fifty-one original dissidents acknowledged that they themselves were "a small group" but added that if their letter of 16 September had been made public from the beginning, if "all 448 priests in this archdiocese" had had the chance to sign, they felt the number of signers would have been larger. This is difficult to judge. But at the least, the fact is that 15 percent of the archdiocesan priests became overtly dissident by requesting the archbishop's resignation.

LIBERALISM, AUTHORITARIANISM, THEOLOGY

INTERVIEWS

The material of this section derives primarily from interviews. One of us was able to interview thirty of the original sixty-eight dissidents, speaking with each of the men from half an hour to two hours. All interviewees were asked to account for the letter-request that the archbishop resign, and all were asked their views on ecumenism, lay participation in liturgy, contraception, and priestly marriage. Otherwise, interviews were unstructured. The first interviewees were several men designated by a number of others (and, also, self-designated) as centrally important figures among the dissidents. Thereafter, a snowball technique was used to have each interviewee nominate others who were centrally important. There is every reason to think that our thirty interviewees stood at the heart of the whole affair. The original intention had been to interview all sixty-eight. But when the resignation of Archbishop Lucey was announced on the morning of 4 June 1969, it became quite evident that this new context would seriously modify the mood and responses of interviewees. Accordingly, after a thirtieth interview that week, interviewing was stopped.

We could not interview an adequate sample of non-dissident priests in the archdiocese. This unfortunate limitation is somewhat mitigated by the availability of relevant data from nonpriestly comparison groups which will be adduced in due course.

It may here be mentioned that when interviewing ceased in June 1969, morale was generally at a low ebb among those dissidents who remained in the city of San Antonio. A very few were hopeful of rectification of what they considered specific injustices by the new, incoming Ordinary, Bishop Furey of California, but many felt that any cause of church reform had little chance of success in the foreseeable future.

LIBERALISM

As would be expected, the thirty dissident priests are inclined in "liberal" directions on a number of fronts. One is the unavoidable front of authority, to which they constantly recurred and which, indeed, they simply refused to let alone. They were deeply disturbed over what they saw as arbitrary authority exercised by their archbishop in disregard of the feelings of subordinates. This concern is mentioned here as a component of "liberalism," but it reflects what we believe might turn out to be a crucial element in the outlook of the dissidents and it will inevitably be referred to in further course.

There is "liberalism" on a second front, too, in that there is a general inclination to "tolerant" views on ecumenism, lay participation in liturgy, contraception, and priestly marriage. All these priests are *for* ecumenism and interfaith conversation, with some reservations about the utility or likelihood of success of ecumenist attempts and with some very occasional wariness about possible dilution of Catholic doctrine. None had a negative word to say about lay participation in liturgy. On the matter of contraception, several men were unsure or did not care to comment, but the majority were clearly inclined to be skeptical of the view that every marital act should be open to the possibility of procreation. There was a strong consensus that the future church would contain married priests, and virtually all felt that marriage should be optional for individual priests.[2]

In close connection with this front of liberalism, these men are attracted or say they are attracted by the writings of liberal theologians such as Rahner and Schillebeeckx. Some mention Hans Küng, Yves Congar, and Teilhard de Chardin. One stressed that he was deeply moved by the book of Charles Davis entitled *A Question of Conscience*.[3] This book was also mentioned by others. Davis is a well-known British theologian who left the Catholic Church in 1966, after twenty years of priesthood. While he left the church, it appears unlikely that all of San Antonio's dissidents will do so. Nevertheless Davis's book expresses lucidly many of the dissidents' forebodings and it will be referred to again.

A general liberal tendency is discernible for the dissidents on a third front also. They champion the causes of disadvantaged Mexican-Americans and Negroes. Some of them, as intimated above, castigated the archbishop for what they took to be his too abstract love for minority groups, a love unmanifested in an effective desire for closeness and contact. The thirty have a deep compassion for the poor and for ill-paid agricultural workers. A number were critical of what they regarded as inept distribution of priestly talent in San Antonio. The ablest diocesan priests were placed in affluent parishes, not in San Antonio's poor and "ethnic" West Side where it was felt they were most needed.

PSYCHOTHERAPEUTIC ETHIC

We now turn in more detail to the anti-authoritarian component in this liberalism. The central problem the men saw in the Lucey affair was that of authority, and authority is constantly associated with, or assimilated to, "structure." Phrases such as "the panic-stricken structure of the church" and "the pathology of church structure" occurred repeatedly and it appeared repeatedly that authority was at the heart of structure. Structure is constantly and insistently contrasted with "person." In the same vein, "formalism" is used in a depreciative way, as are "paternalism," "mechanism," "institutionalism," and of course "authoritarianism." One man is pessimistic about structures and optimistic about people, and another speaks of "dictated values" versus "personal values," or "legalism" versus "personalism."

One priest reported, and our observations concurred, that the signers of the request for the archbishop's resignation were men with a personalistic orientation, interested in psychotherapy. He added that values should not be imposed but that priests should probe for *others'* values and seek somehow to work with them. A model of human relations much affected by psychotherapeutic notions and practices begins to emerge. One *listens* to another. (It was a common complaint about Archbishop Lucey that he did not *listen* and did not hear.) One lets the other tell what is on his mind. One does not tell the other what to think. One lets the other unfold, come to self-expression, develop his creativity. This is therapeutic and at the same time likely to lead to productive human relations. "Authoritarianism" and "institutionalism" are thought to destroy all this. Those who sustain the latter not only fail to listen but thereby, of course, also fail to hear and thereby cut themselves off from vital information at the same time as they hurt, and suppress, and help to sustain inequity and iniquity. The general view thus suggested was sometimes anchored in a particular prestige-name in psychotherapy, sometimes not. It was sometimes expressed with eloquence, sometimes only rather inarticulately. But it was very widespread among our dissidents and it received repeated stress from the same individuals.

There is nothing like a serious effort by any of the dissidents to integrate this model of human relations into a larger, systematic outlook that would tell us, say, how a human society can absorb and make strategically operative this psychotherapeutic vision while providing for indispensable nonpersonal relations—for situations in which one man must order and others unknown to him must obey, and so on. This "psychotherapeutic ethic" seems attractive because it still incorporates important love-values and does so while affording what is vaguely and somewhat confusedly apprehended as a "scientific" grounding for those values. Part of the appeal of the psychotherapeutic model of human relations may well rest in its re-activation, in some sense, of a primitive Christian model; at the same time our men are apparently not inclined to explore possible contradictions between an absolute Christian ethic of love and a psychotherapeutic ethic.

Nor are they inclined to test the limits of making this psychotherapeutic ethic a charter for social institutions. Perhaps none, forthrightly confronted, would have regarded as feasible the notion that the archbishop should love him and be intent on allowing him to "unfold" under *all* circumstances. But they have not so confronted themselves. Charles Davis, who in many ways appears sympathetic to the psychotherapeutic ethic, nevertheless also explicitly remarks: "I see no essential opposition between institution and personal freedom. On the contrary, a person becomes a person only in and through community; and human community is embodied in institutional structures."[4] Yet this does not seem quite to come through to our thirty men. We suggest that at some level and in some sense the thirty "know" it is impossible to turn all of human society into some kind of vast psychological clinic but that they still remain powerfully taken by the psychotherapeutic model because they are fumbling for "something different" in human relations. That model and the ethic it suggests seem to adumbrate the "something different" better than anything else and are attractive despite such confusions as attend reliance upon them.

The three components we identified above *can* be regarded as denoting "liberalism," as we suggested above. But they can also be taken as three elements of a total priestly ideology, inclusive of socio-politico-economic liberalism in a narrower sense, of a somewhat relaxed Catholic theology, and of the psychotherapeutic ethic. The first two of these are entirely familiar and also quite expectable among dissident Catholic priests—which is not to say that they are trivial. The third element—the psychotherapeutic ethic —could *conceivably* be of special importance and it must figure in our account once again.

SELF-ANCHORING AND SELF-EVALUATION

We wanted an instrument to ascertain the images the dissidents had of themselves and the ways in which they saw themselves anchored in their groups, somewhat more delicate and more subtle matters than the interviews could handle. The instrument adopted was the Twenty Statements Test (TST), a device that comes out of the theoretical tradition of symbolic interactionism. One of the postulates in that tradition holds that stability of self-concept depends strongly on stability of relevant social structures and interpersonal networks. The rationale for the TST includes the assumption that the respondent will reveal core components of his self-concept, his most salient self-attitudes, by direct response to the non-directive "Who am I?" query. For both theoretical guidance and techniques of scoring we drew on items of a growing relevant literature.[5]

TSTs were administered to twenty-four of the thirty interviewees ranging in age from 26 to 50, with a mean of 35.6 years and a median of 33.5. All twenty-four men gave twenty responses to the "Who am I?" question. None misunderstood the simple instructions to write down twenty sentences beginning with the words "I am," spontaneously, and without concern for "logic," "order" or "importance."[6] Several of the numerous results obtained should be noted.

LOCUS SCORE

In the paper by Kuhn and McPartland (footnote 5), setting out an empirical investigation of self-attitudes, the authors categorized TST responses dichotomously as either *consensual* or *subconsensual* references. The consensual category included those statements which referred to groups and classes whose limits and conditions of membership were matters of common knowledge. ("I am an assistant pastor ... a hospital chaplain ... a priest.") The subconsensual category included those statements which referred to groups, classes, attributes, traits, or any other phenomena which would require clarification by the respondent to become precise or to enable accurate placement of him in relation to other people. ("I am lonely . . . I need help from others ... I am searching.")

A Locus score, referring to anchorage or self-identification in a social system, was derived from the proportion of consensual responses. The mean dissident-priest Locus score was considerably lower than the mean Locus scores for ten other groups for which comparable data were obtainable.[7] The most nearly comparable mean Locus score among the ten groups was for a group of twenty-eight persons who professed no religion, whose score was still almost twice that of the priests; a group of thirty-eight lay Catholics had a mean score nearly four times that of the priests. This all constitutes one portion, at least, of the evidence that strongly suggests that dissident priests are cut adrift from stable self-identification.

CONCRETENESS OF SELF-REFERENCE

Closely related to Locus score is the indication of the percentage distribution of respondents among four modes—*A*, *B*, *C*, and *D*—referring to the concreteness, or perhaps "imminence" of self-reference. Here we draw on McPartland, Cumming, and Garretson.[8] Each of a respondent's twenty statements is scored and the respondent is categorized according to the mode into which most of his responses fall.[9] *A* statements involve the most concrete level of reference. A man says of himself that he is 6 feet tall or has a certain home address or eye color. No socially important "others" are implied at all. *B* statements point to so-called institutionalized statuses or roles and imply the notion of a generalized other or of an institutional pattern. "I am a priest," "I am a student" are fair enough examples. Also included are statements that give a status-like form to self-references that point less definitely to a generalized or institutionalized pattern (such as "I am a music-lover"). *B* statements point to self-experience in terms of involvement in patterned social networks in which relations are mediated by internalized norms. *C* statements present ways of feeling or responding or performing in social interaction. A man says, "I am moody sometimes" or "I like to be with people." Normative regulation is still not ruled out, nor are consensually supported goals ruled out, but the "others" implied in *C* statements are not very definitely, unequivocally conceived as "generalized others" within a strongly structured context of sanctioned things to do and ways to do them. Fourth, *D* statements, illustrated by "I hope for the best" or "I would like to try to be better" or "I am one with God," imply none except very vague social or interactive contexts or implicitly postulate "others" (such as "mankind" in the statement, "I am just one among billions"); these are perhaps better called "transcendental" rather than "generalized" in the sense of Mead.[10] Table 2 exhibits percentage distributions of the four modes among the twenty-four dissidents and five comparison groups.

Thus, 83 percent of the priests were *C* mode; they show a very low incidence of *B* modes. (None of them was classed as an *A* mode respondent.) While there are difficult interpretative questions here, our data in toto (inclusive of the interviews) suggest that the priests were initially fairly well satisfied with their roles in the church social system and, having located their identity within that system, were appreciably *B* mode; that in time they became disenchanted with the system, loosened their ties thereto, and moved toward the *C* mode; that the *C* response represents for them both a kind of declaration of independence from social structures and a possibly temporary retreat pending more acceptable social anchoring if that can be managed.

Table 2 shows that McPartland and Cumming's "lower class" adults have, after the priests, the highest percentage of *C* mode respondents. These authors explain their results as a function of the "lower class" respondents' looser involvement in institutionalized social relations, lesser activity in voluntary associations, and disadvantages in competition for power and prestige in such areas as work and school.[11] In their present state the dissidents can plausibly be argued to be experiencing some of the correlates of being "low men on a totem pole." They definitely feel a certain powerlessness[12] and even loss of prestige, and of course their dissidence has loosened their church bonds. They see themselves, at any rate, as disadvantaged. They have a relatively strong propensity to identify themselves "in terms of personal characteristics, without reference to position in groups."[13]

TABLE 2

TABLE 2

Percentage Distribution of *A, B, C,* and *D* Mode Respondents

	NUMBER	A	B	C	D
Social Categories					
Dissident priests	24	0	4	83	13
Former mental patients	146	8	18[a]	31[a]	42[a]
College undergraduates	1653	2	51[a]	31[a]	16
Mental patients	100	21	15	31[a]	33
"Middle-class" adults	137	3	65[a]	27[a]	5
"Lower-class" adults	36	0	33[a]	53[a]	14

Sources: Priests: this study; former mental patients: Hartley, "Self-Concept . . . Mental Patients" (n. 5); college undergraduates: Hartley, "Self-Conception" (n. 5); mental patients; McPartland, Cumming, and Garretson, "Self-Conception and Ward Behavior" (n. 5); middle- and lower-class adults: McPartland and Cumming, "Self-Conception . . . and Mental Health" (n. 5).

[a] Differences between priests and others tested by chi-square and significant at level $p < .05$.

SELF-EVALUATION

Additional evidence constrains us to the view that the dissidents are not only, as said, cut off from stable self-identification but are also peculiarly marked by self-appraisal, self-criticism, and self-objectification. The self-appraisal and self-criticism may be barely suggested by pointing to the very high Self-Evaluation scores of the priests. Fifty-four percent of their statements involved self-evaluation, compared with percentages of self-evaluative statements for seven other comparable groups ranging from 15 percent (for a group of Unitarian ministers) to 31 percent (for a group of social work students).[14] As regards self-objectification, Mead, addressing himself to the problem of adjustment to social and interpersonal instability, considered "the function of making one's self an object" to be necessary to "readjustment of responses."[15] The dissident priests may on the basis of our data be said to be agonizing self-evaluative and incessantly involved in self-objectification, making themselves objects of reflection and inquiry.

SUMMARY OF TST FINDINGS

The material emerging from the TSTs is strongly congruous with the interview results. The dissidents are again revealed as groping men. They had undoubtedly been looking for a "readjustment of responses," but they had not— or not yet—achieved it. Given their stances toward authority but continued profound involvement in the interpersonal aspects of human life and the social world, it is small wonder that they should seek for an anchor in something such as the psychotherapeutic ethic. (The reader should be reminded that we lacked a control group of non-dissidents. Our special characterization of the dissidents is not *definitive*. It receives some support from a preliminary, unpublished work by Ralph Nemir, which indicates that *non*-dissident priests tend toward B rather than toward C modes and are relatively non-self-evaluative.)

DISCUSSION

The above materials raise a variety of issues or questions of which three in particular can be briefly discussed. The first has to do with the ideological element represented by the espousal of what we have called the psychotherapeutic ethic. Is there an authentic reaching out for "something new" here? Much of the significance of Catholic dissent for both the Catholic Church and for a larger society as well depends on whether or not notions of the type involved in the ethic develop into something more systematic and full-blown than they now are. Is there a potentially challenging ideological content here; or are we in the end going to find, in attending to the psychotherapeutic ethic and similar constructions, that we deal only with minor, romantic, groping, and rather banal ideological efforts whose lack of substantial content might suggest that much dissent, Catholic and other, is at bottom a transitory distemper? We put the matter in this way precisely for the sake of a certain sharpness.

Second, the material reviewed plainly points beyond itself and indeed beyond Catholicism. As is well known, college students in the United States today often stress the "authoritarian" and "impersonal" and "mechanical" and "formal" character of school experience and teaching.[16] This is evident on the evaluation sheets on which they estimate their teachers. Even where there is some recognition that in principle it is not possible to turn every classroom into a clinic or the scene of a love feast if the classical objects of teaching are to remain in being, a highly personalized model of human relations seems to be widely espoused.[17] We confine ourselves to students and to these broad statements about them. But at least one other resemblance of students and priests is evident. The dissidents say with great frequency that the church has become irrelevant.[18] The accusation of irrelevance is of course often levelled at college and university by dissident or alienated students. The most superficial inspection of pertinent attitudes of priests and students, then, suggests "common denominators," perhaps very important value agreements. It is by now indeed a commonplace notion that the dissidence within Catholicism is part of a bigger phenomenon—part, as it were, of a larger cultural tremor. It is *possible* that much that looks like a "Catholic crisis" has nothing in particular to do with "Catholicism" or even "religion" but rather represents the coming to expression *within* Catholicism of trends also expressed elsewhere, whose primary significance is not "religious." (This does not deny that something of a religious "coloring" may be expected in a religious sphere.) For Emile Durkheim, in his classic study of suicide,[19] it will be recalled, there were features common to various sets of suicides, so that he could in the end formulate several main types cross-cutting common-sense divisions. Presumably various forms of dissent have their affinities too. They still await the kind of exploration that will enlighten us greatly about Catholic dissent, college dissent, non-college youth dissent, and so on, while typing, ordering, and generally clarifying these (or better conceived categories) in relation to one another and perhaps to a "larger cultural tremor."[20] The subjects of social research provide us in what they "say" with indispensable clues to a variety of matters. But they do not say "enough" and clearly cannot do the job of the social researcher for him. That job, we must observe in the present context, ultimately involves going both "beyond Catholicism" and "beyond priestly statements" about what is occurring, what is empirically "right" or "wrong," and so on.

Third, if our material constrains us to look "upward," as it were, to the larger social framework, it inevitably also suggests that there are matters of considerable interest "downward," toward the emotional side of the dissident experience. Perhaps the dissidents have been objectifying themselves prior to a self-disposal that will put them into new, firm social contexts or reestablish them in older ones. Or possibly at least some of them are involved in a certain lasting deprivation of social anchoring that will be acutely felt emotionally. (This indeed looked like more than a mere possibility in a number of cases.) Our data with regard to C modes of response also suggest the possible emergence of a personality type (although this may be too ambitious a term given the modesty of the relevant evidence we have) which would be relatively highly adaptable, change-oriented, and imbued with relatively low emotional commitment to strongly structured social relationships. Here we can only suggest that inquiry on the lines this hints at might be strengthened by simultaneous consideration of strategic components of total priestly ideology. We may be allowed to reiterate our sense that the psychotherapeutic ethic is the component in total dissident ideology that most needs "watching" for its possible importance.

NOTES

[1] In a letter of 30 October 1967, sent to San Antonio's archdiocesan priests' senate, the archbishop reacted with sharp negative criticism to a statement by Father John L. McKenzie, a Jesuit theologian at Notre Dame, to the effect that "authority in the Church belongs to the whole Church and not to particular officers." See *The Alamo Messenger*, 8 November 1968.

[2] Our inquiry, incidentally, convinced us of the simplistic character of "explanations" for dissidence that would merely impute it to a powerful urge to marry. There is no particular reason to doubt the claim to thorough accommodation to bachelorhood made by a considerable number of the thirty dissidents (with a mean age of about 35). It is worth noting also that some still believe in the value of celibacy as witness to the truth of Christianity, as a token and a symbol that there is a world beyond the flesh and of higher value than the

flesh. Celibacy may thus be praised by men who have not the slightest desire to impose it.

3 New York: Harper & Row, 1967.

4 DAVIS, *A Question*, p. 78. Later (p. 185), Davis writes that, "There is still need for institutional structures, despite their ambiguity and limitations."

5 The detail of procedures and findings would entirely burst the bounds of the present paper. Guidelines were provided by the following: CARL J. COUCH, "Self-Attitudes and Degree of Agreement with Immediate Others," *American Journal of Sociology* 63 (March 1958): 491–496; COUCH, "Self-Identification and Alienation," *Sociological Quarterly* 7 (Summer 1966): 255–264; WYNONA HARTLEY, *Self-Concept and Social Functioning of Former Mental Patients* (Kansas City, Mo.: Greater Kansas City Mental Health Foundation, 1968), mimeo.; HARTLEY, "Self-Conception and Organizational Adaptation," paper presented at Midwest Sociological Association meetings, April 1968; SIDNEY JOURARD, "Healthy Personality and Self-Disclosure," in *The Self in Social Interaction*, ed. Chad Gordon and Kenneth Gergen (New York: Wiley, 1969), pp. 423–434; MANFORD H. KUHN, "Self-Attitudes by Age, Sex, and Professional Training," *Sociological Quarterly* 9 (January 1960): 39–55; KUHN and THOMAS S. MCPARTLAND, "An Empirical Investigation of Self-Attitudes," *American Sociological Review* 19 (February 1954): 68–76; *Manual for the Twenty-Statements Test* (Kansas City: Greater Kansas City Mental Health Foundation, 600 East 22nd St., 1965), mimeo.; MCPARTLAND and JOHN H. CUMMING, "Self-Conception, Social Class and Mental Health," *Human Organization* 17, no. 3 (1958): 24–29; MCPARTLAND, CUMMING, and WYNONA S. GARRETSON, "Self-Conception and Ward Behavior in Two Psychiatric Hospitals," *Sociometry* 24 (June 1961): 111–124; CARL R. ROGERS, "The Significance of the Self-Regarding Attitudes and Perceptions," in *Feeling and Emotion: The Moosehart Symposium*, ed. Martin L. Reymert (New York: McGraw Hill, 1950) pp. 374–382; WILLIAM R. ROSENGREN, "The Self in the Emotionally Disturbed," *American Journal of Sociology* 66 (March, 1961): 454–462; RAYMOND L. SCHMITT, "Major Role Change and Self Change," *Sociological Quarterly* 7 (Summer 1966): 311–322; KENT SCHWIRIAN, "Variations in Structure of the Kuhn-McPartland Twenty-Statements Test and Related Response Differences," ibid. 5 (Winter 1964): 47–59; SHELDON STRYKER, "Role-Taking Accuracy and Adjustment," *Sociometry* 20 (December 1957): 286–296; STEPHEN SPITZER, "Test Equivalence of Unstructured Self-Evaluation Instruments," *Sociological Quarterly* 10 (1969): 204–281.

6 Time for response ranged fairly closely around eight to ten minutes. (The general norm in similar studies has ranged roughly from six to fifteen minutes.) The responses were coded independently by two trained coders. The intercoder reliability coefficient was .96.

7 See KUHN and MCPARTLAND, "An Empirical Investigation," for relevant data on groups of Catholics (nonpriests), sect members, Jews, and so on for seven other categories. Differences were at $p < .05$ as between priests and other groups. Differences between means were tested for significance with the t test, one-tailed.

8 "Self-Conception and Ward Behavior."

9 Thus, a man giving seven *A* responses, six *B*'s, 3 *C*'s, and 4 *D*'s would be classified as an *A* mode respondent. *See Manual for the Twenty-Statements Test*, 16.

10 MCPARTLAND, CUMMING, and GARRETSON, "Self-Conception and Ward Behavior," 114–116.

[11] MCPARTLAND and CUMMING, "Self-Conception, Social Class, and Mental Health," 24–29.

[12] This feeling, as was intimated previously, reached a high point at the end of interviewing.

[13] MCPARTLAND and CUMMING, "Self-Conception, Social Class, and Mental Health," 26.

[14] Differences in percentages were significant at the level indicated in fn. 7. Percentage comparisons were tested with chi-square. The comparison data summarized are taken from KUHN, "Self-Attitudes," and SCHMITT, "Major Role Change."

[15] GEORGE H. MEAD, "The Process of Mind in Nature," in *George Herbert Mead on Social Psychology*, ed. Anselm Strauss (Chicago: University of Chicago Press, 1964), p. 96.

[16] See, e.g., SEYMOUR M. LIPSET and PHILIP G. ALTBACH, "Student Politics and Higher Education in the United States," in *Student Politics*, ed. Lipset (New York: Basic Books, 1967), p. 213.

[17] We should not be understood to be suggesting that the relevant complaints of priests and students lack all real foundation.

[18] Cf. also DAVIS (one of innumerable others to make the same claim that the church is irrelevant), *A Question of Conscience*, pp. 7, 13.

[19] EMILE DURKHEIM, *Suicide* (Glencoe: Free Press, 1962).

[20] At least a few theoretical resources for the kind of work suggested can be found in present-day conceptions of social structure that order it according to levels of values, norms, collectivities, roles. See TALCOTT PARSONS, "An Outline of the Social System," in *Theories of Society*, ed. Parsons et al. (Glencoe: Free Press, 1961), pp. 30–79; NEIL J. SMELSER, *Theory of Collective Behavior* (New York: Free Press, 1963).

❖❖❖❖❖❖❖❖❖❖❖❖❖❖❖❖❖❖

Beth, Greg, Diane—What Went Wrong?

J. MURRAY ELWOOD

A letter on the desk awaits your return from the Student Union. From Ken and Marge, Beth's parents. It announces what you already knew—her marriage will take place in a local park later on in the month. Maybe there will be a minister there, more likely not. Beth and her betrothed will take "private vows" in the presence of their friends. And so her parents write a sad sort of letter. Not belligerent, or hostile, just sad: "...it makes us want to cry just thinking of it. Ken and I will not be there and Beth knows this. We feel our presence would be an approval of something which we cannot sanction...."

Normally, you can make some sense out of such strange behavior patterns among these young Catholics. Blame it on the home, an absent father, a repressive high school, an inadequate CCD program in the local parish— you can use any of a dozen rationalizations to explain it to yourself. "Well, she never had the faith to begin with." But you know these words and explanations don't fit Beth's case. You're confused.

You hold the letter in your hand and think back three years to Freshmen Open House when Ken and Marge proudly introduced their daughter to you for the first time. They were different, these parents. Both professional people, both graduates of Catholic colleges with an attitude toward their children—and especially toward Beth, the eldest—that was refreshing. None of the suspicion of many parents, no requests to the priest to "take good care of our daughter," no plea: "tell us if she doesn't go to Mass." Just a deep love, a genuine trust and a calm assurance that the university would do well by their daughter.

She was different, this daughter. A Catholic secondary education that could only be rated superior. None of the common hang-ups or hostility. She had received an outstanding education and was proud of it; proud of her school. She was talented and bright and alert. So Beth plunged into the Newman Center's social action program for the homeless, the parish council felt her presence, visitors at Sunday liturgies remarked on the beauty of her voice. All that was three years ago.

Her Mass attendance had become sporadic toward the end of her sophomore year. She came to tell you that she felt it was more relevant to go

---

Monsignor J. Murray Elwood is chaplain of the Newman Center at the State University of New York at Oswego.

during the week. She did, for a time. She dropped in once or twice at the beginning of her junior year, but something had changed. Her manner of dress was now sloppy, more "grubby." She was working as a student resident assistant, had counseled abortion for several students and this bothered her. She was on pot, but not too much, she assured you. Only now and then. The grapevine rumored she was also shooting speed and the subculture she now gravitated toward contained many acid-heads. Early one Sunday morning, on your way to pick up a paper, you saw her in jeans, work shirt, no bra and newly frizzled hair, drifting back to the dorm with her boyfriend. Later on you learned that she was spending almost every weekend with the same boy. Then her mother's letter and news of the wedding. What went wrong?

Then there was Greg. Greg, like Beth, had come to the campus as a freshman, straight from a brothers' high school in the New York area. He was different, too, and you remember him walking into the Center soon after his arrival and asking if there was anything he could do to help. He helped. Discussion groups, art work around the Center—he was always there. In his sophomore year, he pledged a fraternity and you began to miss him at Mass. Then he was in student government, listed in *Who's Who in American Colleges and Universities*. And somewhere about this time, a beautiful note. He didn't feel the same—nothing personal, because you were still friends— but the hypocrisy.... A request, senior year, for material to use in his nondenominational wedding. Upon graduation, his outstanding talents were put to use by the university in an administrative position. Greg's now attending law school and a letter arrived as he left the locale to say thanks for being his friend and offered hope of a future return with the words "maybe some day we can talk about the faith." What went wrong?

Diane's mother had been a classmate of yours at Catholic High. She had also brought her daughter to the Center to be introduced, the first day of college. You had even known Diane's grandmother when, as a boy serving Mass, you had watched her walk up to receive the Eucharist on cold winter mornings at your parish church. Later, as a priest, you assisted this good woman as she lay dying. Because yours was an even closer relationship to Diane and her family, you did not hesitate to ask why, when she began to be numbered among the missing. She was hostile, said she no longer considered herself Catholic, and gave as the reason "the injustices I suffered from the nuns." You remembered that Diane's mother and you, in those days before the renewal, had suffered many real injustices from several "holy tyrants" who had taught you. But your hurts didn't seem that important. You hadn't carried a grudge. Diane did. What went wrong?

Beth, Greg, Diane. There are days when the list seems endless and the spiritual breakups tragic. New faces, new names, but always the same phrases, the same clues, assert themselves in conversation—"My parents are Catholic," "I was raised as a Catholic," "I used to be Catholic."

How does one evaluate present trends? Is today's religious decline among young Catholics all that unusual? After all, there has always been some leakage. It is identified more readily in the campus situation. The college provides the chaplain with religious affiliation cards which name, fairly accurately, about 98 per cent of the incoming Catholic freshmen, even the most nominal. Many of these, like Jennifer Cavilleri in the movie version of *Love Story*, although baptized and brought up Catholic, can honestly say by the time they enter college, "I never really joined the Church." Some never will. Then there is the openness of the campus community, where students have no inhibitions in talking about their spiritual crises. And good lines of communication run from the campus milieu back to the Center. So maybe this drift is not that unusual, only we are more aware of it.

Also, one can always find husks of hope like Eugene Kennedy's "Here Lies Community: Deo Gratias!" (A.M. 8/22/70). He interprets the current phenomenon in terms of the death-resurrection mystery of the Church and feels that what we are witnessing in the present is the necessary death of one cultural expression of the faith and the birth of another. The point is well made. But what of the human factor, the individuals who are caught up in this cultural transition? Is the cultural explanation completely adequate for the case of Beth, who came, not from a traditional culture, but from an educational and familial climate that offered the best of the post-conciliar years? Can it explain the case of Greg, who was sophisticated enough to discriminate between old and new, who had no observable hang-ups, was full of good will, but who sadly judged that he no longer wanted any part of the past?

Another voice of optimism is that of Andrew M. Greeley in *Religion in the Year 2000*. He asserts that organized religion, in the years to come, will not suffer a numerical decline and that church attendance will persist at the levels reported in the sociological surveys of 1952–1965. But if there will be worshipers present for the Eucharistic celebration in the year 2000, as Fr. Greeley believes, who will they be? Will the pews be occupied by Beth, Greg and Diane? By their children and grandchildren? By those of the present age who feel the crisis most acutely? ... The failure to make an accommodation in the past for native customs and the subsequent imposition of alien cultural forms is not without precedent within the Church. Chinese catechumens, to cite one obvious example, as late as this century were presented with a Christianity packaged in the wrappings of bourgeois French Catholicism. Are our own "natives," Beth and her friends of the Woodstock Generation, also expected to adopt a certain middleclass culture, elements of which are questionably Christian, before they, too, can be counted as first-class Catholics?

Beth's private ceremony in the local park is a good example among many. Honestly convinced that the open-air wedding has meaning for her, if she had desired the presence of a priest, how easily would this type of simple ceremony have been arranged? How much "hassle" would have been involved? An incredible amount, it seems, from this observer's experience with young couples from many different Eastern areas and parishes. Liturgical law and sacramental discipline are necessary and, indeed, required. The question is: does our present unwillingness to make some accommodation for the sake of these "natives" reflect a true ecclesial concern or a cultural intransigence? In an age when belief does not come easy for many, are we placing unnecessary and unneeded obstacles in its way? Is the "Chinese rites" controversy that dead a chapter of the past?

Fortunately, the Church has never lacked those "marginal men" who were willing to move out of their own culture to proclaim the Kingdom to another people with a stranger's tongue. One thinks instinctively of Ricci, de Nobili and, in this century, Père Lebbe. Intuitively, these men could distinguish between core content and the cultural context of Christianity. There have been recent, hopeful signs that charism continues. One hears of priests in jeans circulating among street people; nuns opening storefront clinics offering pregnancy tests, venereal disease treatment, help for drug "bummers"; young Jesuits, once again on the road, living out of knapsacks, working at crash pads. These are specialized roles, entailing risk, but absolutely necessary to serve the needs—at this stage of their pilgrimage—of Beth and her friends.

There are days when the natives get a bit too restless, especially for a straight priest born in one culture, but trying to serve the other and be a bridge to both. Like tribal drums, conflicting calls for allegiance sound their incessant beat across campus: Abortion on Demand, Free Our Black Brothers, Gay is Groovy, Disarm the Campus Cops, Down Male Chauvinist Pigs, The Harrisburg Six, Chicago Seven, Attica Eight, Catonsville Nine....

To regain my sense of perspective, I sometimes retire to the peace provided by some nearby Benedictines. When I entered the monastery chapel recently, I was surprised to discover one of my campus freaks. The student sat cross-legged on the sanctuary floor, oblivious to everything else, playing wild psalms on a wooden flute. The impromptu concert lasted over an hour. He had come here ahead of me, apparently to refresh his own spirit from cultural and religious wellsprings that reached back at least ten centuries. In this climate he felt comfortable. Here he was accepted. He could be free. One hopes that as the whole community becomes more completely catholic, other members of campus cultures will also feel that same sense of belonging, be they Greeks, Meeks or even Freaks.

THE END OF AMERICAN CATHOLICISM?

WILLIAM C. MCCREADY   ANDREW M. GREELEY

That there have been dramatic changes in the Catholic Church since 1960 has become a cliché. The Mass is in English, we eat meat on Friday, the exodus of priests and nuns—frequently to marry one another—has reached massive proportions. Most of the clergy and laity reject the traditional birth control teaching. Priests talk back to bishops and parish councils talk back to priests. An organization which seemed to many on the outside to manifest a high level of organizational control now shows signs of coming apart at the seams.

But there has been no effort to monitor the impact of these changes on the Catholic population. Pontificators, be they episcopal or journalistic, know what the laity think without having to ask them. Hence the controversy about what the laity think of the postconciliar Church has been quite unencumbered by empirical evidence. Since the American hierarchy has made the alarming discovery that social research frequently discovers unpleasant things, it is most unlikely that there will be any serious attempt on their part to study the changing attitudes and behavior of the laity. An organization with fifty million members will blunder into the future with only the haziest notions about its present condition.

The present writers are beginning a yearly monitoring program, using data contained in the 1963 NORC parochial school study (*The Education of Catholic Americans*) as a bench mark. Each year the attitudes and behavior of Catholics on certain critical issues will be reported to provide trend information. It is hoped that periodically more comprehensive follow-up reports will be possible.

This first preliminary report will provide very little consolation for those who had hoped that Catholicism was not on the path to becoming virtually indistinguishable from a Protestant denomination. American Catholicism as it was known before 1960 seems to be finished.

Table 3 gives the frequency of church attendance for the Catholic population in 1963 and 1972. Two major points are demonstrated by this table. First of all, weekly Mass attendance has declined considerably. In 1963, 71 percent of the Catholics in the country went to Mass at least once a week,

William C. McCready and Rev. Andrew M. Greeley are with the National Opinion Research Center in Chicago.

TABLE 3

Frequency of Church Attendance Among
the Catholic Population—in Percentages

HOW OFTEN RESPONDENT WENT TO CHURCH:	1963	1972
More than weekly	9%	6%
Weekly	62	49
Several times a month	7	12
Once a month	4	5
Several times a year	7	11
Once a year	4	9
Less than yearly	6	8
	99%	100%
Total Responses:	2,071	410

while in 1972 only 55 percent of the Catholics in the country attended Mass once a week or more. Perhaps more telling is the figure that in 1963 only 21 percent of the Catholics attended Mass "once a month" or less, while in 1972 this percentage increased to 33. Given the fact that there was no change in the Church precept requiring Catholics to go to Mass every week, this change in behavior is truly considerable. This decline in church attendance could be interpreted in several ways. It may be a general decline for all Catholics, or it may be that some Catholics' church-going has declined more than others.

Table 4 shows the frequency of Church attendance for Catholics in 1963 and 1972 according to age groups. Much of the decline in church attendance can be attributed to those in the two youngest age groups. The decline actually has two components. The first one is the fact that the new cohort of Catholics between the age of twenty and twenty-nine in 1972 is attending church much less frequently than did the cohort of the same age group in 1963. There

TABLE 4

Percentage of the Catholic Population Attending
Church Several Times a Month, by Age Groups

AGE GROUPS:	1963	1972
20–29	76%(337)	46%(109)
30–39	78 (619)	66 (81)
40–49	80 (639)	76 (80)
50–59	79 (332)	80 (75)

[Base-number in ( )s]

is a difference of thirty percentage points between these cohorts. A second component is the fact that the cohort that was between the ages of twenty and twenty-nine in 1963, and that is now between the ages of thirty and thirty-nine, declined ten percentage points in frequency of church attendance. Therefore, we can see that the decline in church attendance for American Catholics is largely attributable to those under forty rather than the entire Catholic population.

Table 5 shows the church attendance of Catholics compared to that of the Protestants, divided by age. The main story of this table is that there are only eight percentage points separating the Catholics and the Protestant respondents between the ages twenty and twenty-nine. For all the other age groups, there is at least a twenty percentage point difference. In other words, young Catholics are beginning to look more like young Protestants in terms of their church attendance.

TABLE 5

Frequency of Church Attendance of Catholics and Protestants by Age Groups—in Percentage Attending Several Times a Month or More

AGE GROUPS:	CATHOLIC	PROTESTANT
20–29	46% (109)	38% (223)
30–39	66 (81)	44 (169)
40–49	76 (80)	50 (191)
50–59	80 (75)	50 (166)

Admittedly, church attendance is not the only measure of religious behavior. However, Catholics have traditionally been more frequent churchgoers than Protestants. These data indicate a sudden shift occurring in that pattern. One conclusion to be reached is that the Church is no longer meeting the needs of younger members sufficiently to keep them interested in the ritual activity of weekly Mass. It is not even necessary to postulate that weekly Mass is an important theological or religious phenomenon. What it did represent was an expression of one's self-definition as a Catholic. Whether or not these young people still define themselves as "Catholics" is a question yet to be determined. What is clear is that weekly Mass is less likely to be a part of that definition in the future than it was in the past. The most likely interpretation of these data is that fewer young people who have been raised Catholic are going to continue to define themselves as members of an organized church.

What has been the effect of the last ten years on attitudes towards various moral questions? Table 6 shows the attitudes of Catholics, Protestants and Jews toward the morality of premarital sexual behavior. Catholics and

TABLE 6

Attitudes of the 3 Major American Religious Groups Toward
the Morality of Premarital Sexual Intercourse—
in Percentages

PREMARITAL SEX IS:	CATHOLIC	PROTESTANT	JEW
Always wrong	38%	38%	9%
Almost always wrong	12	13	6
Wrong only sometimes	26	22	32
Not wrong at all	21	24	48
No opinion	3	3	5
	100%	100%	100%
	(410)	(1027)	(54)

Protestants are quite like each other in their attitudes about the morality of premarital intercourse. (This phenomenon has also been noticed in a recent study of American high school students. Students from Catholic schools and from public schools have very similar attitudes about the morality of sexual behavior.) The only interesting differences show up in the last two categories. A few more Catholics think premarital sex is wrong "only sometimes," and a few less are willing to say that it is "not wrong at all." In other respects the two groups are almost identical.

If we break down the Catholic opinion by age groups, do we find significant differences among them? Table 7 gives an affirmative answer to this question. It presents the attitudes of Catholics about the morality of premarital sexual behavior according to different age groups. As age decreases the percentage of Catholics who say premarital sexual relations are "always wrong" steadily dwindles, 58 percent of those over sixty years of age will say that it is "always wrong," while only 14 percent of those under 30 make the same

TABLE 7

Attitudes of Catholics Toward the Morality of Premarital Intercourse
by Age Groups—in Percentages

PREMARITAL SEX IS:	UNDER 30	30–39	40–49	50–59	60 AND OVER
Always wrong	14%	34%	48%	49%	58%
Almost always wrong	9	7	13	22	8
Wrong only sometimes	35	29	25	15	22
Not wrong at all	36	24	13	12	9
No opinion	6	6	1	2	3
	100%	100%	100%	100%	100%
	(111)	(81)	(79)	(75)	(64)

statement. Over one-third of the Catholic population under 30 say that it is "not wrong at all."

Attitudes about sexual morality show a slightly different pattern from church attendance. Catholics and Protestants are quite alike in their attitudes about the morality of sexual behavior. However, young Catholics are much more likely than older Catholics to adopt a permissive stance. Over 70 percent of those under 30 and 50 percent of those between thirty and forty express some qualification or situational perspective on the morality of pre-marital sex. The traditional teaching on sexual behavior has been one of the Church's strong suits. The kingpin in this position has been the prohibition of intercourse to those who are not married. At the present time a majority of young Catholics seem to reject this teaching.

Another important traditional teaching has concerned the morality of abortion. Table 8 shows the percentage of Catholics and Protestants who approve of legal abortions under specific circumstances. This table is further

TABLE 8

Attitudes of Catholics and Protestants Toward Legal Abortions Under Specified Circumstances and How They Have Changed From 1965 to 1972—in Percent "Yes"

CIRCUMSTANCES UNDER WHICH A LEGAL ABORTION MAY BE OBTAINED:	CATHOLIC		% change	PROTESTANT		% change
	1965	1972		1965	1972	
If the woman's health is seriously endangered by the pregnancy	61%	80%	(+19)	73%	83%	(+10)
If the woman became pregnant as the result of a rape	47	70	(+23)	57	74	(+17)
If there is a strong chance of a serious defect in the baby	45	67	(+22)	56	76	(+20)
If the family has a very low income and cannot afford more children	16	36	(+20)	20	45	(+25)
If the woman is not married and does not want to marry the man	14	32	(+18)	15	39	(+24)
If she is married and does not want any more children	13	28	(+15)	13	37	(+24)
	(325)	(410)		(1024)	(1027)	

<table>
<tr><td>Average change for Catholics = 19.5%</td><td>Average change for Protestants = 20.0%</td></tr>
</table>

divided into opinions expressed in 1965 and 1972. Two comments can be made about this table. First, there is a marked similarity between the Catholic and Protestant patterns. The average change is almost the same for both groups. This indicates that Catholics and Protestants have changed their attitudes about abortion during the past seven years and that there is not nearly the religious difference over this question that conventional wisdom has intimated. Secondly, there are some differences in the patterns when we consider the circumstances surrounding the need for an abortion. Catholics have changed more than Protestants when it comes to approving of legal abortions for women whose health is endangered, whose baby will probably be defective, or who have become pregnant by rape. These might be termed "involuntary" abortions since the situation has many elements outside of the woman's control. Protestants have changed more than Catholics when it comes to approving abortions for those who for reasons of poverty or more selforiented reasons do not want a child. These might be termed "voluntary" abortions since they are more or less a matter of the choice of the woman.

It ought to be noted that both Catholics and Protestants have changed much more on the issue of "involuntary" than on "voluntary" abortions. The similarity between the Catholic and Protestant response is even more interesting when one stops to think that the morality of legal abortion was not even widely discussed in Catholic circles until a few years ago. It was simply taken for granted that it was, and always would be, an immoral and unacceptable practice in our society. These data suggest that the Catholic population of the country is no more resistant to change on this question than is the Protestant population. This does not mean that Catholics would have abortions themselves nor that they think it is a "right thing to do." But it may indicate that they are bonafide members of the pluralistic society in which they live, and that they understand the workings of the system.

Table 9 shows the change within the age cohorts of the Catholic population from 1965 to 1972 on the abortion issue. In other words, most of the people who were in the under 30 category in 1965 are in the 30 to 39 category in 1972. What kind of changes did these age cohorts undergo during this time? Although it is clear from these data that the youngest cohort has undergone the largest change, the average change for each of the first three cohorts is very nearly the same: approximately 20 percent. Meanwhile, the oldest cohort, with an average of 4, has changed little.

Table 10 presents data for Catholics and Protestants under 30 in 1972 as compared to those who were under thirty in 1965. Again we see that the attitudes of the young Catholics resemble those of the young Protestants much more today than they have in the past. The average difference in 1965 was 15 percent, while in 1972 it is 7 percent. As is the case with the general Catholic population, Catholics of this age group are slightly more opposed to abortions when the woman wants no more children and when

TABLE 9

Change Within the Age Cohorts of the Catholic Population Toward the Permissibility of Legal Abortions in Specific Circumstances—in Percent Change (All Positive) Since 1965

CIRCUMSTANCES UNDER WHICH A LEGAL ABORTION MAY BE OBTAINED:	AGE IN 1972			
	30–39	40–49	50–59	Over 60
If the woman's health is seriously endangered by the pregnancy	13%	27%	14%	1%
If the woman became pregnant as the result of a rape	24	21	28	12
If there is a strong chance of a serious defect in the baby	28	20	19	1
If the family has a very low income and cannot afford more children	34	16	14	2
If the woman is not married and does not want to marry the man	18	22	17	2
If the woman is married and does not want any more children	21	17	13	5
Average change for each cohort from 1965–1972:	23%	21%	18%	4%

she does not want to marry. In the other situations, Catholic youth are very much like Protestant youth.

This change has added impact, owing to the fact that young people make up more of the Catholic population in 1972 than they did in 1965. In 1965 those under thirty comprised about 21 percent of the total Catholic population, while in 1972 they comprise about 27 percent. A large and increasingly well-educated segment of the Catholic population is not at all well-disposed toward the traditional Catholic stand on the issue of legal abortion.

These data indicate some of the changes currently going on among the Catholic population of the United States. They can be summarized as follows: (1) Young Catholics are not attending Mass with the traditional regularity of their parents. (2) Young Catholics do not accept the traditional moral teachings of the Church regarding sexual behavior as readily as did the generation preceding them. (3) The majority of Catholics would approve of a legal abortion for a woman who had become pregnant by rape, who expected a defective child or whose life was threatened by the birth of the

TABLE 10

Attitudes Toward Legal Abortion in Specified Circumstances of Catholics and Protestants Under the Age of 30 in 1965 and in 1972—in Percent "Yes"

CIRCUMSTANCES UNDER WHICH A LEGAL ABORTION MAY BE OBTAINED	1965			1972		
	PROT-ESTANT	CATH-OLIC	(DIFF.)	PROT-ESTANT	CATH-OLIC	(DIFF.)
If the woman's health is seriously endangered by the pregnancy	81%	66%	(15)	90%	89%	(1)
If the woman became pregnant as the result of a rape	61	42	(19)	76	77	(1)
If there is a strong chance of a serious defect in the baby	66	43	(23)	84	74	(10)
If the family has a very low income and cannot afford more children	21	4	(17)	50	43	(7)
If the woman is not married and does not want to marry the man	16	8	(8)	44	32	(12)
If the woman is married and does not want any more children	16	8	(8)	45	32	(12)
	(1024)	(352)		(1027)	(410)	

Average difference between Protestants and Catholics:

			15.0			7.2

child. While changes in attitudes toward abortion have occurred in Catholics of all ages, save those over sixty, the greatest change has occurred among Catholics under thirty, who are practically indistinguishable from Protestants of the same age.

These are three recent shifts in the opinions of American Catholics. They are shifts that the official Church neither recognizes nor appears to care very much about. Perhaps it is possible for some churchmen to write off the young as either scatterbrained or unsettled or simply not knowing what they want. It is frequently suggested (or hoped) that when the young get older, settle down and start raising a family, they will become good Catholics again. It is a bit more disconcerting to try to incorporate the attitudes of older, more settled Catholics into this framework. Perhaps the most startling statistic is the proportion of those Catholics over sixty who favor legal abortion in one of the first three circumstances. Between one-half and two-thirds of those over sixty years of age are in favor of legal abortion in circumstances where a health danger, rape or defective child is involved. What does all this mean?

One possible interpretation is that Catholics are becoming more like the rest of the population in terms of their opinion on critical and controversial issues. They are less readily identifiable as a separate block whether we look at church attendance, moral issues or attitudes about the legality of controversial practices. These changes are recent, and we will not know for several years whether or not this is a slow, steady shift and assimilation into the American culture, or whether it is a sudden and dramatic change.

Whatever the end result, it can hardly be denied that there is evidence of a coming apart of the traditional, tightly knit organization of the Church. The real problem for the Church in this set of circumstances is whether or not there is anything besides superficial ritual holding the Catholic community together. Given changes on the level of symbolic behavior and ritual attendance, what remains?

The answer, alas, seems to be that nothing remains. The collective hierarchy are too busy protecting their power, assuring their career and locking barn doors after horses have escaped to address themselves to the deep religious longings which virtually every observer of young America knows are out there. Electing the present leadership of the hierarchy at a time when the immigrant Church is falling apart was an exercise in indifference to social and cultural reality comparable with Nero's famed violin concert.

Many of the clergy and the religious are so mired in their own delayed postadolescent identity crises that they are quite incapable of addressing themselves to the questions of faith and community that middleclass Americans are asking. At the very time when questions of meaning are more important to Americans than ever before, many priests and nuns have abandoned their role as preachers of a meaning-system (called "the gospel"), and are seeking "relevance" (by which they mean personal validation) in radical political activity, which may (or may not) be a consequence of faith, but is certainly no substitute for it—or in pop psychology that replaces the Word of God with badly understood therapeutic jargon. Our "intellectuals" (most of whom are, in reality, journalists and not scholars) are so used to shouting stridently about the Church that they have not bothered to notice that that Church, which was such a convenient inkblot, does not exist anymore. Many of them keep on shouting because they themselves have nothing to believe in, and they see no reason why anyone else should. It is the supposed role of the religious intellectual not to reinterpret symbols, but to destroy them. One must destroy the Church structure, the influence of the clergy, the faith of the laity and the values—all the values—of the past. When there is nothing left, then maybe something good will start—though the typical self-proclaimed Catholic intellectual has no idea what. . . .

Immigrant Catholicism had its weaknesses, heavens knows; but then so do all human religious enterprises. It at least provided a series of answers to fundamental religious questions which enabled millions of men and women to give meaning to their existence during an extraordinarily difficult period of adjusting to a new culture. The immigrant Church also generated an organizational loyalty that, for all its narrowness, produced much enthusiastic creativity. If our data are any indication of what more extensive research will discover (and there isn't much reason to think that there are any indicators which will reverse the findings we have presented in this paper), the loyalty is gone, the creativity is gone and the meaning system is gone or at least going. The remarkable thing is that no outside foe destroyed us; we destroyed ourselves.

Yet the deep and powerful questions of the era remain. Surely, for example, there is more to be said in response to the agonizing need for symbols to interpret the meaning of human sexuality. Is there nothing in the Yahwist symbol system which will illumine the dilemma of the agonizing human quest for fidelity and intimacy?

The present writers believe there is but must report that as far as we are aware no one is working on this or similar questions. To paraphrase a remark of our good friend, the distinguished Mariologist Gregory Baum, if the Blessed Mother expects us American Catholics to survive this mess, she had better send us leaders and prophets—damn soon.

(The present writers do not believe that one can determine the goodness of moral values with public opinion polls. All survey research does is to provide some idea of what, in fact, are the values of substantial segments of the population. We have no intention of asserting that it is a good thing that one-fifth of the Catholic population over 30 has changed its mind on abortion in the last eight years. Much less are we asserting that abortion is a good thing because the majority think it is licit. We are merely asserting the fact of the change and suggesting that the fact of change is one more sign of the crisis in the culture and structure of American Catholicism.)

✜✜✜✜✜✜✜✜✜✜✜✜✜✜✜✜✜✜

The Experience of Being a Roman Catholic in a Time of Change

SISTER ELAINE M. PREVALLET

In this attempt to reflect upon "the experience of being a Roman Catholic in a time of change," I shall try to do two things: First, I shall try to stay in touch with my own experience; and, second, I shall try to relate broader theological issues to that experience. At the outset, I should probably say that my experience is not exactly typical—if indeed there be any such thing as typical. It is conditioned by my profession as a teacher of theology in a college which has very rapidly changed from a rather conservative Catholic college for women to an independent coed institution with a religiously heterogeneous student population—with the revision and revamping of my own teaching approach and a refocusing of questions demanded by the changed context here. My profession, in any case, demands that I stay in touch with students' questions and perceptions, and hence effectively ensures that my own thinking be consistently challenged and changing. Secondly, my experience is conditioned by the fact that I am a sister, and some groups of sisters have been among the most aggressive and progressive in making the changes we felt were necessary to bring our Christian dedication into the twentieth century. This has been especially challenging for me, because it necessitated a rather thorough rethinking of the tradition of spirituality in which I was reared, a consistent attempt to separate the peripheral and nonessential from the core of my commitment, the accidental trappings from the substance. What went on for me in that context is perhaps a miniature of what is and has been going on in the whole Church—an attempt to distinguish the essential from the peripheral. Yet my experience may be different from that of many other Roman Catholics in that my thinking and rethinking was done within and for a community of intelligent and dedicated persons, whose challenge hopefully kept and keeps me from too timid settlements with any given status quo.

My position, then, is only more or less similar to that of other persons within the Roman Catholic community. But precisely here we can note a significant change in the picture—and in the experience—of Roman Catholicism: a shift from a very stable, well-ordered group who all knew and

Originally presented at a regional meeting of the American Academy of Religion, Denver, Colorado, April 1972. Published with the author's permission.

Sister Elaine M. Prevallet is a member of the Theology Department of Loretto Heights College in Denver.

professed the same faith in the same words—the Catholic monolith—to groups of persons who have found or are finding communities of support and coming to find their own faith and take their own stand. We have, all of us, I imagine, felt ourselves shaken, our security threatened, our faith called into question. As one might expect, there are different ways of reacting: Some will become impatient with the slowness of change, decide the Church is antiquated and hopeless, and drop out. Some will sever affiliation but for the opposite reason: The Church has changed so fast and so radically as to be unrecognizable as the Church one knew and loved, so radically changed that one feels no identification with it, is disillusioned and disappointed by it—and so drop out. It could, no doubt, be called an identity crisis: It is no longer so easy to know what it means to be a Roman Catholic, no longer so easy to say what a Roman Catholic believes or holds on various issues.[1] One is thrown much more upon one's own resources, and one is turned much more toward one's brother in faith. From that standpoint, an identity crisis can be a valuable prelude to a new level of self-consciousness, commitment and community. Or perhaps it is a question, as Dan Berrigan has expressed it, of a kind of "geography of faith."[2] Roman Catholic experience now includes a variety of poles and positions, and one has to search to find one's own home ground.

Perhaps one can speak with some accuracy of a relativistic perspective as having had great impact upon Catholic consciousness.[3] Contemporary historical consciousness is one factor in the kind of de-absolutizing we have undergone; the experience of plurality is another. Ecumenical awareness is surely part of this perspective: We have had, in the last decade, to admit that the Spirit of God is not bound by the structure of the Roman Catholic or even the Christian churches; we have had to admit that Protestants—and even Jews, Buddhists, and Moslems— may turn up in heaven and that not in spite of but because of their religious beliefs and practice. Experientially, this has meant a modification of many absolutist attitudes among Roman Catholics: from thinking we knew it all, no doubt with some arrogance, to greater humility before the truth; from believing that everyone had to believe it and say it our way to an attitude of openness to one's Christian or non-Christian neighbor as a possible source of insight into truth; from thinking that once we had mastered the Baltimore catechism we "knew our faith" to what Gordon Allport calls a "heuristic approach" to faith,[4] allowing for growth, change, provisionalness, doubt, discovery.

Equally, in the area of morality, focused in the birth control controversy but helped along by changes such as that in the law of Friday abstinence and the possibility of fulfilling one's obligation by going to Mass on Saturday instead of Sunday, there is less trust of ecclesiastical laws as absolutes. It may sound preposterous to equate the issues of birth control or abortion with the issues of whether or not one eats meat on Friday and goes to church on Sunday, but in point of fact, deviations from the Church's stance on all those were taught to us as mortal sins, equally absolute in deserving damnation. It was, of course, a naive and unnuanced moral sensitivity; yet the change has spawned distrust and even cynicism: If a thing could be a mortal sin deserving of hell one day and nothing at all the next, simply by ecclesiastical fiat, then how trusting can we be of any ecclesiastical laws or moral pronouncements at all? And again, there are varieties of responses: those who learn to think through their moral positions and arrive at a more carefully nuanced and personally appropriated moral sense and those who retire into positions of negativism. Experientially, the former has meant bearing the responsibility for much more serious thought and information gathering, making many more decisions, and, of course, living with many more unanswered questions.

Another powerful influence within Roman Catholicism is the movement to find the meaning of the Church and the focus of the gospel in terms of social justice. Roman Catholicism has, even in this country, precedent in radicalism set by persons such as Dorothy Day who spans the last decades as witness to radical concern for the poor and the pacifist movement. The Berrigans can be said to stand in that same tradition. The movement toward a social-gospel interpretation of Christianity, the challenge to radicalism, is now a powerful force—from Vatican II and its document on the Church in the modern world down to the Harrisburg Seven. Many Catholics, of course, are not even conscious of the Berrigans; many regard them as mixed up, as priests gone astray, are embarrassed that they are Catholics, let alone priests. But for others, and among them a growing number of priests, they seem to have effected a kind of consciousness raising, a courageous and challenging summons to be "on the margin," to stand off from the status quo, to criticize one's involvement or implication in the structured evils in our society. I think I am not naive when I say that there is a growing social conscience in the Roman Catholic community which presents yet another challenge to established systems, habits, works, thought patterns. For those who hear the challenge, it often complicates their relationship to the Roman Catholic establishment.[5]

And finally, the most evident, perhaps: the change in Roman Catholic attitudes toward authority. That is, of course, part of the larger picture of a changing world and society. It has been noted that in a stable society, a rigid hierarchical system is adequate, because its task is simply to provide instructions on how to behave in a framework in which the major outlines of conduct are already agreed upon by all. But in a society of rapid social change, it seems clear a hierarchy will have to assume a different style and role.[6] Recently there has appeared a declaration signed by thirty-four Roman Catholic theologians from different countries, all of them well-known and reputable theologians (their spokesman said they aimed at quality instead of quantity in this case) which spoke of the Church as suffering from a crisis of leadership and confidence.[7] Church authorities, it says, "seem to know only how to warn and lament or to take arbitrary reprisals." The crisis, it suggests, "is largely due to the ecclesiastical system which in its development has remained behind the times and still exemplifies monarchial absolutism: Pope and bishops remain for all practical purposes the exclusive rulers in the church, combining the legislative, executive and judicial powers in one hand." Clearly, the style of leadership which has characterized the Roman Catholic Church seems out of joint in a society which is undergoing such rapid social change as we are, and in which participation and intelligent assent must be the keynote of advance. Yet there is an obvious dilemma, for there are those in the Church who hope for an answer-giving kind of leader.[8] These are disappointed, for if Rome or the bishops give some answers, they do not give nearly enough to allay these peoples' fears. For others, they give too many and in areas where their silence would be better appreciated. In short, they can't win. Perhaps it is enough to say here that people do not know what to believe about authority, whether or when to believe if authority does speak. Credibility, the declaration of the theologians suggests, has dropped to a disquieting degree.

But perhaps we can look at their statement as instance of the vigor and health which persist in Roman Catholicism. They call first of all for a return to the gospel of Jesus Christ and give some practical guidelines to help overcome what they identify as a situation of stagnation and resignation: Do not remain silent; do something yourself; act together; seek provisional solutions; and, finally, don't give up.

It is good to hear these voices speaking of courage and hope. The task—reform both of society and of the Church—seems so massive as to be paralyzing. And so, if one has to speak of the experience of being a Roman Catholic in a time of change, one necessarily speaks of confusion and uncertainty, unsettledness and doubt, disillusion and frustration. But one can also speak of personal conviction and commitment, challenge and inner growth, courage and hope. All of these are our individual and collective experience. Our theologians say, "Why should we continue to hope? ... There is hope because we believe that the power of the Gospel of Jesus Christ shows itself time and again as more powerful than all our human failures and foolishness in the church, stronger than all our discouragement." That is where we are. It is a time when this story, relayed by Thomas Merton from his contact with the Buddhists, has a lot of meaning for us:

> This friend of Merton's had to leave Tibet or be killed when the Chinese Communists took over all the Tibetan monasteries. The Lama was isolated in the mountains, living in a peasant's house and wondering what to do next. He sent a message to a nearby abbot friend of his saying, "What do we do?" The abbot sent back a strange message: "From now on, brother, everybody stands on his own feet."
>
> Merton comments on this message, "We can no longer rely on being supported by structures which may be destroyed at any moment by a political power or political force. You cannot rely on structures. The time for relying on structures has disappeared. They are good, and they should help us, and

we should do the best we can with them. But they may be taken away, and if everything is taken away, what do you do next?

"From now on, brother, everybody stands on his own feet."[9]

NOTES

[1] For instance, in "On So-Called 'Partial Identification' with the Church," HEINZ SCHLETTE strongly challenges the model of "total identification" with the Church which used to characterize Roman Catholic thought and ideal. In *Perspectives of a Political Ecclesiology* (*Concilium* Series, vol. 66), ed. Johannes Metz (New York: Herder and Herder, 1971), pp. 35–49.

[2] DANIEL BERRIGAN and ROBERT COLES, *The Geography of Faith* (Boston: Beacon, 1971).

[3] JAMES KELLY, "The New Roman Church: A Modest Proposal," *Commonweal*, December 3, 1971, pp. 222–226.

[4] GORDON ALLPORT, *The Individual and His Religion* (New York: Macmillan, 1950), p. 81.

[5] DANIEL BERRIGAN discusses his relation to the Catholic radical tradition, as well as his relation to the Roman Catholic establishment in *The Geography of Faith*, op. cit., pp. 124–132.

[6] D. HAY, "The Natural Selection of Hierarchies," *New Blackfriars* 51 (March, 1970): 140.

[7] Reprinted in *The National Catholic Reporter*, March 31, 1972, pp. 8, 17.

[8] Terminology used by ANDREW M. GREELEY, "Sociology and Church Structure," in *Structures of the Church* (*Concilium* Series, vol. 58), ed. T. Urresti (New York: Herder and Herder, 1970), pp. 27–28.

[9] JAMES V. DOUGLASS, *Resistance and Contemplation* (Garden City, N.Y.: Doubleday, 1972), p. 55.

CHAPTER 6

⁕⁖⁖⁖⁖⁖⁖⁖⁖⁖⁖⁖⁖ ⁖⁖⁖⁖⁖⁖⁖⁖⁖⁖

American Judaism

Jewish immigrants, at first almost entirely from Germany and later from Poland and Russia, were prominent among the millions of European settlers who came to these shores between the close of the Civil War and the beginning of World War I—the period known as the "great migration" to the United States. Numbering only 15,000 in 1840—a mixture of Spanish, Portuguese, Dutch, and German, many of whom were among the nation's earliest immigrants—Jews grew to a population of over 2 million by 1914.

By religious background, many immigrant families were by no means Orthodox. Jews, influenced by the ideals of the Enlightenment, had undergone considerable emancipation from traditional Jewish observances. German rabbis in this country responded by developing Reform Judaism, which emphasized a liberal humanism and employed ritual practices reminiscent of American Protestantism. By the end of the nineteenth century, however, a reaction developed among Jews who, dissatisfied with this pattern, wished to return to a measure of Jewish tradition but not, however, to strict Orthodoxy. Thus was born Conservative Judaism. Fidelity to Jewish law, literature, and language was a keynote yet it had a flexibility deemed appropriate to Jews adjusting to a new cultural setting. In the words of Marshall Sklare:

> The essence of the Conservative position, then, is liberalization. While Conservatism believes that liberalism is its own justification, it also holds that liberalization makes possible the promotion of observance.... In addition to

liberalization, the Conservative platform has two additional planks. One is "innovation," the development of new observances or procedures which are required when there is a need to substitute for, modify, or extend the traditional *mitzvoth* [the commandments of the Jewish sacred system]. The other is "beautification," the requirement that the *mitzvoth* be practiced in an esthetic a manner as possible—"the Jewish home beautiful." In sum, the Conservative position is that liberalization—in combination with innovation and beautification—will succeed in averting the evil decree of non-observance.[1]

The eastern European Jews who formed the second wave of Jewish immigrants at the beginning of this century, however, were a curious mixture of the devoutly Orthodox on the one hand and the proponents of radical social change (such as socialists and anarchists) on the other. Conservative Jews, therefore, have played a kind of "moderate" role between the Orthodox Jews and Jews of a more secular, even radical, outlook.

Like other immigrant groups, Jewish Americans witnessed a considerable departure from Jewish tradition among their second- and third-generation members. This did not entail necessarily a loss of Jewish identity

> ...for even if you ceased to think of yourself as Jewish, the larger society was still prepared to define you as a Jew unless you became formally a member of a gentile denomination, something which few Jews were willing to do. Secondly, the disaster of the Second World War to European Judaism produced a reaction in most American Jews that precluded any denial of their Jewishness.[2]

Post-World War II Judaism, then, saw perhaps a majority of American Jews experiencing a heightening sense of identity *as a people*—an identity further strengthened by the emergence of the State of Israel and particularly its striking victory over the Arabs in the 1967 Six-Day War. Religious practice in terms of frequent synagogue attendance and regular observance of dietary customs, however, has not been a characteristic of the average American Jew.

This does not indicate a diminished importance of the synagogue or temple. The first reading, by prominent Jewish sociologist Marshall Sklare, analyzes several functions of the contemporary synagogue. First, synagogue affiliation varies inversely with the size of the Jewish population. In communities where Jews number less than 25,000 or so, affiliation tends to be well over 50 percent and ranges as high as 80 percent. In large metropolitan areas with sizable Jewish populations, affiliation is considerably diminished. Sklare attributes this pattern to differential pressures toward assimilation. In small communities each person or family is usually asked to join: "...he is forced into casting his ballot. A refusal to join means placing himself in the assimilationist camp." Such solicitation and a consequent reduction of pressure to make a decision for "survival" are much less likely in large Jewish communities. Thus in large communities, such as New

York, synagogue membership is considered unnecessary for identity as a Jew. Sklare also points to the educative function of the synagogue as a religious center. Even less-committed Jews are induced to affiliate because of the desire to enroll their children in religious education classes as well as to attend services themselves on the High Holidays. Additional ties are effected by congregational sponsorship of clubs for high school students, young adults, and young married couples. Whether or not the synagogue stimulates more than social affiliation, whether it serves to deepen Jewish religious faith in the consciousness of its membership, is a debatable issue discussed by Sklare. He feels that the congregational structure of American Judaism guarantees the freedom of dissatisfied Jewish groups to establish synagogues embodying the orientations they desire.

The second reading, "Motivations for Attending High Holy Day Services," by Arnold Lasker, shows a variety of goals stated as reasons for attendance. Conservative and Reform Jews sampled tended strongly to emphasize identification with Jewish people and Jewish tradition as primary reasons for attendance, although regular attenders leaned much more toward thanking God and expressing a relationship to the Divine. Orthodox members ranked "relationship with God" and "influencing God" as highest categories.

Selections P and Q, "The Essence of My Commitment" by Danny Siegel and "The Crisis in American Jewry" by Nathan Glazer, provide interesting contrasts. Siegel insists that the desires for political and social security have blunted the Jewish tradition of prophetic challenge to contemporary evils. A painful dilemma arises, but Siegel urges Jews to "identify ourselves with the true struggles for freedom around the world." Glazer is more cautious: In his thoughtful essay he sees two tendencies in American Judaism as it moves away from traditional moorings. First, Jews have incorporated "those aspects of Jewish life that were in fact ethnic, national, folk, into the structure of religion, rather than maintain them in their own right"— unlike some other ethnic minorities. Second, Jews have strongly advocated liberal political and social ideals, particularly in areas such as equality of opportunity and reduction of discrimination. Yet in the black power movement's repudiation of white liberals and in the positive identification of some militant blacks with Arab (particularly Algerian) struggles for independence, Jews find themselves suddenly in opposition to the minority group whose rights it has long championed. Is, then, radicalism the course to follow? Glazer thinks not and here perhaps differs from Siegel and the generation he represents. Revitalized liberalism and ethnic attachment, Glazer feels, are still capable of generating altruistic social ideals. The problem is how to communicate these renewed traditions to the young; that is, how can they be shown convincingly that these traditions "do indeed provide the best patterns to organize our lives on earth"?

NOTES

[1] MARSHALL SKLARE, *Conservative Judaism: An American Religious Movement* (New York: Schocken, 1972), p. 269. Reprinted by permission of Schocken Books, Inc., from Marshall Sklare, *Conservative Judaism*. Copyright © 1955, 1972 by Marshall Sklare.

[2] ANDREW M. GREELEY, *op. cit.*, pp. 198–199.

THE AMERICAN SYNAGOGUE

MARSHALL SKLARE

From the attendance statistics of New York City, Boston, and numerous other communities we might expect that the American synagogue is a struggling institution that is banished to the periphery of Jewish life and located predominantly in neighborhoods where the foreign-born reside. Nothing could be further from the truth. The American synagogue is a vital institution; it is by far the strongest agency in the entire Jewish community. Many hundreds of new synagogues—Reform, Conservative, and Orthodox—were built as a consequence of population movement after World War II. The process continues. As new Jewish neighborhoods and suburbs develop, new synagogues are established or old synagogues are transferred to new locations. Not only have synagogues been built in areas where Jewish life is intensive but sooner or later they are organized even in places that attract the more marginal Jewish families.[1] The number of synagogues, the value of their buildings, and their location in all areas where the Jewish population totals more than a handful of families all attest to the predominance of this institution in American Jewish life.[2]

We already know that only a minority of American Jews can bring themselves to patronize the synagogue with any degree of regularity in connection with its function as a house of prayer. Yet the continuing construction of new buildings, as well as the prosperity of established institutions suggests that the American synagogue must be more than a house of prayer. To help us discover its real nature, we must first know what proportion of America's Jews are affiliated with a synagogue.

There are no reliable nationwide statistics on affiliation. The most notable aspect of synagogue affiliation is that it varies greatly with the size of the Jewish population. In small communities affiliation commonly reaches well over 80 percent, despite the high intermarriage rates characteristic of such communities. In Flint, Michigan, for example, where the Jewish population is under 3,000, a total of 87 percent of the Jews in the community are affiliated with a synagogue.[3] In communities of intermediate size (10,000 to 25,000 Jewish population), the level of affiliation is lower—commonly over 70 percent

From Marshall Sklare, *America's Jews.* Copyright © 1971 by Marshall Sklare. Reprinted with the permission of Random House, Inc.

Marshall Sklare is on the faculty of American Jewish Studies, Department of Near Eastern and Judaic Studies, Brandeis University.

are synagogue members. Thus in Providence the figure is 77 percent, in Springfield it is 76 percent, in Rochester, N.Y., 71 percent, and in Camden it reaches the exceptionally high figure of 82 percent.[4] In large Jewish communities the rate of affiliation is much lower, commonly running at about 50 percent of the Jewish population. Thus in Detroit 49 percent are affiliated while in Boston the figure is 53 percent.[5] New York is *sui generis*—while no study is available observation suggests that the affiliation rate is measurably lower than it is in any other large city.

Unlike the observance of many *mitzvot*, which as we have seen tend to be concentrated in one segment of the population, synagogue membership is widely diffused. Irrespective of community size, membership is common in all segments of the population, with the following exceptions: it is somewhat more concentrated among the prosperous as well as among those with children between the ages of five and fifteen. Significantly, the rate of affiliation among the foreign-born is no higher than among the native-born. Even in the large cities where the rate of affiliation is so low, most nonmembers have belonged to a synagogue at one time or another. Former members include, for example, the widow who resigned after her husband's death and who now lives in reduced circumstances, or the prosperous family that dropped out after their children had a Bar Mitzvah or Confirmation. Furthermore, some of those who have never been affiliated will do so in the future. This is the case with many young marrieds who will join when they move from city apartments to suburban homes, or when they have children old enough to enroll in a Sunday or Hebrew School.

Whatever criticisms former members may have, and whatever the situation of those who have never affiliated, it is hard to find a principled opponent of the American synagogue.[6] Those who are outside of the synagogue are not firm opponents of the institution. Absence from the membership rolls does not generally represent a clear commitment to any rival institution. It does mean of course that the individual has been strongly influenced by the secularization process. But any critical observer would be quick to point out that most synagogue members have been vitally affected by the same process.

The lack of principled objection to the synagogue and the affiliation of diverse segments of the population must be added to our previous findings about wide differences in affiliation rate between smaller and larger communities. There is little to suggest that Jews in smaller communities are more sacred in their orientation than their metropolitan cousins. In fact a case can be made for precisely the opposite conclusion: that they are more secular in orientation, and much less traditional in their thinking. Why then do those who reside in smaller communities affiliate with greater frequency?

The smaller the community the clearer is the threat of assimilation and the clearer it is that the future of Jewish life rests upon the personal decision of each individual Jew. The decision to affiliate with a synagogue, then, means to vote yes to Jewish survival. And the smaller the community the more literal the voting metaphor: since every individual in the small community is asked to join, he is forced into casting his ballot. A refusal to join means placing himself in the assimilationist camp unless of course he has provided clearcut evidence to the contrary by becoming intensely involved with some alternative Jewish agency. The larger the community the less chance of solicitation by significant others, the less pressure to make a decision for survival, and above all, the more remote the threat of assimilation.

Clearly in the largest communities, especially in New York, synagogue membership does not have high symbolic significance. Since many people lack the feeling that Jewish identity requires synagogue membership, non-affiliation does not mean a vote for assimilation. Conversely, one's resignation from a synagogue is not interpreted as meaning disloyalty to the group. In the metropolis, then, the synagogue must appeal on the basis of its instrumental as well as symbolic functions. However, a substantial proportion of the population finds the synagogue unessential to its needs. These people have little interest in the classical functions of the synagogue—religious services and study by adult males of Jewish texts. Nonclassical functions that the synagogue has added also do not attract them. Their children may be too young or too old for Hebrew School or Sunday School. Furthermore they are not interested in the social activities provided by the synagogue, for they already are a part of a satisfying clique. Generally their group is entirely Jewish and dates back to friendships that were cemented in adolescence or early adulthood. Others are not attracted to the synagogue's social activities because they have a rich social life within their family circle. Finally in the largest communities a host of organizations and causes of a specifically Jewish nature are available outside of the orbit of the synagogue.

Whether situated in a large or small community the synagogue is focused upon Jewish survival. It need not have been so—conceivably the synagogue in America could have followed a different course and insisted that as a religious institution it was an end in itself rather than a means for Jewish survival. Such a stance would exclude those who were strongly secular in orientation, or at least require that they accept a subordinate position. But there is religious justification for the synagogue moving in the direction it has: in Judaism the preservation of the Jewish people as a group is an act of religious significance.

The American synagogue has accepted the secular Jew on his own terms; the institution has been more concerned with transforming him than with erecting barriers to his admission. In most congregations membership is open to all; no test of the applicant's religious attitudes or observance of *mitzvot* is required. While in many Reform or Conservative congregations an applicant for membership is generally sponsored by a member of the synagogue or by one of its officials, this is only for the purpose of screening those who have an objectionable moral reputation. The exceptions to the rule are certain Orthodox congregations that are interested in an applicant's observance of *mitzvot*. Such institutions prefer to restrict their roster to those whose behavior is in conformity with certain selected religious norms.

Since the typical American Jewish congregation is formed by local initiative rather than by the authority of a central body, every synagogue is free to determine its own program and ritual.[7] Furthermore, because the polity— the form of religious organization—among American Jews is congregational rather than episcopal, each synagogue is the equal of all others. Residents join together to hold religious services and to establish a school for their children. They raise the funds necessary to build an edifice and to hire a professional staff. The synagogue is organized in the form of a corporate body that holds periodic membership meetings at which the affairs of the institution are discussed and officers and board members elected. The board is responsible for determining the policies of the institution, although on strictly religious questions, as well as in certain other areas, the advice and consent of the rabbi is commonly solicited.

The prototype of the contemporary American synagogue is the "synagogue center." This is the synagogue that compromises with the culture while serving the need for Jewish identification. Recognizing the impact of acculturation this type of synagogue expands its program far beyond the traditional activities of prayer and study. It seeks encounter with the Jew on his own secular level and it strives to reculturate him. The content and procedures of religious services are adapted to give them greater appeal, with Reform synagogues, Conservative synagogues, and Orthodox synagogues each handling the problem of cultural adaptation in characteristic fashion. Although traditionally there is no sermon during the weekly Sabbath service, part of the process of adaptation involves the introduction of this feature. Thus the sermon has become a standard feature of the weekly service in Reform, Conservative, as well as in some Orthodox congregations. The sermon is employed as an instructional as well as a hortatory device.

All synagogues sponsor some kind of program of adult Jewish study, although its character, and the importance attached to it, varies greatly from congregation to congregation. With the exception of some Orthodox synagogues women are free to participate in the program. In many places the traditional textual approach to study has been modified or supplemented. New kinds of courses have been introduced. But Jewish learning for children rather than for adults constitutes the real focus of the congregation's educational efforts. With the exception of certain Orthodox synagogues all congregations sponsor a Jewish school. While the majority of those who attend are of elementary school age, most schools aim to retain their youngsters after the high point of the educational experience: Bar Mitzvah, Bat Mitzvah, or Confirmation.

For the less-committed the opportunity for Jewish education is a strong inducement to affiliate. In most newer neighborhoods of the city, and in the suburbs, the only available Jewish religious schools are those conducted

under congregational auspices. Some congregations make membership manda-
tory for enrollment, while others adjust their tuition fees to provide a financial
incentive for membership.

Another important motivation for affiliation is the desire of secular-minded
Jews to attend religious services on the High Holidays. While daily services,
Sabbath services, and festival services are open to all, the demand for seats on
the High Holidays is so large that admission is commonly restricted to ticket
holders. In some congregations tickets are distributed only to members while
in other synagogues they are sold to the public, but at a higher price than
that made to members. Since most High Holiday services today are conducted
under the auspices of a synagogue, the institution is in a position to attract
individuals who might not ordinarily be interested in an affiliation. The
phenomenon of "mushroom synagogues"—opened during the High Holidays
by private entrepreneurs—is on the wane and the phenomenon is rarely
encountered in more prestigious neighborhoods. It has been replaced by the
practice of established congregations that hold overflow services for the High
Holidays, or of Reform congregations that conduct services on a double shift.

Most congregations sponsor a variety of clubs for high school youth, young
adults, young marrieds, adult women, adult men, and the elderly. These
organizations provide the synagogue member with another tie to the congregation. They are particularly crucial for individuals who are not strongly
involved in the classical functions of prayer and study. Generally the organization composed of adult women (the "sisterhood") is the most vital of these
clubs. Membership in the clubs is so widespread that in the intermediate size
Jewish community they enroll far more members than any other Jewish
organization. In Providence, for example, 53.2 percent of all men age fifty
to fifty-nine are members of a synagogue-affiliated club, as are 55 percent of
the women.[8] Recreational and associational opportunities are not limited to
the synagogue affiliates, however. There are congregational socials and
parties, dinner dances, specialized activity groups, and fund-raising drives.
All strive to increase the interaction among members. In the New York area
in particular many synagogues provide a variety of athletic facilities.[9]

The contemporary synagogue is a large institution by traditional standards.
While older Jewish neighborhoods in the largest cities may contain a dozen
or more small congregations in addition to two or three large ones, an
average synagogue in a newer neighborhood of a metropolis or suburb will
generally enroll over 500 families. Congregations of this size have many
members who confine their participation to specialized activities, or who
participate very irregularly. Given the large size of most congregations and
the specialized, irregular, or even nonparticipation of members, the printed
word becomes a vital part of congregational life. Thus most congregations
publish a bulletin at regular intervals. The bulletin contains the time of services
and the topic of the weekly sermon, the schedules of the clubs, information
about adult education lectures and courses, and news of the school. Of equal
if not greater significance are the personals columns of the bulletin. Births

and deaths are announced, donors are listed, names of active workers are publicized, and significant milestones in lives of members and their families are featured, including birthdays, wedding anniversaries, graduations, and promotions.

While synagogues of the more traditional variety contrast sharply with the synagogue-center type of institution, it is the synagogue characteristic of modern Israel which places the contemporary American synagogue in boldest relief. The core of the program of the Israeli synagogue is the traditional activities of prayer and study. Worship activities are centered on the three daily services and the Sabbath service. Some men remain after the daily services, or come early, for the purpose of studying various sacred texts. They do this either by themselves, in pairs, or in groups. Most synagogues are small. Each has its official, its leaders, and its congregants. However, individuals think of themselves as praying at a particular synagogue rather than being affiliated with it in any formal sense. Most synagogues do not have a professional staff—rabbis are employed by a central authority rather than by a particular congregation. While attendance and participation at services and in the study circles ebbs and flows, and although at certain holidays worshippers appear who are absent at other occasions, the interaction of the group of men who pray and study together constitutes the foundation of the institution.

Unlike the United States, then, the synagogue in Israel offers little other than the classical functions of prayer and study of the sacred system by adult males. Unlike the United States, its existence and prosperity is not interpreted as a promise of Jewish survival at a time when the acculturation process is so advanced as to make survival difficult to assure. And unlike the United States, the Israeli synagogue is not perceived as an emblem of Jewish identity or as the guarantor of the Jewish future. Rather, the nationhood of Israel is viewed as assuring Jewish survival. In essence, then, the synagogue in Israel has little symbolic significance; it exists as an end in itself rather than as a means to an end. Because it does not occupy the unique role that it does in the United States, the Israeli synagogue is a much weaker institution. It reaches a much smaller proportion of the population than its American counterpart.

Even if the American synagogue is generally a means to an end rather than an ultimate value, it is still a religious institution. As such it is subject to evaluation by a unique yardstick—the yardstick of spirituality. Critics of the synagogue, while conceding that it makes a valuable contribution to Jewish life, are prepared to argue that it is nonetheless more of a liability than an asset. Some maintain that the American synagogue protects the individual from the demands of the Jewish religion as much as it exposes him to them. In a scathing indictment of the American synagogue Rabbi Eugene Borowitz, a leading Reform thinker, has commented:

... the average synagogue member ... comes ... to join the synagogue because there are few if any socially acceptable alternatives to synagogue affiliation for one who wants to maintain his Jewish identity and wants his children to be Jewish, in some sense, after him. Though this is not the only motive or level of concern to be found within the synagogue today, the Jew who does not rise above such folk-feeling unquestionably and increasingly represents the synagogue's majority mood. More than that, however, it must be said that he also represents the synagogue's greatest threat.... His newfound affluence and his need for status within the community have made the big building with the small sanctuary, the lavish wedding with the short ceremony, and the fabulous Bar Mitzvah celebration with the minimal religious significance well-established patterns among American Jewish folkways.... What does it say of Jewish life in America when Reform Judaism appeals because it demands so little but confers so much status? when people blandly proclaim that they are nonobservant Orthodox Jews; when Conservative Judaism makes a virtue of not defining the center so that it may avoid alienating those disaffected on either side.[10]

Borowitz believes that the synagogue should become a more sectarian institution, that it should be transformed to become an end rather than a means, and that it should relinquish its function of providing identity for the secular-minded, ethnically oriented Jew. Proponents concede that this policy will mean that many who presently belong will feel compelled to sever their affiliation (or, if not, have it severed for them), but their eventual assimilation is viewed as the price which must be paid for the survival of Judaism. Proponents hope that the loss of the masses will be compensated, at least in part, by the affiliation of those who—they claim—have remained outside or at the margin of congregational life because of an understandable distaste for the American synagogue. As Borowitz sees it:

Clarifying Jewish faith might bring many to the conclusion that they cannot honestly participate in Judaism and the synagogue.... No one wishes to lose Jews for Judaism, but the time has come when the synagogue must be saved for the religious Jew, when it must be prepared to let some Jews opt out so that those who remain in, or who come in, will not be diverted from their duty to God. As the religion of a perpetual minority, Judaism must always first be concerned with the saving remnant, and so long as the synagogue is overwhelmed by the indifferent and the apathetic who control it for their own nonreligious purposes, that remnant will continue to be deprived of its proper communal home.[11]

More ethnically oriented religionists have proposed less drastic remedies. One such idea is the *havurah*, a local group composed of individuals who belong to congregations but find such institutions to be so lax and undemanding that they require other avenues to express their Jewishness. It is claimed that banding together and forming a fellowship or *havurah* will protect and advance the spiritual life of those individuals who are ready for a richer religious diet than the synagogue makes available:

The *havurah* is certainly *not* intended either to supplant the congregation or even to downgrade it. There is no doubt that the congregation serves many vital functions...[but its] insufficiency inheres...in the heterogeneous character of the constituency. And the main aspect of that insufficiency lies in the fact that belonging to congregations is often no more than an innocuous gesture.... Rabbis assume that the vast majority will attend only three times a year. Little—often nothing—is actually required besides the payment of dues. No commitment is asked; none is generally given.

Now, while this may appeal to the escapists and the irresponsible, it does not appeal to those who are looking for a place in which they can take their Judaism seriously in the company of likeminded Jews. Thus, *commitment* is the key to one of the essentials of *havurah*.[12]

The American synagogue is considerably more differentiated than its critics assume. Population size and density permitting, a variety of congregations are commonly established. Even when such congregations are similar in ideological preference they cater to different segments of the community. Such population segments are generally distinguishable by secular differences such as class position and level of general education but frequently they are also separated by differences relating to Jewishness: levels of acculturation, differing conceptions of spirituality, and contrasting degrees of observance of the *mitzvot*.

Lakeville, for example, is served by four Reform synagogues. All of the congregations are distinctive. One of them—the Samuel Hirsch Temple— is highly individual in its approach. In its conscious effort to break with the synagogue-center type, it has been called a synagogue for people who do not like to join synagogues. For a long time the congregation resisted constructing a synagogue building, because the leaders did not want to become involved in the type of activity that a building would entail. Furthermore, the Samuel Hirsch Temple in Lakeville has banned all clubs, and thus it does not have a sisterhood or men's club. The congregation has sought to confine its program to the traditional activities of worship and study, though these activities are of course conducted in a style that differs markedly from the traditional approach.[13]

Differences in the Reform group are paralleled and even accentuated among traditionalists. Far Rockaway, New York, for example, is a community that is as Orthodox in reputation as Lakeville is Reform. Beneath its seeming uniformity there is great diversity among the many small synagogues in the area, and considerable difference between the two largest institutions: the White Shool and Congregation Shaaray Tefila:

The White Shool has developed primarily as a synagogue for the young layman who was once a yeshiva bochur [student in a school for advanced Talmudical learning]....It is unique as an American synagogue in that it numbers among its congregants about thirty-five ordained, non-practicing rabbis. The congregation has no chazan [cantor] but instead uses a battery of its own unusually gifted baaley-tefilah [prayer-leaders] who "work" in rotation. . . . [The rabbi] not only gives more classes . . . than the average rabbi, but he offers them on a generally much higher level. In some areas—such as Gemorah [Talmud]—he may give shiurim [classes] on the same subject to different groups at different levels . . . like the European Rav, the largest part of the rabbi's time is given over to learning Torah and preparing shiurim . . . while a relatively small portion is devoted to the social duties and obligations which take up ninety per cent of the average American rabbi's time.

Shaaray Tefila is tailored . . . to serve the total Jewish community rather than being primarily geared to the intensively Torah-educated Jew. Shaaray Tefila's decorous, dignified service, led by a capable chazan, gives the synagogue and its divine worship an air of sacred reverence and respect for the Almighty. Many White Shool'ers, however, whose own synagogue breathes an atmosphere of an informal camaraderie prevalent in a "second home," feel uncomfortable in the dignified atmosphere of Shaaray. . . . On the other hand, most Shaaray'ites would feel ill at ease in the White Shool, where a considerable amount of conversation goes on during the service. The White Shool, to them, is an "overgrown shtibel" [an intimate setting for prayer and religious study] and far too undecorous.[14]

As we noticed earlier those who wish to change the American synagogue are tempted to do so either by going outside of the synagogue or by somehow convincing established institutions of the error of their ways and seeing to it that they implement higher standards of spirituality. But another option is open to the elitists: they are free to establish their own synagogues. This option is afforded by the congregational structure of American Judaism, guaranteeing as it does the independence of the local synagogue. If this option is exercised the burden of proof will then be on the elitists for they will be compelled to demonstrate the superiority of their institutions over the standard American synagogue center. Since the individual Jew is able to exercise freedom of choice such new congregations will find themselves competitors in the open market of affiliation. The American Jew, then, is free to remain unaffiliated, to retain his present affiliation, or to establish a new institution that offers him a more congenial spiritual atmosphere.

NOTES

[1] Note the case of Park Forest, Ill. See HERBERT J. GANS, "The Origin and Growth of a Jewish Community," in Marshall Sklare (ed.), *The Jews: Social Patterns of An American Group* (New York: Free Press, 1958).

[2] So great is the stress on the building of synagogues that it has drawn the attention of students of art and architecture. See, for example, AVRAM KAMPF, *Contemporary Synagogue Art: Developments in the United States 1945–1965* (New York: Union of American Hebrew Congregations, 1966).

[3] ALBERT J. MAYER, *Flint Jewish Population Study: 1967* (Processed, Flint, Mich.: Flint Jewish Community Council, 1969), p. 45.

[4] See SIDNEY GOLDSTEIN, *A Population Survey of the Greater Springfield Jewish Community* (Springfield, Mass.: Springfield Jewish Community Council, 1968), p. 93.

[5] ALBERT J. MAYER, *Jewish Population Study-Series II* (Detroit: Jewish Welfare Federation of Detroit, 1964–1966), p. 24; and AXELROD et al., op. cit., p. 136.

[6] In Springfield where inquiry was made into reasons for nonaffiliation, the most frequent response was the cost of synagogue membership. Only about one out of ten went so far as to say their reason for nonaffiliation was a lack of interest.

[7] In recent years the congregational unions such as the Union of American Hebrew Congregations (Reform), the United Synagogue (Conservative) and the Union of Orthodox Jewish Congregations of America (Orthodox) have taken greater initiative in forming new congregations.

The most notable exception to the freedom of the local congregation to determine its own affairs are synagogues affiliated with Young Israel (Orthodox). Title to the property of a Young Israel synagogue is vested in the national movement. The purpose of the arrangement is to prevent a congregation from instituting religious practices that violate Orthodox norms.

[8] SIDNEY GOLDSTEIN, *The Greater Providence Jewish Community: A Population Survey* (Providence: General Jewish Committee of Providence, 1964), p. 141.

[9] One important aspect of the synagogue center (very much emphasized in the writings of MORDECAI M. KAPLAN, for example) is the conception that nothing Jewish should be alien to the synagogue—that the synagogue should offer its facilities to all Jewish organizations that make a contribution to Jewish survival and that it should seek to facilitate the work of such organizations. But inasmuch as there are inherent strains in the relationship of the congregation to the community, this is more easily said than done.

[10] EUGENE B. BOROWITZ, *A New Jewish Theology in the Making* (Philadelphia: The Westminster Press, 1968), pp. 45–46.

[11] Ibid., pp. 53–54.

[12] JACOB NEUSNER and IRA EISENSTEIN, *The Havurah Idea* (New York: The Reconstructionist Press, n.d.).

[13] See SKLARE and GREENBLUM, op. cit., pp. 97–178.

[14] MICHAEL KAUFMAN, "Far Rockaway—Torah-Suburb By-the-Sea," *Jewish Life* 27, no. 6 (August 1960), 25–28.

MOTIVATIONS FOR ATTENDING
HIGH HOLY DAY SERVICES

ARNOLD A. LASKER

Being Jewish is a sociological, cultural, and religious condition. Many components, therefore, enter into Jewish self-identification. The meaning of those components to the individual Jew and their relative strengths in his perceptual and motivational structure certainly bear investigation.

The present study is predicated upon the fact that, among those Jewish activities which are most widely carried on by Jews, attendance at High Holy Day services ranks very high. Jews, in very large numbers, make every effort to participate in such services regardless of the cost to them in terms of time, money, energy, and convenience. Presumably, therefore, an analysis of the factors leading to such attendance might very well cast light on what it means to them to be Jews.

Our research was not designed to tap motives that lie beneath the surface of consciousness. [Editor's note: The author asks that readers not overgeneralize from the small population out of which the sample was selected.] Furthermore, even though the questionnaires were administered in such a way as to encourage frankness, it was impossible to overcome completely distortion and self-deception on the part of the respondents. Nevertheless, we feel that the results are enlightening inasmuch as the reasons that people give for their actions constitute in themselves data which should be known.

PROCEDURE

THE INSTRUMENT

Each questionnaire was headed with the sentence, "The goals I look forward to obtaining from attending High Holy Day services are:" Following this were listed thirty possible purposes for such attendance. There were also two spaces thereafter in which respondents could enter additional reasons.

Each of the responses was followed by five letters, one of which was to be

From *Journal for the Scientific Study of Religion* 10, no. 3 (Fall 1971): 241–248. Reprinted with the permission of the publisher and the author. Appreciation is expressed to The Benjamin and Ethel Gittlin Foundation for financial assistance.

Arnold A. Lasker is Rabbi of Congregation Beth Torah, Orange, New Jersey.

encircled as follows: "V—It is *very important* to me; S—It plays a *significant* part; M—It plays some part, but only a *minor* one; N—It plays *no part*; and D—I *dislike* this as a purpose for synagogue attendance." For purposes of statistical analysis, numerical values were given to the responses:

$$V = 4 \qquad S = 3 \qquad M = 2 \qquad N = 1 \qquad D = 0$$

Following the list of items, each respondent was asked to indicate which *three* reasons were *most* important to him and which three were *least* important.

Finally, there was an open-ended sentence-completion test: "If I didn't attend High Holy Day services this year, I'd feel. . . ."

The last page consisted of a personal data sheet.

CHOICE OF SUBJECTS

The study was made among members of three Conservative congregations in 1967. In the first congregation, two randomly selected samples were tested by mail, one before Rosh Hashanah and Yom Kippur and the other after the holidays. A random sample of the second congregation also received their questionnaries by mail, but only before the holidays. In the third congregation, the questionnaires were administered to the members of the Board of Trustees at one of their regular meetings held shortly before the holiday season. While questionnaires were administered to women as well as to men, the present report deals only with male respondents.

Combining all four samples, the data in this paper are based upon 72 questionnaires of a total of 123 distributed. (We have no evidence of the differences between those who returned questionnaires and those who did not.) The four separate samples were largely in agreement, with only minor distinctions.

For purposes of comparison, an Orthodox and a Reform rabbi were asked to chose members of their respective congregations who, in their opinion, represented most authentically their particular "denominations." This resulted in responses from 11 Orthodox and 7 Reform Jews.

Our primary purpose was to learn about the average member of Conservative synagogues but, since we were comparing these "average members" with "authentic" Orthodox and "authentic" Reform Jews, a criterion was sought for the selection of a sub-sample of more intensive Conservative Jews. For this purpose, a separate analysis was made of those who stated, in their personal data sheet, that they attend synagogue services at least monthly (called here the "regular attenders"). There were 19 such from among the total of 72.

ANALYSIS OF RESULTS

The mean ratings by all 72 Conservative respondents of each of the 30 items in the questionnaire are shown in Table 11. Next to that is placed the number of subjects who included each item among the three *most* important (and, similarly, the number of those who included it among the three *least* important) reasons for their attendance.

A similar analysis of the 19 "regular attenders" is given in the second block of figures.

Responses from the Reform sample were seen to be very little different from the Conservative. The Orthodox sample, though, yielded striking differences. They are reported in the third block of figures. The most marked contrasts between the Orthodox and the Conservative are indicated by bold-faced type.

For purposes of greater clarity of analysis, the items have been grouped into nine logical categories (with some being included in more than one such area). These are:

Jewish Identification
The Worship Experience
Relationship with God
Influence on God
Sin and Guilt
Peace of Mind
Humanitarian Concern
Self-Improvement
Social Effect

Each item in Table 11 has next to it a letter indicating the category under which it is subsumed.

Table 12 has all the information included in Table 11, reduced to the nine categories.

(In the following discussion, numerals in parentheses refer to item numbers, using the first rank order given in Table 11. Capital letters in parentheses refer to the categories listed in Table 12.)

THE FINDINGS

All four Conservative groups were primarily motivated by the desire to express their Jewishness, to identify with the Jewish People, and to carry on Jewish tradition (A). Secondarily, they looked to the service as an experience that would be impressive and meaningful (B). The most important aspect of that experience was seen to be the sense of fellowship with the others present (4), all involved in perpetuating an important, beautiful expression of Jewish tradition.

The service was generally looked upon as a positive experience rather than as a refuge from life's pressures (I, particularly 29). Inter-congregational comparisons (based on knowledge of the three congregations) indicated that the less traditional synagogue tends to encourage the feeling of "calm and relaxation" (18), but the more traditional service, being longer, fuller, and more repetitious, was viewed as a (worthwhile) task to be fulfilled more

TABLE II

Ranking, Rating, and Preferences of Reasons for Attending High Holy Day Services

Items	Category[a]	TOTAL CONSERVATIVE N = 72				REGULAR ATTENDERS (CONSERVATIVE) N = 19				ORTHODOX N = 11			
		Rank	Mean Rating	Mosts	Leasts	Rank	Mean Rating	Mosts	Leasts	Rank	Mean Rating	Mosts	Leasts
To carry on Jewish tradition	A	1	3.23	34	0	2	3.33	5	0	8	3.73	3	0
To feel a sense of identification with the Jewish people	A	2	3.07	25	0	5	3.16	5	0	15.5	3.27	0	0
To fulfill my obligation as a Jew	A	3	2.82	19	1	3	3.31	7	0	3	3.95	5	0
To gain a good feeling from participating in a shared experience with the other people present in the synagogue	A,B,F	4	2.79	14	3	8	3.05	2	0	26	2.00	0	1
To enjoy the beauty of the service	B	5	2.72	6	1	18	2.68	0	1	24	2.18	0	3
To be moved, inspired, uplifted, by taking part in the service	B	6	2.63	5	0	6	3.11	2	0	6.5	3.82	0	0
To enjoy the familiar prayers and melodies	B	7	2.60	6	2	12	2.82	1	1	22	2.73	0	3
To express my hopes for a better world	D	8	2.51	8	0	4	3.26	3	0	20.5	2.91	1	1
To thank God for His goodness	C	9	2.45	11	0	1	3.47	7	0	4	3.91	5	0
To feel the closeness of God	C	10	2.34	6	0	13	2.79	3	0	1	4.00	4	0

To gain inner strength for the year ahead	E	11	2.24	3	6	11	1	0	2.95	11	3.55	1	1
To understand God better	C	12	2.24	1	3	7	1	1	3.11	19	3.00	0	1
To develop faith that the world will be better	D	13	2.21	6	4	19	1	1	2.63	23	2.64	0	1
To express my thoughts and feelings to God	C	14	2.20	5	3	9	1	1	3.00	10	3.55	1	0
To comply with God's requirement that we observe Rosh Hashanah and Yom Kippur	C	15	2.17	6	2	10	4	0	2.95	2	4.00	2	0
To evaluate my life, its achievements and failures	E	16	2.14	8	0	20	2	0	2.56	18	3.00	2	0
To get a better understanding of how to live	E	17	2.08	3	7	21	1	1	2.56	20.5	2.91	0	0
To gain a sense of calm and relaxation	I	18	2.07	3	9	23	0	3	2.37	25	2.09	0	2
To seek the health and welfare of others	G	19	2.06	3	3	17	3	1	2.72	17	3.18	0	0
To help, through my prayers, to bring peace to the world	D,G	20	2.04	5	2	14	2	1	2.79	14	3.36	1	0
To be together with people I know	F	21	2.03	2	5	22	0	2	2.42	28	1.82	0	2
To become a finer person	E	22	2.02	1	4	15	0	1	2.79	12.5	3.46	0	0
To obtain God's forgiveness for my sins	G,H	23	1.89	3	10	16	2	1	2.78	5	3.82	7	0
To achieve happiness in the weeks and months to come	G	24	1.77	0	6	25	0	3	2.22	15.5	3.27	0	0

TABLE II (continued)

Item	a	No.											
To ask of God those things which I genuinely desire	G	25	1.66	1	22	26	2.17	0	5	12.5	3.46	0	0
To gain God's favorable attitude toward me	G	26	1.64	1	14	24	2.22	0	2	6.5	3.82	0	0
To please my family or friends who feel I should attend	F	27	1.56	6	26	30	1.39	0	10	30	0.91	0	8
To secure life in the coming year	G	28	1.55	6	14	27	1.94	0	3	9	3.60	1	0
To get away from the pressure of every day life	I	29	1.39	2	27	29	1.56	1	8	29	1.64	0	5
To free myself from feelings of guilt for having done wrong	H,I	30	1.31	0	17	28	1.78	0	2	27	1.91	0	2
Mean rating of all 30 items			2.18				2.66				3.05		

a See categories listed in Table 12.

TABLE 12

Ranking, Rating, and Preferences of Categories of Reasons for Attending High Holy Day Services

Categories	TOTAL CONSERVATIVE N = 72				REGULAR ATTENDERS (CONSERVATIVE) N = 19				ORTHODOX N = 11			
	Rank	Mean Rating	Most	Least	Rank	Mean Rating	Most	Least	Rank	Mean Rating	Most	Least
A—Jewish identification (items 1, 2, 3, 4)	1	2.98	92	4	1	3.21	19	0	3	3.24	8	1
B—The worship experience (items 4, 5, 6, 7)	2	2.68	31	6	3	2.91	5	2	7	2.68	0	7
C—Relationship with God (items 9, 10, 12, 14, 15)	3	2.28	29	8	2	3.06	16	2	1	3.69	12	1
D—Humanitarian concern (items 8, 13, 20)	4	2.26	19	6	4	2.89	6	2	5	2.97	2	2
E—Self-improvement (items 11, 16, 17, 22)	5	2.12	15	11	5	2.71	4	2	4	3.23	3	1
F—Social effect (items 4, 21, 27)	6	2.12	22	34	7	2.29	2	12	9	1.58	0	11
G—Influence on God (items 19, 20, 23, 24, 25, 26, 28)	7	1.82	15	69	6	2.41	7	16	2	3.50	9	0
H—Sin and guilt (items 23, 30)	8	1.60	3	27	8	2.28	2	3	6	2.87	7	2
I—Peace of mind (items 18, 29, 30)	9	1.59	5	53	9	1.90	1	13	8	1.88	0	9

than as a source of serenity. This hypothesis was reinforced by comparisons with the Orthodox on the one side and the Reform on the other side.

For the *average* worshipper, the object of worship—God—was reported to be only secondary to the act of worship itself (C). It is in regard to this aspect—the place of God-consciousness—that there was the sharpest split between the regular attenders and those who frequent the synagogue less than monthly; while the former, on the average, regarded relationship to the Divine as playing a "significant" part in their attendance (average rating of 3.06, see Table 12), the latter considered it only a "minor" factor (average rating of 2.00).

The members of neither classification—the regulars or the infrequents—considered prayer to be a means of influencing God in their favor (G). Despite the use of prayers of petition found abundantly in their prayerbooks, they seemed to feel uncomfortable about asking God for personal benefits, particularly *material* benefits.

If they allowed themselves to petition God for anything, it was for the sake of others rather than for themselves (19, 20). Even so, while they looked upon their prayers as being related to the welfare of humanity (D), they regarded them as more an opportunity to express their *hopes* for a better world (8) than as a means of bringing it about (20).

There was little attention given by our subjects to the impact of the service on their personality and character (E). To the extent to which they were interested in this area, they rated the quest for inner strength (11) and self-evaluation (16) as most important; they had little expectation, however, that they would emerge as finer people (22).

(In the one congregation from which two samples were taken, the post-holiday testing yielded much higher scores in the area of "self-improvement" than did the preholiday testing. Perhaps, the experience of the High Holy Day worship focussed the attention of those present more sharply on this function of the service.)

The key verse for Yom Kippur, repeated again and again, is: "On this day He will atone for you, to purify you from all your sins; before the Lord you will be cleansed." Since our respondents do not seek to affect God through their prayers, they do not seriously strive "to obtain God's forgiveness" for their sins (23). Interestingly enough, the idea of overcoming their own guilt feelings was looked upon with even greater disdain (30). Why this is so—whether there is an absence of guilt feelings or a lack of anticipation of catharsis—is not clear.

There was a general denial among the respondents that they attend services in order to please other people (27). There were, however, a half dozen of them who gave primacy to such motivation; they tended to find little other reason for attendance except to carry on some minimal degree of Jewish tradition and to set an example for their children. Their visits to the synagogue during the remainder of the year were minimal or non-existent.

While the bulk of our respondents reported that they do not feel that their family and friends *push* them toward the worship service, the presence of other Jews in the synagogue—as pointed out above—*attracts* them to it. Yet, they tended to deny that they go there "to be together with people I know" (21). The attraction seems to lie not in friends as such but in Jews who are collectively acting out a vital Jewish tradition with which they can identify.

COMPARISON WITH ORTHODOX SUBJECTS

Orthodoxy teaches that God is a personal Being who has expressed His will to the Jewish People and who responds actively to man's approach to Him in prayer. In keeping with this viewpoint, our Orthodox subjects ranked "Relationship With God" (C) and "Influence on God" (G) as their two highest categories.

Every one of the Orthodox respondents rated "To comply with God's requirement that we observe Rosh Hashanah and Yom Kippur" (15) as a *very important reason* for attendance. Exceedingly high on their scale of motivations were "To obtain God's forgiveness for my sins" (23) and "To secure life in the coming year" (28), goals stressed in the traditional prayerbook but downgraded by the non-Orthodox.

Although—unlike the Conservative—the Orthodox do look forward to "God's forgiveness," they too do not anticipate any release from "feelings of guilt" (30). This fact raises questions about the relationship between the feeling of being under the judgment of God, on the one hand, and the qualms of conscience, on the other.

In keeping with the stress on repentance, the Orthodox also upgrade "Self-Improvement" (E), with a level almost tying "Jewish Identification" (A) for third place.

CONCLUSION

Results based on 72 members of three Conservative congregations in one locality can hardly be generalized to a description of American Jewry as a whole—or even of Conservative Jews in America. Yet, the findings do add to the insights through which the meaning of Jewishness in the life space of the Jew can better be understood. It is in the light of a restricted—yet suggestive—applicability, then, that the following is to be understood.

Inasmuch as Jews express themselves positively as Jews by joining synagogues and attending High Holy Day services, they share a desire to identify themselves with the Jewish People and to carry on Jewish tradition. What that tradition means to them may differ from Jew to Jew and may even be rather nebulous to many, but the idea of preserving their heritage plays an important part in their thinking.

The maintenance of that heritage is seen as requiring a periodic public cultic expression through which the participants collectively testify to and reinforce their sense of belonging to the Jewish People. While the implications of the ritual for the wider aspects of life may be limited, the beauty and inspiration of the observances themselves are regarded as having a worth in their own right.

The extent to which Judaism involves a God-dimension varies in accordance with the background and experience of the individual Jew so that identification with the Jewish People is a much more widespread desideratum than is faith in God. That faith, at least among the non-Orthodox, is not regarded as capable of "moving mountains" since prayer is not taken seriously as a means of affecting reality.

The implications for non-Jewish religious groups of this analysis of the interrelationship of folk, cult, faith, and relevance can well be left to others. One practical result of the study for Jewish worshippers, though, has been the formulation of new prayers and readings by the author, based on these findings, for the High Holy Day services in his own synagogue. No systematic evaluation has been made of the impact of these liturgical selections on the worshippers. Yet, the enthusiasm with which they were received would seem to indicate that the feelings revealed in his study were present and waiting to be tapped at the service.

╬╍╌╍╌╍╌╍╌╍╌╍╌╍╌╍╌╍╌╍╬

The Essence of My Commitment

DANNY SIEGEL

More than most of the peoples of this world, the Jews have longed for security. For centuries, we have lived with the knowledge that today may be our last in this place, that tomorrow we may be driven from our homes. More than most peoples, the Jews have seen in America a chance to realize that dream of finding a permanent home, one in which ideals were part of the reality itself, and where the work to be done involved the construction of messianic mechanisms rather than sustaining the hope for a better future. It is because of this understanding of American life that we have immersed ourselves in it, and it is due to this immersion that we have discovered a range of problems which threatens our people and the survival of its ideals.

The Jew is never to forget his origins in slavery, especially when dealing with oppressed minorities in his own land, nor is he to discriminate against those who have voluntarily accepted "the yoke of God's kingship" although they were not born into it.

This question did not die with the simple inclusion of the phrase, "Remember the exodus from Egypt," in our liturgy. The classic Jewish problem of survival in the face of a hostile majority has been transformed. The question is now at what cost to others can one people pursue the betterment of its physical existence. As Americans, we must confront the results of our labor, the enslavement and embitterment of black people, the widespread use of military power over other peoples and races, the elevation of some at the expense of others, the unchecked pursuit of technology which now threatens to destroy the natural world into which we were born. And as Jews, we must confront all this and more, for we must determine the risks to our security involved in a public examination of these problems.

I remember not long ago attending a meeting of rabbis where the question of supporting the October 15 Moratorium was being debated. Despite the eloquent pleas of one man who insisted that as Jews we must support this effort to bring peace both to the people of Viet Nam and to ourselves, the motion was overruled. The most compelling argument against the support resolution came not over doubts about the ideology of the movement, but

From *Midstream* 16, no. 3 (March 1970): 37–40. Reprinted with the permission of the publisher.

Danny Siegel is rabbi for B'nai Or, a Jewish religious center in a rural area south of Ottawa, Canada.

from a fear that such support would be counted against the Jews when the Nixon administration took up the question of support for Israel. The false god of security for its own sake, the theory that one must "play by the rules" to survive at all costs, was challenging the Jewish position that one must stand by certain minimum ideals even in the world of *realpolitik*. The recent increase in Jewish concern over the American position in the Middle East seems to decisively demonstrate the fallacy of trusting the practitioners of pragmatic politics to be morally consistent.

There is no need here to describe in detail the low state of Jewish life in America. We are all aware of our failure to stimulate and excite the majority of our people in this country. It does seem necessary, however, to suggest a different reason for this situation. We hear much today about a "generation gap," and often the closing verses of Malachi are cited as proof that this gap is a phenomenon which dates back to the beginnings of history. Only Elijah the Prophet, the Messiah's herald, will be able to "turn the hearts of the fathers to the sons and the hearts of the sons to the fathers." Thus, we can be reassured that only the uncompromising idealism of youth, demanding instant satisfaction, makes our problems seem so immediate. In reality, things will change slowly, as always, and the young will mature and be tormented by their children, also as always. The time-honored truths will remain, shortly to be recognized by the children as they also learn the fine arts of compromise and the abdication of moral responsibility.

Indeed, the cost of our security was high, so high that we have forgotten the price, for it is not only the young who challenge American Jewry. Our synagogues are empty most of the year, and it is the adults who dismiss from their pulpits the few rabbis who have the courage to challenge the notion that Judaism must not become involved with the questions of Viet Nam, racism, and poverty. It is not only the young who are disgusted by the displays of wealth so common in our celebrations of "religious" occasions and who are aware of the contradictions involved in having a dinner costing thousands of dollars served by black waiters who earn less in a year than is spent in one night. It is not only the young who have learned that creativity is unwelcome in a Jewish community which blindly insists on preserving religious divisions and forms, preventing the composition of new forms of prayer and religious expression which could add to the meaning of Jewish ritual, and branding as illegitimate (un-*halakhic*) those few attempts which are made. Nothing seems so hypocritical as a Friday night folk-rock service "performed" in Conservative synagogues on Sundays. It is not only the young who understand that Jewish life is empty of real depth because it has accepted a lifestyle which demands silence in the face of evil, submission to the authority of "experts," and surrender of moral accountability for the misfortune of others in exchange for split-level homes, catered affairs, and pious (but very vague) resolutions calling for peace and brotherhood. We have indeed bought into the American economic pie, but we may have done so at the cost of our Jewish souls.

It is certainly true that there has always existed a certain tension between one generation and the next and that this tension continues to be manifested today. It may also be true that it is primarily the younger generation which is calling attention to the problems of contemporary American society and Jewish life. Nonetheless, a generation-gap approach does not sufficiently explain our current situation nor is that situation likely to be resolved simply by waiting for the young to grow older. In fact, the world itself has changed, and changed so radically that its very ability to evolve is threatened. We have absorbed in a few short years more than any other generation in history. We know that man's ability to embark on the systematic extermination of a whole people is beyond question; we know that that decimated people has been capable of a new burst of energy which took it from the depths to the heights and from old age back to youth; we know how threatened that revival is; we know that this earth can be destroyed within a few minutes or that it may die an agonizingly slow death by poison. In short, we know that we may very well not live long enough to be challenged by our children and that this knowledge is being confirmed by growing numbers of people who are over thirty. For many of us it is becoming increasingly clear that in order to have any hope for survival, we must crack the systems which have given us the bomb and are poisoning our wives' milk. We must learn that our real enemies are all those who would destroy the earth in pursuit of profit and national pride. This is neither a generation gap nor the hysteria of youth, it is rather a call both to our elders and our contemporaries to join together in a common struggle to live up to the call of our heritage and to work for the salvation of us all. It is, literally, now or never. . . .

❖·❖·❖·❖·❖·❖·❖·❖·❖·❖·❖·❖·❖·❖·❖

The Crisis in American Jewry

NATHAN GLAZER

If one hears the term, "crisis," in connection with the Jewish community, I believe most Jews will think of two things: one, the threat of anti-Semitism, and two, the threat of assimilation. Now in the last two decades we have been hardly concerned with the level of anti-Semitism, which is quite low, even though there have been some disturbing signs and portents in recent years. We have been considerably more concerned with the possibility of assimilation. But it is neither of these two possible senses of crisis that concern me in this lecture. When I consider the position of the American Jewish community today, I rather think of an internal crisis, a crisis of identity and self-conception, and if you will—I think the term is not too extravagant— a spiritual crisis. . . .

The major unanswered question as to American Judaism—and this is a question that by its nature is not easily to be settled by social surveys— remains, what is Judaism to be? Here I think we can begin to discern an emerging dilemma that to my mind affects Judaism in a special way, and that makes its problems distinct from the crises of religion in America in general. American Judaism, as it has moved further and further away from traditional Judaism, has moved in two directions. One direction has been to make Jewish ethnicity—peoplehood and nationality—in larger and larger degree the major content of Jewish religion. This is not a movement in complete contradiction to traditional religion. Judaism has always emphasized the chosen and distinctiveness of the Jewish people. But there is no question in my mind that American Judaism has emphasized this much more strongly than was ever the case in traditional Judaism.

There were various reasons for this. As Will Herberg pointed out almost twenty years ago, American society tolerantly left room for Jewish religion but was somewhat less tolerant toward long-sustained, long-maintained ethnic, national differences. You could be a member of a religion and a full American. It was somewhat harder to be a member of another national group and a full American, though there were many tendencies in American thinking and practice which argued for this.

From *Midstream* 16, no. 9 (November 1970): 3–11. Reprinted with the permission of the author and the publisher.

Nathan Glazer is a member of the faculty of the Graduate School of Education, Harvard University.

.   .   .

More significant perhaps than this general American tendency to encourage religion at the expense of ethnicity or nationality was the specific impact on American Jewish life of the rise of Israel. The permanent danger to the state of Israel and the close personal, emotional, and historical ties between American Jews and Israelis have made it impossible to create a non-national, non-ethnic form of Judaism. There have been a number of such efforts, which have gained some intellectual respectability—in particular of course classical Reform Judaism and its various later developments such as those represented by the American Council for Judaism. We know what reputation that now has among most Jews. And yet we should recall that the idea of non-national Judaism—Judaism as a humanist religion increasingly divorced from a people with a specific social character and interests—once seemed to make sense to a good number of intelligent Jews.

There has been a second strand in the development of a new content for American Judaism. This is liberalism—liberalism in the form of political and social ideals that emphasized the equality of men, the importance of non-discrimination, freedom of opportunity, and the like. While on the one hand the anti-national side of Reform Judaism failed utterly, the liberal side has been, if anything, continually strengthened. One of the most intriguing parts of Marshall Sklare's study of Lakeville is the section where he asks Lakeville Jews to give him their conception of a good Jew. Various formulations are suggested to the respondents. Obeying the precepts of traditional Judaism is far down on the list. Supporting Israel is higher. But at the very top is to be fair and honest to one's fellow men, not to discriminate, to protect civil liberties, civil rights, and liberal ideals. The result is quite clear—when you ask American Jews what it is to be a good Jew, the answer is, to be a liberal.

My thesis is: the major problems facing Judaism and Jews today lie in the development of certain contradictions, certain dilemmas, inherent in the effort to combine these two tendencies that make up modern American Judaism, the ethnic and the national on the one hand, and the liberal on the other, and the development of these ideals themselves.

Let me explore some of these emerging dilemmas.

First: the main subject of liberal social ideals for twenty-five years has been the condition of the Negro. If we go back and review the various commissions on social justice of the Reform and Conservative denominations, we will see that, alongside the major issue of peace, has been the major issue of the status of the Negro. We are all aware of what a fantastic change has occurred in the thinking and outlook of the Negro—or the black man as he now prefers to be known—in the past five years, changes which have seriously damaged the capacity of liberals and liberal ideals to play a major role in the development of a more satisfactory social position for the Negro in the United States. At one time—only four or five years ago—we saw no contradiction, indeed there was none, between liberal ideals—non-discrimination, equal opportunity, civil liberties and civil rights—and the desires of Negroes. Indeed, in those days all agreed that it was only through the realization of liberal ideals that the desires of Negroes could be fulfilled.

Today, almost all liberal ideals are challenged by the more militant black leaders and their white allies. The dependence on democratic processes and on non-violence; the importance of equal opportunity and fairness to individuals; the hope for integration; tolerance of a variety of viewpoints—all these are anathema to most young blacks, and indeed most black leaders are forced to act as if they agree with them. Five years ago few of us saw any contradiction in being a Jew, in the sense in which so many Jews saw themselves as Jews, and the achievement of equality for Negroes. Today the word liberal is a dirty word among black militants and their white allies. Judaism finds that its kind of liberalism, instead of allying it with the oppressed and deprived and their hopes for a better life, cuts it off from them. This is deeply troubling to Jews, and Judaism.

There is a second reason, aside from the challenge to the value of liberalism, why Judaism is troubled by the radical shift in Negro political attitudes. It is that Judaism's other side, its ethnic-national side, also brings it into conflict with current political attitudes among black and white radicals. Concretely, there is the conflict between the interests of Jews and Negroes in many cities. Here liberal ideals seem to come into conflict with ethnic interests. Perhaps ultimately more dangerous, there is the conflict between Israel and the Arabs, and the way it is reflected in black political attitudes in this country. The Arabs, to blacks, are "Africans," "oppressed," "colonized," victimized by "American Imperialism"—just as the blacks are, in militant eyes. Israel is cast as the imperialist, western, white oppressor.

There are some special and accidental reasons for this black militant view which places Israel in the camp of the enemy of the blacks. After all, Israel in reality has strong links with many black states, and good relations with them. To unravel the image of Israel in black militant eyes would be a task that involves history, myth, and interests in some inextricable mixture. Israel is seen as mirroring the American Jewish landlord, storekeeper, lawyer, doctor, social worker, teacher, who in the past and even today play such a large role in the ghetto.

.   .   .

Thus the liberal side of Judaism and the ethnic side of Judaism both place Judaism in the dilemma of finding that it is in opposition to the group that has been for so long the chief subject and object of domestic liberalism. This is a dilemma and a troubling one.

.   .   .

Perhaps the most serious dilemma relates to the safety of Israel. You will recall that many doves on Vietnam became hawks on Israel. But many Jews must be concerned over recent polls that have shown that Americans are less willing to send troops to defend Israel than many other countries. Even India scored better on this item. The connection between Israel's security and the American military is closer than many of us would like to think. Thus, Israel gets supplies from the United States, and in return provides captured Migs and radar installations for American inspection. It is not only in Arab eyes that the United States is the principal and only military ally of Israel—in many respects the U.S. in reality is, even if rather unwillingly, and even if, as I suspect, our diplomats and military men would prefer to be tied up with the Arabs.

·   ·   ·

If liberalism is challenged as a way of achieving racial harmony and world peace, then I would say that American Judaism itself—as it has become—is challenged, because Jewish identity has come to lean on the pillars of liberalism and ethnicity. When half of all Jews vote, as they may have done in 1969, for Procaccino and Marchi in New York City, that is a crisis for Jewish identity. When many Jews find, as they do in New York, that they are becoming in some sense—any sense—anti-Negro, that becomes a crisis for Jewish identity. When Jews face an intellectual atmosphere in which to be a liberal is to be a sell-out, that is a crisis American Judaism. For if it is not to be liberal, then what is it to be?

·   ·   ·

Perhaps the major problem that Judaism as a mixture of liberalism and ethnicity now faces is the problem of Jewish youth. Jewish youth has been prominent in the upsurge of militant and radical action in the last five or six years; in the South; on the campus; in the anti-War movement. We have often heard and been told that these are the best educated young people we have ever had. And the fact is that what moves them is neither liberalism nor ethnicity—neither of the two main tendencies in American Judaism. They are not moved by Israel—or rather, remarkably few are moved by the great drama of Israel. Even the great wave of emotion of May–June 1967 left Jewish radical youth largely unmoved. Instead of seeing Israel's crisis as that of the heroic defense of a small people, instead of seeing Israel in the model of Cuba and Vietnam, they can identify Israel only with a great power they find hateful, the United States. Nor are they more attracted to the liberal ideals within Judaism. They see liberalism as a failure. It means Johnson, Humphrey, Rusk, and college presidents—and if they were to think of it, rabbis.

This seems a serious matter to me. For on the one hand we would like to claim for Judaism—for the prophetic tradition, for Jewish moralism, for

Jewish education, formal and informal, for the Jewish home—some responsibility for the strong and powerful radical tendencies of so significant a part of Jewish youth. Yet radical Jewish youth disdains the major elements that, for better or worse, now make up the content of Judaism, liberalism and ethnicity.

Recently we have seen the rise of radical Jewish youth movements which, while still rejecting the liberal elements of the contemporary American Jewish mix, have also rejected the universalism that is so common in radicalism, and are willing to, indeed insist on, emphasizing ethnic distinctiveness. They attack the prevalent institutions of the American Jewish community for not being sufficiently critical of those forces in American life that prevent the full development of ethnic distinctiveness. Clearly they are influenced by the growing strength within radicalism of nationalist elements. As against the internationalist radicalism of the First and Second International, and indeed in large measure of the Third International, the radicalism that stems from Mao, third-world revolts, Che and Castro, and American blacks emphasizes the distinct importance of national feeling, and insists that one of the crimes of capitalism is the destruction of national identity as well as the oppression of the working class.

This is in many respects an encouraging development. It means that some radical Jewish youth find it possible to stay within the Jewish community. And yet I think we should understand the limits of this kind of thinking. I think it will and should form part of the pluralist diversity of American Jewishness, but I find it inconceivable that it can become the dominant sentiment among American Jews.

Three factors stand in the way of the American Jewish community replacing its liberalism with radicalism.

First, there are pragmatic interests. It is a community largely of businessmen and free professionals. To such a community, capitalism is not an enemy —it is a benign environment. When radicalism conquers, even if there is not a trace of anti-Semitism in it, the classic Jewish occupations suffer, and Jews individually come upon hard times. Thus, when Castro won in Cuba, most of the Jewish community emigrated—this was no longer a country for businessmen, doctors and lawyers. Nor is this reaction to be interpreted simply as defending selfish interests. To my mind, the arguments in favor of the free market as a means of organizing society are at least as strong as the arguments in favor of Socialism and Communism. In defending the free market, and the occupations it makes possible, Jews are, to my mind, defending freedom as well as their own interests.

Secondly, the antagonism of all the major variants of the left—the Russian, the Chinese, the third-world, and even the more anarchistic variants of Western Europe—to Israel is by now so strong that the notion of a radicalized Jewish community seems very unlikely. One can be radical and pro-Israel. Leading Israeli parties illustrate the possibility. But there is a continual strain in holding together two political positions which in the real world tend to be separated.

Third—and this perhaps is most arguable—the kind of world radicalism wants to bring into being is inevitably a homogeneous, rather than a heterogeneous world. While it makes use of the strong pull of national feeling everywhere in the world, radical Communism still follows Joseph Stalin and his slogan, "national in form, socialist in content." It does not have room for a true and meaningful national and ethnic diversity. It is hostile to different ideas, and suppresses them. And it is, I believe, hostile to ethnic differences unless that difference is expressed in apolitical, innocuous, cultural forms alone. As we know, Jewish difference is not expressed only innocuously. It does serve, very often implicitly, as a critique of dominant values. I do not see a strong role for a Jewish community in a society created by radicals, and I suspect the major elements in the American Jewish community will feel the same way.

Under the present circumstances in American Judaism one is torn between an effort to find a more contemporary, a more "relevant" content to Judaism, and an effort to shore up the old content. I must say, I am not sanguine about the effort to remodel the content of Judaism as it has emerged in the United States. On the one hand, I do not see the strength of a religion of pure traditionalism, strong as tradition is in many respects. Nor do I believe Judaism can be strong as a religion of disembodied humanism, strong as that ideal was in the past.

There is strength in the ethnic-liberal mixture. It is tied to tradition and it is tied to contemporary Jewish reality. The new amalgam gave renewed content, viability, validity, to an old faith for millions.

And on the other hand, the association of ethnic-national feeling and liberalism with religion aided these tendencies too. It prevented the national-ethnic trend from becoming pure chauvinism. I believe Jewish nationalism is still far from chauvinism and protected from getting there by its links to religion. Thus, I am deeply impressed by how Israel's defense has not become infected with hatred of others.

Religion does something for liberalism, too. Liberalism, in some of its tendencies, can become an inhuman kind of scientific and rational concern with simply material matters. The religious component makes this harder.

I end up with no ringing call to replace the inadequate and false idols of ethnicity and liberalism with some new sounder content—internationalism and radicalism, for example, I do not believe that liberalism and ethnic attachment *are* false idols. Rather, our task is to deepen our understanding of what Judaism has in practice become. We must try to give new validity to ethnic attachment and to liberalism, both humanized, or spiritualized, if you will, by association with an old religion. We must become critics and analysts of our beliefs, so we can understand their implications better, hold to them with greater strength, and hope that we can communicate them more effectively to our children. We must be able to convince our children that we hold to these commitments not because we have simply, flaccidly accepted them from our past, or because they serve our interests, but because they do indeed provide the best patterns to organize our lives on earth.

CHAPTER 7

❖❖❖❖❖❖❖❖❖❖❖❖❖❖❖❖❖❖❖❖❖❖❖

Examining the Boundaries

It would be a serious mistake to consider organized American religion only in terms of sharp distinctions between the three major faiths—Protestant, Catholic, Jewish. The boundaries between them, including the boundaries between Protestant denominations themselves, are not altogether rigid. But this entire question is very complex, and sociologists have usually pursued it in two ways. The first is to look at interdenominational or interfaith merger trends. The second is to consider religioethnic groupings and to what extent group members interact across these lines; that is, do they tend to maintain or to disregard the boundaries in both institutionalized settings—marriage, occupations, politics—and less formal ones such as friendship and neighborhood residence?

It is helpful to think of ecumenism as a trend ranging from minimal contact to full union. J. Milton Yinger's diagram, reproduced below, invites us to think of ecumenism in two dimensions: The *extent* of unity may range from toleration through conversation, cooperation, federation, and full integration. The *range* of unity begins with strictly interdenominational relationships within *one* religious tradition (for example, Protestantism or Buddhism) and moves to a theoretical "outer limit" of interfaith or interworld view encounters such as the Christian–communist or the believer–unbeliever.

The causes of ecumenical trends have been widely discussed and catalogued by sociologists. Peter Berger professes skepticism regarding any theological explanation for ecumenical interchange, labeling it as "an *ex post facto* ideological legitimation of a process of cooperation with appreciably more

The extent of interreligious unity		Interdenominational			
		I	II	III	IV
Integration	5	Various Protestant unions			
Federation	4	National and World Councils of Churches			
Cooperation	3	World Fellowship of Buddhists	Various actions of Vatican II		
Conversation	2			Encounter of world religions	Christian- communist dialogue
Toleration	1				

FIGURE 4

Ecumenism defined as a variable. (Reprinted with permission of Macmillan Publishing Co., Inc., from *The Scientific Study of Religion* by J. Milton Yinger. Copyright 1970 by J. Milton Yinger.)

mundane roots."[1] The mundane roots reveal themselves as the increasing homogeneity of Protestantism's (one must add "white") chief "consumers," Mr. and Mrs. Suburban America. Relatively highly literate, mobile, and selective, they will exhibit expectations regarding choice of church which have little to do with traditional denominational loyalties and their accompanying theologies. Church switching among Protestants, especially those who move frequently, is a well-known phenomenon. Second, a sheer rise in financial costs of "every conceivable aspect of church activity, from ministers' salaries to kneeling benches,"[2] and particularly building costs encourages cooperation as an economic "must." Third, the investment policies of denominational bureaucracies, calculated to give them a relative independence from "the ongoing contributions of a frequently reluctant membership,"[3] suggest rational planning in which interdenominational cooperation is an obvious advantage. Berger adds to this analysis a limiting factor: Borrowing again from the economics of cartels, he notes an increasing doctrinal similarity between Protestant denominations. Yet to admit this standardization would involve the denominations singly in "economic bankruptcy." To survive, therefore, involves degrees of "product differentiation" in terms of denominational distinctiveness—a factor that sets some limits on the extent and range of merging.

J. Milton Yinger agrees that "mobility and suburbanization have sharply reduced the sense of denominationalism for many Protestants"[4] but notes that not all who are a part of these changes are equally apt to favor church unity. "The strength of attachment to a traditional group doubtless varies with normal socialization, some people being taught that membership in a particular church is vital, others being taught that many groups offer roads to salvation that are about equally acceptable."[5]

The complicated question of religioethnic membership as a source of American identity has been discussed in Will Herberg's sociological classic, *Protestant, Catholic, Jew*. In an often-quoted passage, Herberg sums up a principal thesis of the book:

> It seems to me that a realistic appraisal of the values, ideas, and behavior of the American people leads to the conclusion that Americans, by and large, do have their "common religion" and that that "religion" is the system familiarly known as the American Way of Life. It is the American Way of Life that supplies American society with an "overarching sense of unity" amid conflict. It is the American Way of Life about which Americans are admittedly and unashamedly "intolerant." It is the American Way of Life that provides the framework in terms of which the crucial values of American existence are couched. By every realistic criterion the American Way of Life is the operative faith of the American people.[6]

Religion then, conceived as this "American Way of Life" is the philosophy or, in Bellah's terms (see Reading 4), the "civil religion" which Americans unitedly confess. They remain *divided*, however, along the conventional lines, *Protestant, Catholic, Jewish*.

James R. Kelly's "Attitudes Toward Ecumenism" is one of the first pieces of survey research bearing on the views of rank-and-file church members, of all three major faiths, concerning ecumenical merger. As Kelly observes, it has been assumed that only church officialdom really cares about merger. The laity are thought to be indifferent or negative.

Mueller's very comprehensive research searchingly examines the Herberg thesis and concludes that a *new* triple melting pot must be considered. "Protestants and Catholics appear to be fusing into a single white Christian group, while the Jews and the Nones form a white non-Christian cluster and the blacks a third group." Mueller's scanning of five major institutional areas—marriage, friendship, residence, occupations, and politics—makes this an unusually stimulating article with implications considerably beyond those of the older Herberg thesis.

NOTES

[1] PETER BERGER, "A Market Model for the Analysis of Ecumenicity," in *American as Mosaic: Social Patterns of Religion in the United States*, ed. Phillip E. Hammond and Benton Johnson (New York: Random House, 1970), p. 180.

[2] Ibid., p. 181.

[3] Ibid., p. 182.

[4] J. MILTON YINGER, op. cit., p. 248.

[5] Ibid., p. 249.

[6] WILL HERBERG, *Protestant, Catholic, Jew* (Garden City, N.Y.: Doubleday, 1960), p. 75.

ATTITUDES TOWARD ECUMENISM:
AN EMPIRICAL INVESTIGATION

JAMES R. KELLY

Although ecumenism is thought to be one of the significant currents in contemporary religion there is not much information about how much grass roots support there is for the movement, nor, an even more fundamental question, how the laity define and evaluate the ecumenical movement. The sociologist Bryan Wilson has suggested that support for the ecumenical movement is limited to the professional clergy.[1] Indeed it seems that even among religious elites there has been an erosion of interest in structural aspects of ecumenism. The Lutheran church historian Jaroslav Pelikan has been quoted as saying that the fundamental question facing Christians is not when or how they should unite but why bother to unite at all?[2] For some, secular ecumenism, the cooperation of the churches on moral and civic problems, is a sufficient goal for the ecumenical movement. To adherents of secularization theology questions of church mergers appear intramural and defensive.[3] The feeling that questions of church union are irrelevant to the larger concerns of contemporary life has been acknowledged even by persons connected with the official life of the churches:

> It seems to many, inside and outside the church, that the struggle for Christian unity in its present form is irrelevant to the immediate crisis of our times. The Church, they say, should seek its unity through solidarity with those forces in modern life, such as the struggle for racial equality, which are drawing men more closely together, and should give up its concern with patching up its own internal disputes.[4]

At least two general questions, then, seem crucial for an understanding of the ecumenical movement. How do the laity define the ecumenical movement and how much membership interest does ecumenism command? The data relevant to the questions of lay definition and evaluation of ecumenism were gathered between the months of May and August in 1968 by the method of mailed questionnaires sent to a randomly selected 25 percent of

From James R. Kelly, "Attitudes Toward Ecumenism: An Empirical Investigation," *Journal of Ecumenical Studies* 9, no. 2 (Spring 1972): 341–351.

James R. Kelly is a member of the Sociology Department at Fordham University in New York.

the adult membership of all the churches in Lexington, Massachusetts. The religious congregations included in the survey are two Roman Catholic parishes, five Protestant congregations (Baptist, Episcopal, Methodist, and two Congregational churches), four Protestant sects, two Unitarian-Universalist churches, and two Jewish synagogues. Sixty-four percent of all subjects selected for the study returned a questionnaire.[5]

DEFINITIONS OF ECUMENISM

Ecumenism is not a univocal term. There is a tendency to label indiscriminately all non-hostile relationships among the churches as ecumenical. Indeed, there are many possible levels of non-conflict relationship among churches, ranging from practical cooperation to full organic unity. Of course, not all Protestant churches accept the position that fidelity to Christianity requires the union of all Christian churches. The self-definition of numerous sects and most Baptist congregations is that local church authority is inalienable and final. Many of the theologians of the main line Protestant churches, however, write that fidelity to the Christian message requires the visible unity of the Christian churches. And since the Second Vatican Council many Protestant authors feel that a Protestant–Catholic union is a future possibility:

> Thus the ecumenical future, on the basis of the ecumenism decree, is an open future. What direction the future takes depends not only on what Catholics do with the decree, but on how Protestants respond to it as well.[6]

Most authors who see one aim of ecumenism as the union of Protestant, Catholic and Eastern Orthodox churches do so not on the basis of a present doctrinal or ecclesial similarity, but in terms of an eventual convergence, a growing together of the churches through a dialogue which will produce a blend of agreement on essentials with liberty on non-essentials. The convergence theory is held by many ecumenists.[7] Let us see if one part of the theory—the growing similarity of Protestant and Catholic beliefs—is also held by the laity. The respondents were asked to agree or disagree with the statement "It seems to me that Protestants and Catholics are becoming more and more alike in their religious beliefs and practices." The responses are given in the following table [Table 13].

With the exception of the Jews (a third of whom say they do not know) the majority of each congregation accepts the convergence theory of Protestant–Catholic doctrinal development. Roman Catholics and Protestants are especially likely to accept this theory, more than three-quarters of both groups agreeing that their respective beliefs and practices are becoming more and more alike. Sect members are almost equally divided on the question, and Unitarians generally agree with the theory but not with the same frequency as Catholics and Protestants.

TABLE 13

Protestants and Catholics Are Becoming More and More Alike
in Their Religious Beliefs and Practices

	BAPTIST	EPIS.	METH.	CONGREG.	TOTAL PROTES- TANT	CATHOLIC
Agree	67%	83	64	76	76	80
Disagree	27	13	23	16	17	15
Neither	5	4	13	7	7	5
number	67	131	53	243	494	357

		SECTS	UNITARIAN	JEWISH	TOTAL
Agree		51%	59	40	70
Disagree		47	27	28	20
Neither		2	14	32	10
number		50	139	115	1155
missing units					8

THE POSSIBILITY OF A FUTURE
PROTESTANT–CATHOLIC–ORTHODOX UNION

The great majority of Protestants and Catholics accept one part of the convergence theory, the growing similarity of Protestant and Catholic beliefs. Let us now examine the second part of the theory, namely that at some future date the convergence of Protestant and Catholic beliefs will allow these churches to unite. The respondents were asked to agree or disagree with the statement "Unity among Protestant, Roman Catholic, and Eastern Orthodox churches will always prove to be impossible" [Table 14].

A future union among Protestant, Catholic, and Eastern Orthodox churches is seen as impossible by the great majority of sect members (72%) and by a slight majority of Unitarians (54%) and Jews (54%). Protestants indicate uncertainty on the question. A sizeable plurality (48%) feel that such a union will always prove to be impossible, but the majority of Protestants express either uncertainty (22%) about the possibility of a Protestant–Catholic–Orthodox union, or think it possible (30%).

The Roman Catholic response differs considerably from that of all other groups. Only 30 percent feel that a union of their church with Protestant and Eastern Orthodox churches will always prove to be impossible. The majority of Catholics either feel that such a union is possible (48%) or are uncertain (22%) as to its possibility.

TABLE 14

Unity Among Protestant, Roman Catholic, and Eastern Orthodox Churches
Will Always Prove to Be Impossible

	BAPTIST	EPIS.	METH.	CONGREG.	TOTAL PROTES-TANT	CATHOLIC
Disagree	19%	33	32	30	30	48
Agree	64	43	47	48	48	30
Don't know	17	24	21	22	22	22
number	65	127	47	221	460	329
missing	2	5	6	24	37	28

	SECTS	UNITARIAN	JEWS	TOTAL
Disagree	22%	23	12	31
Agree	72	54	54	45
Don't know	6	23	34	24
number	47	134	104	1074
missing	3	8	9	89

REACTIONS TO PROTESTANT UNION

As we have seen, most Catholics feel that Protestant–Catholic beliefs are converging, and that a future Protestant–Catholic union is possible. Most Protestants also think that Protestant and Catholic beliefs are converging, but there is great variation among Protestants as to whether a future Protestant, Catholic, Eastern Orthodox union is possible. A sizeable minority (48%) think that such a union is impossible, but the majority are either uncertain (22%) or think it possible (30%).

When asked "How much difference would it make to you if most of the Protestant denominations united to form one church?" only sect members generally said they disliked this possibility.

As Table 15 shows, Jews (73%) and Catholics (51%) generally do not have strong feelings about a united Protestantism, most saying that they would not care if most Protestant churches united. Unitarians are also generally unconcerned about the prospect of Protestant unity, only 32 percent disliking the notion, but only 28 percent liking it. Protestants themselves would like to see a united Protestantism, 51 percent saying they like the idea and only 26 percent disliking it.

The Jewish and Catholic responses are interesting. First of all, Jews and Catholics do not appear to fear a united Protestantism. In more polemical times the possibility of a united Protestantism might have been viewed as a possible threat to either Jewish or Catholic interests. Indeed,

TABLE 15

How Much Difference Would It Make to You if Most of the Protestant
Denominations United to Form One Church?

	BAPTIST	EPIS.	METH.	CONGREG.	TOTAL PROTESTANT	CATHOLIC
Would like this	56%	47	58	49	51	45
Would dislike this	27	36	12	23	26	4
Would not care	17	17	30	27	23	51
number	66	129	50	233	478	344
missing	1	3	3	12	19	13

	SECTS	UNITARIAN	JEWS	TOTAL
Would like this	30%	28	7	41
Would dislike this	57	32	19	21
Would not care	13	41	73	38
number	47	138	109	1116
missing	3	4	8	47

in an earlier period some Protestants advocated a united Protestantism precisely to better protect Protestant interests against a growing Catholic power.[8]
Presently, however, Catholic and Jewish respondents do not appear to think
that a united Protestantism would be injurious to their interests.

The large percentage of Catholics (45%) expressing a liking for intra-
Protestant unity is interesting. A possible explanation of this statistic is that
a large percentage of Catholics view the uniting of Protestant churches as
a first step toward the uniting of Protestantism and Catholicism.

REACTIONS TOWARD A UNITED CHRISTIANITY

When asked "How much difference would it make to you if, sometime
in the future, the Protestant, Roman Catholic, and Eastern Orthodox churches
united to form one church?" the responses were as follows [Table 16]:

Roman Catholic respondents show a decided desire for a future union of
Protestant, Catholic, and Orthodox churches, 69 percent saying that they
would like an eventual union. The Protestant response is less clear cut. A
plurality (46%) say they would like an eventual union among the churches,
but a sizeable minority (35%) say they would dislike this.

Interestingly enough, the Protestant reaction to the possibility of a Protestant,
Catholic, Orthodox union is similar to their reaction toward a union among
most Protestant churches [Table 17]:

TABLE 16

How Much Difference Would It Make to You If, Sometime in the Future,
The Protestant, Roman Catholic, and Eastern Orthodox Churches United
to Form One Church?

	BAPTIST	EPIS.	METH.	CONGREG.	TOTAL PROTES- TANT	CATHOLIC
Would like this	42%	49	48	46	46	69
Would dislike this	48	31	33	33	35	16
Would not care	9	20	19	21	19	15
number	66	127	52	228	473	342
missing	1	5	1	17	24	15

	SECTS	UNITARIAN	JEWS	TOTAL
Would like this	20%	24	7	46
Would dislike this	71	46	39	32
Would not care	9	30	55	22
number	45	134	107	1101
missing	5	8	10	62

In fact, those Protestants who say they would like a union among most
Protestant churches are also the ones who favor a united Christianity. 79
percent of the Protestants favoring a united Protestantism also favor a
united Christianity. As Table 18 shows, Protestants who find the notion of
a united Protestantism attractive also feel the same way about a united
Christianity. Apparently a united Protestantism is not viewed by Protestants
as a union against the threat of Catholicism or closed to a possible union
of these two faiths.

Just as Protestants who desire a united Protestantism generally also favor
a united Christianity, most Catholics favoring a united Christianity also
favor a united Protestantism.

As Table 19 shows, 63 percent of the Catholics favoring a Protestant–
Catholic–Orthodox union also favor a union among most Protestant churches.

TABLE 17

PROTESTANTS	UNION AMONG MOST PROTESTANT CHURCHES	PROTESTANT, CATHOLIC, EASTERN ORTHODOX UNION
Like	51%	46%
Dislike	26	35
Don't care	23	19
number	478	473

TABLE 18

(n: 234)

PROTESTANTS LIKING A UNION AMONG MOST PROTESTANT CHURCHES

Also Liking a Union Among Protestant, Catholic, and Eastern Orthodox Churches	Not Caring	Disliking a Union Among Protestant, Catholic, and Eastern Orthodox Churches
79%	5%	16%

Only 4 percent of the Catholics favoring a united Christianity say they would dislike a united Protestantism.

In brief, the ecumenical movement appears to be of one piece. There is no ecumenical double standard. As we saw earlier, there are few Protestants (16%) who define ecumenism solely in terms of a united Protestantism. Likewise, Catholics generally react to the phenomenon in a consistent fashion, favoring ecumenism whether it be a united Protestantism or a united Christianity.

As we have seen, most Catholics and a plurality of Protestants say they like the idea of an eventual union of Protestant, Catholic, and Eastern Orthodox churches. Of the other religious congregations, only sect members show a dislike for the notion, 71 percent saying they would not like a united Christianity. A sizeable minority of Unitarians (46%) and Jews (39%) also dislike the possibility of a Protestant–Catholic union. But interestingly enough, the majority of Jews (55%) say they do not care. Jewish respondents do not appear to perceive a united Christianity as a danger to the religious or political interests of the Jewish community.

PERCEIVED MEMBERSHIP INTEREST IN OFFICIAL ECUMENICAL DISCUSSIONS

Respondents were asked to agree or disagree with the following two statements concerning officially sponsored ecumenical discussions: "Discussions on Protestant Church unity are of interest only to certain church officials. Most church

TABLE 19

(n: 228)

CATHOLICS LIKING A CATHOLIC–PROTESTANT–ORTHODOX UNION

Also Liking a Union Among Most Protestant Churches	Not Caring	Disliking a Union Among Most Protestant Churches
63%	33%	4%

members are not enthusiastic about them." And "Discussions among Protestants, Catholics, and Eastern Orthodox churches about a future union are of interest only to certain church officials. Most church members are not enthusiastic about them."

Some writers have argued that the ecumenical movement does not exist at the grass roots level and that the movement receives its support primarily from church officials. A leading proponent of this hypothesis is the sociologist Bryan Wilson who argues that since religion in general is on the wane, ecumenism in particular can have little support among the laity.[9] As Tables 20 and 21 show, only about 25 percent of all respondents accept Wilson's

TABLE 20

Discussions on Protestant Church Unity Are of Interest Only to Certain Church Officials. Most Church Members Are Not Enthusiastic About Them.

	BAPTIST	EPIS.	METH.	CONGREG.	TOTAL PROTES-TANT	CATHOLIC
Disagree	41%	50	39	46	46	52
Agree	46	26	26	30	31	18
Don't know	13	24	35	24	23	30
number	63	126	49	215	453	314
missing	4	6	4	30	44	43

	SECTS	UNITARIAN	JEWS	TOTAL
Disagree	44%	41	26	45
Agree	44	23	18	25
Don't know	11	36	56	30
number	47	130	104	1049
missing	3	12	13	125

hypothesis. Most Catholics feel that there is grass roots support both for discussions about Protestant unity (52%) and Christian unity (62%). A majority of Protestants say there is grass roots interest in Christian unity discussions, and a plurality (46%) feel the same way about Protestant unity discussions. Only a minority of Catholics (about 20%) and Protestants (about 30%) agree that most church members lacked an interest in either kind of discussion.

Jewish respondents generally say they do not know whether there is grass roots interest in official ecumenical discussions, sect members are about equally divided on the question, and Unitarians show some variation, although over 40 percent feel that there is membership interest in these discussions.

TABLE 21

Discussions Among Protestant, Catholic, and Eastern Orthodox Churches About a Future Union Are of Interest Only to Certain Church Officials. Most Church Members Are Not Enthusiastic About Them.

	BAPTIST	EPIS.	METH.	CONGREG.	TOTAL PROTES-TANT	CATHOLIC
Disagree	54%	51	39	52	51	62
Agree	38	26	28	30	30	21
Don't know	8	23	33	18	19	17
number	63	124	49	219	455	328
missing	4	8	4	26	42	29

	SECTS	UNITARIAN	JEWS	TOTAL
Disagree	47%	44	27	51
Agree	44	26	18	26
Don't know	9	30	55	23
number	47	130	104	1064
missing	3	12	13	99

CONCLUSION

Most respondents feel that Protestant and Catholic beliefs and practices are becoming increasingly alike, and Protestants and Catholics are especially likely to feel that their respective beliefs are converging. There is less agreement, however, that this convergence will lead to an organizational union among these churches. A moderate minority of Catholics (30%) and a sizeable minority of Protestants (48%) feel that a union among Protestant–Catholic–Orthodox churches will always prove to be impossible. But the majority of Catholics and Protestants either believe that such a union is possible or express uncertainty on the question.

Although a majority of Protestants favor a united Protestantism, very few Protestants endorse a pan-Protestantism as a suitable goal of the ecumenical movement. Most Protestants favoring Protestant unity also favor an eventual union with the Catholic and Orthodox churches.

Finally, most Protestants and Catholics feel that there is grass roots support for both intra-Protestant and Protestant–Catholic unity discussions.

NOTES

[1] BRYAN WILSON, *Religion In Secular Society* (London: Watts, 1966), p. 129.

[2] *Newsweek*, Feb. 5, 1968, p. 83.

[3] ROBERT L. RICHARD, *Secularization Theology* (New York: Herder and Herder, 1967), pp. 179–180.

[4] From a report of Section 1 to the Uppsala Assembly of the World Council of Churches.

[5] This is a high response rate for mailed questionnaire studies. Lexington is a low density, residential suburban community of 31,500 people. The respondents are primarily middle and upper middle class. A study of ecumenism in other areas might yield results which differ from the following. See the author's "Attitudes Toward Ecumenism In A New England Suburb," unpublished thesis, Department of Social Relations, Harvard University, 1970.

[6] ROBERT MCAFEE BROWN, *The Ecumenical Revolution* (New York: Doubleday, 1967), p. 207.

[7] For example, see WALTER MARSHALL HORTON, *Toward A Reborn Church* (New York: Harper & Row, 1949); DOUGLAS HORTON, *Toward An Undivided Church* (New York: Association Press, 1967); PETER DAY, *Tomorrow's Church* (New York: The Seabury Press, 1969); AVERY DULLES, "Dogma As An Ecumenical Problem," *Theological Studies* 29 (Sept., 1968).

It is significant to note that the delegates to the *Consultation On Church Union*, merger discussions among nine Protestant denominations with a combined membership of about 24 million, agreed that the proposed church should not be named the "United Protestant Church" because this name would not indicate the delegates' desire to seek future alliances with the Eastern Orthodox or Roman Catholic Churches. See "9 Groups Ponder Church of Future," *New York Times* (March 21, 1969).

[8] "The denominational system robs Protestantism of its inherent strength in its inescapable competition with a formidable and aggressive Roman Catholicism." CHARLES CLAYTON MORRISON, *The Unfinished Reformation* (New York: Harper & Row, 1953), p. 35.

[9] WILSON, op. cit., p. 77.

✣

✣✣✣

THE NEW TRIPLE MELTING POT:
HERBERG REVISITED

SAMUEL A. MUELLER

One of the best-known books ever written about religion in America is Herberg's *Protestant, Catholic, Jew* (1955; rev. ed., 1960). Starting from a review of this nation's immigrant history, Herberg analyzes the process of religious change in this country from the standpoint of ethnic assimilation. His argument, later echoed by Gordon (1964), is two-pronged. First, Herberg argues, religious boundary lines have replaced national origin lines as the significant form of ethnic differentiation among whites in American society. Social interaction tends to be confined to one's own religious group, and there are only three religious groupings that are important to consider in this way—the three that form the title of his book.

Herberg's second major thesis concerns the way American society has solved the problem of religious pluralism. (For good theoretical treatments of the sociological problems created by religious pluralism, see Lenski, 1965; and Yinger, 1970. Descriptive materials about religious pluralism in other societies are presented for Lebanon by Gulick, 1965; for the Netherlands by Moberg, 1961; and Lijphart, 1968.) Taking the Durkheimian stance that all societies must have some religious base to continue to exist, Herberg (1960) distinguishes between the formal religious structure of a society (the Church or the churches) and the society's operative religion, the set of beliefs and practices that actually perform the Durkheimian task of societal integration.

Herberg's (1960: 78–79) second thesis is that the problems created by religious pluralism have been resolved in this country by robbing all of the various churches of their distinctive historical emphases, replacing them with a vague kind of ideology he calls the "American Way of Life," a diffuse faith and trust in the peculiarly American concepts of democracy and free enterprise. Thus, Herberg concludes, while Americans are interactionally *divided* along religious lines, they are *united* in their acceptance of the tenets of the "American Way of Life" as the basic set of social values necessary for the operation of society.

From *Review of Religious Research*, Fall 1971. Reprinted with the permission of the author and the publisher.

Samuel A. Mueller is a member of the Sociology Department at the University of Akron, Ohio.

. . .

I have evaluated Herberg's (1960) second major thesis in other places (Mueller, 1970: Chs. 3–5; Mueller and Sween, 1969), with the essential conclusion that only the white Christians accept the American Way of Life. White non-Christians (a conglomerate of the Jews and the religious Nones) and the blacks do not share this set of beliefs. The purpose of this article is to provide a systematic evaluation and updating of the evidence relevant to Herberg's first thesis, that Americans are interactionally divided along religious (and racial) lines. Thus, we shall examine the strengths of three religio-ethnic boundary lines, those between white Protestants and white Catholics, between Jews and Gentiles (among whites), and between whites and blacks.[1] These boundaries will be assessed in each of five institutional areas—marriage, friendship, residence, occupations, and politics [Editor's note: This paragraph, not in the original article, was inserted at the request of the author.]

INTERMARRIAGE

The prime empirical basis for Herberg's (1960) hypothesis concerning the interactional separation of American religious groups was the data presented by Kennedy (1944, 1952) in her articles on mate selection in New Haven. She showed that national origin lines within religious categories were fading, but that religion was a powerful social divider. Many other studies (e.g., Hollingshead, 1950; Greeley, 1970) have made the point that religion is a potent factor in mate selection. The most thoroughly analyzed set of data on the topic was collected in the ill-fated Current Population Survey (CPS) on religion in 1957. (See Winch, 1963:327–33; and Glick, 1960, for discussions of these data.) Yinger (1968) has examined these data with great care, and after making several adjustments on them, has come to the conclusion that the number of couples who were of different religious backgrounds—using the gross Protestant–Catholic–Jewish categorization—*at the time of marriage* is much larger than the CPS data would indicate at first glance.

The adjustments that Yinger (1968) made, however, do not take into account several important factors. First, the CPS data are not controlled for race, which is highly confounded with religion and which is a very strong social divider. Secondly, the CPS data refer to all marriages in existence in 1957, and some of these had undoubtedly passed their golden anniversaries. If any assimilative trend at all exists, the amount of intermarriage occurring among couples who became married in 1957 would be above the same figure for all marriages then in existence.

Reiss (1965) assembled a time series of data on the intermarriage of Catholics in the United States from 1943 to 1962, and Wagner (1970) updated Reiss' figures for 1967 and 1969. The source of their data is the *Official Cath-*

olic Directory, which gives the number of *valid* (performed by a priest) Catholic marriages which involve a non-Catholic (who is almost necessarily a Protestant, given the religious composition of American society). While this figure is obviously less than the total number of marriages involving both a Catholic and a non-Catholic, Burchinal and associates (1962) report high correlations between these data and official state data in Iowa, one of but two states in which marriage license applications include religious preference.

Heer (1962) assembled a similar data series for Canada from 1927 to 1957, and Wagner (1970) updated these figures for 1962 and 1965, the last year for which data were available. These data are based on official Canadian government records and are undoubtedly of higher quality than the *Catholic Directory* data. Both the Canadian and American Catholic series are presented in Table 22. All of the intermarriage rates are "group" rates; i.e., they refer to the percentage of marriages of members of a religious group which involve a member of another (Rodman, 1965).

Except between 1943 and 1947, the series for Canadian and American Catholics parallel each other; this fact increases our confidence in the rather crude American data. Both Catholic series seem to be on plateaus from the end of World War II until the early 1960s. Since that time, however, there has been a sharp upturn in the amount of religious intermarriage in both countries. Wagner (1970) argues that this upturn is a consequence of Vatican II, and while it would take other data to support that hypothesis, it is certainly plausible.

The Jewish–Gentile boundary in mate selection is a very strong one. Every study that gives an estimate of the rate of Jewish exogamy that can be compared to those of Protestants and Catholics shows that the Jewish rate is the lowest of the three. There is, however, some evidence that the rate of Jewish exogamy is increasing (Kennedy, 1952; Rosenthal, 1963). There is clearly an increased acceptance of intermarriage among third- and fourth-generation Jews in "Lakeville" (Highland Park, Illinois—an upper-income suburb of Chicago) compared to the first two generations (Sklare and Greenblum, 1967:310). On the Gentile side of the ledger, Stember (1966:104–107) has analyzed public opinion poll data on the question of Jewish–Gentile intermarriage. Among Christians, the percentage responding that they "definitely would not" marry a Jew fell from 57 in 1950 to 37 in 1962. Thus, while the Jewish–Gentile boundary line in mate selection is still strong, it appears to be in the process of weakening.

But if Jewish–Gentile intermarriage in this country is still uncommon, black–white intermarriage is almost nonexistent. Heer (1965) argues on the basis of the sparse official data that exist on this topic that the general trend is upward. The upward trend, however, has not progressed very far, nor is the slope of the trend line very sharp. By extrapolating the available trend data under twelve sets of assumptions, Heer (1965) found that under the most liberal set of assumptions amalgamation would occur in about thirteen generations, or 350

TABLE 22

Group Rates of Intermarriage in Canada and the United States

| | CANADA | | | U.S.A. |
YEAR	PROTESTANT	JEWISH	CATHOLIC	CATHOLIC
1927	9.5%	5.8%	13.5%	
1932	12.5	5.4	17.2	
1937	12.7	5.2	15.4	
1942	15.2	9.3	20.0	
1943				31.7%
1944				30.8
1945				31.0
1946				28.9
1947	16.7	8.4	20.0	26.9
1948				27.0
1949				26.2
1950				27.6
1951				26.1
1952	19.1	11.1	20.5	27.1
1953				27.5
1954				26.4
1955				27.1
1956				27.3
1957	20.7	12.7	20.6	26.9
1958				27.0
1959				27.6
1960				27.3
1961				27.3
1962	23.6	14.3	20.8	28.1
1965	26.8	14.4	23.2	
1967				32.8
1969				33.8

Sources: Heer (1962); Reiss (1965); Wagner (1970); Heer's (1962) "individual" rates have been transformed to "group" rates (Rodman, 1965).

years. Under the most conservative set of assumptions, amalgamation would not have occurred after 1000 generations, or about 27,000 years. Thus, the slope of the trend line is near zero.

The available intermarriage data, crude as they are, can be used to make a direct comparison of the strengths of the boundary lines. To do this, one first computes the number of intermarriages he would anticipate on the basis of chance. This figure can then be used as the divisor for the actual number of intermarriages in a percentage calculation. Using Wagner's (1970) latest figures and adjusting them to reflect all Protestant–Catholic intermarriages

(Yinger, 1968; Reiss, 1965), the number of marriages between Protestants and Catholics approaches half of its random expectation, given the marginal distribution of religious preference in this country. Adjusting the data further for race and other factors raises this parameter to approximately 55 per cent, and possibly higher than that.[2] By contrast, the parameter calculated for Jewish–Gentile intermarriage from the 1957 CPS survey was only about 12 per cent of random expectation. Finally, using Heer's (1965) latest data from Michigan as an empirical base, the number of marriages that cross the black–white line is less than one per cent of random expectation.

FRIENDSHIP PATTERNS

The formation of friendship bonds across ethnic lines has not been investigated as often or as thoroughly as the process of mate selection. This is unfortunate, since friendship, being a much less permanent and free-floating structure than marriage, may actually be a more sensitive indicator of ethnic cleavage.

Lenski (1961:37) used close friendship as one of the components of his index of "religious communalism," the degree to which an individual's primary relationships are confined to members of his own religious group. He characterized the strength of the communal bonds in each of the four major religious groups in his Detroit study as "strong" for Jews and Negroes and "medium" for white Catholics and white Protestants.

Greeley's (1962) case study of a community in Chicago at about the time of Lenski's research in Detroit provides further evidence of a deep Protestant–Catholic cleavage in an upper-middle class community. While Greeley (1962) uses the fictitious name of "Westwood," it quickly becomes obvious that the data are drawn from Beverly, the highest income area within the city limits of Chicago (Kitagawa and Taeuber, 1963: 3–5). This semi-suburban community is roughly half Catholic and half Protestant, and Greeley shows that there is virtually no interaction of a primary nature across this religious line.

Greeley's (1962) most convincing evidence comes from an analysis of interaction patterns on the golf course at the local country club, the religious composition of which matches that of the community as a whole. Greeley (1962: 54–55) examined the starting sheets for the golf course during July, 1950. During that month, 2,408 rounds of golf were played, 1,293 by Catholics and 1,115 by Protestants. When the religious composition of the twosomes, threesomes, and foursomes that played golf together was examined, however, the picture changed radically. Almost all the groups were either *all*-Catholic or *all*-Protestant. Two-thirds of the religious mixing that did occur on the links could be attributed to a total of seven men.

Both Lenski's (1961) and Greeley's (1962) data, however, refer to the 1950s. A later comparison can be drawn from the work of Laumann (1969), based on 1966 interviews in the Detroit metropolitan area. Since Laumann (1969) used a technique of multidimensional scaling to analyze his data, exact comparisons between his research and Lenski's (1961) are impossible to draw, but several points may be noted. First, Laumann did find a significant Protestant–Catholic cleavage in terms of friendship relations in Detroit, but he was quick to point out (1969:188) that this factor alone yielded a very poor description of friendship patterns. At least two more factors were necessary— social status and a "liturgical" factor. The failure of the Protestant–Catholic cleavage to describe the patterns adequately, together with the emergence of the other two factors as secondary bases of friendship interaction, gives credence to the view that there was some degree of closure between Detroit Protestants and Catholics during the period between Lenski's (1961) and Laumann's (1969) studies.

Both Lenski (1961) and Laumann (1969) would agree that the Jews—and in Laumann's case, the religious "Nones"—are still far removed from both the Protestants and the Catholics in terms of friendship interaction. Stember (1966:99–102) has analyzed public opinion poll data on Jewish–Gentile friendship relations between 1938 and 1962. The data on this aspect of inter-ethnic contact are not conclusive, but Stember does surmise that ". . . it seems reasonable to assume that the proportion [of the Gentile population having close contact with Jews today] is considerably greater than it was a few decades ago." Stember (1966:107) also documents similar trends in terms of the degree of isolation of Jews from Gentiles in several other areas of life, including intermarriage, neighboring, and admittance to colleges and employment. But while these trend lines exist, data from Stember (1966), Laumann (1969), and others (especially Baltzell, 1964) would indicate that the Jewish–Gentile cleavage is still much deeper than the Protestant–Catholic cleavage.

Lenski (1961) characterized the black Protestants as being strongly enclosed within their own communal boundaries. This brief treatment of the issue is one of the very few pieces of sociological literature in which friendship patterns across racial lines have been formally investigated. Social distance data (Bogardus, 1958) indicate that blacks are the farthest removed of all ethnic categories from white Protestants, and that there has not been much movement over a span of several decades.

The best recent study of black–white interaction on a personal level (Molotch, 1969) is about South Shore, a residentially integrated community in Chicago. Despite the fact of residential integration, interpersonal contact across the racial barrier is confined to the most formal of settings, such as commercial establishments. Even in such cases, the clientele of most stores is racially selective. Suttles (1968) reaches a similar conclusion in his study of Chicago's Near West Side.

Another locus of close personal interaction is the voluntary association. Only churches have been studied in sufficient detail to warrant discussion here. Loescher (1948: 76–78), writing about Protestant churches, estimated that only about 500,000 of the 8,000,000 Negroes in the country at the time were members of predominantly white denominations, and most of these were gathered into segregated congregations. In 1946, the number of Negroes who were actually worshiping with whites in Protestant sanctuaries was only about 8,000, or about 0.1 per cent of all Negroes in the United States.

Reimers (1965:178) updated Loescher's (1948) figures through 1964. About 10 per cent of the congregations in predominantly white Protestant denominations had Negroes worshiping with whites, although the integration was, in most cases, no more than token. (See Molotch, 1969:886–88, for some data on the churches of South Shore.) Reimers (1965) estimated the total number of integrated Negro worshippers as no more than one per cent of all Negroes in the United States, up only slightly from the 1946 figure.

Lamanna and Coakley (1969) present Catholic data on the same issue. While there are relatively few black Catholics in the United States, they are more integrated into white parishes than are their Protestant counterparts. As early as 1928, 46 per cent of 200,000 Negro Catholics in the United States were worshiping with whites, and the number of black Catholics since that time has been rising faster than the number of all-black parishes (Lamanna and Coakley, 1969:153, 171).

Both the Protestant and Catholic trends in this area, then, are in the direction of assimilation of the blacks, but neither slope is very steep. It is possible to argue that the ecclesiastical segregation of blacks is due to their residential segregation (see below), but works like Clark's (1965) indicate otherwise. Pope (1957:104–105) argues, however, that the churches actually have a better record on this topic than most voluntary organizations in this country. His point is underscored by a resolution of the national convention of the Elks Lodge in 1969, in which the Elks reaffirmed their traditional policy of refusing membership to Negroes (reported in the Chicago *Sun-Times*, August 4, 1969). Additional data on the exclusion of blacks and other ethnic minorities from voluntary organizations and leisure-time activities are given in Baltzell (1964:357) and *Rights Magazine* (1962).

RESIDENTIAL SEGREGATION

The specialization of residential areas has long been a major concern of urban sociologists, and sociologists have paid attention to each of the ethnic boundary lines under discussion in this paper. Greeley (1962) and Lenski (1961:69–73) found mild degrees of separation of the residences of Catholics and Protestants, but in neither case could this pattern be termed discrimination. Helper (1969: 282) cites realty industry sources to the effect that Christians—a term including Catholics—were acceptable in all parts of Chicago, while Jews were not. Within recent times, then, Catholics have not been the objects of discriminatory real estate practices.

This conclusion accords with Cowgill's (1960) study of Wichita, the only city for which detailed information on intra-Christian segregation patterns exists. The Catholics were the least segregated religious groups in the city. Protestant denominations were segregated from each other, the pattern of segregation following the familiar class structure of Protestant denominations (Gockel, 1969). Catholics—the largest single denomination—were spread throughout the status structure of the city and were thus integrated with Protestants. Upper-class Catholics, however, were likely to live next door to a different kind of Protestant from their lower-class co-religionists.

Cowgill (1960) found that Wichita's small group of Jews was concentrated into a single neighborhood. Goldstein and Goldscheider's (1968:46–49) study of the Jewish population of Providence, R.I., is further evidence. In that metropolitan area, Jews constituted 35 to 50 per cent of the population in four contiguous census tracts. Of the remaining 102 tracts, Jews accounted for as much as 10 per cent of the population in only six, and less than 2 per cent in 83 tracts. Jews comprised 4 per cent of the population of the metropolitan area.

There is evidence (Goldstein and Goldscheider, 1968) that large numbers of Jews have migrated to Providence's suburbs since World War II, and that they are dispersing through the Gentile population. Providence may be different from other cities in this respect. Mueller (1966:143) notes that the suburbanization of Jews around Chicago has been destined for a very few small areas in which Jews constitute the bulk of the population, and Clark (1966: 99–100) makes the same point about Toronto, the most "American" of Canadian cities. Thus, while legal barriers to the residential integration of Jews are dead (Helper, 1969:282), and while Gentile attitudinal barriers are dying (Stember, 1966:95–98), there appears to be no major influx of Jews into Gentile areas at the present.

In their definitive study of patterns and trends in the residential segregation of Negroes from whites, the Taeubers (1965) find virtually total segregation. The index of dissimilarity (computed on a block basis) between Negro and white residences typically ranges around 90, meaning that 90 per cent of either the white or the black population in a typical city would have to be moved to achieve racial balance. Farley and Taeuber (1968; see also Clemence, 1967) have attempted to update the Taeubers' (1965) analysis of 1960 census data. It was possible to compute indices of dissimilarity for 13 cities of over 100,000 population which had special censuses conducted since the 1960 census. The index of dissimilarity (computed on a tract basis) increased between 1960 and the special census in 11 of the 13 cities. Thus it appears that black–white residential segregation increased during the 1960s, but we must await the results of the 1970 census to obtain a more definitive picture.

THE OCCUPATIONAL WORLD

It has long been known that there are major differentials in socioeconomic status (SES) among Protestant denominations (Cantril, 1943; Schneider, 1952:228; Pope, 1948; Bogue, 1959; Lazarwitz, 1961, 1964; Gockel, 1969). Very little of this variance, however, is attributable to discrimination in the Duncans' (1968) sense, i.e., differentials that persist after "social origin" and subcultural variables have been taken into account (Mayer and Sharp, 1962; Rhodes and Nam, 1970).

Protestant–Catholic differentials are of more sociological interest than intra-Protestant differences, in light of their bearing on Weber's (1958) classic Protestant Ethic formulation. Sociologists have paid a great deal of attention to this issue in recent years, and empirical studies can be found on both sides of the thesis that the Protestant Ethic formulation is applicable to the present situation. Lenski (1961:76–77) and Goldscheider (1969) provide favorable evidence for the thesis; a large number of other writers (Mack, Murphy, and Yellin, 1956; Lipset and Bendix, 1959:48–57; Rosen, 1962; Greeley, 1963a, 1963b; Glenn and Hyland, 1967; Jackson, Fox, and Crockett, 1970) present essentially *un*favorable evidence. To bring some order out of this disagreement, I have assembled the available published cross-tabulations of religion (Protestant vs. Catholic) from national samples where race is controlled, and which refer to males in the labor force. The indices of dissimilarity (D) between white Protestant and Catholic occupational distributions on the Edwards (1938) scale for each eligible study are shown in Table 23. D is computed twice for each sample, once including farm occupations and once excluding them. This was done because there are large differences between Protestants and Catholics in the proportion of each group engaged in farming. In addition to providing a control for this difference, this device also serves the pur-

TABLE 23

The Trend in Protestant–Catholic Occupational Differentials

| | | | INDICES OF DISSIMILARITY BETWEEN PROT. AND CATH. | |
| | | | With Farmers | Without Farmers |
INTERVIEWING AGENCY	Source	Date		
Michigan SRC	A	ca. 1930	31.3	15.6
Gallup Organization	B	1954	17	9
Michigan SRC	A	1957	17.3	11.0
Current Population Survey	C	1957	11.0	7.2
Gallup Organization	D	1962	11	7
Gallup Organization	E	1964	8.6	4.4

NOTE: Comparisons are restricted to employed white adult males. The first line represents the fathers of respondents interviewed in 1957.
Key to sources:
A—Jackson, Fox, and Crockett, 1970:54.
B—Lipset and Bendix, 1959:50.
C—Goldstein, 1969:622.
D—Crespi, 1963:131.
E—Glenn and Hyland, 1967:79.

pose of applying a crude control for the degree of urbanization of the two groups.

D does not indicate the direction of the difference between the two groups; it is interpreted as the percentage of either Protestants or Catholics who would have to be moved from one occupational category to another to achieve a distribution identical to the other group (Taeuber and Taeuber, 1965:229). In the original distributions from which the Ds were calculated, however, the Protestants have a clear advantage on the Catholics in all but one of the comparisons summarized in Table 23, the single exception being the 1964 sample reported by Glenn and Hyland (1967) in the "farmers included" analysis. When the data are arranged in time series order, a striking pattern of convergence can be noted, and this pattern would indicate that the long debate about Protestant–Catholic differentials in the occupational world is rapidly becoming moot.

The two studies for which it is possible to obtain D for Jewish–Gentile occupational differentials are summarized in Table 24. Like the Protestant–Catholic comparisons, the Jewish–Gentile comparisons are restricted to white males in the labor force. Because of the extremely urbanized nature of the Jewish population, the Jewish–Gentile comparisons are restricted to those which exclude farm occupations.

Two studies only seven years apart are not a very firm basis for establishing a trend, but some points can be made, nonetheless. First, the Jews rank much higher than the Gentiles in the original distribution tables from which the Ds were computed. The sheer sizes of the differentials can be given meaning by comparing them to the black–white occupational differential. The Jewish–Gentile difference is actually larger than the current size of the black–white difference (see below). Finally, the limited trend evidence in Table 24 indicates little change over time in the size of the Jewish–Gentile differentials.

Black–white occupational differentials have been studied in much greater

TABLE 24

Jewish-Gentile Occupational Differentials

			INDICES OF DISSIMILARITY BETWEEN	
INTERVIEWING AGENCY	Source	Date	Jew and Prot.	Jew and Cath.
Current Population Survey	A	1957	35.0	42.1
Gallup Organization	B	1964	37.8	37.0

NOTE: Comparisons are restricted to employed white adult males. Farm occupations have been excluded.
Key to sources:
A—Goldstein, 1969:622.
B—Glenn and Hyland, 1967:79.

TABLE 25

The Trend in Black–White Occupational Differentials

YEAR	TYPE	INDICES OF DISSIMILARITY
1910	Negro vs. all other	39.5
1920	Negro vs. all other	40.4
1930	Negro vs. all other	42.7
1940	White vs. nonwhite	47.8
1950	White vs. nonwhite	40.9
1955	White vs. nonwhite	36.4
1960	White vs. nonwhite	38.5
1961	White vs. nonwhite	35.2
1965	White vs. nonwhite	33.0
1968 (June)	White vs. nonwhite	31.9
1969 (July)	White vs. nonwhite	28.4
1970 (July)	White vs. nonwhite	27.4

For sources, see text. Comparisons are restricted to adult employed males.

detail than space allows reporting in this paper (Broom and Glenn, 1965: 110–115; Glenn, 1969; Price, 1969). The existence of census data, however, makes a very long time series possible, and Table 25 presents this series as far back as 1910. For 1910, 1920, and 1930, the Ds (which include farm occupations) were computed by combining data from Hayes (1962) and the U.S. Bureau of the Census (1958), and these Ds refer to the dissimilarity between Negroes and all other persons. From 1940 on, the Ds reflect the dissimilarity between whites and nonwhites. The Ds for 1940, 1950, and 1960 derive from the decennial censuses, while those for the other years derive from the monthly CPS as reported in the Bureau of Labor Statistics' *Employment and Earnings.* For 1955, 1961, and 1965 the Ds are annual averages (U.S. Department of Labor, 1966:107), while those for the latest years are for individual months.

The discrepancy between white and nonwhite occupational distributions increased steadily until 1940 (although part of the large increase in D between 1930 and 1940 may be due to the change in the nature of the data series), but it has been declining steadily ever since. Further, the rate of the convergence has been accelerating in recent years. The index declined by less than 3 points between 1950 and 1960; the change from 1960 to 1970 was over 11 points. Put another way, about 43 per cent of the inequity between whites and nonwhites that existed in 1940 has been eliminated, and over half of this change has occurred in the last 10 years. Thus, in contrast to the private spheres of life where nonwhites are largely excluded, they are entering the mainstream of American economic life at an increasingly rapid pace.

THE POLITICAL WORLD

There are two questions that we shall raise about each of the ethnic boundary lines with respect to the political world. First, we shall examine the degree to which ethnic preferences in voting for particular candidates exist, and secondly, we shall be interested in the extent to which persons of the various ethnic backgrounds are actually found in positions of power in this country.

There is no doubt that the Protestant–Catholic cleavage was in evidence in the 1960 presidential election (Converse, 1966). Protestants voted in numbers greater than expected for Nixon, and the number of Catholics who voted for Kennedy was also higher than expectation. Yet, while this effect did exist, there is evidence (Baggeley, 1962) that indicates that the Protestant–Catholic cleavage was not as great in 1960 as in 1928, the only other time a Catholic received a major party's presidential nomination. Using Wisconsin counties as units of analysis, Baggeley (1962) regressed the percentage voting for the Democrat—who was, fortunately for the research, the Catholic in both instances—on the percentage of Catholics in the population. After constructing the regression line, Baggeley extrapolated it to the end points on the independent variable. In effect, he was asking how a completely Catholic and a completely non-Catholic county would have voted, if they had existed. He then took the difference between the two estimates as an estimate of the Protestant–Catholic differential in voting. For the 1928 election, the estimated religious impact was 60 percentage points, and for the 1960 election, it was only 26 points. A similar estimate for the 1956 election, in which there was no religious issue, was 7 points, indicating that while there was a religious factor at work in 1960, it was of far smaller magnitude than in 1928. While these results are based on ecological correlations, the 1960 figures are, happily, supported by Scoble and Epstein's (1964) analysis of sample survey data on the 1960 election in Wisconsin.

To gain an even better perspective on the 1960 election, we may compare it with the 1968 election. In that year two Irish Catholics were leading contenders for the Democratic presidential nomination. While neither won the nomination, *neither of them lost it because of his religion*, and a Polish Catholic received the Democratic nomination for vice-president. The religious backgrounds of Robert Kennedy, Eugene McCarthy, and Edmund Muskie were rarely mentioned in the press, and none of these men faced the type of question that John Kennedy had to answer almost every day during the 1960 campaign: "Mr. Kennedy, *as a Catholic*, what do you think of . . . ?" In 1968, no one seemed to notice.

A common political axiom is that tickets must be ethnically balanced, i.e., that in New York, for example, a party's ticket must include a Protestant, a Catholic, a Jew, and perhaps a Negro and a Puerto Rican. In the one place in which the effects of such ticket-balancing has been investigated (Glazer and Moynihan, 1963:304–310), however, a deliberate attempt at ethnic balance on a ticket failed miserably in the case of the Jews.

The propensity of blacks to vote for other blacks is not well documented in the literature, but this is probably because few blacks have managed to be placed on the ballot in times past. Hadden, Massotti, and Thiessen (1968) analyzed precinct voting statistics in three elections in Gary, Cleveland, and Boston where a significant racial issue was involved. They document a deep racial cleavage in all three cases. This conclusion is supported by data from the 1968–69 Area Project of Indiana University. A sample survey of the population of Gary, Indiana, after the election of Richard Hatcher, a black Democrat, as mayor, indicated that 97 per cent of the blacks voted for Hatcher, while 77 per cent of the whites voted for Radigan, Hatcher's white Republican opponent.[3] This latter figure is especially surprising in view of Gary's long history as the most important stronghold of the Democratic Party in Indiana.

Our second political question concerns the degree to which members of various ethnic categories actually find themselves in positions of power and influence. Using information supplied by the Friends Committee on National Legislation, I have tallied the religious affiliations of members of Congress (both houses) in early 1962 and 1969. There were 98 Catholics in Congress in 1962, but in 1969 this figure had risen to 109. For Jews, the comparable figures were 11 and 19. The Catholics are still slightly underrepresented in Congress according to their proportion in the population; Jews are almost exactly evenly represented. The increase in the numbers of Catholics and Jews in Congress (at the expense of the Protestants) is particularly impressive when one considers the fact that there were many more Republicans in Congress in 1969 than in 1962.

As in the other institutional areas examined in this paper, blacks lag far behind the other groups with respect to political representation. This picture, however, is changing rapidly. The U.S. Commission on Civil Rights (1968) credits the Voting Rights Act of 1965 for providing up to 560,000 blacks in the South with their first opportunity to vote, and they attribute a sharp increase in the number of black elected officials in the South to this increased registration. Many other black officials have been elected in the North, including Mayor Hatcher of Gary, Mayor Stokes of Cleveland, and Senator Brooke of Massachusetts. While blacks are still far from having proportionate representation in political offices, there certainly has been a very recent increase of black penetration into the political structures of this nation.

An interesting sidelight on this upsurge in black political representation is provided by a study of informal power and influence in the Boston-to-Washington megalopolitan region (Miller, 1970). During 1968 and 1969, Miller asked 178 formal leaders in that vast region to name a set of leaders who could "best represent the Boston-to-Washington region in the shaping of urban policy and programming for the region." About 200 men received nominations. Mayor Lindsay and Governor Rockefeller led the list of nominations, but in third and fourth positions were Bayard Rustin and Whitney Young. A. Phillip Randolph was in eighth place, Kenneth B. Clark in ninth, Roy Wilkins in 11th, the Rev. Leon Sullivan in 12th (Sullivan was incidentally, the highest-ranked religious leader; the only other religious leader in the top 25 was Cardinal Cooke in 22nd place), Walter Washington in 13th, and Robert C. Weaver in 24th place. Thus, of the top 25 persons nominated, eight were blacks, and seven of these were in the first 13 places. This pattern indicates a very significant entrance of blacks into the American political structure.

A RECAPITULATION

The summary chart in Table 26 is an attempt to place the literature reviewed here into perspective. It portrays in capsule form the strength of each ethnic boundary line with which we have been concerned in each of the five institutional areas. Where possible, an indication of the trend in each ethnic differential is also given.

The line between the white Protestants and Catholics is the weakest of the three. In residence, occupations, and politics the Catholics have been assimilated into the Protestant structures. A noticeable cleavage still exists in marital and friendship relations, but the trend data on intermarriage suggests that even these cleavages are disappearing.

The Jewish–Gentile line is much stronger than the Protestant–Catholic boundary but several points can be noted. The Jews are now well represented in the political arena, and they are, of course, much higher than Gentiles in terms of occupational prestige. A sharp separation between the Jews and Gentiles still exists in the three more intimate areas, but there is evidence to indicate that the Jews stand on the threshold of assimilation in each of these areas, and the full assimilation of the Jews is probably the next major event to be anticipated on the American ethnic scene.

There is virtually total cleavage between blacks and whites in marriage, friendship, and residence, and there are no signs of a black–white convergence in any of these areas. Recent black gains in occupations and politics are, however, impressive, although the separation of blacks from whites in these areas is still wide.

A note should be added concerning one more group—the religious "Nones." Enough information exists to comment on their position in two institutional areas, friendship (Laumann, 1969) and occupations (Glenn and Hyland, 1967). In both of these areas the Nones are surprisingly similar to the Jews, even though most of the Nones come from Christian—and predominantly Protestant—backgrounds (Stark and Glock, 1968:195).

This is an interesting pattern, since it allows a major restatement of Herberg's (1960) triple melting pot thesis. The white Protestants and Catholics appear to be fusing into a single white Christian group, while the Jews and the Nones form a white non-Christian cluster and the blacks a third group. Herberg's (1960) three categories must therefore be modified to fit this pattern. *There are still three groups, but they are no longer Protestant, Catholic,*

TABLE 26

Summary of Ethnic Differentials in Various Institutional Areas

ETHNIC DIFFERENTIAL

Institutional Area	Protestant–Catholic	Jewish–Gentile	Black–White
Marriage	Moderate cleavage; converging at fairly rapid pace.	Wide cleavage; some signs of convergence.	Virtually total cleavage; no signs of convergence.
Friendship	Moderate cleavage; probably converging, but good trend data are lacking.	Wide cleavage; some signs of convergence.	Almost total cleavage; good trend data lacking.
Residence	Complete convergence has occurred.	Wide cleavage evident; but definite trend toward convergence exists.	Almost total segregation, no sign of convergence.
Occupations	Very rapid convergence, Catholics now equal to Protestants.	Jews much higher than Gentiles; scanty trend data indicate stability in relationship.	Blacks much lower than whites, but trend has been converging since 1940; gains since 1960 are impressive.
Politics	Catholics now appear to have been fully absorbed into political system. 1960 election appears to have been turning point.	Jewish representation in Congress is now proportionate to number in total population.	Blacks are still largely outside the political structure, but very recent gains are impressive.

and Jew. The new triple melting pot is comprised of white Christians, white non-Christians, and blacks.

NOTES

The author wishes to thank Robert F. Winch for suggesting the general approach of this paper and Rockwell C. Smith and Scott A. Greer for their comments on earlier drafts. The author's colleagues at Indiana University, especially Peter J. Burke and Elton F. Jackson, provided a substantial amount of methodological advice and criticism. This paper is Research Report No. 105 of The Institute of Social Research at Indiana University.

[1] The term "ethnicity" is used in this paper to refer to a higher level concept that subsumes race, religion, and national origin. This is different from the standard usage, in which the term refers to race and/or national origin. Whenever one or both of these variables is intended, the lower level terms will, for the sake of terminological consistency, be employed. The present usage is consistent with that of Gordon (1964).

[2] Calculations based on crude estimates of some of the necessary parameters given by Thomas (1969: 224) yield a figure of over 70 percent of random expectation for marriages between Catholics and non-Catholics, and this figure does not take the racial factor into account.

[3] The author is indebted to Sheldon Stryker, Director of the Area Project in 1968–69, for these data.

REFERENCES

BAGGELEY, ANDREW R. 1962. "Religious influences in Wisconsin voting, 1928–1960." American Political Science Review 56: 66–70.

BALTZELL, E. DIGBY. 1964. The Protestant Establishment. New York: Random House.

BOGARDUS, EMORY S. 1958. "Racial distance changes in the United States during the last thirty years." Sociology and Social Research 43: 127–135.

BOGUE, DONALD. 1959. The Population of the United States. New York: Free Press.

BROOM, LEONARD, and NORVAL D. GLENN. 1965. The Transformation of the Negro American. New York: Harper & Row.

BURCHINAL, L. C., WILLIAM F. KENKEL, and LOREN E. CHANCELLOR. 1962. "Comparisons of state- and diocese-reported marriage data for Iowa, 1953–57." American Catholic Sociological Review 13: 21–29.

CANTRIL, HADLEY. 1943. "Educational and economic composition of religious groups: an analysis of poll data." American Journal of Sociology 48: 574–579.

CLARK, HENRY. 1965. The Church and Residential Desegregation. New Haven: College and University Press.

CLARK, S. D. 1966. The Suburban Society. Toronto: University of Toronto Press.

CLEMENCE, THEODORE. 1967. "Residential segregation in the mid-sixties." Demography 4:562–568.

CONVERSE, PHILIP E. 1966. "Religion and politics: the 1960 election." Pp. 96–124 in ANGUS CAMPBELL, PHILIP E. CONVERSE, WARREN E. MILLER, and DONALD E. STOKES, Elections and the Political Order. New York: Wiley.

COWGILL, DONALD O. 1960. "The ecology of religious preference in Wichita." Sociological Quarterly 1: 87–96. (Reprinted in Schneider, 1964.)

CRESPI, LOUIS. 1963. "Occupational status and religion" (letter). American Sociological Review 28: 131.

DUNCAN, BEVERLEY, and OTIS DUDLEY DUNCAN. 1968. "Minorities and the process of stratification." American Sociological Review 33: 356–364.

EDWARDS, ALBA. 1938. A Social and Economic Grouping of the Gainfully Employed Workers in the United States. Washington: U.S. Bureau of the Census.

FARLEY, REYNOLDS, and KARL E. TAEUBER. 1968. "Population trends and residential segregation since 1960." Science 169: 953–956.

GLAZER, NATHAN, and DANIEL P. MOYNIHAN. 1963. Beyond the Melting Pot. Cambridge: M.I.T. Press.

GLENN, NORVAL D. 1969. "Changes in the social and economic conditions of black Americans during the 1960's." Pp. 43–54 in Norval D. Glenn and Charles Bonjean (eds.), Black in the United States. San Francisco: Chandler.

GLENN, NORVAL D., and RUTH HYLAND. 1967. "Religious preference and worldly success: some evidence from national polls." American Sociological Review 32: 73–84.

GLICK, PAUL C. 1960. "Intermarriage and fertility patterns among persons in major religious groups." Eugenics Quarterly 7: 31–38. (Reprinted in Schneider, 1964.)

GOCKEL, GALEN. 1969. "Income and religious affiliation: a regression analysis." American Journal of Sociology 74: 632–647.

GOLDSTEIN, SIDNEY. 1969. "Socioeconomic differentials among religious groups in the United States." American Journal of Sociology 74: 612–631.

GOLDSTEIN, SIDNEY, and CALVIN GOLDSCHEIDER. 1968. Jewish Americans. Englewood Cliffs, N.J.: Prentice-Hall.

GORDON, MILTON. 1964. Assimilation in American Life. New York: Oxford University Press.

GREELEY, ANDREW M. 1962. "Some aspects of interaction between religious groups in an upper-middle class Roman Catholic parish." Social Compass 9: 39–61.

——— 1963a. Religion and Career. New York: Sheed and Ward.

——— 1963b. "Influence of the 'religious factor' on career plans and occupational values of college graduates." American Journal of Sociology 68: 658–671.

——— 1970. "Religious intermarriage in a denominational society." American Journal of Sociology 75: 949–952.

GULICK, JOHN. 1965. "The religious structure of Lebanese culture." International Yearbook for the Sociology of Religion 1:151–187.

HADDEN, JEFFREY, L. H. MASSOTTI, VICTOR THIESSEN. 1968. "The making of the Negro mayors, 1967." Trans-Action 5: 21–30.

HAYES, MARION. 1962. "A century of change: Negroes in the U.S. economy, 1860–1960." Monthly Labor Review 85: 1359–1365.

HEER, DAVID M. 1962. "The trend in interfaith marriages in Canada, 1922–1957." American Sociological Review 27: 245–250.

——— 1965. "Negro–white intermarriage in the United States." New Society, August 26, 1965. (Reprinted in R. F. Winch and L. W. Goodman, eds., Selected Studies in Marriage and the Family, 3rd ed. New York: Holt, Rinehart, and Winston, 1968.)

HELPER, ROSE. 1969. Racial Policies and Practices of Real Estate Brokers. Minneapolis: University of Minnesota Press.

HERBERG, WILL. 1960. Protestant, Catholic, Jew. Garden City, N.Y.: Doubleday Anchor (first edition, 1955).

HOLLINGSHEAD, AUGUST B. 1950. "Cultural factors in the selection of marriage mates." American Sociological Review 15: 619–627.

JACKSON, ELTON F., WILLIAM S. FOX, and HARRY J. CROCKETT, JR. 1970. "Religion and occupational achievement." American Sociological Review 34: 48–63.

KENNEDY, RUBY JO REEVES. 1944. "Single or triple melting pot? Intermarriage trends in New Haven, 1870–1940." American Journal of Sociology 49: 331–339.

——— 1952. "Single or triple melting pot? Intermarriage trends in New Haven, 1870–1950." American Journal of Sociology 58: 56–59.

KITAGAWA, EVELYN M., and KARL E. TAEUBER. 1963. Local Community Factbook, Chicago Metropolitan Area, 1960. Chicago: Chicago Community Inventory.

LAMANNA, RICHARD A. and JAY J. COAKLEY. 1969. "The Catholic Church and the Negro." Pp. 147–193 in Philip Gleason (ed.), Contemporary Catholicism in the United States. Notre Dame, Ind.: University of Notre Dame Press.

LAUMANN, EDWARD O. 1969. "The social structure of religious and ethnoreligious groups in a metropolitan community." American Sociological Review 34: 182–197.

LAZARWITZ, BERNARD. 1961. "A comparison of major United States religious groups." Journal of the American Statistical Association 56: 568–579.

——— 1964. "Religion and the social structure in the United States." Pp. 426–439 in Schneider, 1964.

LENSKI, GERHARD. 1961. The Religious Factor. Garden City, N.Y.: Doubleday.

——— 1965. "Religious pluralism in theoretical perspective." International Yearbook for the Sociology of Religion 1: 25–42.

LIJPHART, AREND. 1968. The Politics of Accommodation: Pluralism and Democracy in the Netherlands. Berkeley: University of California Press.

LIPSET, SEYMOUR MARTIN, and REINHARD BENDIX. 1959. Social Mobility in Industrial Society. Berkeley: University of California Press.

LOESCHER, FRANK. 1948. The Protestant Church and the Negro. New York: Association Press.

MACK, RAYMOND W., RAYMOND MURPHY, and SEYMOUR YELLIN. 1956. "The Protestant ethic, level of aspiration, and social mobility." American Sociological Review 21: 295–300.

MAYER, ALBERT J. and HARRY SHARP. 1962. "Religious preference and worldly success." American Sociological Review 27: 218–227.

MILLER, DELBERT C. 1970. Report of the Eastern Leadership and Environment Quality Study. New York: Resources for the Future.

MOBERG, DAVID O. 1961. "Social differentiation in the Netherlands." Social Forces 39: 333–337.

MOLOTCH, HARVEY. 1969. "Racial integration in a transition community." American Sociological Review 34: 878–893.

MUELLER, SAMUEL A. 1966. "Changes in the social status of Lutheranism in ninety Chicago suburbs, 1950–1960." Sociological Analysis 27: 138–145.

——— 1970. The New Triple Melting Pot: Race, Religion, and National Origin as Components of Ethnicity. Unpublished Ph.D. dissertation, Northwestern University.

MUELLER, SAMUEL A., and JOYCE A. SWEEN. 1969. "Omnis America in partes tres divisa est." Christian Century 86: 1342–1344. (See also Letters, Christian Century, January 7, 1970.)

POPE, LISTON. 1948. "Religion and the class structure." Annals of the American Academy of Political and Social Science 256: 84–91.

——— 1957. The Kingdom Beyond Caste. New York: Oxford University Press.

PRICE, DANIEL O. 1969. "Occupational changes among Whites and Nonwhites, with projections for 1970." Pp. 55–64 in Norval D. Glenn and Charles M. Bonjean (eds.), Blacks in the United States. San Francisco: Chandler.

REEVES, RUBY JO. 1944. See Kennedy, 1944.

REIMERS, DAVID. 1965. White Protestantism and the Negro. New York: Oxford University Press.

REISS, PAUL. 1965. "The trend in interfaith marriages." Journal for the Scientific Study of Religion 5:64–67.

RHODES, A. LEWIS, and CHARLES B. NAM. 1970. "The religious context of educational expectations." American Sociological Review 35: 253–267.

Rights Magazine. 1962. "A study of religious discrimination by social clubs." Reprinted as pp. 106–114 in Raymond W. Mack (ed.), Race, Class, and Power, 2nd ed. New York: Van Nostrand Reinhold, 1968.

RODMAN, HYMAN. 1965. "Technical note on two rates of mixed marriage." American Sociological Review 30: 776–778.

ROSEN, BERNARD C. 1962. Review of Lenski, The Religious Factor. American Sociological Review 27: 111–113.

ROSENTHAL, ERIC. 1963. "Studies of Jewish intermarriage in the United States." American Jewish Yearbook 64: 3–53.

SCHNEIDER, HERBERT. 1952. Religion in Twentieth Century America. Cambridge: Harvard University Press.

SCHNEIDER, LOUIS. 1964. Religion, Culture, and Society. New York: Wiley.

SCOBLE, HARRY M., and LEON D. EPSTEIN. 1964. "Religion and Wisconsin voting in 1960." Journal of Politics 26: 381–391.

SKLARE, MARSHALL, and JOSEPH GREENBLUM. 1967. Jewish Identity on the Suburban Frontier. New York: Basic Books.

STARK, RODNEY, and CHARLES Y. GLOCK. 1968. American Piety. Berkeley: University of California Press.

STEMBER, CHARLES H. 1966. Jews in the Mind of America. New York: Basic Books.

SUTTLES, GERALD D. 1968. The Social Order of the Slum. Chicago: University of Chicago Press.

TAEUBER, KARL E., and ALMA F. TAEUBER. 1965. Negroes in Cities. Chicago: Aldine.

THOMAS, JOHN L., S.J. 1969. "The American Catholic family." Pp. 215–238 in Philip Gleason (ed.), Contemporary Catholicism in the United States. Notre Dame, Ind.: University of Notre Dame Press.

U.S. Bureau of the Census. 1958. Occupational Trends in the United States, 1900 to 1950. Bureau of the Census Working Paper No. 5. Washington: U.S. Government Printing Office.

U.S. Commission on Civil Rights. 1968. Political Participation. Washington: U.S. Government Printing Office.

U.S. Department of Labor. 1966. The Negroes in the United States: Their Economic and Social Situation. Bureau of Labor Statistics Bulletin 1511. Washington: U.S. Government Printing Office.

WAGNER, CAROL. 1970. "Religious intermarriage in the United States and Canada." Unpublished paper, Department of Sociology, Indiana University.

WEBER, MAX. 1958. The Protestant Ethic and the Spirit of Capitalism. New York: Scribner (first published in 1904).

WINCH, ROBERT F. 1963. The Modern Family, rev. ed. New York: Holt, Rinehart, and Winston.

YINGER, J. MILTON. 1968. "A research note on interfaith marriage statistics." Journal for the Scientific Study of Religion 7: 97–103.

———— 1970. The Scientific Study of Religion. New York: Macmillan.

PART THREE

Religion and Social Conflict

CHAPTER 8

❖❖❖❖❖❖❖❖❖❖❖❖❖ ❖❖❖❖❖❖❖❖❖❖

Religion and Black Liberation

Minority groups who have experienced a history of discrimination adopt a variety of strategies in attempting to cope with the hostile world surrounding them. Sociologists sometimes categorize these strategies into acceptance, avoidance, and aggression. Aggression, in the form of the black liberation movement (succeeding "black power" of a few years ago) is selected partially because blacks, since the civil rights movement, are aware that gains *can* be achieved, partially because improvements have not kept pace with their hopes and with the promises of white leaders, and partially because cultural traditions, such as the religious themes to be examined in this chapter, lend support for major demands.

As black sociologist E. F. Frazier surveyed the history of the black church in the United States,[1] he noted that in the absence of Negro educational and other socializing institutions outside the home, the church became the principal source of leadership development. This is not new; Americans witnessed Martin Luther King's initial leadership in the civil rights movement and heard the challenges to white supremacy flung down by Malcolm X, a member of the Black Muslim sect.

Since their deaths, however, the scene has changed considerably. No leadership comparable with King's seems yet to have arisen from the Southern Christian Leadership Conference; the Muslims appear to play a minor role in contemporary expression of protest. Since 1968, however, several highly articulate black theologians have emerged. Men such as James F. Cone and Albert B. Cleage (Selection S), casting black liberation in a militant Christian theological framework, mirror the strong separatist thrust currently gaining strength in the black community. But will the black church (more accurately, churches) become the primary *organizational* base for black separatism, as men like Cleage hope it can? Secular groups seem to be in the forefront at present, from political caucuses of black elected officials to urban coalitions with some religious underpinnings, such as Rev. Jesse Jackson's "Operation Breadbasket" in Chicago. In any case, the black protest movement will probably continue to be inspired by the "freedom" motif characteristic of black spirituals and black preaching throughout black history in this nation.

Ronald Johnstone's "Negro Preachers Take Sides" illustrates the principle of structural constraints to be further elaborated in the social protest chapter. Three types of black preachers emerge: militant, moderate, and traditionalist. Although the militants are in the minority among preachers in Detroit, they interact with far more congregational members than do their moderate and traditionalist counterparts. Yet Johnstone points to only a *potential* leadership contribution by Negro clergymen, attributable principally to the time-consuming tasks of ministering to their primary responsibility, the local congregation. The ministers in general are also unorganized politically in the city and so affect governmental and other civic structures only as individuals, thus reducing their potential impact upon the centers of power.

The widow of Martin Luther King, Jr., Coretta Scott King, paints the legacy of her husband's creed of nonviolence. Passages such as those from the "Letter from Birmingham Jail" are already American classics.

A different world altogether—and a measure of the growth of militant religions—is shaped by angry theologian Albert B. Cleage, Jr., of Detroit's Black Madonna Church. The message is clear, even repetitive. "The Christian Church has served the Black man poorly, and certainly a white Christ sitting in heaven at the right hand of a white Father God could not be expected to champion the Black man's cause...." But Cleage moves beyond denunciatory diatribe. He proposes a key role for the church: "We begin with the basic premise that the Black church is essential to the Liberation Struggle, because it is controlled by Black people and is capable of being restructured to serve the Black Revolution."

NOTES

[1] E. F. FRAZIER, *The Negro Church in America* (New York: Schocken, 1963).

✣

✣✣✣

NEGRO PREACHERS TAKE SIDES

RONALD L. JOHNSTONE

INTRODUCTION

"Come weal or woe, my status is quo." So a nameless old Negro preacher is supposed to have summarized his philosophy of making do. In so speaking he was typifying the accommodating, peace-making, don't-ripple-the-waters style of Negro preacher—one who knew he was to keep his place, encourage submission and fatalistic acquiescence on the part of his flock, and preach an other-worldly gospel. If he did his job well, he knew his choir would receive an invitation to sing spirituals in a white church or two and he could look forward to a little free coal for his church in the winter.

This is the "Uncle Tom" style of clerical leadership many Negroes have been repudiating in recent years; this is the stereotype of Negro preachers in general that the present inherits from the past 150 years. But how accurate is such a description of Negro clergymen today? What are the social characteristics of Negro preachers today? Are they what they were? Are there important differences among them?

Here we have the components of an important question clamoring for empirical data—data we shall shortly present in summary fashion. A second question immediately follows. In brief it asks: "So what?" That is, regardless of who and what Negro clergymen are today, of what significance is this category of people in our contemporary changing social world? In particular, where do they and where can they be expected to fit in the agitation and activity called the "civil rights movement"?

However, before we make such assessments, predictions, and extrapolations, we need data to give answers to the prior question of who Negro preachers are and what characteristics and diversity they represent. In gathering data from personal interviews with a 25 per cent random sample[1] of all Negro clergymen in Detroit, it soon became highly obvious that Negro clergymen today are far from alike on most any issue one might want to name. In fact, three distinct types emerged—Militants, Moderates, and Traditionalists.[2]

From *Review of Religious Research*, Fall 1969. Reprinted with the permission of the author and the publisher.

Ronald L. Johnstone is a member of the Sociology Department at Central Michigan University.

THREE TYPES
OF NEGRO PREACHERS

A *militant* says:

> The black man has endured, yes suffered, about all he can take. One of my major jobs as a minister is to help lead him out. If that causes trouble or embarrassment for some white people, that's too bad. Action is what we need and I must be in the forefront. My people need leadership and prodding.

Here are the Negro preachers who identify themselves as members of inner core planning and executing civil rights action groups—men who are aggressive, take-charge civil rights protagonists who are not only outspoken on the civil rights issue but are committed to action on the basis of their beliefs and commitment. In these ranks are the Negro preachers who organized and successfully carried through economic boycott programs against several major retailing firms in Detroit, Philadelphia, and elsewhere. Here are the Negro preachers who demonstrate, march, and picket.[3] Although this style and role of the Negro preacher was not completely unknown in the past, the Negro preachers who combined both indignation and the daring to engage in aggressive action to challenge the system were few and arose only sporadically. The increasing numbers as well as the success of such militant preachers has become a new thing (Washington, 1964; Meier, 1963; Cox, 1950; Wilson, 1960; Thompson, 1963).

The *moderate* is clearly distinguishable from the militant. He is inclined to be the peacemaker, the gradualist, the treader-down-the-middle-of-the-road. He may protest inwardly. Certainly he is well aware of conditions. He knows the plight of so many of his people. But he is more conciliatory and accommodating than the militant as he evidences a protest that is much less audible, overt, and active than that of his militant brother. Improvement of the lot of the Negro, certainly, but carefully, quietly, slowly, without alienating the white brother—such is the moderate's philosophy.

"The most important thing as a minister is to carry out that part of my work which puts me away from all political things. I ought to do spiritual work and preach." So speaks the *traditionalist*—the Negro preacher who is passive with regard to challenges to the prevailing social order, preferring never to enter the battle arena. His attitudes and thoughts will rarely be framed in protest even to himself, nor will he join in attempts at aggressive action. Some actually are relatively unaware of problems; some have given up hope of changing prevailing conditions; most appear to be satisfied with the system since they are able to do what they want to do—make a living and preach the Gospel. In any case, they are acquiescent.

SOCIAL AND RELIGIOUS CHARACTERISTICS (CORRELATES) OF THE THREE TYPES

As these three types have been outlined in broad strokes and as the reader can probably think of examples of each type at work in his community, obvious questions arise concerning the significance of each type. Which is most representative? Is one type growing at a faster rate than the others? How much leadership potential is there from the Negro clergy ranks? Although answering such questions of significance and impact is the ultimate objective of this paper, it is exceedingly important to know more precisely who these Negro preachers are before attempting any overall assessment. That is, who are the men in each category, and what social correlates to each type can we find? Discovering the characteristics and correlates will not only advance knowledge about a category of people on whom there has been little data available before, but it will contribute much toward answering questions of possible future impact.[4]

1. AGE

The militant Negro preacher is almost certain to be a relatively young man. In Detroit, 32 per cent of the militants are under 40; none of the traditionalists is this young; and only 19 per cent of the moderates are under 40. On the other hand, only 25 per cent of the militant preachers are over 55, while 45 per cent of the traditionalists and 37 per cent of the moderates are 55 or older. Young, older, old describes the continuum of militant–moderate–traditionalist almost perfectly. Does this suggest that the degree of involvement in the civil rights movement and concern for the attendant issues among Negro clergymen is a function of age? In part, yes, but only in conjunction with other features.

2. EDUCATION

Education is another prime factor. The militant Negro preacher is clearly differentiated from his fellow clergymen in terms of the dramatically superior education he has received. Similarly, the moderate has generally attained a higher level of education than traditionalists, though significantly less than the militants. In fact, whereas over half (58 per cent) of the traditionalists have no more than a high school education, none of the militants stopped there, and only 31 per cent of the moderates did not go beyond high school. On the other hand, five out of every six militants have a college and/or graduate degree, with all militants having at least two years of college training. But only 16 per cent of the traditionalists and 38 per cent of the moderates have graduated from college.

Militants are clearly not only significantly more highly educated than the moderates and particularly the traditionalists; they have attained an education level that ranks high regardless of the standard of comparison or evaluation used. We thus see that militants are highly educated young men; traditionalists are poorly educated older men; moderates fall between on both counts.

3. SOCIAL STATUS BACKGROUND

These preachers similarly can be differentiated on the basis of their social status background. Militants are much more likely than either moderates or traditionalists to have come from a higher family status background with fathers in the professional, proprietor, and skilled craftsmen categories. Traditionalists and moderates have fathers who were predominantly from the ranks of tenant farmers or unskilled and semiskilled laborers.

Clearly the degree of involvement in and commitment to active participation in civil rights activities on the part of Negro preachers is related very directly to their age, level of educational attainment, and social status background. Although in no sense direct one-for-one causes of militance or its absence, obvious strong dispositions are evident.

But of almost equal interest and significance are other characteristics that correlate highly with militancy. Among these are theological stance, denominational affiliation, number of members attracted to one's congregation, view of the role of clergymen today, and political party affiliation.

4. THEOLOGICAL STANCE

As might be expected from the evidence above, militants are inclined to display greater theological liberalism than their traditionalist or moderate counterparts. Nearly all militants (92 per cent) but only one-third of the moderates and traditionalists accept the possibility of error in Scripture and reject the traditional conservative view of biblical inspiration and inerrancy. Also, militants are significantly more likely than the others to reject the idea of the physical reality of hell.

5. DENOMINATIONAL AFFILIATION

Militants (with moderates a close second) are much more likely than their traditionalist brethren to be members of mainline Protestant denominations such as Episcopal, Congregational, Presbyterian, and Methodist churches. The traditionalists, however, are much more likely to be members of Pentecostal and more nearly sect-type religious groups. Of the traditionalists, 84 per cent are either Baptist or Pentecostal; nearly half of the militants are neither Baptist nor Pentecostal.

6. CONGREGATIONAL SIZE

The size of congregations served by these Negro preachers varies considerably also. Whereas exactly two-thirds of the traditionalists serve small congregations, only 17 per cent of the militants serve such congregations of 200 or fewer members. At the other extreme, half the militants serve large congregations of 600 or more adult members while only 10 percent of the traditionalists and 12 per cent of the moderates have large memberships in their churches. To put it even more graphically, the average number of adult members served by militants is 752. For moderates it is 308, and for traditionalists 213.

7. VIEW OF MINISTRY

The three types of Negro preachers also exhibit distinctive views of the ministry and their responsibilities as ministers. The militants overwhelmingly support the view that their role is as spiritual leader but equally important as leader and advocate for their people in the social, political, and economic realms. Moderates see themselves primarily as spiritual leaders but with some attendant responsibilities for their members as social beings. Traditionalists almost to a man think of their task solely as a spiritual one—preaching, converting, and leading to heaven, with of course some purely administrative responsibilities along side. These differences would be expected from our earlier definition and description of the three types. Militants, for example, are civil rights activists and planners. But it is important to know that such participation is not by accident. It follows from their concept of the ministry and their role as minister. Similarly the traditionalists' lack of participation, perhaps even lack of interest, in civil rights activity stems from an explicit rejection of such involvement as a part of their role as clergymen; "My job is to preach the Gospel."

8. VOTING BEHAVIOR

With regard to political attitudes and activities we should point up two important areas in which Negro preachers differ significantly among themselves: (1) voting behavior, (2) evaluation of the effectiveness of the political process.

Although Negro voters generally have switched from a post-Civil War attachment to the Republican Party to a large majority identification with the Democratic Party, primarily since the appearance of Franklin D. Roosevelt, Negro clergymen do not accurately reflect such a shift. They are *not* so closely attached to the Democratic Party as the Negro population generally. It is important to note, though, that the obverse does not hold. Those who do not identify as Democrats are little inclined to affiliate with the Republican Party. Instead they claim the status of Independents. Our data reveal party preference as follows: Democratic (48.5 per cent); Republican (13.5 per cent); Independent (39 per cent). However, actual voting behavior of these preachers in all major elections in Detroit (presidential, gubernatorial, and mayoralty) between 1956 and 1962 does give an edge to the Democratic side. Those voting essentially Democratic (only one crossover)—59.3 per cent; those voting essentially Republican (only one crossover)—11.9 per cent; those about evenly divided between Democratic and Republican candidates—27.8 per cent.

Our primary interest is in comparisons among our three types of clergymen. Fully 100 per cent of the militants voted a mixed pattern. Such consistency of inconsistent voting patterns is matched by only 58 per cent of the moderates and 45 per cent of the traditionalists. We thus have a picture of militant Negro preachers tending to assume a clearly independent stance, certainly a more independent stance than the moderates and traditionalists.

• • •

SUMMARY

There are many other differences among Negro clergymen that we shall not take the space to list. A sufficiently clear pattern has emerged, however, to enable making two observations and then to proceed to some broader projections and evaluations. (1) There is clearly today no single type of Negro preacher. Rather, there are vast and significant differences on a wide range of features. We have capsuled the major differences into the three summarizing types of militant, moderate, and traditionalist. (2) Some apparently highly capable and potentially influential men are in the ranks of the Negro clergy; these men tend to assume a militant stance insofar as civil rights are concerned.

IMPLICATIONS OF DATA FOR CLERGY LEADERSHIP IN CIVIL RIGHTS MOVEMENT

Now, what does the existence of three quite clearly delimited types mean? Particularly what can be said about the relationship of Negro clergymen to the civil rights movement in the future? Will the ranks of Negro clergymen become a more significant reservoir of leaders for the movement? Is the stereotyped traditionalist gradually declining in number and influence?

MILITANTS' INFLUENCE DISPROPORTIONATE TO THEIR NUMBERS

Only 20 per cent of the Negro clergymen in Detroit are militants but over half (nearly 53 per cent) are traditionalists.[5] Already knowing the quiescent, non-involved, spiritually oriented character of the traditionalists, we might be ready to conclude not only that militancy is a relatively minor and unimportant stance among Negro clergymen but also that Negro clergy ranks in general would be a nearly blind-alley source for leaders to bring about change. As checks on such hasty conclusions, however, several points need to be made. First, although more in number, traditionalists are much lower in influence than the militants. We have already noted the vast differences in the size of congregations as related to ministerial type. Although the amount of influence a preacher has over his congregational members is almost a moot question, the fact is that militants address and counsel with far more people than their traditionalist and moderate counterparts. And remember that these militants not only hold direct action civil rights views, but they also admittedly endeavor to communicate them to others. Such communication is part of their role definition.

Relevant data show militants belong to an average of 54 associations and organizations outside the strictly religious sphere, compared with an average of only one for traditionalists. Further, three out of four militants have personally spoken with public officials about specific problems or issues; only one in three traditionalists has ever done so. What these facts suggest is that both the potential and real influence of the militants exceed their proportion in the ranks of Negro clergymen.

It is also revealing to discover that militants are much more likely deliberately to bring politics into their churches and attempt to stimulate action on the part of their parishioners. Over half of the militants but only a quarter of the traditionalists invite or allow political candidates to address their people and use their facilities. Fully 83 per cent of the militants permit campaign literature to be distributed from their churches, while only 42 per cent of the traditionalists grant such permission. Further, while over half (58 per cent) of the militants admittedly attempt to influence their members' votes by specifically suggesting particular candidates to them, almost none (13 per cent) of the traditionalists recommend candidates by name to their members.

It was interesting and important to discover that many traditionalists seem to have a secret though somewhat intangible respect for at least some aspects of the militant stance and for militant ministers themselves. In nominating their opinion leaders, they selected militants six to one over traditionalists. They seemed to sense a need for such militancy for their people even if they did not see it as part of their task to join the militant ranks.

THE POTENTIAL FOR MILITANT INFLUENCE

Our conclusion at this point is that there is more potential for militancy and influence by militants among Negro clergymen than the simple proportion of militants in Negro preacher ranks would indicate. That is, we dare not dismiss the possibility of a significant contribution to and involvement in the civil rights movement by these clergymen. There would appear also to be the possibility of a spread of the militant stance among Negro preachers in the future. Witness the secret respect for militancy that can be inferred on the part of traditionalist preachers and the consensus expressed by several dozen community leaders and politicians we interviewed who said that militancy has been on the uptrend among Negro preachers during the past ten years.

The evidence seems to point to at least a *potential* contribution by Negro clergymen to civil rights agitation and progress in the days ahead. They have made some widely acknowledged contributions in the past. They spearheaded several successful economic boycotts against allegedly discriminating manufacturing and processing firms and played a successful and noticeable role in the 1961 mayoralty campaign. But what about the future? Several factors will limit their potential.

LIMITATIONS ON THE POTENTIAL

First, organizations of Negro ministers, whether denominational or non-denominational, are not entering the political arena to any substantial degree. They are not entering the political arena as independent organizations, but only as part of a broad community effort, and even then not all of them by any means.

Second, Negro preachers tend to remain noticeably independent entrepreneurs. Most activities directed toward affecting the political and governmental structure of the community are carried on by individual ministers acting out of personal motivation, as representatives of their local congregations, or as citizen members of various local community organizations. Thus, an individual minister may speak to a civic board or official about a personal grievance; he may come to the Housing Commission because his church is headed for demolition by the city's urban renewal program and remuneration for the church's property is not viewed as adequate; or he may be part of a local parents' group protesting segregation or overcrowding in the local high school. But in none of these instances is he representing or working with a category or group of people called "Negro preachers." In a few instances clergymen have organized a fairly large proportion of their fellow ministers behind particular efforts, but no permanent organization persists. At best they have been able to achieve "crisis" or "issue" unity that does not maintain momentum.

A third factor that tends to minimize the impact of Negro preachers beyond the walls of their churches stems from the nature and demands of their occupational role. For one thing, the time and energy required to foray significantly outside their churches are minimal. The traditional primary responsibility of these men, by definition, lies with their local congregations. The attendant activities and tasks are not only many, they are time consuming. Also, whether by default or design, many Negro preachers must assume tasks that in many white churches are handled by laymen—such functions as handling congregational business affairs and building maintenance. Nor dare we ignore the traditionally strong norm of separation of church and state in this country which may have been more deeply absorbed by the Negro than by the white churches. Although this norm of separation does not preclude clergymen from becoming politically involved, it does take strong motivation and a carefully thought-out philosophy to go counter to the familiar pattern of non-involvement by clerics, whether Negro or white, in the sphere of politics. Another factor that tends to inhibit an active and organized moving outward of Negro preachers centers around the tendency of Negro religious groups to approach the sect end of the church–sect continuum; the sect's inherent tendency is toward withdrawal from community and political issues while focusing on spiritual and other-worldly matters.

A fourth broad factor that tends to limit the potential for civil rights leadership and activity by Negro preachers centers in their vast diversity and the lack of consensus among themselves. The differences along the militant–traditionalist continuum are both many and of considerable magnitude. Further, they have been almost totally unable to agree on priority problems. Even the militant preachers who are consistently similar, even alike, on so many dimensions, evidence no consensus on which one or two problems facing the Negro citizen are most crucial. Although employment rates the most frequent choice, only 32 percent could agree that it was most pressing. In fact, one traditionalist clergyman could not identify one single problem facing his people. No more than one-fifth of the preachers could agree on the best general approach to solving problems facing Negro citizens.

ASSESSMENT OF LEADERSHIP POTENTIAL FOR THE FUTURE

In short, we see in the Negro clergy as a total category or group no significant or sustaining leadership source for continuing civil rights agitation. This is not to deny that Negro preachers can still serve as a useful source of grass roots support for programs developed by other leaders. In fact, they conceivably can serve a crucial middle-man function. There is a readiness among them to support civil rights programs and tactics once these tactics are communicated and understood.

Minimizing their leadership potential and function outside spiritual realms also does not deny that the Negro clergy are a potential reservoir of civil rights leadership—leadership at positions above the level of the local church or neighborhood. Although this reservoir is quite small, there are Negro preachers (militants) who by desire, commitment, and training are capable of filling roles of policy making, planning, and organizing at levels above their local congregation or denomination. They have achieved a few fairly notable successes in recent years and they have an outreach and influence disproportionate to their numbers. In all likelihood, however, they will have to be co-opted by other organizations and drawn out of the local responsibilities associated with serving a neighborhood church and its band of believers if they are to make a sustained and significant impact on civil rights.

NOTES

[1] The 25 per cent sample comprised 75 ministers, 59 of whom were successfully interviewed. Of the 16 nonrespondents 7 had moved to known parishes in other cities, 2 had moved and left no forwarding address, 2 were seriously ill, 2 had died, and 3 were ultimate refusals. Data from these 59 clergymen provided the basis for this study.

In addition, we interviewed 10 Negro clergymen who were not in our sample but were frequently mentioned as clergy leaders by the men in our sample. As an outside check on our data and conclusions as well as expanding our perspective, we interviewed 40 Detroit community leaders both white and black. These were members of the Detroit Common Council and the Board of Education, the Detroit Police Department, the Urban League, the National Association for the Advancement of Colored People, the Metropolitan Church Federation, the Detroit Commission on Community Relations, Wayne State University faculty, and labor union leaders, politicians, attorneys, businessmen, and the religion editors of 4 Detroit newspapers.

[2] Our initial categorizing device was the relationship each preacher had to a clearly militant civil rights organization composed solely of Negro clergymen in Detroit. This organization, the Negro Preachers of Detroit and Vicinity, planned and expedited several "boycotts" of major Detroit companies that were designed to bring and did bring the companies to the bargaining table with the militant preachers and ultimately increased the proportion of Negroes employed at all levels within these firms.

Three possible relationships to this organization were utilized to categorize the preachers in our sample: (1) the inner core planners and bargainers (militants), (2) the rank and file members of the organization who supported its goals and urged members to support the boycotts (moderates), (3) those who disclaimed membership in or even awareness of the existence of the Negro Preachers of Detroit and Vicinity organization (traditionalists). Such behavioral and action data proved highly predictive in the course of the study.

[3] We conceive of militance as implying a commitment to aggressive protest against the existing social order that results in specific challenging actions.

[4] Although scant even then, the best hard data on Negro clergymen are from studies 35 or more years old: Mays and Nicholson, 1933, and Fry, 1930. Although Lenski (1961) gathered data on Negro clergymen in Detroit as part of his study, relatively little information on Negro clergymen that relates directly to our study was actually reported.

[5] The precise distributions in our sample were: militants—20.3 per cent; moderates—27.1 per cent; traditionalists—52.6 per cent.

REFERENCES

COX, OLIVER C. 1950. "Leadership among Negroes in the United States." Pp. 228–271 in Alvin W. Gouldner (ed.), Studies in Leadership. New York: Harper & Row.

FRY, C. LUTHER. 1930. The U.S. Looks at Its Churches. New York: Institute of Social and Religious Research.

LENSKI, GERHARD E. 1961. The Religious Factor. New York: Doubleday.

MAYS, BENJAMIN, and JOSEPH NICHOLSON. 1933. The Negro's Church. New York: Institute of Social and Religious Research.

MEIER, AUGUST. 1963. Negro Thought in America, 1880–1915. Ann Arbor: University of Michigan Press.

THOMPSON, DANIEL C. 1963. The Negro Leadership Class. Englewood Cliffs., N.J.: Prentice-Hall.

WASHINGTON, JOSEPH R. 1964. Black Religion. Boston: Beacon.

WILSON, JAMES. 1960. Negro Politics. Glencoe, Ill.: Free Press.

✢•✢•✢•✢•✢•✢•✢•✢•✢•✢•✢•✢•✢•✢

The Legacy of Martin Luther King, Jr.:
The Church in Action

CORETTA SCOTT KING

Sometimes—yes sometimes—the good Lord ... I say the good Lord ... accepts his own perfection, and closes his eyes, and goes ahead, and takes his own good time, and he makes himself a man. Yes! And sometimes that man gets hold of the idea of what he's supposed to do in this world, and he gets an idea of what it is possible for him to do. And that man lets that idea guide him as he grows and struggles, and stumbles, and sorrows ... until finally he comes into his own God-given shape, and achieves his own individual and lonely place in this world. It don't happen often. Oh, no! But when it does, then even the stones will cry out in witness to his vision, and the hills and towers will echo his words and deeds, and his example will live in the breasts of men forever.... So you look at him awhile, and be thankful— that the Lord let such a man touch our lives, even if it were only for a little while.

When Ralph Ellison wrote those beautiful and profoundly meaningful words, he must have been talking about a man like Martin Luther King, Jr. The legacy of Martin Luther King, Jr., to mankind was a life totally committed to the pursuit of truth, love, justice, and peace: a true servant of humanity. Through the living of his own life and his leadership in the non-violent movement for social change in America, he demonstrated that the noble ideals of our Judeo-Christian heritage could be incorporated into our everyday lives, that the true practice of Christianity could be a dynamic and transforming force in the life of the individual as well as the whole of society. Indeed he was a Christian statesman, a moral and spiritual leader who (perhaps more than any other individual) became the conscience of our nation, speaking and fighting against the evils of racism, poverty, materialsim, and militarism.

The significance of Martin Luther King's impact on the last half of the twentieth century will not be assessed adequately for decades, even centuries. His legacies were numerous, and for the initial lecture of this series I have chosen one of those which is dearest to my heart. I should like to speak with you from the caption, "The Legacy of Martin Luther King, Jr.: The Church in Action."

From *Theology Today* 27, no. 2 (July 1970): 129–139. Reprinted with the permission of the author and the publisher.

Coretta Scott King is president of the Martin Luther King, Jr., Center for Social Change in Atlanta.

As a minister, Martin was strongly influenced by the social gospel. He said:

The gospel at best deals with the whole man, not only his soul but also his body, not only his spiritual well-being but also his material well-being.

A religion that professes a concern for the souls of men and is not equally concerned about the slums that damn them, the economic conditions that strangle them, and the social conditions that cripple them, is a spiritually moribund religion.

Like the master teacher to whom Martin Luther King totally submitted his life, he suggested to a world complacent with conformity, a world filled with man's inhumanity to man, and a world unable to extricate itself from war, that we return to the *militancy* and *courage* of the early Christians: "You have heard that it was said, 'You shall love your neighbor and hate your enemy!' But I say to you, Love your enemies and pray for those who persecute you, so that you may be sons of your Father who is in heaven" (Matthew 5:43–45, RSV).

Two thousand years after Christ had given that injunction, Martin Luther King, Jr., dispersed an angry mob who wanted revenge when his home had been bombed. He told the would-be avengers that hate would only multiply hate. He further stated that hate would only scar the soul and distort the personality. On that evening of January 30, 1956, when Montgomery, Alabama, could have become an uncontrollable holocaust, a then obscure black Baptist minister, weaponless except for his unshakable belief in the words of Christ, changed the course of history and gave twentieth century meaning to the words, "But I say to you, Love your enemies and pray for those who persecute you." "Christian love," he told the hundreds who had gathered outside his bombed home, "can bring brotherhood on earth. There is an element of God in every man." This undaunted stand made by a single minister of the gospel was analogous to the great shot at Concord—except that words were used, not bullets. The Montgomery bus boycott became international news because fifty thousand Negroes in that city had listened to and believed in the man they had chosen to lead them.

For countless victims of indescribable brutality, this would not be an elementary undertaking. For the *leader* there would be moments of despair and depression, and fervent prayers that he might be spared the agony of so awesome a responsibility. In 1958, Martin Luther King, Jr., said:

History has thrust upon our generation an indescribably important destiny— to complete a process of democratization which our nation has too long developed too slowly. How we deal with this crucial situation will determine our moral health as individuals, our cultural health as a region, our political health as a nation, and our prestige as a leader of the free world.

Love of enemies, one phase of Martin Luther King's legacy of the church in action, solidified the black community in an unprecedented manner, for King fused the spirit and motivation of Christ with the method of Gandhi.

During the twelve and a half years of his leadership, no violence was ever perpetrated against the oppressor, notwithstanding the wanton violence of every conceivable form which was suffered by the oppressed. Churches were bombed, innocent children were slaughtered while at Sunday School, homes were dynamited, jobs were inexplicably terminated, entire families were forced to flee the land on which they had been for generations. Civil rights workers mysteriously disappeared only to be discovered later, brutally killed; their murderers were never brought to trial.

Martin Luther King, Jr., the eminent twentieth-century prophet, said to his opponents: "We shall match your capacity to inflict suffering by our capacity to endure suffering. We shall meet your physical force with soul force. Do to us what you will, and we shall continue to love you. . . ." The hooded night riders who sought vainly for an Achilles' heel were bitterly disappointed because Martin King's legacy included a deep truth: "Blessed are you when men revile you and persecute you and utter all kinds of evil against you falsely on my account. Rejoice and be glad, for your reward is great in heaven, for so men persecuted the prophets who were before you" (Matthew 5:11–12 RSV).

The history of the church is filled with lay movements which have grown up within the institutional church and then either been forced out into the world or voluntarily moved out into the world in order to witness more effectively. The Montgomery Improvement Association was such a movement. It was born of the persecution of an outstanding lay woman of the church, Rosa Parks, and it was nurtured by my husband and the pastors of the city within their churches. When there was no denominational response and when the institutional forms of church life proved their inability to deal with the problem, it was necessary to organize The Southern Christian Leadership Conference as a missionary action arm of the church to continue the much needed ministry to the southern United States. The initial motto was: "To redeem the soul of America" through non-violent action and the power of the ballot. This was the church in action.

·   ·   ·

Martin Luther King's legacy—the church in action—gives Christians everywhere a broad arena in which to operate. In "Letter from Birmingham Jail" which was addressed to local white clergymen and rabbis who criticized his action in Birmingham, he wrote,

> I must make two honest confessions to you, my Christian and Jewish brothers. First, I must confess that over the past few years I have been gravely disappointed with the white moderate. I have almost reached the regrettable conclusion that the Negro's great stumbling block on his stride toward freedom is not the White Citizens' Councilor or the Ku Klux Klan, but the white moderate, who is more devoted to "order" than to justice; who prefers a negative peace which is the absence of tension to a positive

peace which is the presence of justice; who constantly says: "I agree with you in the goal you seek, but I cannot agree with your methods of direct action"; who paternalistically believes he can set the timetable for another man's freedom; who lives by a mythical concept of time and who constantly advises the Negro to wait for a "more convenient season." Shallow understanding from people of good will is more frustrating than absolute misunderstanding from people of ill will. Lukewarm acceptance is much more bewildering than outright rejection.

I had hoped that the white moderate would understand that law and order exist for the purpose of establishing justice and that when they fail in this purpose they become the dangerously structured dams that block the flow of social progress. I had hoped that the white moderate would understand that the present tension in the South is a necessary phase of the transition from an obnoxious negative peace, in which the Negro passively accepted his unjust plight, to a substantive and positive peace, in which all men will respect the dignity and worth of human personality. Actually, we who engage in non-violent direct action are not the creators of tension. We merely bring to the surface the hidden tension that is already alive. We bring it out in the open, where it can be seen and dealt with. Like a boil that can never be cured so long as it is covered up but must be opened with all its ugliness to the natural medicines of air and light, injustice must be exposed, with all the tension its exposure creates, to the light of human conscience and the air of national opinion before it can be cured.

．　　．　　．

In his final "testament" he also expressed his hope for the American Negro:

I have come to hope that American Negroes can be a bridge between white civilization and the non-white nations of the world, because we have roots in both. Spiritually, Negroes identify understandably with Africa, an identification that is rooted largely in our color; but all of us are a part of the white American world, too. Our education has been western and our language, our attitudes—though we sometimes tend to deny it—are very much influenced by western civilization. Even our emotional life has been disciplined and sometimes stifled and inhibited by an essentially European upbringing; so, although in one sense we are neither, in another sense we are both Americans and Africans. Our very bloodlines are a mixture. I hope you feel that out of the universality of our experience, we can help make peace and harmony in this world more possible.

SELECTION S

✛✛✛✛✛✛✛✛✛✛✛✛✛✛✛✛✛

The Gospel of Black Liberation

ALBERT B. CLEAGE, JR.

A revolutionary Black church that seeks to explore new directions cannot hope to take everyone along on the journey. But certainly in a world in which people are dissatisfied with the church—as most Black people are, because they are finding less and less relevance in both its message and its program— there ought to be an increasing number of Black people willing to make the sacrifices necessary to structure a revolutionary church totally committed to the Black Liberation Struggle. We begin with the basic premise that the Black church is essential to the Liberation Struggle, because it is controlled by Black people and is capable of being restructured to serve the Black Revolution. We also assume that a Black Revolution is impossible unless Black people are able to build an entire system of counterinstitutions, created and designed to serve the interests of Black people as all American institutions now serve the white-supremacy interests of white people. To build a system of counter-institutions we must first build one basic black institution which has the accept-ance of the masses of Black people, facilities and economic stability not directly dependent on the hostile white world, and the capacity to spin off all the other institutions needed for the establishment of a Black Nation within a nation.

These basic concepts are a source of general confusion to many young Black revolutionaries who have rejected religion in general and the Christian religion in particular—because it is a white man's religion, is counterrevolu-tionary, and serves to perpetuate the Black man's enslavement by teaching otherworldly escapism and distracting his attention from his powerlessness, exploitation, and oppression. The Christian Church has served the Black man poorly, and certainly a white Christ sitting in heaven at the right hand of a white Father God could not be expected to champion the Black man's cause against the cause of his own people, who owe their present white supremacy at least in some measure to the inspiration of his divine whiteness. White Christianity is a bastard religion without a Messiah and without a God. Jesus was not white and God is not white. Jesus was a Black Messiah, the son of a Black woman, a son of the Black Nation Israel. Historical and anthropo-

The Rev. Albert B. Cleage is a clergyman of the United Church of Christ and is pastor of the Shrine of the Black Madonna in Detroit.

logical evidence abounds to prove the Blackness of Jesus, so let us not waste time whipping a dead horse (or a nonexistent white Messiah).

Historically Christianity is a Black man's religion created out of the experiences of Black people in Africa. This is not to say that Christianity was the one and only Black man's religion. It was the religion of a small, numerically insignificant, mongrel tribe of nomads who wandered for centuries mixing, intermingling, and intermarrying with all the peoples of Africa and the Fertile Crescent. They were a Black people racially, culturally, and religiously. All Black people in America do not derive from these Israelite tribes, but some do. Neither do all the Black people in America derive from any other African tribal or religious group. The ruthless white slavers took slaves wherever they could find them. All the great religions of the world came from the deep spirituality of Black people. Black Coptic Christians kept Islam from moving below the Sahara for more than two hundred years. Black Jews scattered throughout the world after the fall of Jerusalem and the fort of Masada. White European and Russian converts to Judaism still bear the marks of their African blood in their physical features and hair textures, as many white Jews will admit. Only one point is really important. Black people have a legitimate right to be Christian or Jewish if they wish. Historically both religions belong to us. A Black man in America can follow any of the historic religions of the world and be confident that he worships as his Black forefathers in Africa worshipped at some time in the Black man's past.

Christianity is not a white man's religion. He has only distorted it, used it for his selfish purposes, and for a time concealed from us its true origins. We have now reclaimed our covenant as God's Chosen People and our revolutionary Black Messiah, Jesus. Slave Christianity which we learned from our white masters is counterrevolutionary and has served to perpetuate our enslavement. The revolutionary teachings of the Black Messiah commit us to revolution and Nation building. Today our task is clear. We must free the Black church from slave Christianity and call it back to the original teachings of Jesus, and we must liberate the Black church as an institution and restructure it so that it can become the center of the Black Liberation Struggle. Young Black revolutionaries who cannot put aside their ideological hangups (largely inherited from white people) and be about this very serious business must stand accused of frivolity and of playing games with liberation. Elderly, middle-of-the-road, integrationist Black Christians—who cannot put aside their love for a nonexistent blue-eyed white Jesus, the dream of a heaven off somewhere in the wide blue yonder, and their identification with their white oppressors, to follow a revolutionary Black Messiah, the Jesus of history— obviously love whiteness more than truth and are willing to accept the white man's *declaration of Black inferiority*. Neither of these segments of the Black community will play a significant role in the Black Liberation Struggle, because neither realizes that it is Nation-building time and we struggle for our very survival. Neither is willing to accept historical, philosophical, theological, or pragmatic truth. Neither is willing to submerge his individualism in the emerging Black Nation, accepting discipline, accountability, and the simple faith that nothing is more sacred than the liberation of Black people. Neither is willing to pursue liberation for Black people by any means necessary. . . .

Any liberation struggle must involve confrontation and conflict. There is no such thing as a peaceful, calm, quiet liberation struggle. Even Dr. King's nonviolent phase of our liberation struggle involved conflict. Every time he went into a city and organized a mass demonstration and brought Black folks out to protest in the streets, white people confronted them and there was conflict. The fact that they kept marching and protesting day afer day made it conflict in spite of the fact that they did not strike back. This not striking back was an early phase of our struggle. We had not yet learned that you cannot fight effectively without striking back. It takes time to learn. We had not yet learned that you can't fight a war with the enemy in key positions of leadership in your army. You cannot win if the enemy is directing his army and yours as well. All our organizations and institutions had white folks running them. We thought we had picked good white folks and therefore they were on our side. Their position was impossible because they were a part of the system of oppression under which we suffered and from which we were excluded. But we were learning, and the conflict and the struggle were essential to the learning process. In seeking new directions for the Black church, we are not unaware of the simple fact that the day will come when Black people who are seriously engaged in the Liberation Struggle can no longer tolerate a Black church which is preaching a counterrevolutionary message and exerting a counterrevolutionary influence. In some way it must be redirected and its programs reoriented so that it can begin to deal with the realities of the Black man's existence.

. . .

The first task of the Black church is to liberate the Black man's mind. It must be willing to deal with truth and stop telling fairy tales to men and women. If the Black church is to move in new directions it must learn the nature of reality and become committed to truth. The Black church must become a teaching church. It cannot be a church that says what people want to hear. It must help Black people begin to think realistically about everyday problems. This is the process by which we will move from a gospel of salvation to a gospel of liberation. We must define liberation, define struggle, analyze tactics, and develop methods for the struggle. We must look at history to find out what works and what does not work. The Black church must define liberation in terms of reality. Then we must put together the organization and structure to make it effective. We must learn to deal with individuals. We seek to bring all Black people together in one Black Nation so that we can struggle together for liberation. We will not all start at the same stage of development; some of us will be more emancipated from our white identification than others. But no prizes will be given for the kind of individualistic personal pride and arrogance which uses a little knowledge to destroy the unity of a group. The submergence of intellectual pride is difficult, but the individual who uses his knowledge and skills to destroy the Nation will, as Jesus suggests, be put out of the Nation and treated as a Gentile. The Nation must become a group working, thinking, and planning together. One of our basic problems is the development of a process which will make this possible.

. . .

Black unity must mean that we are willing to bear with one another's weaknesses and share with one another ideas as well as dollars. The new Black church will not ask for faith in Jesus, a mystical Saviour, but for faith in one another and commitment to walk in the footsteps of Jesus, as we join in the Black Liberation Struggle as defined by the Black Christian Nationalist movement.

CHAPTER 9

❖❖❖❖❖❖❖❖❖❖❖❖❖❖❖❖❖❖❖❖❖❖❖

Religion and Prejudice

A great deal of research has been devoted to the relationships among religious beliefs, values, attitudes, and prejudice. Much of this research has been done by social psychologists, notably the late Gordon Allport and, more recently, Milton Rokeach. The results have been dismal indeed for the churches. "Religious people" as measured by affiliation as well as by regular attendance score higher on measures of authoritarianism and intolerance than nonbelievers and nonchurchgoers. These results are not explainable by controlling for other factors; for example, the lower educational attainments of many regular church attenders are insufficient to explain higher scores on intolerance.

As Allport and later investigators discovered, however, the overall relationships between church attendance and bigotry is curvilinear. Those exhibiting highest tolerance are on either extreme of a curve: They consist of the "absolutely never attend/belong to no church" group on the one hand and, among attenders, the "more-than-weekly" group on the other. The lowest tolerance seems to belong to the church "regulars"—once a week to once a month.

These findings led Allport to construct a hypothesis that has become classic in the sociology of religious prejudice. Persons may develop, he suggested, one of two general religious orientations that he labeled intrinsic and extrinsic. In his words:

> Extrinsic religion ... is something to *use* but not to *live*. And it may be used in a variety of ways: to improve one's status, to bolster one's self-confidence, to enhance one's income, to win friends, power, or influence. It may be used as a defense against reality, and, most importantly, to provide a supersanction

for one's own formula for living. Such a sentiment assures me that God sees things my way, that righteousness is identical with His....

Intrinsic religion ... is not primarily a means of handling fear, or a mode of conformity, or an attempted sublimation of sex, or a wish-fulfillment.... Quandaries, predicaments, cross-purposes, guilt, and ultimate mysteries are handled under the comprehensive commitment. This commitment is partly intellectual, but more fundamentally motivated. It is integral, covering everything in experience and everything beyond experience; it makes room for scientific fact and emotional fact. It is a hunger for, and a commitment to, an ideal unification of one's life, but always under a unifying conception of the nature of all existence.[1]

Rodney Stark and Charles Glock, in their own recent studies in the religion–prejudice relationship, examine the structural location of prejudice on the official or bureaucratic level, among the clergy, and at the level of the laity. The laity are influenced, they conclude, by the theological element of particularism, that is, the conviction that one's faith is *the* true religion, as well as a "radical free-will image of man," which makes many persons unable "to perceive the effect of those forces outside the individual which may utterly dominate his circumstances." Thus the disadvantaged are seen as "there" through their own failure to appropriate the means of upward mobility open to all. Finally, the "miracle motif," or idea that individual conversion to Christ will cure social evils, breeds suspicion of efforts to reform major social institutions so that they serve all in a spirit of justice. They conclude with suggestions for a sharp alteration of church teaching and policy.

"The Church Alive and Changing" sketches what the author regards as a moderately successful program to bring about social change in white suburban congregations—the very ones seemingly most resistant to changes. Under certain conditions, it seems, changes are possible, but the desire of even socially active laymen to have the church function as a comforter—"a rock in a weary land"—must be taken into account.

NOTES

[1] GORDON W. ALLPORT, "Behavioral Science, Religion, and Mental Health," *Journal of Religion and Health* 2, no. 3 (April 1963): 193. Quoted in ANDREW M. GREELEY, op. cit., p. 208.

PREJUDICE AND THE CHURCHES[1]

RODNEY STARK   CHARLES Y. GLOCK

. . . How much prejudice exists within the churches? The answer to this question depends very much on the level at which the churches are examined: at the official, or bureaucratic, level; among the general clergy; or at the level of the laity. At each level, it is important to assess religious prejudice, that is, prejudice against persons of other faiths or denominations; racial prejudice; and, finally, the view of the role of the churches in combatting prejudice.

THE OFFICIAL CHURCHES

At the official level of churches—i.e., the national bureaucratic and organizational apparatus, consisting of church leaders, commissions, agencies, governing bodies, councils of bishops, and the like—there is virtual unanimity: nearly all the major denominations have spoken out forcefully and repeatedly against prejudice, both religious and racial. In the area of religious prejudice, all major denominations are officially opposed to anti-Semitism. Furthermore, while the recent Vatican Council statement condemning the widespread belief that Jews are collectively guilty for the Crucifixion received considerable publicity, similar statements had been made a good deal earlier by most American Protestant bodies. Indeed, at the present time only the Lutheran Missouri Synod and the Southern Baptists seem to be having difficulty taking this position officially. On religious prejudice against other non-Christian groups, the churches have been less specific, but there is a growing moral sensitivity. At its 1968 national convention, for example, the Lutheran Church in America adopted a position on religious liberty which explicitly includes atheists and agnostics.

On matters of racial prejudice, the churches have been even more unanimous and outspoken. All major denominations have issued sharp condemnations of racial prejudice and specifically opposed discrimination in schooling, housing, and jobs. In addition to noble words, church bodies have also done

From Rodney Stark and Charles Y. Glock, "Prejudice and the Churches," in *Prejudice, U.S.A.* ed. Charles Y. Glock and Ellen Siegelman. Copyright © 1969 by Frederick A. Praeger, Publishers.

Rodney Stark is a member of the Sociology Department at the University of Washington in Seattle. Charles Y. Glock is a member of the Sociology Department at the University of California at Berkeley.

some impressive deeds—from rewriting Sunday school and devotional materials to developing agencies devoted to action to oppose prejudice and discrimination.

THE CLERGY

When we look behind the superstructure of the churches and consider the views of the entire clergy rather than only those of religious leaders, we must make some important qualifications to the picture we have just sketched. If the official churches unanimously denounce prejudice and are committed to an active role in opposing it, the clergy as a whole are not unanimous on these same matters. It is unfortunate, but surely not surprising, to discover that a substantial minority of the clergy displays religious and racial prejudice.[2] Furthermore, even among unprejudiced clergymen there is a minority that does not believe the church ought to take an active role in the struggle for brotherhood. Nevertheless, the majority have relatively enlightened attitudes toward persons of other religions and races and do support the official actions of the churches. To give substance to these general remarks, let us consider some relevant research findings.

As already mentioned, officially the churches denounced the notion of collective and continuing Jewish guilt for the Crucifixion. The majority of the clergy support the official denunciations, but a minority continue to accept even the extreme forms of these notions. A recent national study of Protestant clergymen, conducted by Jeffrey K. Hadden, revealed that 6 per cent of the Methodist, 7 per cent of the Presbyterian, 21 per cent of the American Lutheran, 22 per cent of the American Baptist, and 38 per cent of the Missouri Synod Lutheran clergymen in his sample agreed with the statement that "The reason Jews have so much trouble is because God is punishing them for rejecting Jesus."[3]

As with attitudes toward Jews, clerical attitudes toward blacks are also mixed. Again, however, what data there are reveal that the majority of Christian clergy have fairly enlightened attitudes. For example, 80 per cent of the Protestant ministers in the Hadden study rejected the statement that "Negroes could solve many of their own problems if they were not so irresponsible and carefree about life," and only about one in ten opposed the civil rights movement. Among Roman Catholic diocesan priests, also about 10 per cent disapprove of the civil rights movement, according to Joseph Fichter's recent study of America's priests.[4]

The clergy, by and large, also supports an active role for the church in the struggle against discrimination. Here again one finds a minority that denies that the church has any business trying to reform society. However, a substantial majority does support an activist role for the churches and the clergy.

THE LAITY

When we turn to rank-and-file church members, we get an entirely different perspective. The facts are that Christian laymen, as a group, are a rather prejudiced lot. It is perfectly obvious that large numbers of people in the churches, for whom Christian ethics provide an important basis for love, understanding, and compassion, are not prejudiced. But the majority of church members are prejudiced; furthermore, they deny the right of the churches to challenge their prejudices.

Looking first at religious prejudice, the following picture emerges: from half to two-thirds of American Christians would deny civil liberties to a person who does not believe in God. They would bar him from holding public office and remove him from a teaching position in the public schools. Similarly, half of American Christians continue to blame the Jews for the Crucifixion despite official pronouncements to the contrary. Worse yet, 33 per cent of American Christians score high and another 40 per cent score medium-high on an index made up of strongly anti-Semitic statements.[5]

Religious prejudice varies from denomination to denomination. Catholics are a bit less prone to such prejudice than are Protestants, and conservative Protestant bodies are somewhat more prejudiced than liberal Protestant groups. Nevertheless, religious prejudice is sufficiently widespread among laymen in all Christian bodies to constitute an important problem.

Turning to racial prejudice, one sees no change in this depressing picture. Among white Protestant and Catholic church members in the San Francisco–Bay Area of California, nearly half say they would move if several Negro families moved into their block. A third think Negroes are less intelligent; nearly half blame Communists and other radicals for racial tension.[6] These data were collected in 1963 before any of the riots. Undoubtedly things are worse today. Indeed, a recent national survey conducted by the National Opinion Research Center for Jeffrey Hadden, 1967, showed that 89 per cent of the Christian laity felt that Negroes ought to take advantage of the opportunities society offers them and quit their protesting. And sadly, too, only those who rarely or never attended church dropped significantly below this proportion.[7] By way of contrast, only a third of Protestant clergy would support this view of Negro protest.[8]

This brings us to a final point about the contemporary Christian church member. Not only does he differ sharply from the official church and the clergy on the matter of his prejudice, he strongly opposes the role being played by the churches in overcoming discrimination. Thus, 70 per cent of the laity in the Hadden study denounced clerical involvement in social issues, such as civil rights. Indeed, data from a variety of recent studies indicate that the majority of laymen want their church to tend to the private religious needs of its members and to stay out of such questions as peace, social justice, and human rights.[9]

.   .   .

RELIGIOUS INFLUENCES ON PREJUDICE

It seems clear that many Christians are able to justify racial and religious prejudice despite the official opposition of the churches to which they adhere. Thus, one must ask if it is possible that the churches are perhaps unwittingly doing something that contributes to this ability to rationalize prejudice. And further, is there anything the churches can do to reduce prejudice among their adherents? These are the questions that will guide the remainder of our discussion.

Broadly speaking we are concerned with two classes of factors that influence prejudice among the laity. The first of these is theological, i.e., teaching and doctrine that bear upon racial and religious prejudice and, in some aspects, seem to promote prejudice while in others appear to provide the churches with powerful means for overcoming it. The second class is represented by institutional constraints. These are features of the organization of the churches that affect the power of religious leaders to influence the views of the laity.

THEOLOGICAL FACTORS

The idea that Christian beliefs may be a source of prejudice is likely to be rejected out of hand by theologians and churchmen. Their view of the faith rules out the possibility of such a connection. Nevertheless, there can be a link between theology and prejudice, especially as doctrine is comprehended in the pew. Interpretations of the faith that are widespread among laymen are often not conducive to tolerance; they serve, instead, as a supporting dynamic for prejudice. This is true of both religious and racial prejudice, although the theological elements active in the two types are sometimes different.

Examining first the prejudice of Christian laymen toward persons of other faiths, such as Jews or Hindus, or even between Catholics and Protestants, a significant theological buttress for such prejudice is what we have called particularism—the notion that only one's own religion is true and legitimate and that others are therefore false.[10] In contemporary Christianity, particularism continues to flourish in interpretations of the doctrines that Christ offers the only way to salvation and that to reject him is to be condemned to eternal damnation. Unless such notions are held with a degree of sophistication that seems beyond the capacity of many laymen, they readily support prejudice. If others are seen as committed to a false religion and thus condemned to hell, it is but a short step to seeing them as inferior and immoral. Indeed, a commonly held particularistic doctrine holds that only through Christian teachings is morality made possible.

The greater the strength with which particularistic theological views are held by Christians, and the more narrowly they are defined, the greater the hostility Christians harbor toward persons they see as religious outsiders: for example, Jews, Hindus, Moslems, and, of course, atheists and agnostics. Indeed, particularism generates hatred between Catholics and Protestants, and even between some Protestant groups.

When particularism is combined with the belief that the Jews crucified Christ and thus called down on themselves a collective and eternal curse, Christians display considerable vulnerability to general anti-Semitic beliefs. A Christian who sees the Jews as religiously illegitimate finds it difficult to resist other negative images of Jews.

These days few, if any, theologians would advocate a narrow particularism that would deny all religious virtue to non-Christians, and so far as we know no church officially endorses such doctrines. Indeed, the statements on religious liberty issued by various churches in the past several years uniformly condemn intolerance toward persons of other faiths. Nevertheless, these actions have had little impact upon rank-and-file Christians. A great many laymen continue to find theological support for their religious prejudices in such doctrines as the necessity of accepting Christ in order to be saved. Many feel that persons who refuse to accept the glad tidings have only themselves to blame for subsequent misfortunes.

Turning from religious to racial prejudice, the part played by theology is not so obvious. Christian particularism, while a potent source of prejudice toward Jews and other non-Christians, does not generate prejudice toward Negroes. Negroes by and large are Christian and not susceptible to the charge of rejecting Christ. Nor is any other theological rationale for racial prejudice immediately apparent. For example, only a few extremists argue that racial inferiority and segregation are proper Christian views, basing their view on certain interpretations of passages in the Old Testament.

In our initial investigations we failed to detect any very important relationships between customary measures of religious commitment and the considerable racial prejudice of church members. We found a higher incidence of racial prejudice among those who held conservative theological views, and among those who participated in church activities, private devotions, and the like.[11] These relationships were weak, however, and did not reveal any theological factor that contributed significantly to racial prejudice. The evidence of widespread racial prejudice among professing and practicing Christians, however, and the opposition among parishioners to active church involvement in civil rights, seemed nevertheless to hint that a subtle theological factor might be at work despite appearances to the contrary. Thus, we pursued the matter. Our investigations[12] are still not complete but, briefly, here is what we have discovered so far:

Underlying traditional Christian thought is an image of man as a free actor, as essentially unfettered by social circumstances, free to choose and thus free to effect his own salvation.[13] This free-will conception of man has been central to the doctrines of sin and salvation. For only if man is totally free does it seem just to hold him responsible for his acts, to punish him for his sins, and to demand repentance. Correspondingly, to the extent that a man's destiny is fixed by external forces, to that extent the notion of guilt is unjust. It has been widely recognized that this conception of human nature has been a mainspring in the development of Western civilization and has greatly influenced our attitudes on personal accountability and the ingredients of personal success. An image of man as free and responsible lies behind such notions as rugged individualism, the self-made man, and the justification of wealth on the basis of merit. In short, Christian thought and thus Western civilization are permeated with the idea that men are individually in control of, and responsible for, their own destinies. If I am really the "captain of my soul" and "the master of my fate," then I have no one but myself to thank or to blame for what happens to me.

In the modern world, of course, these radical notions of unfettered free will have been somewhat modified. Still, a great many persons adhere to them in relatively pristine form, and they serve as lenses through which these people view and judge the behavior of others. The significance of this for prejudice is that radical and traditional Christian images of man prompt those who hold them to put the blame for disadvantage upon the individuals who are disadvantaged. A radical free-will image of man makes for an inability to perceive the effect of those forces outside the individual which may utterly dominate his circumstances. Thus, efforts to change the condition of the disadvantaged through social reforms appear irrelevant at best. Instead, one is led to dismiss the misery of the disadvantaged as due to their own short-comings.

In pursuing this line of thought in our empirical studies we found that such an image of man tends to prevail among more active Christian church members and is strongly reflected in their disproportionate commitment to conservative politics.

The results of our empirical analysis lend themselves to the following inter-pretation: a free-will image of man lies at the root of Christian prejudice toward Negroes and of negative attitudes toward the civil rights movement; it also underlies the rejection of programs underwritten by the church and the government to improve the situation of minorities. The simple fact seems to be that a great many church people, because they believe men are mainly in control of their individual destinies, think that Negroes are themselves largely to blame for their present misery. It is not that these Christians con-done the social forces that deprive black people, but rather that they simply do not recognize the existence of such forces in the world. They do recognize that Negroes are collectively disadvantaged. But the conclusion that logically follows from their theology is that this disadvantage must be the result of a racial shortcoming. For how else can one explain such a widespread racial circumstance, if one sees the world in primarily individualistic terms?

The flavor of this perspective on reality is perhaps best conveyed by those who accept it. Here are several comments written at the end of our ques-tionnaires by Christian church members who took part in one of our major studies.

These are the views of a Protestant dentist:

When I see the pictures of the poverty of Negroes on the TV and in the press I feel as sorry as anyone. But I am more depressed by all the "social-engineering" schemes that are being proposed to improve the lot of Negroes and others. Not only will these schemes destroy our free-enterprise heritage, but they will take away the only chance for the Negroes to live better lives. They do nothing about the real problem. The Negro is lazy, and short-sighted. He does not save his money or work to the future. And this is the only way anyone ever betters himself. If we turn to socialism for the answer we will simply make it impossible for the Negro to ever be better off, because under socialism individual initiative is destroyed, not created. We will all live in slums. Will that make Negroes feel better?

A Catholic housewife wrote: "The Irish came to this country way after the Negro and had it just as tough. Today we have an Irish president of the United States. The difference is hard work and the blessings of religion."

.   .   .

Our analysis showed that the conception of man as wholly free was related to racial prejudice, but it was even more closely related to opposing social action to improve the lot of disadvantaged minorities. Most lay opposition to church and clerical participation in human rights activities stems from the conviction that people get what they deserve in this life and the next.

A second interpretation of Christian doctrine that reinforces opposition to efforts to improve the lot of the disadvantaged is what we call the "miracle motif." This is the belief, most prevalent among evangelical Protestants, that if all men are brought to Christ, social evils will disappear through the miraculous regeneration of the individual by the Holy Spirit.

Billy Graham exemplifies this theological posture in his response to the social evils of our day. Recently, in answering critics' charges of indifference, Graham claimed to be a revolutionary. He argued that far from being unresponsive to the growing crises in human affairs—war, annihilation, inequality, hatred, and despair—he is actively pursuing a complete reconstruction of society. He claimed that he differs with his critics primarily on means, not ends. For Graham, the means are a miraculous revolution through individual salvation.

The perhaps unintended consequence of a preoccupation with individual salvation is a suspicion of, and often a hostility to, social and political efforts for reform. So long as there are men who have not been won to Christ, a sinful society is inevitable. Therefore, any attempts to reform society that do not require conversion to Christ are doomed to failure.

The power of Christian faith to transform individual lives is evidenced by Christian saints and martyrs of the past and present. There is less evidence, however, that faith applies wholesale and that the vast body of persons calling themselves Christians have been so transformed. Nonetheless, individual conversion is the orientation which many Christians feel the church should take in confronting the problems of secular society.

· · ·

Thus far we have concentrated on theological factors that seem to foster prejudice. Obviously this would be an extremely biased assessment if we did not also give attention to the capacities of theology to serve as a bulwark against prejudice. Christian claims about the stimulus for brotherhood, compassion, and love provided by the teachings of Christ are hardly partisan distortions. Rather, the ethical and moral teachings of the New Testament are rightfully used as a basis for all official church pronouncements on brotherhood. In our culture, such central ethical notions as "Love thy neighbor" and "Do unto others . . ." are pre-eminently religious teachings. Consequently we have also investigated the power of commitment to Christian ethics as a bulwark against prejudice, both religious and racial. Our findings produce an ironic contradiction, a basis both for future hope and for present disillusion.

First of all we find that as one might both hope and expect, individual commitment to Christian ethics provides a powerful antidote for prejudice. Persons high on ethical commitment are much less likely than others to hold religious and racial prejudices. *But the contradiction arises from equally persuasive evidence that commitment to Christian ethics is not related to other forms of Christian commitment.* Thus, while the ethics taught by the churches are a potent weapon against prejudice, it is not at all clear that the churches can claim direct credit for this fact. Instead, we found that those church members who accepted the other doctrines of the church, or who more regularly attended church or participated in church activities, were somewhat less likely to accept Christian ethics than those who were less orthodox in their beliefs and less regular in their participation.[14] That is to say, *Christians who are somewhat poorer church members judged on other criteria were more likely to be committed to the ethical teachings of the New Testament than were those who were otherwise better and more active members.* Thus, one is faced with the fact that Christian ethics is a powerful weapon against prejudice, but it is not clear that the churches are presently playing an important role in wielding this weapon.

We must emphasize that a great many devout Christians do accept Christian ethical teachings and are undoubtedly thereby inspired in their resolve to oppose prejudice. One need not look far to find many splendid examples. But when the whole range of Christians is examined, ethical commitment is, seemingly, not the typical product of religious devotion. When the churches search for support for their ethical teachings they are slightly more likely to find it among their most dormant members than they are to find it among the most active. Thus, the churches have not been effective in getting ethical doctrines across.

· · ·

WHAT CAN BE DONE?

In conclusion, we would like to give some attention to the implications we see in our findings for the future policy of the churches. We are not theologians, and many of these problems require considerable theological understanding. Nevertheless, one may find some general lessons here for prejudice reduction.

The first lesson, in our judgment, is that ideas are important social forces. There has been a tendency in our society, encouraged by social science, to regard the ideas men hold somehow as epiphenomena, as simply reflections of other variables such as class and education, or of deeper psychological forces such as authoritarianism, anxiety, anomie, and the like. This tendency has been especially pronounced in regard to religious ideas. Even a good many churchmen have come to think that religious ideas play little part in the way men evaluate and act upon the world around them. It may well be true that religious ideas have little influence on some aspects of modern life. The main conclusion of our studies, however, is that theological notions and convictions play an important role in religious and racial prejudice. It matters greatly whether or not Christians hold particularistic conceptions of Christianity, blame the Jews for the Crucifixion, hold a radical free-will image of man, or on the other hand are strongly committed to the ideals of Christian ethics. These beliefs considerably influence prejudice, quite independently of the effects of class, education, authoritarianism, anomie, and similar factors which have preoccupied social scientists.

If we accept the evidence that religious ideas are important in prejudice, we must then face the fact that at present they more commonly function to sustain prejudice than to overcome it. From this observation it follows that if the churches are morally committed to conquering prejudice, they must take theological issues seriously. We would pose the following as some central questions for theological consideration:

1. Do the churches mean for their adherents to believe that only Christians can be saved? How can doctrinal reformulations that are meant to provide religious legitimacy to non-Christians be stated simply so they can be widely understood and accepted?

2. Is a free-will image of man, as we have earlier described it, essential to contemporary Christian doctrine? If not, what can be done to supplant such notions, since they are widespread among both clergy and laity and play a powerful role in supporting prejudice?

3. Is contemporary Christianity really committed to the miracle motif in human affairs? How can the notions of an active God be more effectively made to harmonize with the need for direct human action?

4. How is it possible for persons who ardently proclaim their Christian orthodoxy to reject the doctrines of Christian ethics? Is this not heterodoxy? If so, is it not pertinent to suggest that ethical proclamations ought to be so inextricably implicated in confessions of faith and in true orthodoxy as taught

by the churches that such a separation is no more possible than would be a belief in the divinity of Jesus but not in the existence of God? Could the churches undertake emergency measures to give as much emphasis to the ethical demands of the faith as they do to its promise of salvation?

Speaking as nontheologians, we suspect that particularism, radical notions of freewill, and extreme "miracle motifs" are not essential to contemporary Christian thought. If this is so, then we believe it is crucial that the churches concentrate on convincing their members of this fact. By doing so they could make an extremely important contribution to reducing our capacities to hate one another.

Indeed, of all the major institutions in society, the churches may be in the best position to make deep inroads on contemporary prejudices. This is true partly because of past failures. For on Sunday morning those Americans who most need to have their prejudices shaken are more likely to be found in church than at home reading the newspapers or watching the football game of the week. But in addition, the church alone among society's institutions is specifically concerned with sin and righteousness. It is the avowed task of the churches to ask men the moral significance of their thoughts and actions.

This leads to our final consideration—the extent to which the churches can reasonably be expected to act on these suggestions. Although ideally the churches are primarily concerned with transcendent matters, they are also formal organizations subject to the mundane forces that bear upon all such organizations. Given the built-in constraints that oppose the authority and the ability of the churches to confront questions of prejudice, can we expect them to act more vigorously and effectively than they have? We cannot anticipate how the churches will take up this problem of authority. In the final analysis it seems likely that the course followed by the church will depend upon how it really sees itself and its mission.

If the church is willing to settle for being a successful organization, in terms of buildings and budgets, then perhaps it cannot really do more than it has. But if there is widespread conviction among churchmen that the Christian church is primarily a moral instrument, a unique servant of righteousness, then perhaps the churches will be willing to run some risks. Given the fact that it presently rests upon a disproportionately comfort-seeking base, the church will have to take some risks—including the risk of losing some members—in order to act. But by taking these risks the churches may be able to activate some of those presently dormant Christians who share the official views of what the churches ought to stand for. One way or another such measures would almost certainly cause some convulsions within the churches. But at this moment there are convulsions throughout our society. Dare the churches remain aloof?

NOTES

[1] The University of California Five Year Research Program on Patterns of American Prejudice was supported by a $500,000 grant from the Anti-Defamation League of B'nai B'rith. Initial findings on the role of religion in prejudice have appeared in CHARLES Y. GLOCK and RODNEY STARK, *Christian Beliefs and Anti-Semitism* (New York: Harper & Row, 1966), and in GARY T. MARX, *Protest and Prejudice* (New York: Harper & Row, 1967), Chap. 4.

[2] See JEFFREY K. HADDEN, *The Gathering Storm in the Churches* (Garden City, N.Y.: Doubleday, 1969).

[3] HADDEN, op. cit.

[4] See JOSEPH FICHTER, *America's Forgotten Priests: What Are They Saying?* (New York: Harper & Row, 1968).

[5] For example, "Jewish boys were less likely than Christian boys to volunteer for service in the armed forces during the last war"; "Jews are more likely than Christians to cheat in business"; "Jews, in general, are inclined to be more loyal to Israel than to America." GLOCK and STARK, op. cit., pp. 124, 202.

[6] Some of these findings appear in GLOCK and STARK, op. cit. A fuller treatment of religion and racial prejudice based on the same data will appear in RODNEY STARK and CHARLES Y. GLOCK, *By Their Fruits: The Consequences of Religious Commitment* (Berkeley and Los Angeles: University of California Press, forthcoming).

[7] See HADDEN, op. cit.

[8] See HADDEN, op. cit.

[9] See EARL R. BABBIE, "A Religious Profile of Episcopal Churchwomen," *The Pacific Churchman* (January, 1967); CHARLES Y. GLOCK, BENJAMIN B. RINGER, and EARL R. BABBIE, *To Comfort and To Challenge* (Berkeley and Los Angeles: University of California Press, 1967). Findings from the Berkeley project which also support this tendency among laymen will appear in RODNEY STARK and CHARLES Y. GLOCK, *The Poor in Spirit: Sources of Religious Commitment* (Berkeley and Los Angeles: University of California Press, forthcoming).

[10] See GLOCK and STARK, *Christian Beliefs and Anti-Semitism*.

[11] See STARK and GLOCK, *By Their Fruits*.

[12] These will appear in STARK and GLOCK, *By Their Fruits*.

[13] Our initial discussion of free-will doctrines appeared in CHARLES Y. GLOCK and RODNEY STARK, *Religion and Society in Tension* (Chicago: Rand McNally, 1965), Chap. 15.

[14] See RODNEY STARK and CHARLES Y. GLOCK, *American Piety: The Nature of Religious Commitment* (Berkeley and Los Angeles: University of California Press, 1968).

SELECTION T

✣·✣·✣·✣·✣·✣·✣·✣·✣·✣·✣·✣·✣·✣·✣·✣

The Church Alive and Changing

JOSEPH C. HOUGH, JR.

The church is alive and changing in southern California—that is the conclusion we draw from more than two years of research and action in "Project
Understanding," an effort financed by a $210,000 grant from the Irwin-
Sweeney-Miller Foundation. At the School of Theology in Claremont, Dan
Rhoades and I set up an experimental educational project aimed at bringing
about social change in predominantly white suburban congregations—and
it goes without saying that white racism was the nub of the problem. Altogether, we worked in more than 35 congregations having a combined
membership of 20,000 persons. Twenty seminarians were involved as full-
time staff, and about a dozen seminary professors and some 50 clergymen
cooperated in the project.

A report on the results of this undertaking is being prepared for the
sponsoring foundation. Meanwhile, having examined this considerable crop
of data, we can make some general statements about what we learned and/or
confirmed concerning local churches.

In a word, we believe that the collage put together by recent critics of the
church is in part a caricature, and that another side of the life of the local
church should be emphasized to counter the one-sidedness of the sociological
perspective current in the United States. Further, we believe that our research
points to significant possibilities for the future of the local church....

There are signs that rather large numbers of white laymen share the
impatience of younger clergy and some minority laity. Hadden's study
surprised many, for they had not suspected that a relatively significant percentage of laymen supported church participation in social action. Furthermore, in the action research we have just completed at Claremont, we
discovered that so-called "liberal" laymen were themselves surprised at the
number of others who are committed to similar goals. Therefore the Winter-
Berger-Glock-et al. picture is misleading when taken alone. In fact there is
widespread commitment to the prophetic function within the churches,
straight through all levels of church life. As Hadden's study indicates, this
raises tensions that threaten to bring about a schismatic situation; in fact
there can be little doubt that elements of schism are already present in spite

Joseph C. Hough, Jr., is dean of Graduate Studies at the School of Theology at
Claremont College, California.

of ecumenical talk and strategy. The only remedy, Hadden argues, is more effective communication and evangelization by prophetic leadership, particularly focused on the local congregation. This is an ambitious strategy, to say the least.

But is communication the real problem? On the basis of the Hadden and Glock studies, we can say that communication has not been effective enough to inform the members about the stands denominational agencies have taken in favor of equality or justice; and communication has apparently been even less effective in regard to more specific policy statements. This may result in part from blockages in the communications process from the national to the local level, but it may also indicate that communication has not been seriously undertaken at the local level.

On the other hand, it might be that, even if the national councils and the national denominational bodies successfully communicated all their decisions to their constituents, no significant social change would occur in the local church. The results of our research are relevant here. We can at least offer some well documented generalizations about the possibilities and the problems of change in the local church.

In the first place, we are convinced that a good bit of the talk about the church's dying is simply rhetoric. In fact, many congregations are experiencing the liveliest time of their existence. This, we believe, is due to churchmen's increasing willingness (or at least their recognition of the need) to face conflict and controversy as part of congregational life. It is certainly true that most congregations are encountering difficulties, but I doubt that even a well organized plan of attack could kill the churches. They are here to stay, much alive and, in some cases, undergoing significant changes.

Further, we have scientific data and personal testimonials which offer some evidence of the effectiveness of our antiracist programs in changing attitudes. While there was no miraculous communitywide improvement in those attitudes, at least the people of God in the project churches did not conform to the caricature of "God's frozen people."

Yet our experience did confirm one of the findings arrived at by Glock from his more limited sample in 1952. In almost every church, we met resistance to our antiracist programs on the grounds that people seek relief from the pressures and conflicts of life in the services of the church. Anything that emphasized problems or highlighted issues was considered counter to the group's religious needs. We concluded that this kind of resistance is quite different from a protest made in the name of institutional preservation or of group harmony as the norm of church life, and different also from a protest based on blatant racism. Genuine, felt religious needs often form the basis for resistance to the introduction of conflict-producing change into the life of the church. People do suffer, die, have anxieties, and they need comfort. Religion is still seen as a "rock in a weary land," a comfort to the weak and heavy-laden, and a presence to the lonely. Interestingly enough, we discover that a number of laymen who are active in secular social change organizations shared this fundamentally quietistic and comfort-oriented view of the role of the church today.

It is difficult to deny the importance of this function of religion in a society where, ironically, the more sophisticated the instruments of control, the less control we have over our personal destiny; a society where we are most alone when we are most crowded. Still this view of the function of the church is troublesome, for it can be a part of a pacification program and hence an antichange force in serious tension with a more socially conscious Christianity.

Such tension, however, can have surprising effects. We have found that tensions arising over the prospect of social change often provide impetus for a new kind of ecumenicity which may be one of the factors in the growth of underground churches. In our project we sought to legitimize this "underground" ecumenicity and to institutionalize it as support for social action groups across denominational lines. Our effort succeeded in six ecumenical clusters and four single churches. Hence, while pressure on social issues was indeed schismatic in local congregations, it was also ecumenical in the sense that it prompted like-minded groups to form around specific issues. We believe therefore that, if a strategy for legitimizing such groups is successful, the churches can become much more effective in relating themselves to their members' social concerns. At the same time, they can embrace those whose religious needs are more adequately met by a ministry of worship and healing. Thus churches could avoid the *either-or* choice between "comfort" and "challenge." A plural understanding of religious needs and a legitimation of pluralistic expressions of religious vitality could enable the local church effectively to do both.

That this can happen is confirmed by our experience during the past two years. For example, in one location conflict developed over a local church task force on fair housing. The result was that the entire church undertook a self-study on the nature of its mission. Subsequently, the congregation decided to adopt pluralism as a norm. It deliberately chose this norm in opposition to its old, implicit norm (brought to light by the self-study)—that of harmony. Under the new norm, the congregation will legitimize various types of religious involvement and expression.

Further, our project led to the institutionalization of ecumenical social action ministries in five other church situations. Money has been raised and staff engaged to continue the focus on white racism as a moral-religious issue. Thus, while the local churches in these clusters will carry on the traditional ministries, they have formally adopted a new style of social change ministry.

We also discovered that local churches can be effective bases and agencies of change in their communities. In two locations, project churches intervened at the level of city government (on housing and policy issues) and effected actual policy changes. In another location the project members were able to initiate through the church, an antiracist program involving the entire staff of the city's public school system. Of course, some churches do not have the connections or the power to forward this kind of change, but we found that, more often than not, the problem was not lack of political connections or power but lack of mobilization.

In fact, mobilization is critical for developing a social-change ministry in local churches. A key factor in mobilization, we have found, is the "event of discovery"; the discovery, that is, of other persons in the local church who are interested in ministries for change. Lay participants in our project often told us that they felt isolated and helpless. Indeed, in many congregations the penchant for harmony has all but silenced prophetic laymen, and there are few structural bases in the church organization for these people to occupy. Social concern groups are notoriously underfunded and inactive. Therefore, when a commitment to a specific action program is reported to the congregation at large, it immediately proves a magnetic attraction to which prophetic types are drawn. And if the program involves several congregations and interdenominational groups, the impact of the discovery of like-minded people is magnified and accentuated. This event in itself is important for change. In fact, on many occasions the formation of ecumenical support groups for Project Understanding teams proved inspiring. Even at the early stages of group organization, a new sense of community and potentiality emerged.

But still more important as an "event of discovery" was the realization on the part of old white social-action liberals that *they* are the problem of white racism. Utilizing the "new white consciousness" training model developed by Douglass Fitch and Bob Terry, we tried to move from a purely social-action stance to a clearer understanding of the subtle and not so subtle manifestations of white "liberal" racism. The aim of this model is to help persons move beyond guilt to positive action in implementing new values. In our case it was very effective as a training device in that it prevented our task groups from jumping into a purely "social action" stance. And it was a constant reminder of the need for theological and psychological self-appraisal and renewal. However, when this "new white consciousness" model was used in isolation from actual involvement, it degenerated into just one more group-dynamics technique. We found, then, that the "event of discovery" was possible only when gathered groups of committed persons kept a healthy dialectical tension between action and reflection on action. This tension allowed the event to maintain its integrity and to avoid the twin pitfalls of self-righteous activism and refined personal pietism.

In spite of our heavy emphasis on lay involvement, we found that the clergyman is still a key actor. In churches where his commitment to social-change ministry is low, the problem of mobilization is greatly complicated, even when there is enthusiastic and committed lay support. In this connection it is interesting to recall Hadden's suggestion that the "gathering storm in the churches" will be precipitated by a serious division between liberal clergy and conservative laity. Our experience indicates that this is only partly true. In some cases the resistance to change was indeed strongest among powerful lay people. In other cases it was the ministers themselves who resisted change, very often because they did not appreciate the congregation's willingness to entertain the possibility of change. Again, in some cases ministers who spoke out most passionately on social issues resisted organization for change in the church. Underlying this curious phenomenon, there seemed to be a tacit understanding between congregation and minister which allowed him to champion social justice while they held to the status quo. Also, there seemed to be an agreement between the minister and the congregation that nothing should be done in the church's name which would impair the functioning of the necessities for the maintenance of church life. Hence, in some cases, the contradiction between the public image of a minister who was very liberal and an operational style which tended to be very conservative. This operational style, we found, hampered any effort to organize new programs which might not be under the complete control of the congregation or the administrative control of the church staff.

Part of the problem here is related to the lack of a rewards system in the ministerial profession. The minister's rewards come either from the congregation or from the church bureaucracy. In either case, they are largely given on the basis of his performance of what Campbell and Pettigrew (*Christians in Racial Crisis*) call "maintenance functions"; that is, the management of the congregational participation and finance so that both are kept on an upward curve. Creative ministries in social action or congregational development are seldom recognized in the same way by those who administer the rewards, and the profession itself has no system whatever for providing recognition. Hence it is not surprising that the formation of ecumenical support teams in our project was an important factor in mobilizing clergy as well. Moreover, in the case of two congregations that chose to adopt a pluralistic norm, there were significant changes in ministerial style, with more attention given by the minister to the role of social change in his concept of his task.

However, just as often as ministerial reluctance the overriding factor was a lack of skills at promoting social change. The average minister knows little about organizing for change. In several cases we found that the introduction into the project staff of trained change agents not only facilitated the development of antiracist programs; the sharing of their skills with the local ministerial staff was an important factor in significantly altering the minister's own professional style.

All this points to the necessity of better training for social change ministries in all phases of theological education. We found that the most effective method for this kind of education united serious theological and social-psychological reflection with actual involvement in supervised change-oriented task groups. We found also that this method was best implemented by a combination of teaching agencies which included local churches, church training organizations, and seminary faculty.

Let me conclude by saying that our research has convinced us that, whatever the problems, the churches represent one of the best options for maintaining a counter-systemic pressure on the total American system. From a political point of view alone, the churches represent the best possibility for utilizing large voluntary associations in the society as loci of dissent and criticism.

From the standpoint of their self-understanding, the churches are symbols of hope and comfort and joy to large numbers of people. Even prophets of change recognized that without these symbols of hope, problematic though they be, there is no opening to the future; and where there is no opening to the future, there is no prospect for change. Hence the continuing presence of the church *in both its priestly and its prophetic style* is essential to the development and maintenance of an open society. On the basis of our experience in Project Understanding during the past two years, we believe that such a double presence is a concrete possibility for local congregations.

CHAPTER 10

❖❖❖❖❖❖❖❖❖❖❖❖❖❖❖❖❖❖❖❖❖❖❖

Religion and Current Social Protest

The function of religion by which it challenges the status quo is the prophetic. The great German sociologist, Max Weber, contrasted far eastern religions in this respect. The absence of a personal, transcendent, and ethically demanding God in oriental religions meant that the "prophet" in these religions was "exemplary," that is, showing by the example of his life the proper way to salvation. The Israelite God, Jehovah, on the other hand, was ethically demanding. He bade all men obey the Ten Commandments under penalty of severe sanction.[1] A prophet in the Judaeo-Christian tradition, then, will act in the manner of Old Testament prophets: calling to judgment both men and institutions insofar as they fail to live up to the divinely assigned code of ethics.

The histories of both Judaism and Christianity are replete with players of the prophetic role. Sociologists, of course, are interested in conditions that underlie the development and "outbreak" of prophetic or challenging patterns in the course of religious history. In a sense, some conditions are at hand almost constantly: Morally sensitive individuals (Weber called them "virtuosos") are generally present in all historical periods within religious institutions; social conditions, particularly in rapidly developing industrial societies, are apt to involve denial of socal justice for considerable segments of the society.

In periods of relative calm and prosperity, however, religious institutions are more likely to support the status quo and to be supported by it. Prophetic protests are less likely to occur, and if they do, to be suppressed by church and/or secular officials. In times of upheaval affecting either the religious institutions(s) or the society at large, charismatic individuals are more apt to arise to condemn, urge, point out new directions. Examples in American history are abundant. Northern Protestant churches were very active in the abolition movement during the Civil War; they took a leading role in the temperance movement and in municipal reform at the turn of the century (Social Gospel Movement). Roman Catholicism has been less "prophetic" (because of conditions described in Chapter 5), a defensive posture combined with an ideology of adapting as quickly as possible to American democracy. Judaism's prophetic stance is well known, expressed in the liberal, civil-rights-conscious ethos of Jewish religious organizations, particularly on the national level.

The turbulent America of the 1960s was fertile soil for outbreaks of prophetic protest. The civil rights movement, begun under auspices of Martin Luther King's Southern Christian Leadership Conference, galvanized many white clergymen into overt protest activity. The Vietnam war had a similar effect. The war on poverty stimulated many churchmen (and churches) to side with the poor by participating in or even leading community organizations against "the establishment." From within religious institutions, both cultural and structural developments eased the way for prophetic activity. Culturally, a personalistic ethic that blossomed in the 1960s percolated into religious institutions, legitimating the clergyman's pursuit of his "call" over any contrary interpretations of his church. Structurally the breakdown of Roman Catholic authority facilitated the engagement of individual priests in similar activities. In addition, the creation of special urban ministries, farm worker chaplaincies, and the like enabled clergymen to involve themselves in activities and movements in a way impossible had they been financially dependent on a local congregation or parish. Prophetic clergy involvement is much more common now, but it should be remembered that these enabling developments have occurred only within the last ten years.

The relationship between laymen's beliefs and their disposition to be active regarding social issues has been explored in research recently published by sociologist James D. Davidson.[2] Members of two Baptist and two Methodist congregations in Indiana were surveyed in the spring of 1968. Those members strongly emphasizing "vertical beliefs" (those beliefs embodying man's relationship to the supernatural without reference to the social order) saw their religion in predominantly comforting and consoling terms; those interpreting their religion "horizontally" (stressing beliefs having to do with man's relationship to his fellow man) saw its consequences in terms of social action. (Those holding "vertical beliefs" rated "social consequences" very low.) Altogether, fewer than one-third of all respondents scored high on the topic of social consequences. "One implication is that if church leaders wish to increase the social involvement of church members, they might explore ways of making the social significance of vertical beliefs more explicit."[3] Also, "this finding supports the contention that religion today is oriented to personal and family matters more than it is oriented to social and community problems."[4]

Jeffrey Hadden describes in further detail the conditions for clergy involvement in social protest, such as denominational affiliation and peer support. But he is also alert to lay reaction against clergy involvement—a reaction eloquently set down in J. Howard Pew's "Should the Church 'Meddle' in Civil Affairs?" Hadden concludes that churchmen should devote more time than they have "toward changing men's hearts."

Antiwar protest is the theme of Selections V and W, focusing on perhaps the best known of clerical war resisters, the Berrigan brothers. Implicit in these selections is the feedback effect of the prophetic ministry on religious institutions themselves. A Daniel Berrigan can serve to legitimate authentic, if less spectacular, protest activities and statements on the part of clergy and laymen throughout the American religious landscape.

NOTES

[1] MAX WEBER, *The Sociology of Religion* (Boston: Beacon, 1956), especially Chapter IV, "The Prophet," pp. 46–59.

[2] JAMES D. DAVIDSON, "Religious Belief as an Independent Variable," *Journal for the Scientific Study of Religion* 11, no. 1 (March 1972): 65–75.

[3] Ibid., p. 74.

[4] Ibid.

CLERGY INVOLVEMENT IN CIVIL RIGHTS

JEFFREY K. HADDEN

... Granted that clergy express deep concern for blacks and have quite liberal attitudes about issues of civil rights and social justice, how much have they been willing to do in order to match their words with deeds? This is not an easy question to answer because (1) the data available are much less systematic and (2) ambiguities accrue in measuring involvement. Is the clergyman who marches anonymously in a large group more involved than the minister who would not dream of carrying a picket sign, but is not afraid to hit civil rights issues head-on from the pulpit? The answer to the question is not at all obvious.

However, it does seem clear from the data available that clergy involvement in overt actions of protest for the cause of social justice is much greater than is generally believed by the American public. The average American thinks of the social actionist clergy in terms of a very small minority of "nuts" or "kooks." There are reasons for this misconception of reality. One important dimension is the fact that many clergy participate anonymously—sans collar or other clerical identification and without the knowledge of their constituency. But a second important reason is that the image of a clergyman involved in protest is so foreign that the average person simply refuses to believe it.

I encountered firsthand experience of this selective perception very early in my studies of clergy involvement in protest. Picking up a newspaper, I commented to a desk clerk in the hotel where I was staying, "I see there were some ministers arrested in the demonstration yesterday." "Yeah," he replied, "I saw it on the news last night. They arrested Father X. They ought to lock him in the can and throw away the key." I then asked him if he was aware that there were thirty-nine clergymen arrested during the demonstration. Surprised, he replied, "You're kidding. There might be a few more nuts in the world like that Father X, but not right here in this town." This man watched the television news report of that event. At least ten of the arrested clergy wore clerical collars.

Although systematic samples of clergy participation are not available, nu-

From *The Annals of the American Academy of Political and Social Science*, January 1970, pp. 118–127. Reprinted with the permission of the author and the publisher.

Jeffrey K. Hadden is a member of the Department of Sociology and Anthropology at the University of Virginia.

merous case studies offer information on the extent of clergy involvement in civil rights activities. Since 1963 there have been three events in which large numbers of clergy have participated. The first was the 1963 Civil Rights March on Washington. The second was the Selma march in the spring of 1965. Because no records exist, it is impossible to determine just how many clergy were involved in each of these marches. Newspaper accounts vary widely, ranging from two thousand to more than ten thousand clergy participating in each of these marches. In the spring of 1967, approximately 2,600 clergymen and seminary students participated in a Clergy Mobilization March on Washington to protest the Vietnam War.

Local conflict situations are perhaps more revealing of the uneasiness of clergy about the civil rights crisis in this nation and of the extent of their mobilization in moments of crisis. In Cleveland, 221 clergymen (40 per cent of the metropolitan area's white Protestant clergy) became involved in the Emergency Committee of Clergy for Civil Rights during the educational crisis in that city in 1964. An indeterminate but not insignificant number of this group participated in picketing. Sixty per cent of the group signed a statement released to the press demanding the resignation of the Board of Education. During the summer of 1965, 444 civil rights demonstrators were arrested in two days of protesting in Chicago. One quarter of this group were clergymen and nuns. In 1966, 132 Detroit clergymen signed a statement pledging civil disobedience and submission to arrest if Mayor Jerome Cavanagh did not respond to housing demands of the poor.

These are but examples. The evidence seems clear that involvement of clergy is considerably more extensive than "a very small minority." The nature of involvement, of course, varies enormously. Similarly, activists do not emerge at random from the ranks of the clergy. We have already noted that younger and theologically liberal clergy tend to have more liberal views about civil rights. Hence, we would expect them to be more involved in activist roles, and, indeed, this is the case. Social-structural variables, however, seem to be more important in determining whether or not a clergyman will play an activist role. In my case studies, I was able to isolate three critical factors.

The first is the stance taken by his denomination, or in the case of a Catholic priest, the position of his bishop. The stronger the denominational position, the greater the probability of a clergyman's involvement. The second, and most critical structural factor is the type of position the clergyman occupies. Nonparish clergy are much more involved in direct protest action and militant strategies than those clergymen who serve a congregation. The third factor is the presence of group support. Group interaction serves to reinforce the members' sense of the legitimacy of the concern and also tends to raise the level of the commitment of individual members. In several cases that I observed, clergy initially joined together for the purpose of discussing a problem without any intention of taking action. But the group reinforcement and the perception of the problem as critical then led to collective action.

Involvement, of course, may not be the result of interaction with other clergy. In many cases, the involvement emerges through efforts to minister to persons or groups of minority status. For example, the inner-city clergyman who is attempting to relate to a gang may find that his credibility with the group is dependent upon getting involved. Protest is a symbolic gesture of his commitment and concern for their problems. But, even here, the group process is the same. The group reinforces the legitimacy of the cause—supports, and indeed encourages, what they perceive as appropriate behavior. Having identified with the group, the clergyman must act in accordance with the group's expectations or be rejected.

In the attitudinal data above, we saw that three-quarters of the laity say that they would be upset if their minister became involved in social protest. Dozens of case studies indicate that they frequently become upset enough to dismiss the minister. But just as selective perception takes place in viewing the media's reporting of clergy involvement in civil rights protests, so, too, does this happen in interpreting conflict in the local congregation. For every minister who had been dismissed because his stance on issues of social justice was too bold, there are several others who were dismissed for "neglecting their parish duties" or some similar charge. Also, in some denominations, built-in expectations of relatively frequent pulpit changes have obviously quenched many a brewing fire.

THE YEARS AHEAD

The civil rights movement, as it was symbolized and personified by Dr. Martin Luther King, Jr., is now dead. For the moment, at least, blacks are largely committed to going it alone. These developments had the immediate effect of taking the pressure off clergymen to find overt expression for their consciences. But the lull did not last long. While blacks were busy working out their own thing, clergy began to heed the call of students to resist the war effort in Vietnam.

Virtually every war in history has been fought in the name of a deity. This nation has never experienced more than token resistance to its military efforts from the clergy. But all this is now prologue. Although clergy are much more divided on the war issue than they are about civil rights, there is a growing sentiment among them that the war is morally wrong, and consequently, they have become an important part of the war-resistance movement.

Quinley's California data again provide evidence that clergy involvement in the antiwar movement is not an isolated development by a very small minority.[1] Twenty-nine per cent of the clergy in his sample were classified as hawks. The theologically conservative Southern Baptists and Missouri Synod Lutherans, who represented only 18 per cent of the sample, accounted for more than half the hawks. Among the theological liberals, only 8 per cent were hawks.

Of those who are most dovish (about 35 per cent of the total sample), 85 per cent believe it is appropriate to express one's convictions by participating in an antiwar protest march. Moreover, almost three-quarters approve of civil disobedience. Nineteen per cent have actually participated in an antiwar protest, and 7 per cent have committed acts of civil disobedience. These are the most extreme forms of protest behavior. A substantial number have engaged in "lesser" forms. More than a third have joined peace organizations. Almost half have attended a protest meeting. The same proportion have organized study groups. Four-fifths have delivered sermons on the war. More than half have signed a petition, and almost the same percentage have written a public official.

These figures certainly indicate a fairly high level of participation. Quinley does not report differences in participation by place of residence. It is clear, however, that clergy residing in metropolitan areas were more involved than clergy from smaller communities. One can only speculate, but the participation rate among clergy in the San Francisco Bay area must have been very high.

The Vietnam war is much more complex than the civil rights issue. Ideologically, it is much more an unsettled issue. The cross-pressures have resulted in laity's expressing somewhat greater tolerance of clergy involvement than has been the case with civil rights. Nonetheless, Quinley reports that local parishioners were more than twice as likely to discourage a minister's antiwar activities as they were to encourage him. One-quarter of the doves report losses in financial contributions to their churches, and approximately the same proportion report some loss of membership. About one in ten indicated that there had been an organized effort to have him removed from his pulpit.

These data lend support to my thesis that the civil rights movement of the late 1950's and early 1960's unleashed a deep sense of social consciousness among clergy that must find expression in social action and an ongoing commitment to the creation of a more just world. The data also reaffirm the layman's uneasiness about the widening gap between his perceptions and those of the clergy on the meaning and purpose of the church.

In the spring of 1969, the churches faced a new crisis—perhaps with more far-reaching implications than any development of a decade that was already unprecedented in turmoil for religious institutions. On April 26, James Forman presented a "Black Manifesto" to the National Black Economic Development Conference (NBEDC). The assembled voted to adopt the Manifesto by a 3 to 1 margin. The following week, Mr. Forman presented the Manifesto to the General Board of the National Council of Churches. The core of the Manifesto: a demand that the churches of America pay $500 million in reparations to blacks for injustices resulting from slavery.

The American public responded to the Black Manifesto as though it were a sick joke. The NCC's General Board responded in deadly earnest:

The General Board records its deep appreciation to Mr. James Forman for his presentation of an explanation concerning the Black Manifesto and shares the aspirations of the Black people of this country from which it sprang.... The

Board urges that the communions [denominations] give serious study to the Manifesto, expecting that each communion will act on the matter in its own way.

In the months that followed, Forman and the NBEDC did not collect very much of the demanded reparations—which were raised to $3 billion—but the churches were trembling at their foundations. Again and again, as the denominations held their annual meetings, the Black Manifesto was the key item on the agenda. The schisms cut in several directions, but, again, the deepest rift was between clergy and laity.

In August, the *New York Times* reported the results of its own study of church finances, showing that the national programs of the major Protestant denominations are suffering their first cutback in funds since the depression.[2] Hardest hit are the social-action programs. Perhaps even more significant is the fact that these cutbacks largely occurred *before* the appearance of the Black Manifesto. Denominational offices are being flooded with mail from laymen who are enraged that their church could even consider responding to Forman.

As the 1960's come to a close, the stage is set for the unfolding drama of the 1970's. There seems to be little hope for altering the course of conflict. The average church layman in America is not much different in his social views from the average John Q. Public. The large majority of Americans believe that black militants and college demonstrators have been treated too leniently. Nearly two-thirds believe that police should have more power and that constitutional rights should be denied those who are accused of criminal acts.[3] Although we do not have an end-of-decade study of clergymen's views on these subjects, all the evidence indicates that they are largely at variance with these views. Clergy did much in the 1960's to aid institutional and legislative change in the area of human rights. If the churches are to survive the 1970's, the clergy must devote much more of their energies toward changing men's hearts.

NOTES

[1] QUINLEY, "Hawks and Doves Among the Clergy: Protestant Reaction to the War in Vietnam," *Ministry Studies*, vol. 3, no. 3, 1969.

[2] *New York Times*, August 10, 1969.

[3] *Newsweek* 74, no. 14, October 6, 1969.

❖❖❖❖❖❖❖❖❖❖❖❖❖❖❖❖❖

Should the Church "Meddle" in Civil Affairs?

J. HOWARD PEW

Of all the institutions of human society, the Christian church is surely the most amazing. Standing like a rock amid the shifting currents and cultures of the ages, it has occupied a unique place in man's life for almost 2000 years. While other institutions have come and gone, political and economic systems waxed and waned, the church, alone among them all, has endured.

I have no worry that it will not continue to endure. I do worry, however, when leaders of the church show signs of jeopardizing its power and influence by taking it away from its main mission. To be specific: as an active churchman for more than 40 years, I am concerned that many of the church's top leaders today—especially in what are called the "mainstream" denominations—are sorely failing its members in two ways: (1) by succumbing to a creeping tendency to downgrade the Bible as the infallible Word of God, and (2) by efforts to shift the church's main thrust from the spiritual to the secular. The two, I believe, are related.

FIXED STARS

The strength of the church in the past has been its reliance upon the Bible as the basis of ultimate, eternal truth. From the time "holy men of God" spoke and wrote "as they were moved by the Holy Ghost," the Scriptures have been accepted as the one changeless guide to faith, morals and life. They were so accepted by Christ himself: "Ye do err, not knowing the Scriptures."

If there is one thing that modern man needs more than anything else, psychologists are agreed, it is fixed stars to guide him. Modern man has too few such fixed stars. The philosophy of our day makes all the truth relative. Standards, values, ethics, morals—these, we are told, are subject to change according to the customs of the times.

The effect of that kind of thinking has been devastating to the morals of our times. I'm convinced that much of the jittery, uncertain mood of youth today is traceable to the lack of something firm and unchangeable to stand

Used with permission from J. Howard Pew, "Should the Church 'Meddle' in Civil Affairs?" *Reader's Digest*, May 1966, pp. 49–54. © 1966 by the Reader's Digest Assn., Inc.

The late J. Howard Pew served as chairman of the board of Sun Oil Company and president of the board of trustees of the General Assembly of the United Presbyterian Church in the U.S.A.

upon. As one brilliant but confused young man said to me recently, "The trouble is, we're being asked to play the game of life without any stable ground rules."

.   .   .

Evangelism, traditionally interpreted as the means used to bring men and women to Christ and the church, has been given a completely new definition. Says Dr. Jitsuo Morikawa, secretary of evangelism of the American Baptist Convention, "Contemporary evangelism is moving away from winning souls one by one, to the evangelism of the structures of society." Says Dr. D. T. Niles, one of the World Council of Churches' leading figures, "The heart of Christianity is not concern for the soul but concern for the world."

Expressing this "concern," the church's new-type evangelists, without any notable competence in either statecraft or economics, are leaping headlong into such fundamentally secular concerns as federal aid to education, civil rights, urban renewal, the nation's foreign policy, and plugging for such controversial issues as the admission of Red China to the United Nations, disarmament, higher minimum wages, forcible union membership, etc.

As *Newsweek* recently noted, clergymen last year "defied police barriers to march in Selma, Ala., paraded before the Pentagon to protest the Vietnam war, condemned prayers in public schools, rallied Mexican and Filipino laborers in their strike against California fruit growers." From high church commissions and councils come regularly such sweeping statements as "A church that denies responsibility in economic affairs can offer no acceptable worship to God."

.   .   .

No one would seriously deny that the individual Christian must relate his conscience to the problems of the secular society of which he is a part. It is plainly his duty as a citizen to express his Christian convictions in economic, social and political affairs. Likewise, no one would deny the pulpit's right to speak out on civil issues where moral and spiritual principles are clearly involved.

However, action to correct existing ills in the secular society should be taken through secular organizations: political parties, chambers of commerce, labor unions, parent-teacher associations, service clubs and many others which can supply skilled leadership and techniques to do the job. To commit the church, as a corporate body, to controversial positions on which its members differ sharply is to divide the church into warring camps, stirring dissensions in the one place where spiritual unity should prevail.

When any individual or church council, largely dominated by clergymen, issues statements on complex economic and political matters, giving the public the impression that it is speaking for the whole membership, the result is justifiable indignation on the part of the laity. "When I joined the church," writes one layman from Park Ridge, Ill., "I stated my faith in Jesus

Christ as my personal Saviour. I was not asked to subscribe to any special political, economic or social view. Is that now about to be changed?"

I find it difficult to understand that such protests do not seem to bother the church's self-styled "God's avant garde." "We will get real schisms over the church-in-the-world issue," admits the Rev. Donald Benedict of Chicago. "Some congregations are going to be split right up the middle in the next ten years."

Also less than pleased these days by the church's overwhelming preoccupation with civil affairs are America's lawmakers and civil authorities. I have a file full of letters from members of Congress expressing resentment over church pressures. Says one: "Separation between church and state is a principle deeply embedded in our tradition. Yet church leaders who would raise the loudest outcry if government attempted to interfere in any way with church matters see nothing contradictory in maintaining Washington lobbies and trying to dictate to Congress the kind of legislation which should be enacted on almost every conceivable economic, social and political subject."

From another distinguished Senator comes this: "I have been particularly distressed by the actions of many of our clergy and other church leaders who justify their violation of federal, state and local laws on the grounds that these are 'bad' laws and that the only way to correct them is to break them. Once it has been stated that any law need not be obeyed unless it is a 'good law,' the beginning of an end to rule by law has been initiated."

HIGHEST PRIORITY

By what Scriptural authority does the modern Christian church make this turnabout from its ancient mission? Christ himself made a clear distinction between the concerns of temporal and spiritual natures. He refused to enmesh himself or his followers in the economic, social and political problems of his day—problems certainly as serious as those we face today. When the Pharisees sought to entangle him in politics, asking him whether they should pay taxes to Rome, Jesus gave the classic answer: "Render unto Caesar the things that are Caesar's, and unto God the things that are God's."

At no time did he countenance civil disobedience or promote political pressure either to correct social evils or to advance his spiritual mission. His highest priority was given to measures for changing the hearts of men and women, knowing full well that changed men and women would in time change society—as indeed they have done all down the ages. He made it crystal-clear that we are to seek "first the kingdom of God and His righteousness"—carefully pointing out that "the kingdom is within you."

The church, during periods of its greatest influence, has always followed that lead. Only when, as during the Middle Ages, it forsook its spiritual mission to gain temporal power, has its real power languished. Succeeding church fathers, having learned from the Middle Ages, brought the church back to its rightful realm and insisted that it stay there. John Calvin, father of the Reformed tradition, was one among many who stated flatly that "the church has no Scriptural authority to speak outside the ecclesiastical field," warning that "meddling in politics" was divisive and inimical to the church's success.

If the church's "social activists" are to be halted from plunging the church again into areas where it has no jurisdiction, its concerned laymen and clergymen will have to make their voices heard more clearly in the high councils of their denominations.

To me, the church is the hope—perhaps the only hope—of the world. If it proclaims the Bread of Life, as it did in the past, it will so affect society that many of our prevalent social ills will disappear. But, as a visiting Church of England theologian remarked after extensive observation of U.S. churchmen's frenetic devotion to "social action," "It would be tragically ironic if the church, grown skeptical about God's power to redeem society by transforming human nature, were to fall into the same ideological error as communism and attempt to transform man by altering his environment."

❖•❖•❖•❖•❖•❖•❖•❖•❖•❖•❖•❖•❖

The Berrigans

FRANCINE DU PLESSIX GRAY

... The prosecution began its summation. The Catonsville Nine were accused of willful depredation of government property in excess of one hundred dollars, of willful seizure and mutilation of documents of Maryland Draft Board No. 33, of interference with the Selective Service Act of 1967. "They were candid," government attorney Arthur Murphy said, "they were frank, they were honest, we even said they were sincere ... but, members of the jury, for this kind of offense, the social, the religious, the political, or the moral views are no defense." With a pleading look at the defendants, Mr. Murphy went on to name all the activities which the Nine could have engaged in to express their condemnation of the Vietnam war. "You are allowed to speak at public places. You can write all the letters you want to your Congressmen, to your legislators. You can write letters to the editors ..." His lean brown hand waved approvingly in the direction of the street, where the protests were continuing. "You can picket. You can debate. You can write books. You can write articles ..." And then the prosecutor went on to dissect a crucial word of the Catonsville trial, "motive." "Motive is that which prompts an individual to do a thing ... Intent is what you really do, as distinguished from what you may do accidentally, or by inadvertence. I may have a motive to feed my family and to keep a roof over my family, or the person in the ghetto might have that same feeling. The motive there is what? Give his family food and shelter. But that motive may become so strong, because the man is unemployed, that he goes out and robs a bank. Is he to be excused because the motive was good? No, he is not to be excused. And this is the situation you have with these defendants."

"Ladies and gentlemen of the jury," William Kunstler said as he began the summation for the defense, "we feel that this is essentially an historic moment for all of us." Stalking the courtroom like a large sleek panther, a lock of black hair straying over his forehead which he tossed back with a boyish gesture, he was determined to draw the last ounce of emotion from the impassive jurors. "We are present at one of those moments in history that suddenly crystalizes for at least one brief and shining moment certain issues.

From Francine du Plessix Gray, *Divine Disobedience*. Copyright © 1969, 1970 by Francine du Plessix Gray. Reprinted with the permission of Alfred A. Knopf, Inc. First printed in *The New Yorker* in slightly different form.

Francine Gray is a staff writer for *The New Yorker* magazine and contributes regularly to the *Washington Post* and the *New York Review of Books*.

As I and my co-counsel have said throughout this trial ... we do not think it is just a simple burning case. We feel that it is something quite different. Just as we never really believed that the trial of Socrates was merely a question of whether he was trying to confuse and destroy the youth of Athens; or the trial of Jesus, that he was attempting to overthrow the Roman Empire ... We agree wholeheartedly with the prosecutor as to the essential facts of the case. The defendants did participate in the burning of records. They produced a substance called napalm ... They used the cans you saw. They went to Catonsville. They took certain files out . . . and you must have understood, because it was said openly here, that the Selective Service System is an arm of the Federal Government for the procurement of young men to be put into military service . . . to be used, as one defendant said, as cannon fodder, if that be the government's dictates. This is not a question of just records which are independent of life. It is not driving licenses we are talking about here ... there are no other records which so directly affect life and death on a mass scale, as do the Selective Service records ..."

... The defense lawyers finished making their exceptions, and the court, in normal procedure, should have been recessed until the jury was ready to deliver its verdict. But the normal course of procedure was altered at this point by a totally extraordinary event. William Kunstler stepped towards the bench and said that the defendants asked permission to address the Court directly.

"All right," Judge Thomsen said amiably. A mutter of amazement spread through the courtroom. However, the shock, the surprise of this unheard-of proceeding was restricted to the spectators and the press. For Judge Thomsen, in one more admirable tactic of pacifying the peace movement, had agreed earlier in the day, during a meeting in his Chambers with the defense, to allow the defendants themselves to take exception to his charges—a privilege which, traditionally, is strictly reserved to lawyers. Judge Thomsen thoughtfully rubbed his spectacles with his handkerchief, put them back on, leaned his elbows attentively on his desk, and smiled. The Catonsville Nine rose to their feet as a single man, and there ensued a forty-minute colloquy between the judge and the defendants which, as Judge Thomsen himself admitted later with some pride, was totally unprecedented in the history of legal proceedings.

"Your honor," Daniel Berrigan said early in this dialogue, "we are having great difficulty in trying to adjust to the atmosphere of a courtroom in which the world is excluded, and the events that brought us here are excluded deliberately by the charges to the jury."

"They were not excluded," Judge Thomsen pleaded, "the question ..."

"They were," Daniel Berrigan insisted, "the moral passion was excluded. It is just as though we were in an autopsy, and we were being dismembered by people who were wondering whether or not we had a soul. But your honor we are sure we have a soul!"

These words came out weightily from the boyish man in black, spoken with the fanatic intensity of an inquisitor probing a heretic's faith, turning the judge into the accused.

"It is our soul that brought us here," he continued, "it is our soul that got us in trouble. It is our conception of man. We really cannot be dismembered in such a way that it can be found eventually that our cadavers are here, and our soul is elsewhere, and our moral passion is outside the consideration of this Court, as though the legal process is an autopsy on us."

"Well I cannot match your poetic language," Judge Thomsen said, and was interrupted with frenetic applause. He stiffened. "Any further demonstrations and the courtroom will be cleared," he barked out with uncharacteristic fierceness, "and I mean that, the whole crowd!"

The noise stilled, and he continued: "I think that you all for some reason, either because your lawyers have not gotten it over to you or for some other reason, simply do not understand the functions of a court ... I happen to have a job in which I am bound not only by an oath of office, but by a long tradition of which we are proud in this country."

"Yes sir," Daniel Berrigan said.

"We are proud of the Constitution of the United States," the judge continued crisply. "If this had happened in many countries of the world, you would not have been sitting here. You would have been in your coffins long ago."

"Your honor," said Daniel Berrigan, "may I ask just one more question, and then I will be silent?"

"Yes indeed," the judge said.

"I think you spoke very movingly of your conception of your vocation," Daniel Berrigan said softly, "and I wish merely to ask whether or not one's reverence for this tradition of law or of religion or of any worthwhile human inheritance does not also require us constantly to reinterpret this and adjust it to the needs of the people here and now; in order that this does not remain a mere inheritance which is deadening us, but a living inheritance which we offer to the living here and now. So that it may be possible, even though the law has excluded certain very enormous questions of conscience, that we admit them for the first time and, thereby, rewrite the tradition for the sake of our people."

The Jesuit had suddenly gained control of the courtroom. The Berrigan magic had scratched through the black carapace of the law to touch the judge's naked conscience. For Roszel Thomsen took off his glasses, looked wistfully at the Jesuit, and began to talk about his distaste for the Vietnam war.

"You speak to me as a man and to me as a judge," he said softly. "To me as a man, I would be a funny sort of man if I had not been moved by your sincerity on the stand and by your views. I doubt if any of these jurors has great enthusiasm for the Vietnam war. It seems to me that most of the people in the United States now want to terminate the war ... I am as anxious to terminate it as the average man, perhaps more than the average man ... Because I agree completely with you, as a person, that we can never accomplish what we all would like to accomplish in the way of giving better life to people in this country, if we are going to keep on spending that much money. We certainly are not going to do it. We have not done it, and I do not believe that we will be able to do it."

The courtroom was hushed in a moment of exquisite satisfaction. The Jesuit's teach-in had exposed the nation's schizophrenia. And Roszel Thomsen, realizing that he had gone awfully far as a man, swiftly urged everyone to deal with the nation's disease by voting for the right candidate. . . .

"Your honor," said Philip Berrigan, "I think that we would be less than honest with you if we did not say that, by and large, the attitude of all of us is that we have lost confidence in the institutions of this country, including our own bureaucratic Churches ... we have no evidence that the institutions of this country, including our own Churches, are able to provide the type of change that justice calls for, not only in this country, but also around the world."

"If you are advocating revolution," Judge Thomsen retorted with a sharpness he had not yet displayed towards men of the cloth, "I suggest that you consult your counsel before you say it ..." He softened a little. "Let me say that they will not do it as fast as you would like, but within the next four years the young people of this country are going to have a tremendous percentage of the vote. I would imagine that that is going to make a substantial difference on a good many issues."

"But how much time is left in this country," said Philip Berrigan, and suddenly the habitual impatience was restored to his worn face. "How much time is left in this country, as our casualties inch towards 20,000 men, and Vietnamese casualties, perhaps 175,000 civilian casualties every year, and then nuclear war, of course, staring us in the face ..."

"Well, I assure you that I am concerned about it," Judge Thomsen said, looking increasingly helpless, "selfishly for my grandchildren, as well as for everybody else. It is a serious thing ..."

It was Daniel Berrigan who stepped forward, and, with a grim courtesy, put an end to the colloquy.

. . .

"Could we finish with a prayer, your honor?" Daniel Berrigan asked. "We would like to recite the 'Our Father' with our friends."

Judge Thomsen sat back in his chair, eminently shaken, and a few seconds passed before he answered.

"I will be glad to hear from the chief legal officer of the United States as to his advice," he answered curtly.

There was a flurry at the back of the courtroom. Several Federal marshals who had been patrolling the hall outside swung through the door to observe this new improvisation of the Nine's living theatre. The Chief District Attorney for the State of Maryland, Stephen Sachs, a short, dark young man who had been standing at the back of the room for the last few minutes of the colloquy, walked towards the bar, his head thoughtfully lowered, his hands jammed in his pockets.

"The government, your honor, has no objection whatsoever," he said quite amiably when he reached the bar, "and rather welcomes the idea."

The Catonsville Nine made the sign of the Cross. Then they joined hands, as they had on that May day in Catonsville, and in grave, heavy voices, began to recite the "Our Father." The spectators and both teams of attorneys rose to their feet like one man and joined in the prayer. The judge stood motionless in his black robes, suddenly transformed, by the Nine's dramatics, into a Congregational minister, his bench metamorphosed into a pulpit, his ornate courtroom into an affluent suburban Church. There were stifled sobs from many young priests and students, and from a large black woman, a former parishioner of Philip Berrigan's, who sat in the front row, a "Free the Nine" button pinned to her coat. The marshals, more stupefied than ever, confused as to whether they should participate in the prayer, joined in at every second word, looking pleadingly at the judge to follow his lead. And the words of the Lord's Prayer—boldly trespassing upon the separation of Church and State, brazenly intruding into the formal language of the law— seemed, in that courtroom, like the marvelous tongues given to the Apostles at Pentecost. The Nine led the prayer on to include the Anglican formula: "And thine is the kingdom, and the power, and the glory, forever and ever, Amen." "We thank you very much," Daniel Berrigan said in his friendly, boyish voice, turning towards the judge's bench. Judge Thomsen fled down from his pulpit, his black robes flapping like the wings of a startled bird. The audience filed out of the courtroom to await the jury's verdict. A bevy of priests and students clustered, as usual, around Daniel Berrigan, who looked arrogant, triumphant, amused. "Did you ever see so many marshals?" he said. "They were guarding Our Father."

❖❖❖❖❖❖❖❖❖❖❖❖❖❖❖❖

America Is Hard to Find

DANIEL BERRIGAN

Hard to find;
   wild strawberries swans herons deer
      those things we long to be
   metamorphosed in and out of our sweet sour skins—
      good news housing Herefords holiness
      wholeness
   Hard to find; free form men and women
        harps hope food mandalas meditation
Hard to find; lost not found rare as radium rent free
   uncontrollable uncanny a chorus
   Jesus Buddha Moses founding fathers horizons
   hope (in hiding)
Hard to find; America
        now if America is doing well you may expect Vietnamese to
      do well   if power is virtuous the powerless will not be
      marked for death   if the heart of man is flourishing so will
      plants and wild animals   (But alas alas so also vice versa)
   Hard to find. Good bread is hard to find. Of course. The hands
   are wielding swords The wild animals fade out like Alice's cat's
   smile Americans are hard to find The defenseless fade away like
   hundred year pensioners The sour faced gorgons remain. . . .
But listen brothers and sisters this disk floats downward a flying saucer
in the macadam back yard where one paradise tree a hardy weed sends
up its signal flare (spring)!
       fly it! turn it on! become
     hard to find become be born
     out of the sea Atlantis out in the wilds America
       This disk like manna miraculous loaves and fishes
        exists to be multiplied savored shared
        play it! learn it! have it by heart!
Hard to find! where the frogs boom boom in the spring twilight
   search for the odor of good bread follow it

The Rev. Daniel Berrigan, S.J., is a peace activist and poet.

man   man is near (though hard to find)
      a rib cage growing   red wild as strawberries   a heart!
imagine intelligence   imagine peaceable caressing food planting   music
making
     hands   Imagine   Come in!
       P.S.   Dear friends   I choose to be a jail bird (one species is
       flourishing) in a kingdom of fowlers
                         Like strawberries   good bread
    swans   herons   Great Lakes   I shall shortly be
      hard to find
an exotic uneasy inmate of the   NATIONALLY ENDOWED ELECTRONICALLY
                                      INESCAPABLE ZOO
     remember me   I am
      free   at large   untamable   not nearly
   as hard to find   as America

PART FOUR

Religion and Contemporary Change

CHAPTER 11

‡-‡-‡-‡-‡-‡-‡-‡-‡-‡-‡-‡-‡-‡-‡ ‡-‡-‡-‡-‡-‡-‡-‡-‡

Today's Search for Meaning:
Some Cultic Examples

Charles Glock suggests that felt deprivation is the key precondition for the rise of any social movement, whether religious or secular.[1] In addition, the deprivation must be shared; no alternative arrangements can be perceived within the range of existing institutions; and leadership must emerge with fresh ideas for building a responsive movement. If the nature of the deprivation is *social*; that is, if groups of people perceive themselves as severely lacking in prestige and acceptance, another kind of deprivation usually accompanies these social experiences: *psychic* deprivation, or a concern for meaning, sought for its own sake.

A *religious* response is considered likely to these experiences if "the nature of the deprivation is inaccurately perceived or where those experiencing the deprivation are not in a position to work directly at eliminating the causes."[2]

In relating these theoretical strands to some prominent contemporary religious movements, it is helpful to recall the frustrating experiences of large segments of American youth during the late 1960s and early 1970s. Racism, economic exploitation, the violence of the Vietnam war, and destruction of the environment appeared as overwhelming problems to which America's leaders and the major political and economic institutions they represent seemed largely unresponsive or, when they did respond, repressive rather than open. Adding to these experiences the new philosophies of sexual freedom and drug usage has resulted in a large-scale collective alienation from "mainstream"

American values. The values most cherished by "middle America" and which many students continue to struggle against are well expressed by David Warren:

> . . . a belief in monogamous sexual relationships within and without marriage; the creed that life's primary responsibility is work, not leisure; the articulated faith that corporate capitalism is the only righteous form of organizing an economy; and the declaration that the law and its flag demand unblinking allegiance irrespective of circumstance.[3]

Together, then, these conditions combine to produce severe sociopsychic deprivation—social in that many young people see no place for themselves within the dominant culture's standards of work, play, worship, and politics; psychic in that institutions such as the churches, which formerly provided meaning, no longer seem capable of doing so.

Some are convinced that this overall cultural crisis is even more profound. Allan Eister maintains that advanced societies such as our own suffer from jolting "dislocations" in institutions responsible for "building and maintaining discourse."[4] More fundamental than churches or schools, "orientational institutions" are charged with establishing and legitimating signs and symbols to be used in communicating and identifying rules of reasoning, as well as with "the task of *supplying one or more definitions* of the 'conditions of human existence.' "[5] These are precisely the institutions that have broken down, according to Eister. (Examples of participants in a society's orientational institutions are "painters, poets, editors, novelists, journalists, dramatists, composers and others. . . ."[6] "It is not just religious dogmas that have been challenged, but many ideas, including scientific propositions, have had to be recast in different language. Ideologies have had to be restated."[7] Skepticism and confusion result regarding "orientations once thought to be stable and reliable."[8]

Cults may be predicted to flourish in such circumstances and attract many seeking a firmer system of meaning in their lives. Less structured than a sect, which relies on borrowing elements from extant religious traditions, cults may draw and hold members "more on the basis of affect and of immediate gratification than might be the case for other types of movements or organizations."[9]

This chapter's readings illustrate a number of these theoretical themes. William Shepherd portrays a cultic response in discussing countercultural involvement as a new expression of religiosity. "Pot smoking and drug taking do assume a ritualistic status" which "produces, or at the very least, greatly reinforces, a sense of social 'belongingness' to a group not part of the established culture." Its membership may consist of those most seriously disoriented by the communication crisis elaborated by Eister.

Jack Balswick points to the combination, among the Jesus people he studied, of two "very unlikely bedfellows, fundamentalist Christianity and the 'hippie' style of life." Countercultural and drug scene terminology is retained to describe one's relationship with Jesus; revolutionist phraseology is adapted so that one can speak of "Jesus power." Involvement in the movement appears to allay the loneliness, frustration, and general alienation experienced by many young people and appeals to those desiring a strong sense of direction—as opposed to the "do your own thing" philosophy of the counterculture. Yet opposition to tradition remains in the form of challenge to more conventional churches. Whether organized Christianity will absorb the Jesus movement or the latter will itself become institutionalized are possibilities discussed.

Robbins' and Anthony's provocative analysis of the Meher Baba cult suggests a further function of cultic involvement. Relying on theories of adolescent development that stress the unpreparedness of youth for the instrumental roles required of bureaucratic occupational milieus, the authors note that "dropping out" is often a way of extending an atmosphere of expressive, loving life styles as found in the street–drug cultures. The latter disappoint many, however, because of drug dependency's increasing trend toward instrumental relationships, which precipitate such distinctly unloving experiences as stealing, being sold bad drugs, and the paranoia of "getting busted." The Meher Baba cult rejects drug usage yet continues the philosophy of loving relationships. Furthermore, by enjoining "social service" as an ideal, the cult bestows meaning on the larger society's work ethic and thus acts as a means of resocialization into conventional work roles.

A great deal of research remains to be done in this area. Not only must the larger cultural conditions under which sects and cults flourish be identified, students must, as Eister suggests, probe the particular meaning systems they provide, the symbols used, the role of charismatic leadership in them, and the kinds of emotional and cognitive appeals they make. Social psychologists must also study personality characteristics of cult adherents. Eister himself stresses the plurality of possible responses to perceived orientational dislocation. Why do some choose cult membership as a response (and why a particular cult?) while others select different ways of seeking out and reaffirming meaning in their lives?

NOTES

[1] CHARLES Y. GLOCK, "The Role of Deprivation in the Origin and Evolution of Religious Groups," in *Religion and Social Conflict*, ed. Robert Lee and Martin E. Marty (New York: Oxford University Press, 1964), pp. 24–36.

[2] Ibid., p. 29.

[3] DAVID L. WARREN, "A State of Quiet Calamity," *Commonweal*, March 3, 1972, pp. 521–522.

[4] ALLAN W. EISTER, "An Outline of a Structural Theory of Cults," *Journal for the Scientific Study of Religion* 11, no. 4 (December 1972): 319–333.

[5] Ibid., p. 324, fn. 4 (emphasis in the original).

[6] Ibid.

[7] Ibid., p. 325.

[8] Ibid., p. 327.

[9] Ibid., p. 329.

RELIGION AND THE COUNTER CULTURE—
A NEW RELIGIOSITY

WILLIAM C. SHEPHERD

Max Weber once described himself as "religiously unmusical," meaning that religion didn't "tick" for him, that he didn't "swing" with it. I think that this phrase is intriguing. Properly unpacked, it says a good deal about the modern Western cultural and religious situation. But I shall argue that it has less to do with any of the standard forms of Western religion than with a genuinely new variety of religiosity emerging among the counter culture of the young in America and other Western nations. The implications of this phenomenon may be profound because they go beyond the sheer abandonment of orthodoxy in the direction of forming a novel religious ethos, one quite different from the traditional avenues to salvation the West has known. Sociologists and anthropologists have developed fruitful categories for understanding the characteristics of religion and the forms of the religious life, and I believe that the religiosity of the counter cultural young is as open to such interpretation as any other religious body, however much more amorphous it may appear on the surface.

One way to elucidate the religious aspect of the youth counter culture is to show how it differs from traditional types of Western religion, and that is the tack I take in this essay. I first analyze the concepts of being religious and being "musical" and pursue the question of the extent to which the two concepts are analogous. In the second section, I try to emphasize how central doctrines or religious truth claims have been in the Western tradition. And in the final part, I argue that drugs and rock music provide both symbolic forms and the stuff of ritual behavior within the counter culture and that, as a consequence, a deep sense of social solidarity is produced and sustained. Since a set of symbols, certain ritual practices, and the production of social cohesion are all cardinal marks of religious systems, it is fair to say that our counter cultural young have developed a genuine form of religiosity, indeed a quite new form for the West because it does not include doctrines or truth claims about supersensual entities.

From *Sociological Inquiry* 42, no. 1 (Spring 1971):3–9. Reprinted with the permission of the author and the publisher.

William C. Shepherd is a member of the Department of Religious Studies at the University of Montana.

MUSICAL EXPERIENCE AND WESTERN RELIGION

An analogy between "being religious" and "being musical" is implied in Weber's self-analysis. One might say that the ability to respond affirmatively and appreciatively to things religious is said to be like the ability to "hear" music, to spot recurrent themes, to take in a piece of music as a whole, to "understand" its complexity and thereby profit from it as an integral aesthetic experience. If responding to religion is something like this, then Weber can say that he has a "dead ear" for it. Doubtless there are parallels between music and traditional religions. One's musical tastes are a matter of choice and, in a pluralistic, secular culture, so are one's religious allegiances or lack of them. Emotional and to some extent intellectual needs are satisfied by both. Certain communal needs are also fulfilled, more obviously in the case of religion, but with regard to music too—a phenomenon like the Woodstock Arts Festival clearly makes the point and so does the "community" of symphony goers in a given locality, for they share a distinct and meaningful arena of discourse. Generations and families are often split by differing religious affiliations and by disparate musical tastes as well.

A list of similarities between music and religion could be extended, and of course a substantial amount of overlapping also occurs: there is a musical use of religion and a religious use of music. But the similarities do not add up to an analogy between music and traditional monotheistic religions in the West. For to say that they are analogous overlooks a crucial distinction between theistic religions (though not all religions, excepting for example Confucianism and Theraveda Buddhism) and music. The important difference is that theistic religions make truth claims not only about the character and composition of reality, but also about non-empirical entities; while music on the other hand ordinarily does neither. Even if a composer wishes his music to make some claim or other about the way the world is, as was the case, say, with Wagner and many folk and rock writers today, I don't think it can be argued that such a claim is crucial to the production of a musical or aesthetic experience. But the reverse is so with regard to the Western religious traditions, including Islam for my purposes here. In Judaism, Christianity, and Islam at least two major truth claims are asserted regardless of all the other differences among them: a personal God exists in some way ontologically different from the way men or other "natural" things exist; and this God is benevolent toward all or some of mankind, no matter how difficult it is to verify this assertion empirically. It is true that the "death of God" theologians in Germany and America appear to be exceptions to my generalization—I return to them later on in a somewhat different context.

The lack of correspondence between music and Western religion on this point holds also with regard to art. To provide one brief example, it has been argued (by David Kelsey, 1967) that Tillich's doctrine of *analogia imaginis* is invalid. The doctrine of *analogia imaginis* declares that the "picture" of Jesus as the Christ in the New Testament is genuinely like a picture in the sense that one "gets in on it" analogously with the way one "appreciates" a painting. I agree with Kelsey that a logical difficulty is involved with the whole concept of a verbal icon in Tillich's sense: pictures don't make truth claims, while on the other hand Jesus appears to have made many and to have assumed a whole host of others commonly shared by his compatriots in first century Palestine (for instance, "Yahweh intervenes in history"; "the world will come to an end soon by Yahweh's apocalyptic action"). And certainly the ensuing Christian traditions have hugely elaborated claims about what populates the universe and about what the "real" character of the world is. The same goes for Judaism even in its Reform variety (Rubenstein perhaps notwithstanding) and surely for Islam, which is literalist and fundamentalist about its scripture. Pictures do not and cannot make claims in this way, although they, like music, stand available for men to make claims *about* them. To speak of what a picture or a piece of music "says," however, is metaphorical and not to be taken in the same sense, or even in an analogous sense, to what a religious truth claim about Yahweh or Allah says.

I believe that religious people would readily agree with me about the centrality of religious truth claims to the Western religious traditions, and most, I think, would disavow for themselves a direct analogy between musical experience and religious experience. Where one might find opposition to this point is in the academies and among the theologians. Many theologians appear to say that religious experience is the central thing and that religious language then becomes the real problem for religious people. If religious people, they think, could just once and for all get straight about the functions of religious language, then religion could once again become relevant to the modern world even in thes guise of the traditional religious orthodoxies because it's the experience that counts and the language used in religious contexts need not be referential.

I don't however, find religious people outside the universities to be much concerned over religious language per se. I find instead of a concentration on religious language that there is a concern with the realities to which religious language appears to refer, namely God, the Holy Spirit, grace, Allah, eternal life or whatever. Surely this is the case among the professionally religious, the priests and ministers and nuns dedicated to the truth of their particular tradition; I doubt that many would feel themselves professionally akin to an orchestra conductor or to a rock and roll singer, precisely for the reason that they feel themselves to be serving a higher truth. An appeal to the importance of religious language and its functions in religious experience, as opposed to strictly propositional or assertive or dogmatic claims about God or Christ or Allah, cannot, then, validate an analogy between music and Western religion. Religious language in the Western traditions is really intended by most who use it to do more than mediate (or produce) a religious experience. Neither language itself nor experience itself is enough, and both together are not enough for them. Stated bluntly, I am arguing that the concepts of religious language and religious experience in what is (or was) a monotheistic cultural context cannot make sense apart from the claim that there are non-empirical entities which are external to the self and to which religious terms refer. Even in its most demythologized form, Christian language, for example, cannot make sense apart from the claim that there is a God who gives grace or who provides salvation. This is the orthodox husk left in Bultmann's thought (e.g., 1958) and I think that one can find the same in Tillich despite his somewhat misleading tendency to speak of a God "beyond the God of theism" (1951; 1952).

THE CHARACTER OF WESTERN
RELIGIOUS TRUTH CLAIMS

In this section I offer a brief account of the Western tradition's insistence on emphasizing truth claims which ostensibly refer directly to supersensual entities. Against this background the very different character of youth counter cultural religiosity should become apparent, especially with reference to an analogy between religion and music.

The relationship between religious experience and dogma or religious truth claims of a binding nature has always been fairly explicit in Roman Catholicism and still is, I think, regardless of the appeal that Protestant liberalism holds for some Catholic thinkers. No doubt there are many quite sophisticated Roman Catholics who are terribly well versed in studies about the motivations for religious behavior and the functions which religions have performed in the societies of mankind. Yet it is hard to conceive of any Roman Catholic, no matter how sophisticated, who would say that religious experience is the primary thing and that the content of dogmatic assertions is irrelevant. Most in fact would say that apart from the truth of the dogmatic claims there could be no specifically Catholic religious experiences. One does not have visions of Mary, for instance, apart from the truth of the claim that God assumed her bodily or that in some way she "lives still." An even more obvious point: one does not ordinarily have a vision of Mary unless one believes that Mary is important in the first place. A Buddhist monk, the content of whose religious experience was formed by Mary, would doubtless be exceptionally hard to find. My point is simply that for Roman Catholicism, including its entire tradition up to the present time, religious assertions or religious truth claims have held a distinct primacy over religious experience. Any "new" religious experiences, for example those of Francis of Assisi, not only occur in an already well-defined dogmatic context, but also are regarded simply as supplements, special "charismas" which enhance but do not supersede the main tradition. The same primacy of dogma over experience holds even for the post-Vatican II church, since what modernization means for the liberal in the church is not so much the excision of dogmas as it is an attempt to get non-dogmatic items treated in a non-dogmatic way by the authoritarian hierarchy. Traditional customs about a celibate clergy and about the prohibition of mechanical means of birth control are only the most obvious examples. Modernizers in the church do want to maintain the standard dogmas (suitably reinterpreted but hardly in such a way as to do without the crucial referents, God, Christ, etc.); they are pressing for freedom merely as regards the *adiaphora*, the non-essential things. The difference between the modernizers and the traditionalists has to do with how many ecclesiastical laws and customs that have been handed down to the modern day church are counted as essential: for the most liberal churchmen (e.g., Küng), very few; for the staunch traditionalists (e.g., Ottaviani), everything, including Latin in the liturgy.

In the Protestant tradition, the relationship between religious assertions regarding the character of the world and religious experience is somewhat more complex, but in all cases, except for the Barthian wing perhaps, different from the Roman Catholic view. Luther's insights basically had to do with the primacy of the experience of justification by grace through faith, although in his mind there was of course no question of denying the reality of "grace" or of the God who gives it. In the modern situation still, I think, experience is rated more highly by Protestants than Catholics. The Bible-belt fundamentalist, however full of truth claims about the literal validity of biblical views of the world and of biblical assertions in general, will nevertheless invariably put the crucial emphasis on experience—only when the abject sinner experiences redemptive grace is he able to make the decisive "decision" and to follow through on it with a turnabout in his life style. The situation is clearly different in the tradition of Protestant liberalism stemming from Kant through Schleiermacher and Ritschl to Bultmann and the death of God adherents today. What is really different, however, is simply that biblical fundamentalism is rejected. For Kant, as for Schleiermacher and all the rest of their modern followers, the subjective experience of "grace" or "conversion" is again the primary thing. Here again the crucial significance of the experience is not questioned. What does come into question is the reality or existence of a supernatural source of such experiences. Yahweh is the source for Bultmann; man's own ideal projections of himself are for Feuerbach and his modern followers who reject theism altogether. But this point once more invalidates an analogy between religion and music even in Protestant liberalism. The Protestant liberals who remain "churched," emphasize experience as they may, nevertheless are finally forced to reintroduce, however surreptitiously, at least some of the traditional truth claims. Schleiermacher merely interprets dogmas as religious feelings set forth in speech and promptly proceeds to incorporate the whole dogmatic tradition in this way. Kierkegaard simply assumed the truth of the Lutheran dogmatic tradition, then set about his characteristic business of relating how the lonely, alienated self could appropriate it unhypocritically and with due intensity. Bultmann, as I mentioned above, is left, despite all his modernizing efforts, not only with the *experience* of grace but also with a distinct claim that Yahweh produces the experience. Of course he would not allow us to *explain* the experience as the result of the external operation of a supernatural agent on a natural, finite one, because as a good existentialist Bultmann argues that explanation inevitably falsifies experience. Such a position, however, does not detract from Bultmann's core proposal that, in whatever way he may do it, Yahweh is responsible for justification and forgiveness. The same in general is so for Buber: although we cannot without falsification say how Yahweh is operative in the production of I–Thou encounters, the fundamental claim is that his action is the necessary condition for them to occur at all.

My point is that Protestant liberalism and religious writers influenced by existentialism come closest to an espousal of sheer experience as the crucial and primary religious thing; but even they cannot reject all religious assertions about supersensual realities. The analogy between religion and music may apply most closely to this influential group, but it does not apply fully, or even strictly enough to be counted as a loose analogy. The aspect of religious assertions or dogmas or truth claims is too important. All the Western religions, even in their most extreme liberal presentations, cannot avoid making, and holding as significant, the two basic theistic claims that a personal God exists and has been known to be or still is benevolent toward some or all. Those death of God theologians who try to avoid such assertions as these are logically wrong even as they are psychologically in tune with the times; for if there ever were a God with anything like the attributes that Christianity and Judaism have applied to Yahweh, and Islam to Allah, he *could not* have died. This position therefore simply begs the question of whether a being with such attributes does (or could) exist in the first place. And, although I admit the following is an *ad hominem* point, the psychological and ideological strain involved in retaining Christian or Jewish discourse and attitudes while denying the durability of Yahweh strikes me as very great, and for this reason the movement probably cannot last.

COUNTER CULTURAL RELIGIOSITY

I can now state my final and major argument. While the analogy between religion and music is invalid with reference to the standard forms of religiosity in our culture, it seems to me valid with reference to a newer form of religiosity emerging among the young in America, France, England, Italy, and Japan—in short among the young in all industrialized countries of the West or under Western influence. I would argue that we are witnessing the birth of a new religious life style in which religious experience *is* precisely analogous to the aesthetic experience of music. For the incompatible elements so basic to other sorts of Western religiosity, dogmas or truth claims about supernatural entities, are truly missing here. If the analogy between religion and music fails as regards traditional theistic religions, even of the very liberal variety, it succeeds as regards the emerging religiosity among a good proportion of our young, especially, of course, on the West and East coasts in America and in the large urban and university centers in other countries. I shall try to say why.

Clearly the young are greatly in need of some unifying experience, some deeply felt focus for their lives; and, perhaps for the first time on such a wide scale, they reject the possibility of finding such a unifying focus in any of the available traditional forms. Christianity and Judaism have failed them in this way, and Marxism, really the only competitor, has for the most part failed to substitute except with obviously forced symbolism (Mao and Ho portraits at SDS conventions, commune terminology in building takeovers and the like). Science and technology, and needless to say, technocratic culture in general, have been anything but successful in establishing new values—Roszak (1969), Slater (1970), and Reich (1970) have provided accounts of this failure in their recent books. In fact, none of the available "world views" appear to be acceptable to many of the young, partly because the gap between religious or Marxist ethics and actual social conditions is so great, partly because religious and Marxist claims about the way the world is find no reference point in concrete personal experience. The alienated young accordingly feel themselves forced into scepticism about any totalistic world views and sometimes also into a moral solipsism. For them there is no way to vindicate hope on a grand scale and there are no universally compelling symbols to act as motivations for either public or private action.

As we all know, quite frequently the young turn to drugs in response to an otherwise hopeless cultural situation. Not only is the actual use of drugs important to them, but also there has grown up around drugs a whole new arena of discourse—"acid," "trip," "freak out," and so forth. Drugs are used, I suggest, to fill a vacuum in personal experience, the vacuum caused by a lack of a shared, unifying focus for life and by the apparent unavailability of vocational goals which are uncontaminated by what radical youth see as the greed, myopia, callousness and hypocrisy of business and government and academia. I call drug-induced experiences, as well as the whole ethos built around drugs in the youth counter culture "religious." It may be that the experiences in themselves would deserve the label "religious" because of the mystical qualities they manifest and because they add a new dimension to life and put ordinary experience in a different perspective. But to my mind it is the novel ethos, the shared group experience, that is important as a religious phenomenon. The youth-drug counter culture fulfills genuinely religious functions which are no longer being fulfilled by the traditional religions or by any substitute ideology. Whether religious needs are universal I do not know, but that they exist among the anti-Establishment youth of the industrialized West I have no doubt; and none of the available religious alternatives have been able to satisfy them.

Following Durkheim (1915) and modern sociologists of religion such as Bellah (1970) and Berger (1967), I take the production of social solidarity and the creation of a symbolic universe to be the chief of these religious needs and functions. In the counter culture, drugs act as both symbol and ritual in forging a sense of social cohesion. Pot smoking and drug taking do assume a ritualistic status in the lives of many, analogous perhaps to the several-martinis-before-dinner syndrome for more contented Americans. But much more important is the fact that the ritual produces, or at the very least, greatly reinforces, a sense of social "belongingness" to a group not part of the established culture. Of course, the group is defined also by age and dress and protest, but I think that the drug aspect is crucial as a kind of social cement. Using drugs seems to be the one crucial criterion for acceptance into the counter culture; this is a primary function for a basic symbol in any group. *Extra ecclesiam nulla salus*, or in the phrase of Kelsey's Merry Pranksters, you're either on the bus or you're off the bus. Not participating in this symbolic rite of drug usage means that one is definitely off the bus. Drug usage also creates a whole new in group terminology, which operates symbolically by bolstering social cohesion in the absence of other attractive and workable symbols and by helping to define and identify the members of the group.

When the drug phenomenon is considered together with youth's devoted allegiance to rock music, then I think that the essential contours of the counter culture begin to emerge. Rock music, in conjunction with drugs, provides the context for counter cultural ritual activity. Rock festivals supply the occasion for the celebration of self-expression and for the reinforcement of a new social ethos. Perhaps it would be as well to say that the counter cultural social ethos is not so much new as it is the reemergence of an old social ethos, the *Gemeinschaft* type of face-to-face, small group communality. But it is difficult indeed to develop this sort of sociality in the midst of our decidely *Gesellschaft* type of life in the wider society. That just this is happening, however, is amply attested by the wildly proliferating growth of communes all across the country, and one could say that a rock festival is the celebration of communal life writ large. I should argue that what makes this communal style of life a possibility are the symbolic and ritualistic reinforcements of drugs and rock. Drugs and rock music in all their various forms supply the means of identification, the primary vehicles for conceptualization of meaning, and the impetus for living out an "erotic sense of reality," to use N. O. Brown's phrase. When one is under the influence of drugs, rock music can appear to beat out colors and other sensory stimuli. The combination of music and drugs can cause one to alter ordinary attention patterns so that things are attended to differently. And memory residues are activated that would not be in "straight" circumstances. These experiences are interesting and important, but even more so is the fact that they are shared, and generally occur in a group. They can become the very stuff of counter cultural group or *Gemeinschaft* life.

Besides drugs and rock, few other symbols appear to have gained counter cultural adherence, although the peace symbol, for instance, is a widely shared badge of identification. Further, patternless psychedelic lighting nicely emphasizes the non-rational and non-totalistic character of the religious ethos the young are creating—precise, rationally stated ideological views about identity and destiny and cosmos are not to be had. Even the apparently literalistic use of divination tools such as the I Ching or tarot cards or astrological data does not produce an ideology. The popularity of these resources for divination in fact can illustrate that the quest for a stable identity within the counter culture must be regarded as a kind of game. To put the point another way, the seriousness of such a quest depends on the existence of some shared fundamental assumptions about value and upon the notion that life in society is at least passably rationally organized. Neither of these is the case for the counter culture, and a consequent emphasis on present experience becomes paramount. But deeply felt private experience stimulated by drugs and rock can then be shared even in a non-verbal way; it is shared because one knows that the others are experiencing something like what he is. And this sharing among those "on the bus" definitively marks them off from the ordinary life of established culture which knows nothing of what they know. Needless to say, persecution on the part of the established society against the counter culture (illustrated graphically in the film *Easy Rider*) only serves to reinforce the bonds of social solidarity felt among counter cultural young—the blood of martyrs has not infrequently been the crucial factor in any anti-Establishment group's ability to survive and grow.

If we are no longer tempted to define religion naively and incorrectly in such exclusively Western terms as belief in God, then we are in a position to analyze youth counter culture as a religion, or better perhaps, as a new religiosity, a new religious style of life. But if we think of a religion in terms of systems of symbols and rituals, and their function in providing social cohesion for a reasonably well-defined group then the phenomenon of the youth counter culture fulfills the criteria. And once the supernatural element is removed from the picture, the analogy between this new religious experience among the young and aesthetic experience becomes valid. For in this context the problem of religious assertions or dogmas does not arise. Furthermore, if aesthetic experience is "artificially induced" by external stimuli, so also is this form of religious experience induced, in this case by drugs primarily. What counts in both cases is the integrity of the experience, the depth with which it is felt, the needs it fulfills, the unifying or patterning functions it provides. That one does have such experiences is the important thing; the content of them is not so important. One's own thing, whatever may be the actual thing, is the central notion here; not the thing but that it is one's own—hence again the peculiar nature of the symbols utilized, for by intensifying experience of the most private sort, the drugs and rock music enhance group solidarity. The *form* of the experience is shared if not its precise content. Finally, if a code of ethics is said to be a necessary component of a religion, the new youth culture, with its emphasis on honesty, integrity, gentleness, and personal freedom, surely does have one, although it is vague and largely borrowed.

The historical situation that comes closest to producing a widespread phenomenon with similar religious characteristics is the Hellenistic world. There again we find a pronounced quest for individual salvation, the availability of numerous options for life commitment, and in general the cultural or political irrelevancy of which one a man adopted. Until the Constantinian settlement, virtually anything was permitted in the religiously and ethnically mixed melting pot of the Hellenistic milieu. But I think that even this situation differs from today's in that most available choices involved elaborate schemes, mythologies, and, again, truth claims of various sorts pertaining to non-empirical entities. Gnosticism is only the most extreme example; the mystery cults ran a close second, along with Christianity and Judaism. For many of the modern student generation, however, such schemes are not compelling. The experience itself and that it is one's very own are the things that count. Such an ethos stresses this-worldly salvation, to be sure, but that does not diminish its importance or centrality to those who seek it.

We are watching, then, the unfolding among the young of a new religious culture in which religious experience is truly analogous to the aesthetic experience generated by music for those able to "hear." An obvious, but not necessarily the only, case in point is the Woodstock festival held in the late summer of 1969. Hundreds of thousands of the young were drawn to it. It was to be an aesthetic "happening," certainly; but it turned out to be a religious one as well. The music was an experiential inducement to all; drugs to a reported ninety-five per-cent. Perhaps it is not possible to differentiate which experiences were produced by what, the music or the drugs; probably they must go together. But it is clear that inner, personal experiences themselves are primary in this new non-ideological religious ethos. And I hope I have shown that the ramifications of the phenomenon go beyond personal experience. The media are still marvelling over the social solidarity produced at Woodstock, not to mention the actual implementation there of Christian and Jewish ethical ideals about peace and gentleness, charity and compassion.

The analogy that I have discussed between music and religion is relevant to the counter culture of the young in another important sense. Weber himself may simply have been stressing that the "felt" side of religion is a crucial one for the individual; but this aspect at its most intense pole is mystical. And I find a new mysticism emerging among the young in the developed countries, one not constrained by an already well-defined religious context, and certainly not by a quest for union with God as in the Western traditions. It is closest, however, to the mysticism nurtured by Zen Buddhism, which is decidedly non-theistic and marked by the phenomenon of questing deep within the psyche. It stresses plumbing the depths, not of a god but of one's own psychic experience; and if the reports are to be believed, drug induced experiences among the counter cultural young also take one on a mystical quest within the ego. And since in this context rock music is also crucial, we may be witnessing an escape from the traditional Western stress on the visual, the ethos McLuhan (1962; 1965; 1967) calls "linearity," and its devotee "print man." If the West is industrializing the East, the West ironically may at the same time be turning away from the values that underlie industrial progress, namely the importance of productive work and the emphasis not only on financial security but also on money as an end in itself. By the same token, as McLuhan insists, the West may also be awakening to an Eastern ethos characterized more by contemplative interiority than by frenetic external worldly activity, and by communal, extended family sort of living than by our typical individualistic each man to his own wife, house, and car pattern. Particularly the counter cultural young among Westerners, then, may be the agents in a process of "reorientalization" occurring within our own culture, and that may be the harbinger of spring, of a new value consensus that could conceivably heal the wounds so evident in our badly polarized and fragmented culture.

REFERENCES

BELLAH, ROBERT N. 1970. Beyond Belief: Essays on Religion in a Post-Traditional World. New York: Harper & Row.

BERGER, PETER L. 1967. The Sacred Canopy: Elements of a Sociological Theory of Religion. New York: Doubleday.

BULTMANN, RUDOLF. 1958. Jesus Christ and Mythology. New York: Scribner.

DURKHEIM, EMILE. 1915. The Elementary Forms of the Religious Life. London: Allen and Unwin.

KELSEY, DAVID H. 1967. The Fabric of Paul Tillich's Theology. New Haven: Yale University Press.

MCLUHAN, MARSHALL. 1962. The Gutenberg Galaxy. Toronto: Toronto University Press.

―――― 1965. Understanding Media: The Extensions of Man. New York: McGraw-Hill.

―――― 1967. (with Quentin Fiore) The Medium Is the Massage: An Inventory of Effects. New York: Bantam.

REICH, CHARLES A. 1970. The Greening of America. New York: Random House.

ROSZAK, THEODORE. 1969. The Making of a Counter Culture: Reflections on Technological Society and Its Youthful Opposition. New York: Doubleday.

SLATER, PHILIP. 1970. In Pursuit of Loneliness: American Culture at the Breaking Point. Boston: Beacon.

TILLICH, PAUL. 1951. Systematic Theology, Vol. I. Chicago: University of Chicago Press.

―――― 1952. The Courage to Be. New Haven: Yale University Press.

THE JESUS PEOPLE MOVEMENT:
A SOCIOLOGICAL ANALYSIS

JACK BALSWICK

The Jesus people movement, which began quietly on the West Coast during the late 1960s, has developed into one of the most dynamic forces in the youth counterculture today. By 1971, the movement's impact upon the whole youth scene was so great that virtually every major mass-media magazine had presented it in one of their feature articles. The findings reported in this paper are based upon participant-observation research among the Jesus people in California during the summer of 1971. My acceptance by the Jesus people was aided immensely by my businessman brother who, among other things, manages a gospel rock group, co-owns a Jesus people Christian house, and maintains personal contact with many of the leaders in the movement.

Jesus people are recognized, and recognize themselves, by several different names, such as "Jesus people," "street Christians," "God's forever family," or "Jesus freaks." Although most would prefer to think of themselves as people, rather than freaks, they see nothing wrong with being thought of as a freak for Jesus Christ. The Jesus movement contains very diverse, loosely organized groups and is not a social movement in any unified sense. The peculiarly unifying feature is the belief that man can overcome his alienation and find real meaning in life only through a personal relationship with Jesus Christ. Since almost all Jesus people are recruits from the youth counterculture, this belief in Jesus is expressed with the style of the wider counterculture through "gospel rock" music (but not *Jesus Christ Superstar*, which is considered purely humanistic), psychedelic art forms, underground Christian newspapers, and an emphasis upon subjective religious experience.

HIPPIE FUNDAMENTALISM

The most curious aspect of the Jesus movement is that it combines the two very unlikely bedfellows, fundamentalist Christianity and the "hippie" style of life. Religious fundamentalism is the branch of Christianity in America which has been the most nonreceptive of the hippie symbols—long hair,

Revision of a paper presented by the author at the annual meeting of the American Sociological Association, 1972. Reprinted with permission.

Jack Balswick is a member of the Sociology Department at the University of Georgia.

beards, rock music, and a questioning of the American way of life. The one outstanding similarity between Christian fundamentalism and the youth counterculture is an emphasis upon subjectivism and a suspicion of rationalism and the rational approach, even as it is represented in the scientific approach. The anti-intellectualism within fundamentalism goes back to the early 1900s, when it was shaped through its attempt to preserve "historic" Christianity from the dual foes of modern scientific thought and modernism or liberal Christian theology. Fundamentalism, through an emphasis on the "fundamentals" of the faith (a belief in the virgin birth, miracles, the bodily resurrection of Christ, the Bible as the inerrant verbally inspired word of God), developed into a movement which was built upon the negation of modernism as a theological approach to Christianity. Modernism, which held to the basic tenets that man is not sinful by nature, and that utopia could be achieved on this earth by merely correcting evil social structure, was quite soundly shaken by two world wars and the great depression. With the decline of modernism as a viable option, fundamentalism, without a foe, lost its reason for being, while continuing its negative ethic. Contained in the negative bag of ethics were a renunciation of things of the world—secular music, entertainment, cards, movies, alcoholic beverages, tobacco, and dancing; and an anti-intellectualism and suspicion of secular education with its reliance upon the scientific method. The religion of the Jesus people corresponds very closely to this fundamentalist negative ethic. As traditional fundamentalists attempted to live the "separated life" by abstaining from "worldliness," the more sectarian of the Jesus people groups, like the Texas-based "children of God," attempt to cloister themselves from the world by retreating to rural communes. Jesus people are also similar to traditional fundamentalists in emphasizing the personal gospel, stressing man's need for salvation, and almost totally neglecting the social gospel, with its emphasis upon the need to change evil social structures.

USE OF COUNTERCULTURE SYMBOLS

Having accepted Christianity, Jesus people often carry with them the symbols and terminology which they have acquired in the youth counterculture as a whole, and within the drug scene, specifically. Thus a personal relationship with Jesus is expressed as "having an eternal high," or "turning on with Jesus," or "taking a trip with Jesus." Echoing the student radicals who talk of the coming revolution, the Jesus people describe their movement as a revolution. The problem with institutionalized Christianity, they say, is that it has sold itself out to the values of a materialistic, conformist-oriented society; and it is not preaching the true gospel, which is actually radical. As the words "radical" or "revolutionary" imply drastic, total changes, so the heart of man is seen as being in need of change, not just reform. Thus the Jesus people argue that they are the only truly revolutionary segment of the youth movement today. As the political revolutionaries speak of "people power," or "black power," or "student power," so the Jesus people speak of "Jesus power." As the opponents to the war in Vietnam symbolize[d] with a raised hand with two fingers thrust upwards, the hope of the ultimate victory of their views, so the Jesus people symbolize by a raised hand with one finger pointing upward that the only real answer to life is through a personal relationship with Jesus. This gesture symbolizes "one way," the one way to Jesus being the only ultimate, lasting answer to alienation, war, racial prejudice, and hatred.

THE SUBJECTIVE RELIGIOUS EXPERIENCE

Most Jesus people have emerged out of the wider youth counterculture which rejects rationalism (especially as a means to finding meaning in life) and, instead, emphasizes subjectivism. Part of the counterculture hippie morality is the belief that "meaning" and life's full potentials are to be found within the individual. Jesus people have usually gone the subjective route in searching for their meaning in life through drugs, sex, Eastern mysticism (usually Zen Buddhism) and have found these to be temporary or bad trips. Considering what the stresses have been within the youth counterculture, it should not have been too surprising that it would turn, in part, to a subjective interpretation of Christianity.

Jesus people often describe their conversion in terms of the experiential feelings which it produces within them. This subjective conversion experience is cognitively described as "Jesus coming to dwell within the heart." The believer reaches his "high" with Jesus to the extent that he yields his own life (usually thought of as "will") to the direction and leaning of the Holy Spirit.

In understanding the Jesus people, it is important to understand their subjective emphasis upon the "spirit which dwells within." It is common to hear past or expected behavior explained as: "The Holy Spirit led me to talk to him about Jesus," or "The Spirit is leading me to go...," or just "I felt led...." To the Jesus people, after one becomes a believer, "Jesus power" comes to be expressed as "Spirit power." The institutionalized church is seen as having a hangup both in becoming emotional about Jesus and also in regard to its lack of emphasis upon the Holy Spirit, the third person of the Christian Trinity.

This subjective emphasis upon the role of the Holy Spirit probably helps to explain why part of the Jesus movement has a strong Pentecostal emphasis. Pentecostalism, as it is presently found in the United States, had its origin in the early 1900s among the less educated and economically less well-to-do. The term *Pentecostal* comes from Pentecost, the occasion described in the Bible (Acts 2) when the Holy Spirit was sent, in the absence of Jesus Christ, who had ascended into heaven, "as a dove from heaven" to dwell in the lives of Christian believers. Within most of Pentecostalism there is a stressing of charismatic gifts such as a physical healing or glossolalia (speaking in tongues). Pentecostalism emphasizes that the believer needs to be "baptized with the Holy Spirit," at which time he becomes empowered by the Holy Spirit through this experience of speaking in tongues.

The emphasis on "speaking in tongues" fits in nicely with the counter-cultural emphasis on spontaneity and yielding to impulse through disregarding intellectual control. Rosak, in his book *The Making of a Counter Culture* (1969:128), describes Ginsberg's conception of poetry as "an oracular outpouring [which] can claim an imposing genealogy that reaches back to the rhapsodic prophets of Israel. Like Amos and Isaiah, Ginsberg aspires to be a *nabi*, a mutterer: one who speaks with tongues, one who permits his voice to act as the instrument of powers beyond his conscious direction." The emphasis on speaking in tongues also fits in with the youth counter-culture's emphasis on "doing your own thing."

The most recent convert can speak in tongues and in so doing establishes his status in the Jesus people community. He need not endure years of studying his Bible, nor be of service to his fellow men in the ghetto, nor attempt to change evil social structures, for speaking in tongues proves his spirituality.

RELIGIOUS PRAGMATISM

The theology of the Jesus people movement is very pragmatic, deemphasizing both the highly existential emphasis of neo-orthodox Christianity, and the highly historical and rational emphasis of orthodox (reformation) Christianity. Jesus is a worthy recipient of one's faith, not because He is the "ground of all being" (Tillich), nor because historical evidence points to the authenticity of His claims, but rather because He "works" in one's life. Thousands of former drug addicts testify that when they entered into a personal relationship with Jesus they were able to kick the drug habit. Others explain that with Jesus they no longer feel lonely, or alienated, or un-loved, or unloving. Several excerpts from the "Letters to the Editor" section of one issue of the largest of the Jesus people papers, the *Hollywood Free Paper* (July 8, 1971), illustrate this pragmatic emphasis:

> I was on "speed" for a little over a year—you know, a tab once in a while just to keep awake. But then I started doing it heavily. I was dropping between 8 and 12 tabs each time which sometimes was a couple of times an hour. This kept going on for about 5 months until I really overdosed. I was in the hospital—scared and dying. It was the first time in my life that I ever prayed and man, did I ever. I prayed to God that he would take away the withdrawal pains, and he did. After that night I gave my heart completely to God. It was really wonderful. I received the Baptism... [speaking in tongues] ...the following week. Man, it was really kind of wonderful. I never before experienced this kind of feeling. I really felt the Spirit of God coming over me—it's really wonderful.
>
> Around the beginning of February, I asked Jesus to take control of my life.

This radical change in my life occurred after a friend of mine explained to me how the Lord had changed his life and how he was having no trouble now that he had let Jesus into his heart.

In the year 1968, my Lord Jesus the Christ released me from the bonds of an addiction to narcotic drugs that had me in enslavement for more than 10 years. From the age of 13 when I had my first shot of heroin, until after my 23rd birthday when I found the WAY, my life was devoted to and centered around the cravings for narcotics. Prior to my acceptance of Christ, I had gone the whole route of "cures," been to the USPS Station in Forth Worth, Texas, to reformatories and prison a number of times, seen psychiatrists, psychologists, medical doctors, tried ZEN, YOGA, and Spiritualists . . . needless for me to say—all of the foregoing was to no avail. It was not until I asked Jesus Christ to enter my heart and change my life that I had any hope at all of a cure . . . and I am here today to attest to the WORD of GOD as written in JOHN 8:32—"And ye shall know the truth, and the truth shall set you free." PRAISE THE LORD!!!

Dear Brothers and Sisters in Christ, I would like to testify that our Heavenly Father can and will deliver us from all afflictions, illnesses, and hang-ups. He set me free from one of the most controversial—Homosexuality. . . . You can't lead a "Gay Life" and serve God too. I know from experience.

BIBLICAL AUTHORITY

An area in which Jesus people are very similar to both fundamentalist and orthodox Christianity is in the acceptance of the Bible as the inerrant Word of God, to be used as the ultimate authority. Along the lines of traditional Protestantism, each believer is encouraged to read the Bible himself. As Jesus is the "one way" to meaningful life and to God, and the Bible and the Holy Spirit are the authoritative guides for living. The use of the Bible by the Jesus people does not parallel the Christian existentialist who understands the Bible not as the Word of God but as becoming the Word of God through the Holy Spirit's revelatory work as it is read; nor does it parallel the traditional orthodox view, which considers the Bible to be the Word of God in propositional truth but subject to the Holy Spirit's illumination as the reader attempts to *systematize* God's truth. Jesus people use the Bible more in the manner of the Christian fundamentalist, who accepts the Bible as the Word of God without being too concerned about working towards any "systematic theology," and who rather subjectively interprets Scripture as he understands how it relates to his life at that moment. Similar to the Christian existentialist, Jesus people rely upon their *feelings* in interpreting Scripture, but unlike the existentialist they accept the Bible as undoubtedly being the Word of God (God's true revelation to man). The traditionalist who attempts to systematize scriptural truths may be accused by Jesus people of undue theologizing, rather than letting the Holy Spirit illuminate God's truth through a simple reading of the Scripture. A common practice of this sort in reading the Bible is "proof texting," citing scriptural verses to support a point one is trying to make. This can result in a misleading interpretation of the Bible when one verse is heard in isolation from the context of the total passage from which it was taken.

The youths within the counterculture movement are a product of a society and an educational system which has largely taught them a cultural relativistic view. To a large extent this cultural relativistic view is reflected in "hippie" morality, and there may even be a kind of reverse ethnocentrism, in which the aspects of other, more exotic cultures are seen as less contaminated by modern industrialism. The hippie morality includes very few absolutes beyond the injunctions that one should love and that one should be self-expressive in each living moment of experience, which is, of course, subject to a range of interpretations. The Jesus people, in adhering to a rigorous view of biblical authority, may be reacting against a very permissive hippie morality which they feel does not work. They have seen and experienced the rejection of traditional sexual morality in favor of a nebulous ideal of love and in the process have seen and experienced sexual exploitation. They have thrown off societal tradition, rules, regulations, and restraint in pursuit of freedom and liberty, and in the process have seen and experienced disillusioning chaos and disorder. They have freed themselves from living lives which were held captive to the future and have lived for the moment but in the process have found that, although man does not live by bread alone, he does need bread. All of this is to suggest that life in the counterculture, especially in the drug aspect of it, was found by the Jesus person to be unfulfilling and to leave one without a sense of direction. The Bible, within which are contained absolute norms for living, becomes a means of great security for the young Jesus person. Since the believer has reached his conclusion about biblical authority through a subjective experience with Jesus, no amount of rational attack upon the authenticity of Scripture is going to shake his confidence of authority. The only way a member of the Jesus movement is going to have difficulty in accepting Scripture as the inerrant Word of God is to return to a less subjective and more rationally oriented approach to truth. There is evidence that some of the Jesus people are moving toward a more rational view of truth, and as they do, they often reexamine more objectively what they found subjectively to be true.

REACTION AGAINST THE ORGANIZED CHURCH

It was not only the youth counterculture which gave impetus to what has developed into the Jesus movement but also the fact that much of organized Christianity in the United States is in reality an American cultural religion. Jesus people criticize liberal institutionalized Christianity for its failure to recognize man's alienated state and his need to be rightly related to God before he can be rightly related to his fellow man. They criticize conservative institutionalized Christianity, which they feel pays only lip service to the personal gospel, and is often unloving, intolerant, and racially and socially discriminating. They see Americans as obsessed with building expensive, lavish church buildings, a practice which Bishop Fulton Sheen has called our "edifice complex." They see the church as an organization whose end is to be served, not to serve. The church, when it is not totally preoccupied with itself, has attempted to put evangelism inside the church instead of in the market place. Church services consist of singing eighteenth- and nineteenth-century hymns and then listening to one-way pulpit communication which allows no opportunity for dialogue. This is the organized church as the Jesus people see it, and this is what they are reacting against, as much as the "counterfeit infinity" of the drug scene and the relativistic emptiness of the youth counterculture.

THE FUTURE OF THE MOVEMENT

It is hard to predict what the Jesus people movement's future will be because of its lack of unity and variations in form. A regional variation consists of a much stronger Pentecostal emphasis in southern California than in northern California. Variation in organizational structure ranges from the well-oiled machinery of the Berkeley-based World Christian Liberation Front (WCLF) and the 3000 member Calvary Temple Church in La Mesa, California, to informal collections of Jesus people worshipping in city parks. The quality of Jesus people literature varies from unsophisticated misspelled gospel tracts to the highly sophisticated underground newspaper, *Right On*, produced by the WCLF. Some groups emphasize a permanent communal type of existence, while other groups adhere to the biblical injunction that Christians should be the salt of the earth thus encouraging their members to move out into the world to live and preach the gospel.

Two things which could greatly weaken the Jesus people movement as a distinctive religious movement are: (1) The organized church could preempt the movement by imitating it in an attempt to attract youth; and (2) the movement could go the way of so many spontaneously born religious movements in the past and gradually become institutionalized. There are signs that the organized church has already attempted to use gospel rock music, psychedelic advertising, and so forth in an attempt to appear "relevant." As to the second point, only a few organized Jesus people churches have, as yet, emerged. Also, to some the Jesus trip is only the latest of many fads which will be followed before adulthood is reached. It is impossible to estimate the dropout rate among the Jesus people, although it is undoubtedly high among groups which emphasize a high-emotion and low-content brand of religion.

Some religionists, such as Billy Graham, are predicting that the Jesus movement is the beginning of a religious revival in the United States. Others, like the University of Chicago theologian Martin Marty, are predicting that the movement will have run its course in five years. It is my impression that a majority of the youth in the movement are sincere in their faith and are willing to give up neither their countercultural life style nor their religion. In general, the Jesus people are willing to identify themselves with the few churches they can find that are both theologically conservative and tolerant in allowing long-haired, bearded, and barefooted persons in their pews. Unless theologically conservative churches become more culturally tolerant I would predict that the Jesus people movement may yet be the impetus for the forming of several new religious groups, which eventually will come to be the equivalent of new denominations in the United States. There is probably little chance that the Jesus people movement in its present form can keep its distinctiveness over a period of time. Our Madison-Avenue-geared society, including the organized church, is capable of capitalizing on anything which captures the fancy of youth today.

•‡•‡•‡•‡•‡•‡•‡•‡•‡•‡•‡•‡•‡•‡•

Let's Get One Thing Straight

THE "RIGHT ON" STAFF

"Right On" has one line for the people: Jesus Christ holds the key to the only ultimate solution to any basic human problem you can suggest.

Too much? Well, before you split, you should know what constitutes a real Christian. All of us in the family of "Right On" writers know Jesus, and we want to share His answers with you.

We are not talking about belonging to or going to church, following the ethic Jesus taught, a religious code or rule of heart, self-righteous hypocrites, the atrocities and injustices which some men have committed in the name of Christianity, or even "good" people called Christian because they seem "nice" or moral.

We *are* talking about the change Jesus makes in lives—as shown by the kind of men and quality of life exhibited by those 1st century "love-revolutionists" recorded in history. That life is available today—by an encounter of one's natural life with a new quality of life altogether, an experience where Jesus the Messiah, with all His power and attributes comes to live inside an individual. We *are* talking about allowing Him to replace your limited ability to love, about being totally "unhung" from one's past, including the injustices committed and the guilt experienced, and about having one's own human life linked up permanently and experimentally with the very life of God without the aid of artificial stimulants, pills, or meditation—about going through a spiritual birth just as real and permanent as was your physical birth.

Dig it! Here's how to initiate that experience. You don't have to believe a thing except that God would have to be fair enough to reward those who really want to know Him. Simply express some thoughts like these:

"God, if you're really there and can hear me right now—and although I'm skeptical: if Jesus was right and has something uniquely to do with experiencing you, I ask you, through Him, to make yourself real to me. I make no promises to you, but as best I know my own mind, I do want to experience your Spirit—I simply need you!"

That's it. The rest is up to God. "Too simple," you say. Well, if you want

---

From editorial, *The Street People: Selections from "Right On," Berkeley's Christian Underground Student Newspaper* (Valley Forge: Judson Press, 1971), p. 9. Used with permission.

that to be your hang-up, that's your hang-up. All we can do is tell you we've experienced it. It has transformed the very core of our lives.

Sincerely,
The "Right On" Staff

P.S. We'll tell you more and answer your questions if you'll write us at P.O. Box 541, Berkeley, Calif.

GETTING STRAIGHT WITH MEHER BABA:
A STUDY OF MYSTICISM, DRUG REHABILITATION
AND POSTADOLESCENT ROLE CONFLICT

THOMAS ROBBINS   DICK ANTHONY

THE SOCIOLOGICAL ANALYSIS OF YOUTH CULTURE
AND YOUTH MOVEMENTS

Recently, a sociologist has noted that "youth culture is located at the point of conflict between the bureaucratic ethos and the ethos of modern childhood" (Berger, 1970:34). The separation of family and childhood from the productive process, the shrinkage in family size, and the diminishing likelihood of death during childhood have converged to produce a contemporary middle class childhood which "is vastly more humane than it was before" and which "brings forth more humane individuals" (Berger, 1970:35). Continuity is disturbed, however, because the humanistic and personalistic values fostered by the milieu of modern childhood cannot be carried over into the instrumental processes of the adult occupational milieu. The bureaucratic aspect of many post-childhood occupational and educational milieux is in some ways the antithesis of the "humanistic" patterns of childhood.

.   .   .

In contrast, the adult occupational structure (including preparatory higher educational institutions) increasingly stresses roles which are functionally specific, affectively neutral, universalistic and performance-oriented, in short, "bureaucratic" and "impersonal" instrumental relations (Eisenstadt, 1956). The transition between the familial milieu and the adult instrumental milieu thus becomes increasingly difficult and young people experience sharp role conflict. Within the terms of this analysis, youth movements, although they may have explicit "anti-establishment" overtones, can often be seen as devices to ease the tension of the familial-occupational transition. They do

From *Journal for the Scientific Study of Religion* 11, no. 2 (June 1972): 122–140. Reprinted with the permission of the publisher and the authors.

Thomas Robbins is a member of the Sociology Department at Queens College of the City University of New York. Dick Anthony is a member of the Department of Psychiatry, School of Medicine, University of North Carolina at Chapel Hill.

this by constructing value orientations and normative frameworks which combine elements of both familial and bureaucratic role systems (e.g., bureaucratic universalism and familial diffuseness). Through youth movements, adolescents and postadolescents work out roles and relationships consistent with selected aspects of both "childish" and "adult" milieux.

Eisenstadt's analysis is relevant to recent discussions of the clash of the "counterculture" with "technocracy" (Roszak, 1969; Reich, 1970).[1] It should be noted, moreover, that Eisenstadt and Berger interpret youthful "alienation" as essentially a problem of *community*.[2] There is a dearth of gratifying expressive-communal relationships and roles available for young people in the adult instrumental milieu. Such people face the prospect of being "love-starved." The formations of the counterculture will necessarily cater to these longings (Slater, 1970), and, moreover, can be expected on the basis of Eisenstadt's analysis to manifest an *integrative dimension* facilitating the working out of satisfying expressive patterns within the context of the larger society.

.   .   .

METHODOLOGY

The present study was conducted during the summer of 1970. The first author spent most of that summer at the Meher Spiritual Center in Myrtle Beach, South Carolina. The study utilizes a participant observation or "anthropological" approach, which emphasizes living within a culture until one assimilates its meaning system (Bruyn, 1966). The meaning system is presumed to have been acquired when the investigator can participate in the symbolism, ritual, and patterned interaction patterns of the culture in a way that is deemed acceptable or correct by its members.

This general procedure was supplemented by detailed recording of proto-typical interaction sequences, and by the tape-recording of interviews with people who appeared to be representative of types active within the cult. These interviews were generally informal and involved the respondent's description of his life from his initial involvement with drugs until his drugless cultic present. The interviewer asked questions clarifying various points or seeking responses which would enable him to compare features of the respondent's history to that of other cult members. The respondents were aware of the interviewer's role as researcher, but tended to perceive him primarily as a fellow participant in the cult.[3] In addition, we taped various informal talks given by a cult member for other cult members in the Saroja Library at the Meher Center.

The generality of the conclusions drawn from the observation and interview data collected at the Meher Center was checked against the impressions arising from periodic attendance by both authors at Meher Baba meetings in Chapel Hill, North Carolina, Berkeley, California, and New York City over a period of three years.

.   .   .

AN EXPRESSIVE COMMUNITY OF BELIEVERS

Meher Baba is a recently deceased (January 31, 1969) Indian spiritual master who claimed to be the most recent manifestation of the avataric tradition. According to Baba, Zoroaster, Rama, Krishna, Buddha, Christ and Mohammed were all human manifestations of the same divine being whose appearances on earth have punctuated humanity's movement through an "avataric cycle." Baba is the most recent manifestation of this being, and His advent closes the cycle.

Meher Baba has hundreds of thousands of followers in India. His American following remained small and predominantly adult until the middle sixties, when an interest in Meher Baba developed among young people, including (but not exclusively) drug users and "hippies" (Robbins, 1969). Prominent in His "message" is a doctrine of metaphysical unity among all persons, summarized in the phrase "We are all one" (Meher Baba, 1967). He has also become well known for his opposition to the use of psychedelic drugs (Meher Baba, 1966).

The Meher Spiritual Center in Myrtle Beach was founded at Meher Baba's direction by western disciples.[4] Situated on 500 acres of virgin forest and fronting on about a mile of ocean beach, it is intertwined with paths. There is a random grouping of 15 to 20 residential cabins and communal buildings of one sort or another near the center of the property. Because Baba spent much time there, His "presence" is generally considered by Baba followers to pervade the area. In addition, the two western disciples who manage the Center spent much time in India as His intimate companions. Their advice and counseling is much sought after by young converts. A visit to the Center is frequently, therefore, a formative influence in the emergent life-style of neophyte Baba followers. Young converts come there from all over the United States, and it has been the experience of the authors that styles of interaction inculcated at the Center reinforce and give authority to emergent expressive patterns in small groups of believers around the country.

These patterns seem to be a basis for "expressive community" within these groups, and seem to alleviate the "love-starvation" mentioned earlier. For this reason we shall list briefly characteristics of interaction at the Center which seem relevant to the expressive quality of these nascent "communities."

1. Organizational procedures at the Center are mostly informal and "personal." Group activities are more or less spontaneously arranged by the people who happen to be there at the time. For instance, dining takes place in communal kitchens, all cooking is done by visitors themselves, and

whether this shall be done individually or by groups is left up to the individuals concerned. Resident supervisory personnel live at the edge of the Center, not in the central visitors' area, and are usually seen only by appointment. There are a few rules posted on the cabin walls, but most of these have to do with the exigencies of living in the woods, e.g., carrying a flashlight at night as protection from snakes. A significant exception is a rule against possession of illicit drugs.

2. There is a deemphasis on formal proselytising. The only entrance criterion is some interest in Baba or the "spiritual path." Formal or intellectual belief is not emphasized.[5] Baba is quoted as saying "I came not to teach but to awaken." An interest in Baba is not considered inconsistent with other religious or worldly interests. Insofar as there is anything approaching worship services at the Center, they take the form of casually arranged get-togethers, e.g., to hear an older follower relate anecdotes of his experiences with Baba, to listen to music or sing, or to watch movies of the Master.

3. Interpersonal style at the Center is markedly familial and intimate. Hugs and kisses are customary greetings, occasionally between people just being introduced. This sort of affectionate physical contact is common between people of the same as well as opposite sexes, and is not treated as primarily sexual in nature. There are no shibboleths of membership, and there is a lack of defensiveness toward newcomers. Intimate personal information is openly exchanged between relative strangers, and these exchanges cut across normal affinity boundaries, e.g., class, sex, age. People smile ecstatically at each other for no apparent reason. Occasionally someone cries without embarrassment. Although many converts come from "intellectual" backgrounds, most conversation is simple, concrete, and personal.

The impact that this environment can make on a newcomer can be seen in an excerpt from one of our interviewees.

> I had my doubts. But as the people started coming in for breakfast and cooking their food, I started getting to talk with them more and more and I just started loving them and it just really sparked something in me to want to find out about Baba, seeing what Baba had done to these people...I sensed a peace in them all. All their eyes sparked and their faces seemed to have light in them. They were just so warm. No separateness, really...It was just such a loving environment and they had such a love for Baba.

The Meher Center thus plays a central role in establishing the informal and expressive character of the cult. Followers from all over the country meet and lay the groundwork for longterm friendships. The researchers have observed new acquaintances at the Center eagerly writing down each others' addresses and making plans to visit each other. Thus one follower came to the Center for the first time this summer and subsequently traveled north with two other followers from Miami (whom he had met at the Center) and visited other followers in Boston and Yonkers (whom he had also met that summer in Myrtle Beach). The Meher Center takes on something of the aspect of a *social clearing house*. The nature of the Myrtle Beach Center plus the existence of Baba communities in a number of cities means that a follower who has visited the Center is likely to have friends and acquaintances in various places in which, were it not for his cultic involvement, he would not know anyone. The authors have observed over the last three years that geographically mobile followers tend to resettle in places in which there are Baba communities.

.   .   .

FAILURE OF A PRIOR EXPRESSIVE LIFE–STYLE

The analysis of the Baba cult in the previous section, while adequate as far as it goes, requires further elaboration to explain certain features of the cult's success.

One such feature: Most of our respondents had been involved in other counterculture expressive milieux prior to involvement with the group. And such involvement, while it alleviated certain problems, created others of even greater scope. Our interviews revealed that some degree of disillusionment with these milieux generally preceded cultic involvement. It will be useful, then, in refining our analysis, to compare the Baba cult to the followers' prior drug-oriented drop-out expressive milieux; understanding why these involvements failed may help us to understand why the Baba cult works.

After an initial period of feeling pleasure in their release from bureaucratic educational or vocational milieux, many of our respondents began to feel that these drop-out milieux were not appropriate as permanent life situations for adults. These respondents had internalized residues of a middle-class work ethic such that prolonged dropping out ultimately engendered feelings of anomie. This development is illustrated by the case of one respondent who left school and joined a "clique of long-haired freaks" who filled their days with drugs and sex.

> We had an idea of finding some paradise in the woods or some tropical island and just staying in this paradise forever eating acid [LSD] and smoking grass ...We thought that just doing what we were doing, taking acid, making love, making music and just trying to be happy all the time was really the free life, and we didn't want to get imprisoned in the life our parents were leading.

But the respondent was never entirely at ease in his psychedelic paradise. His gratifying expressive relations seemed somehow illegitimate because they were not linked to instrumental behavior from which the expressive gratifications could be seen to arise as a reward. The respondent felt guilty and parasitic.

> *Respondent:* I was a parasite. You see, I always felt guilty because I'd say all these things and yet I knew I was a parasite. I knew I was just sucking what I could out of it without doing anything for it. It gave me a few guilty feelings.

Interviewer: So you got a feeling that somehow it couldn't be right to just sit around and trip and ball?

Respondent: Yes. Exactly. Exactly. I think all through this trip that I knew deep down that it wasn't for me and I always had a hidden feeling that, you know, this is short lived. It's not going to last. But I just blinded myself, just to get away from the thought of ever having to face work and just getting involved in the whole [routinized, work-oriented] life-style.

The respondent's precultic history resembled that of another respondent who, prior to becoming a follower of Meher Baba, had become friendly with Charles Manson (alleged mastermind of the Sharon Tate murders), and spent some time at his California commune. The respondent was initially fascinated and awed by the uninhibited spontaneity which characterized group relationships: "Everyone was real free... These people are all stoned out on acid and really loose... and I thought their freeness, their looseness or uninhibited selves was a kind of trip, so I hung around for a while." Subsequently, the respondent became disillusioned and saw the commune members as "sad" and their existence as really "drab" because "They did nothing ... they'd sit around all day long... they'd either ball or eat or take dope." Unable to succumb to the charismatic mystique of Manson, the respondent ultimately perceived the totally noninstrumental communal life-style as devoid of meaning.

The cases presented above indicate that a totally expressive drop-out lifestyle may be perceived as conflicting with a conventional adult role-identity. Many otherwise alienated persons have internalized such identities to a degree that simply dropping out is not psychologically viable for them in the long run. For such people, dropping out *requires a special legitimate rationale.* What we will refer to as "psychedelic utopianism" appeared to be a common legitimating mystique or precultic meaning system among our respondents. The inherent contradictions and ultimate failure of psychedelic utopianism as a legitimating mystique constitutes a second dimension of the failure of these respondents' precultic expressive milieux.

Formulated by Timothy Leary, among others, psychedelic utopianism stressed the attainment of vital personal growth and expressive community through psychedelic drugs (Leary, 1968). Later "hippie" versions of psychedelic utopianism stressed the role of drugs and a drug-oriented life-style in operationalizing Universal Love (Yablonsky, 1968). One difficulty with psychedelic utopianism for our respondents was that there are intrinsic potentialities in drug use which are inconsistent with the utopian rationales which they utilized to rationalize drug-oriented life-styles. . . .

1. Drug dependency often involves the proliferation of highly instrumental relationships with peers, which are treated not as ends in themselves but as means for obtaining drugs. Involvement in these instrumental relationships conflicts with the legitimating mystique of spontaneous, expressive, personalist relationships.

2. The contradiction is particularly sharp when the need for drugs instigates

dishonesty—people are "burned" (sold bad drugs) and "ripped off" (stolen from or otherwise cheated)—all of which falls short of "love."

3. The illegal status of drug use tends to breed "paranoia" over the ever-present threat of a "bust." Harassment of drug users also elicits negative stereotypes and vehemently hostile attitudes toward authorities, parents, "straight" nonusers, etc. Many utopiate drug users become aware that these orientations are "unloving" or "separative" and contravene the mystiques of universal love, unity and oneness which legitimate deviant patterns.[6]

The current decline of psychedelic utopianism is probably a consequence of the problems we have discussed above. Drug use continues to be a major social problem and a central feature of adolescence and youth. However, it has been observed by several writers that since the middle sixties youthful middle-class drug abuse has been "secularized" (Robbins, 1970) in the sense that "it is no longer claimed that recreational drugs have extraordinary value for achieving higher social goals" (Schaps and Sanders, 1970). Hence "psychedelic drugs do not now have the spiritual and mystical aura they had several years ago" (Robbins, 1969).[7] The "secularization" of drug use is the immediate sociocultural context of the growth of movements such as the Meher Baba cult. As drugs lose their potency as symbols embodying utopian "love" mystiques, other movements, which become increasingly dissociated from drugs, arise to perform their expressive and communal functions.[8] The Meher Baba cult is one such source of expressive symbolism.

.   .   .

MEHER BABA AS A UNIVERSAL EXPRESSIVE SYMBOL

In previous sections we argued that expressive role patterns rendered most meaningful by modern childhood will be perceived as inappropriate for adults unless an adequate legitimating rationale is constructed. Given the current fragmentation of expressive and instrumental role systems, an effective strategy for legitimating postadolescent expressive roles is to *universalize* them. Such universalizing is essential to the transmutation of specific values into a "sacred cosmos" (Berger, 1967). Moreover, universalized expressive values combine the universalism associated with "adult" modernist instrumental roles with the diffuse solidarity of familial expressive milieux. This combination is a frequent characteristic of youth movements (Eisenstadt, 1956).

Meher Baba is perceived by his followers as a *Universal Saviour*. He is the "Avatar of the Age" and "The Highest of the High." He is a Messiah who incarnates on earth at crucial periods "when the earth is sunk in materialism and chaos as it is now"[9] and who comes to inspire humanity and lead mankind to a higher level of consciousness (Needleman, 1970; Robbins, 1969). We shall see later that Meher Baba is "universal" in a particular sense involving his immanence in all persons.

The essence of Meher Baba's universal message is "love," which, in its purest form "arises in the heart...in response to the descent of grace from the Master" (Meher Baba, 1967). Meher Baba descends to impart this grace and awaken love in humanity. In Baba's case, "the medium is the message" in the sense that He is viewed by his disciples as a quintessentially "loving" Master. One follower commented to a researcher:

> You can look at Baba's picture and know that He loves you and that He'll never leave you.

Baba is thus viewed as a personification of universalized expressivity. Below, a respondent discusses his perception of Baba as an infinitely loving master, the very essence and embodiment of affectivity.

> To me Baba *was* love and with God and love and all, it just seemed a really groovy thing and why didn't somebody tell me about Him before?...I remember reading, well, like He says "I can love you more than you can love yourself." Well, I know a little bit about self-love, hassling with it, and like that really seemed incredible to me...That I was into a love thing and here it was.

Another respondent comments:

> Love *is* God and *love* is Baba. Baba is love. Baba is God, it's like each one of us—we've got it within us. It's just finding it and finding it through Baba is the best way.

Meher Baba's status as the personified embodiment of love is expressed through His relationships with His followers. These role-orientations appear to follow the dimensions of expressivity articulated by Parsons and referred to by Eisenstadt (1956). They are: affective, quality-oriented, diffuse and particularistic. Baba's "loving" relationships to people are depicted in movies of Baba shown regularly at the Meher Center. One such movie shows Baba tenderly washing lepers, whom Baba is said to have called "beautiful birds in ugly cages." Baba is thus perceived as responding *qualitatively* to persons rather than in terms of their apparent circumstances or attainments.

. . .

The interview excerpt below expresses the premise accepted by Baba Lovers that loving interpersonal relationships among themselves are derived from loving relationships to Baba.

> *Interviewer:* Why was it you felt good when you were at the Center?
> *Respondent:* Just because of the feelings. Just because of what people were expressing. I could feel Baba coming through these people. I even felt myself expressing these things which I never thought I would.

Thus, "loving" roles in the Baba community, "loving" relationships among Baba Lovers and "loving" attributes or "vibrations" of a Baba Lover are seen as emanations of Baba immanent within the lovers. In the passage below, the derivation of positive expressive qualities and expressive relationships from inner liaisons with Meher Baba is stated clearly.

> I don't see Charlie as Charlie. Really, I see Charlie as—I see Baba in Charlie. I see Baba in the people in the Center. I see Baba in you. I see Baba in so many of the people in the Center. And it's not the individual Charlie; no, I think it's Baba in Charlie.

Summarizing this section, we have seen that Meher Baba is perceived as having conspicuous expressive role-orientations which, by virtue of Baba's status as universal saviour and immanent divinity, become archetypal and universal. Baba's love is viewed as diffusing through loving relationships among Baba Lovers, which are viewed as derivative from the participants' inner expressive liason with the Divine Beloved. Expressive and affective relationships among followers are thus universalized and achieve a transcendental legitimization.

THE PROBLEM OF WORK ROLES

This paper has undertaken a functional analysis of the Meher Baba cult, which we have viewed in its integrative aspect as embodying an effective strategy for coping with alienation. This analysis is still incomplete. Considering youthful alienation in Parsons-Eisenstadt role-conflict terms, no resolution of alienation is complete without resolution of the perceived tension between instrumental "Establishment" work roles (including preparatory educational roles) and expressive needs which allegedly cannot be satisfied by these roles.

The fact of the integrative consequences of involvement in the Baba cult has been cited earlier and is also discussed in an earlier paper by one of the authors (Robbins, 1969). Numerous Baba Lovers have been led to give up illegal drug use (Robbins, 1969; Dunn, 1968; Needleman, 1970; Townshend, 1970) *and* either resume educational career preparation or exchange casual and primarily menial "odd job" patterns for long-term career involvements. This change usually involves a concomitant upgrading of social respectability. Below a former "speed freak," college drop-out and convicted felon describes his return to college in Chapel Hill after an extended stay at the Meher Center.

> The following year I went back to school. Give it one more try. When I left Chapel Hill, I had been thrown out. Like everybody was just trying to do me in—the administration, the police. They took me down to a cellar, you know, interrogating me. It was really something...So I went back up there, and I talked to the dean, who a year before had made very serious efforts to have me put in prison. He was shaking my hand, saying "Oh, it's so good you're back, you're just the kind of boy we need." That was an experience! He did everything but give me a scholarship.

It is the authors' belief that this transition from social alienation to social integration is accomplished through the particular form of universalized expressivity utilized by the Baba cult, i.e., expressive immanence. As explicated in the preceding section, an expressive community of believers is legitimated by this means. As a result, its members no longer suffer from "love starvation," and thus no longer feel a need to rebel against the impersonal institutions of the larger society. In addition, the logic of Meher Baba being the "real" universal self of all people compels a certain tolerance for people who are not members of the cult. The writer below is describing some of his acquaintances.

> Even without knowing about Baba they live and breathe his love, as does everyone, I suppose, but in them it is a fairy tale of color and good vibes (Townshend, 1970).

Below a respondent manifests this tolerance with distinct prosocial overtones.

> I get along with people more. It used to be, I'd go into the street and I'd see some whitecollar cat walk down the street and right away he's the enemy. I wouldn't go so far as ask him what he thought, he just *looked* like that and I didn't want to have anything to do with him. Or some cat would drive down the street in a Cadillac or something. There'd be no way in the world . . . I didn't want to meet him. But now like I want to talk to people. Even people like that, especially. Go out and tell them about Baba.

.   .   .

In a later segment of the interview, the respondent discussed Baba's modified work ethic. Baba maintains that action in the world is important for spiritual advancement, but to be really beneficial, i.e., to avoid enhancing the individual's sense of separateness from God, which most worldly endeavor reinforces, the spiritual aspirant must cultivate a sense of *inner detachment* from the results of his activity. He must dedicate and surrender his activity to "the Master" and in so doing he "liberates" himself from his own action and from the consequences of his actions, which are no longer his concern (Robbins, 1969; Meher Baba, 1967). A rationale of inner detachment from the results of one's work makes the impersonality of technocratic vocational routines less oppressive.[10]

.   .   .

It can be seen how Baba's ethic of inner detachment, in conjunction with the expressive context of the "loving" Baba community, enables alienated individuals to accept work roles which are not in themselves perceived as intrinsically gratifying or expressive. Moreover, the ethos of "selfless service" actually appears to provide a basis for a limited renewal of personal involvement in interesting and exacting work roles. Some indications of this tendency can be seen in the interview excerpt below.

> The relationship any job brings to spirituality is simply to use what I've been given as selflessly as possible. That is to say, I don't think it's right that if I happen to be a very intelligent person for me to spend my life stringing beads or washing dishes. It has to be put to use and it has to be lined up

with the fulfilling of my own *karma*. . . . I don't think from the point of view of God-realization that it matters whether one were a dishwasher or a great scientist, except that if I could have been a great scientist, then maybe I wasn't fulfilling my karma and that's the reason I won't wash dishes any more.

Thus, the "selfless service" ethos can eventually become a basis for renewed motivation and career orientation. A sort of mutual validation occurs between the emergent work roles of Baba Lovers and the cultic meaning system. The ethos of "selfless service" facilitates the crystallization of career involvements, which, in turn, act out the cultic "love" orientation and make it appear socially relevant. Baba Lovers thus strive to articulate their emergent work roles with their sacred cosmos.[11]

CONCLUSION

In the first section of this paper, we outlined arguments from Berger and Eisenstadt. Berger indicated that children raised in a modern technocratic setting would perceive themselves as love-starved when attempting to make the transition from the familial expressive milieu to the adult bureaucratic instrumental milieu. Eisenstadt has argued that *youth movements which seem to be attempting to perpetuate this expressive milieu in adult life often actually function to integrate the expressive and instrumental systems of role orientation.*[12]

In this paper we have argued that the Meher Baba cult has chosen one of the pattern variables from the instrumental system, viz. universalism, and integrated it with role-orientations from the expressive system. In this way the cult has *legitimated expressive role orientations for adults.* Universalism seems to be a particularly useful orientation for legitimating expressively, as it allows the elaboration of expressive role-orientations into a "sacred cosmos." This sacred cosmos, which presents itself as reflecting the nature and purpose of the universe, naturally supersedes all merely conventional institutions if their mandates should happen to conflict. It is thus an effective device for legitimating structural change, such as those arising from the fragmentation of modern society into a bureaucratic instrumental system and an expressive familial system.

The traditional work ethic, which rationalized the old small entrepreneurial instrumental-expressive synthesis of role orientations, derived expressive values from instrumental ones.[13] The "sacred cosmos" of Baba followers supersedes that ethic, by deriving instrumental values from expressive ones. It thus reduces the tension between conditions of modern childhood and the instrumental roles rationalized by the old ethic.

Other modern youth movements can also be seen as attempting to legitimate expressive role-orientations as a basis for community in adults by universalizing them. Thus we described the hippies' attempt to universalize their drop-out drug-oriented expressive life-style into an ethic of psychedelic utopianism. We saw that this attempt failed, at least for certain of our respondents, for two reasons: (1) the ethic led to behavior which was inconsistent with itself, e.g., use of drugs led to unloving behavior, and (2) it failed to include enough of the instrumental role-orientations in its synthesis, and thus never seemed quite legitimate to many of our respondents.

The Baba cult seems to have escaped these problems in that (1) its ethic does not produce consequences which are obviously inconsistent with it, and (2) it ameliorates the problem of "loveless" work roles in adult instrumental milieux by endowing instrumental role orientations with expressive meaning, not by trying to eliminate them entirely. It could be argued that insofar as a modern youth movement violates the second requirement, it will inevitably violate the former. That is, certain instrumental functions are necessary for the perpetuation of a total culture. If a subculture attempts to legitimate expressive functions by universalizing them, without including vital instrumental functions, it cannot maintain itself except as a specialized subsystem of the larger society. It must then, by its own logic of legitimation, convince the larger society to support it, because its expressive values rather than the larger society's instrumental values are the truly "universal" ones. But if the larger society were to accept this logic, it would adopt the purely expressive values of the subculture, and instrumental functions necessary to its maintenance would disappear. Thus, in order to maintain itself, the adult society rejects the love ethic of the hippies, and an escalating conflict between hippies and "straight" society appears. Hippies thus become Yippies, love-ins evolve into hostile confrontations with "Amerika," and the love ethic has become inconsistent with itself.

The particular form of universalism the Baba cult has chosen to legitimate its expressive values—expressive immanence—seems to have allowed it to escape these problems. This doctrine, which presents the same loving self as the "real" self of all, obviates "seeming" conflicts of opinion and belief. If one "self" is present in all, and that "self" is loving,[14] then people who have "realized" this must act in a way consistent with this awareness. They must attempt to act "lovingly" toward others, whether those others consciously accept their ethic or not.

In order to remain self-consistent, this form of universal expressivity is elaborated into a service ethic, which synthesizes expressive and instrumental role-orientations. The cult's ethic incorporates the instrumental values which allow it to perpetuate itself within the larger society, while maintaining the expressive emphasis which gave it birth.

NOTES

[1] Aspects of EISENSTADT's formulation have been applied to hippies by YABLONSKY (1968) and VON HOFFMAN (1968), who have noted the childhood-familial elements in the hippie "tribal" mystique. EISENSTADT's analysis has also been applied to student radicalism by FLACKS (1970b), who suggests modifications and criticisms. EISENSTADT's role-conflict analysis (whose conceptual components derive from the

system of TALCOTT PARSONS) has been an influential and distinctly sociological perspective on youth movements.

[2] An unfulfilled need for community has often been identified as the general curse of modern society—or modern American society (NISBET, 1956; SLATER, 1970). EISENSTADT, BERGER, and others feel this problem is particularly acute for post-adolescents of the present generation. The most recent statement of this position is by SLATER (1970), who argues that the youthful counterculture necessarily serves those needs which are repressed by the dominant sociocultural pattern. SLATER argues that contemporary American culture systematically frustrates basic human needs for community. This frustration is least tolerable among modern middle-class youth whose environment is more differentiated, organized, and bureaucratized than that of previous generations, and whose evident security and affluence undermines the scarcity premise which legitimates the dominant anticommunal ethos of competitive individualism (SLATER, 1970).

[3] As a movement the Meher Baba cult has no formal boundaries, membership certificates, or criteria. The researchers, who have been interested in the Meher Baba cult for some time, do consider themselves committed to some degree to the cultic meaning system and thus are participants in the Baba subculture (hence there was minimal pretense involved in the interviews or participant observation). For purposes of sociological analysis of the data, the researchers have operated from a premise of what ROBERT BELLAH (1970) has called "consequential reductionism" in which the truth or validity of the meaning system is viewed as irrelevant to sociological analysis. The details and attributes of the cultic meaning system are thus viewed in terms of the functions they appear to serve for participants. BELLAH may be correct in arguing that consequential reductionism cannot capture the real essence or full inner meaning of religious beliefs, but it has led to many sociologically significant insights.

[4] The Meher Center in Myrtle Beach, South Carolina, established at the order of Meher Baba, is a place for "rest and renewal of the spiritual life." It is the only resident Baba center in the United States. Followers of Baba come from all over the country to visit the Center. See DUNN (1968) for a vivid description of the interpersonal atmosphere of the Center.

[5] In this connection the evolution of the Monday night Baba meetings in Chapel Hill is instructive. Initial meetings in the summer and fall of 1967 were highly theoretical in tone and were characterized by intense discussions of Meher Baba's cosmology and eschatology. Current meetings in Chapel Hill seem to have a much more relaxed atmosphere and increasingly take on the appearance of a social gathering with refreshments and gossip. The spiritual symbols and belief system of the cult are still objects of deep attachment, but they have become an implicit rather than an overt dimension of collective gatherings and social interaction involving followers. A shared spiritual meaning system operates as an underlying premise of cult-related social phenomena, but is often not the explicit focus of the gatherings. In the opinion of the authors, this does not imply "secularization" in the sense of diminished attachment to cultic symbols and perspectives. It is, however, indicative of the growing sociocommunal dimension of cultic involvement. Thus the official Monday and Saturday night meetings of various Baba groups in New York City (run by older followers) have very recently been supplemented by "Baba House" in the West Village (run by young followers) which devotes more attention to social and recreational

activities and is currently sponsoring a sensitivity group and a theater workshop.

[6] YABLONSKY (1968) describes hippies cultivating drug-induced sensations of oceanic unity and oneness with everything. He goes on to criticize the hypocrisy of this utopianism which is belied by nonloving behavior (e.g., violence) within hippie communities. Countercriticism of YABLONSKY as writing from an irrelevant "Establishment–Liberal" standpoint (BERGER, 1969) is misleading, because hippies are themselves aware of these inconsistencies and experience and react to the resulting cognitive dissonance—or so our research would seem to indicate.

[7] The secularization of the drug scene has given rise to a number of movements and ideologies which seek to operationalize a mystique of *universal love*, which will legitimate expressive roles and relationships among postadolescents in a manner which evades the contradictions inherent in psychedelic utopianism. This tendency can be seen in the proliferation of postpsychedelic youthful "Jesus freaks" or "street Christians." VACHON (1971) quotes one postpsychedelic convert to Jesus as commenting that in his prior drug-oriented period, "We called ourselves love children, but we sure didn't love cops; now we love everybody."

[8] There are a number of other intrinsic difficulties with a distinctly psychedelic approach to *gemeinschaft*. Hallucinogenic drugs are often used to enhance sensations of interpersonal communion and expressive spontaneity; however, the aftermath of a "bad trip" can leave a user feeling utterly isolated and unable to relate to others (KENISTON, 1968). A number of respondents reported traumatic experiences of this nature.

There is also an intrinsic problem of meaning associated with drugs. Drug-induced sensations tend to be perceived as ego-alien. They cannot easily be identified with. A follower of Meher Baba has recently described this problem in a confessional article in *Rolling Stone*:

> On the surface, then, it seemed I owed a lot to dope. It gave me beautiful girls, it gave me R&B. What it didn't give me was the feeling that any of the above were really *mine*. They were all thanks to dope. That's where the paranoia came it. If I hadn't been stoned that solo would have been a bummer. If I hadn't been stoned, that chick wouldn't have wanted to know [me]. If I hadn't been stoned, the sun wouldn't have come up (TOWNSHEND, 1970).

[9] Quoted from a radio interview of Kitty Davy, co-manager of the Meher Spiritual Center.

[10] The "detached" resolution of the problem of alienation from work roles is congruent with the increasing tendency of middle-class employees to segregate their personal identity from their occupational roles which has been noticed by a number of sociologists (BERGER, 1965; LUCKMANN, 1967).

[11] A somewhat disillusioned former Baba follower commented in an interview:

> "If I were still a Baba Lover, I'd say, 'Oh, Baba found me this job'; like people say, 'Oh, it's because of Baba I found this house; oh, He directed me to....' That's what people do, say it's Baba. People have a way of fooling themselves . . . whenever they're going to do something, they say they're doing it for Baba. You know, I'm saving humanity... Baba has helped me do this. Because of Baba I found this service. But if you really want something, it's there. You can say, 'Well, Baba has helped me find it,' or Jesus or anything."

The respondent's comments indicate the degree to which Baba Lovers continually strive to relate all their worldly activities to their cultic involvement in such a way that the former is viewed as inspired by and derivative of the latter. A process of mutual or reciprocal validation appears to take place whereby the cultic meaning system legitimates worldly roles which in turn reinforce the meaning system.

[12] We consider EISENSTADT's analysis of the function of modern youth movements to be most valuable as a formulation of the conditions which a successful youth movement must fulfill, rather than a causal explanation of all youth movements. It is not then "reductionistic." It provides a principle of "natural selection" defining successful youth movements, rather than positing some mysterious *élan vital* intelligently but unconsciously directing all youth movements. It is simply a descriptive language identifying dimensions and functions of self-regulating social systems, and thus defines the nature of adaptive solutions to change and stress.

[13] PARSONS (1937), paraphrasing WEBER, has pointed out that Calvinism viewed man as an instrument for enhancing God's glory. This instrumental concept of man legitimated the assimilation of one's identity to a specialized instrumental work role.

[14] It is not our intention to explain Baba's "worldly" service ethic and its integrative and resocializing consequences solely on the basis of Baba's immanence. The usual consequences of immanentist doctrines are "retreatist," as they imply the possibility of making direct contact with God through intense spiritual endeavor (e.g., meditation) which usually involves social withdrawal. In the case of the Meher Baba cult, the key factor is the emphasis on "love," and Baba's archetypal "loving" role-orientations. In the context of this theme, immanence operates to facilitate social reintegration. One must love Baba and this involves loving others in whom Baba is immanent. In consequence, one best validates and operationalizes the cultic meaning system by acting lovingly in the world, which precludes retreatism.

REFERENCES

BELLAH, ROBERT. 1970. "Christianity and symbolic realism," *Journal for the Scientific Study of Religion* (Summer): 89–96.

BERGER, BENNETT. 1969. Review of *The Hippie Trip, Transaction* (February): 54–56.

BERGER, PETER. 1965. "Towards a sociological understanding of psychoanalysis," *Social Research* (Spring): 26–41.

———— 1967. *The Sacred Canopy.* New York: Doubleday.

———— 1970. *Movement and Revolution* (with Richard Neuhaus). New York: Doubleday.

BRUYN, SEVERYN T. 1966. *The Human Perspective in Sociology.* Englewood Cliffs, N.J.: Prentice-Hall.

CRENSHAW, RICHARD. 1968. "The hippies: beyond pot and acid." Pp. 99–108 in Martin Ebon (ed.), *Maharishi The Guru.* New York: New American Library.

DUNN, J. A. C. 1968. "Don't worry, be happy—I will help you," *Red Clay Reader.* Charlotte, N.C.: Southern Review.

EISENSTADT, S. N. 1956. *From Generation to Generation.* New York: Free Press.

———— 1961. "Archetypal patterns of youth." Pp. 29–50 in Erik Erikson (ed.), *The Challenge of Youth*. New York: Doubleday.

FLACKS, RICHARD. 1967. "The liberated generation: an exploration of the roots of student protest," *Journal of Social Issues* (July): 52–75.

———— 1970a. "Who protests: the social bases of the student movement." Pp. 134–157 in Julian Foster and Durwood Long (eds.), *Protest! Student Activism in America*. New York: Morrow.

———— 1970b. "Social and cultural meanings of student revolt: some informal and comparative observations," *Social Problems* (Winter): 340–357.

GLASER, BARNEY G., and ANSELM L. STRAUSS. 1968. *The Discovery of Grounded Theory*. Chicago: Aldine.

GREELEY, ANDREW. 1969. "There's a new religion on campus," *New York Times Magazine* (June 1).

———— 1970. "Superstition, ecstasy and tribal consciousness," *Social Research* (Summer): 202–211.

GUSTAITIS, RASA. 1969. *Turning On*. New York: Macmillan.

KENISTON, KENNETH. 1968. "Heads and seekers," *American Scholar* (Winter): 97–113.

LEARY, TIMOTHY. 1968. *The Politics of Ecstasy*. New York: Putnam.

LUCKMANN, THOMAS. 1967. *The Invisible Religion*. New York: Macmillan.

MEHER BABA. 1966. *God in a Pill?* San Francisco: Sufism Re-oriented.

———— 1967. *Discourses* (three volumes). Ahmedegar, India: Adi K. Irani.

NEEDLEMAN, JACOB. 1970. *The New Religions*. Garden City, N.Y.: Doubleday.

NISBET, ROBERT. 1953. *The Quest for Community*. New York: Oxford.

PARSONS, TALCOTT. 1937. *The Structure of Social Action*. New York: McGraw-Hill.

———— 1951. *The Social System*. Glencoe, Ill.: Free Press.

PEACOCK, JAMES L. 1968. "Mystics and merchants in fourteenth century Germany," *Journal for the Scientific Study of Religion* (Spring): 47–59.

REICH, CHARLES A. 1970. *The Greening of America*. New York: Random House.

ROBBINS, THOMAS. 1969. "Eastern mysticism and the resocialization of drug users," *Journal for the Scientific Study of Religion* (Fall): 308–317.

———— 1970. "Characteristics of amphetamine addicts," *International Journal of Addictions* (Summer): 183–193.

ROSZAK, THEODORE. 1969. *The Making of a Counter-Culture*. New York: Doubleday.

SCHAPS, ERIC, and CLINTON R. SANDERS. 1970. "Purposes, patterns and protection in a campus drug-using community," *Journal of Health and Social Behaviour* (June): 134–145.

SLATER, PHILIP. 1970. *The Pursuit of Loneliness*. Boston: Beacon.

TOWNSHEND, PETER. 1970. "Loving Meher Baba," *Rolling Stone* (November): 24–27.

VACHON, BRIAN. 1971. "The Jesus movement is upon us," *Look* (February): 15–21.

VON HOFFMAN, NICHOLAS. 1968. *We Are the People Our Parents Warned Us Against*. Chicago: Quadrangle.

WEBER, MAX. 1964. *The Sociology of Religion*. Boston: Beacon Press.

YABLONSKY, LEWIS. 1968. *The Hippie Trip*. New York: Pegasus.

CHAPTER 12

❖❖❖❖❖❖❖❖❖❖❖❖❖❖ ❖❖❖❖❖❖❖❖❖❖❖❖❖❖

Religion on the Frontier

The preceding chapters have amply demonstrated the interdependence of religion and society. This interdependence is particularly striking in an era characterized by new value systems competing with traditional religious belief systems—or, more appropriately, new viewpoints that criticize received religious perspectives as retrogressive to the progress of a particular movement or emerging group within the larger society. J. Milton Yinger suggests that in such a society there is need of "a highly flexible, undogmatic religion, and one that is dedicated to the free study of society, if religion is to contribute to the solution of our major moral problems."[1]

The concluding readings illustrate religious traditions challenged by movements on the "cutting edge" or frontier of our contemporary world. American Indians are perhaps the most romanticized of ethnic groups currently asserting their rights to distinct cultural recognition and identity. Scholar and Indian missionary Father Carl Starkloff, S.J., suggests that an ecumenical dialogue between American Indian religious traditions and Christianity could replace the previous religious "imperialism" of most missionaries, who have attempted to suppress many ritual and doctrinal features of Indian religion. "Indian religion offers insights to Christians that might long have been neglected. Recent attempts at liturgical celebrations of Earth Day and efforts to develop more esthetic and sensually pleasing worship are cases in point."

The ecology and feminine liberation movements contain prime examples of traditional religious perspectives under attack today. The popularity and, to many, vital importance of these movements strongly suggest that religion will adapt, in the flexible spirit stated by Yinger, and in some manner attempt to reinterpret whatever elements of tradition impede respect for natural resources and full acknowledgement of woman's dignity and equality with men.

NOTES

[1] J. MILTON YINGER, op. cit., p. 532.

AMERICAN INDIAN RELIGION AND CHRISTIANITY: CONFRONTATION AND DIALOGUE

CARL F. STARKLOFF

In undertaking an article to discuss the possible rapport or "ecumenism" between Christianity and American Indian religion (more specifically here Arapaho religion[1]), I am well aware of the limitations involved. Apart from the white man's inevitable tendency to misinterpret Indian actions and statements—a tendency that increases with what one is tempted to call "understanding," there are also growing manifestations of another obstacle. Indians themselves now often show indifference or hostility towards efforts by whites to meddle in their internal affairs, of which religion constitutes the Holy of Holies. I need not expatiate on the problem of the growing emphasis on separation and distrust that has arisen out of centuries of broken faith in white North America's dealings with Indian peoples. Vine Deloria, in his angry, sarcastic, sometimes unfair but basically accurate book, *Custer Died for Your Sins*,[2] has already covered ground that this writer could not presume to violate. The Sioux Deloria's unequivocal rejection of white society's efforts on behalf of Indians could well be a deterrent to further overtures at dialogue. And yet dialogue we must; the alternative is hatred and suspicion. If this article makes any contribution to such dialogue, it will be by advocating a policy of mutual enrichment and fulfillment between the Indian religious tradition and the Christian, in my own case Roman Catholic, tradition that has so often suppressed it and contributed to the religious vacuum of which Deloria speaks. I would in fact speak more cautiously about "Christian Indians," if this corresponded to the real situation, and would then advocate dialogue along the lines of what is taking place between Christians and other religions of the world. But there are so many actual situations dealing with Indians who are also Christians and wish to remain so, that it seems important to explore the possibilities of one's being a Christian according to traditional tribal religious practices. There are indeed precedents—Ricci in China and de Nobili in India, to name just two. This study, however, could also be

From Carl F. Starkloff, S.J., "American Indian Religion and Christianity: Confrontation and Dialogue," *Journal of Ecumenical Studies* 8 no. 2 (Spring 1971): 317–340. Reprinted with the permission of the author and the publisher.

Carl F. Starkloff is a member of the Theology Department of Rockhurst College, Kansas City, Missouri. He spent two years as chaplain at Haskell Indian College in Lawrence, Kansas.

applied simply to an investigation of the intrinsic value of Indian religion in itself.

Religion to the Indian people is perhaps the only possession which gives them insulation against the massive culture shock of the last three centuries or more. If the loss of these practices and traditions, for those who still follow them or have returned to them, is implied in "ecumenism," they will reject the overtures out of hand. If ecumenism means that whites can lay profane hands upon the sacred things of Indian belief, in order to "integrate" these into white society, the response will be that "Go back to Europe!" often heard today on reservations. The writer's experience with the Native American Church on the Wind River Reservation is a case in point. Although several influential Arapaho men, friends of mine for a decade, had planned to "put up" a peyote meeting for two of us Catholic priests, this plan was vetoed through the efforts of a committee of the Native American Indian Church,[3] with the argument that what a white man writes, especially if he is a priest, cannot likely tell the truth about any Indian practice or custom. My disappointment over this development, given time to settle, gave way to a grudging admission that such a charge is probably well-founded and accurate, even in the case of one who may be highly sympathetic and supportive. Over the years, I had become friendly with many Arapaho families and other Indian people, and count many of them among my friends (to employ a very risky and clichéd phrase!). Yet, all of these are persons reared at least nominally in a Roman Catholic or other Christian tradition, and consequently I could not lay claim to an understanding of the mentality of the Indian whose native religion is his exclusive "ultimate concern" (and the number of these is growing). Hence my decision to write almost exclusively as an outsider looking in, and even as one willing for now to suspend efforts at integration, in favor of a preliminary exchange of ideas and attitudes. It may be that both sides need to separate and reconnoiter for a time.

There is a guarded remark in Vine Deloria's book, at the end of his invective against Christian missionary efforts, that an Indian Christianity could be of great value to our society. To *allow* this to happen would be the duty of Christian denominations, first, by ceasing to be "denominations" (the overriding scandal in Christian history), and second, by permitting the rise of a national Indian Christian Church. "Such a Church would incorporate all existing missions and programs into one national church to be wholly in the hands of Indian people."[4] The role of the Church, ideally operated by an Indian clergy and assisted by Indian lay boards, would be to implement the redemption and growth of reservation society; the Church would be integrated into the ongoing life of the tribe. This is Deloria's challenge to the churches, calling them back to unity and to a genuine role in the improvement of religious life without destroying native cultures.[5] The present writer is himself skeptical about such a possibility ever being realized. Nevertheless, as a Christian convinced of the vocation of men to unity with diversity (an

Indian ideal as well), I have taken up the challenge in at least a small effort at dialogue.

. . .

It would not be honest to deny that Indian religion, like all religions, needs reform and revitalization. As we shall see later, there is decadence here, no doubt generally caused or occasioned by the invasion of foreign cultures. Most American Indian tribes retain at least vestiges of traditional practices, and many tribes, such as the Sioux, Arapaho, Shoshone in the north and Navajo, Apache, Pueblo in the south, have held onto many rites in their purity. Yet, the general situation of Indian religion is like the situation of Indian culture as a whole: it exists largely in the memory of the elders, not without a vestige of despair about its future. Among Indian youth there is not yet widespread interest in revival. But the various tribes are probably closer to their identities than are white Americans, with encouragement, a renaissance is possible— a renewal that could benefit both Indian and White. Young Indians in some areas are showing renewed interest in returning with college degrees to their reservations to work for their people, and religion figures large in their plans. Hence, the most practical plea for reform of White and Indian alike should no doubt be a mutual search for valid forms of thought, symbol, worship and community life. The result may be, hopefully, not "Christianity" as we now know it in its fragmented form, but the "assembly of Christ," realized beyond present decadence and confusion on all sides. If this writer shares Deloria's pessimism about any near realization of this cooperation, he still feels under the Pauline injunction to "redeem the time." The redemptive process may turn out to be a combination of inspired activity by white Christians along with that immense admiration of the Indian for all that is sacred, especially for the sacred figure of Jesus the Christ. If the Christian seems to be unwilling to relinquish this in his search for ecumenical dialogue with the Indian, it is because he believes that Christ is transcendent to all tribes and cultures, but demands of none of them that they relinquish their identities.

By way of introducing a format for discussion, we should first take cognizance of the superb posthumous work of Hartley Burr Alexander, *The World's Rim*. This book, which ends with Tertullian's ringing and much disputed "Eclamant vocem naturaliter Christianam" (their cry is by nature Christian),[6] offers us as fine an effort at comparative study of American Indian religion as is available today. The author draws us a poignant picture of the plains Indian standing with arms extended on the "rim of the world, about which walk the winds," covered over by the sky-dome, descending upon the earth at its four cardinal points, praying to the Spirit and spirits who govern all of life.[7] In his ensuing descriptions of important Indian rituals and their rationale, which we shall leave mostly to the reader's own initiative here, Alexander makes strikingly evident what John Bryde has included in his monograph written for the education of Indian children: the Indian is a seeker for integrity, with God, with himself, with his fellow man, and with the world.[8] His search is for the I–Thou in the most extensive and deepest sense. All of Alexander's discussion contributes to this—the Sacred Pipe, the Symbol of the Tree of Life, the Sioux myth of the Abiding Rock whereon stood the Great Elk whose baying summoned the first morning of the world.[9] There are various agricultural myths and rites whose sophistication and poetic content are not exceeded by the classics of Greek and Eastern mythology. One also finds among the Indians, says Alexander, a sense of a "world time" (*kairos* in the New Testament is a similar concept) that transcends chronological time, demonstrating that man's destiny is not profane but sacred, and that, while creation is not God, neither is it so secularized as to lose its redemptive value.[10] As the Kurahu tribe prayed in its contemplation over the life cycle of the earth, "This is very mysterious; we are speaking of something very sacred, although it happens every day."[11] Man will ultimately be granted transcendence even over this cycle, according to most tribes, in a life to come.[12] Thus, to the Indian, nature is sacramental, life is sacramental, and man only shares in these "for an allotted span of petition and proof."[13] There is therefore a deep sense of the mystery of death, dramatized by Indian ritual, for the Indian spirit, like all spirits, protests against death's ultimate victory and love's seeming defeat.[14]

Within the pattern of the Indian sense of self and universe then, we find an integrity that brings all things into one and recapitulates them, to use a Pauline image. In order to discuss the Indian religion, and especially, from personal experience, the Arapaho tradition, in an orderly manner, I have chosen to employ three "categories" used by Joachim Wach. In his *The Comparative Study of Religions*, Wach evaluates religions according to the way in which they respond to man's ultimate concern in *thought*, in *action* and in *fellowship*.[15] The remainder of this article will be an attempt to relate the religion of the Arapaho people to this pattern.

.   .   .

CREATION

One dare not proceed into Arapaho religion before he has clarified the question of the unicity and sovereignty of the Supreme Being (a term which, incidentally, does not seem to be an abstraction to the Arapaho), because in myth and symbol many supernatural and preternatural beings emerge, along with apostrophes to the elements under human titles.[16] Thus the narratives are not theologically explicit affirmations of monotheism. However, everything but the One Above comes under the concept of creaturehood, with a strong awareness of the "otherness" of God, who gave men all of creation as a gift. St. Paul's denunciation of those gentiles who confused creature and Creator in Romans 1:25 finds a parallel in the Arapaho conviction that, while nothing created is wholly "profane," neither is any creature divine. A sense of this appreciation of man's creaturehood is voiced in every Arapaho prayer, which is always an integral expression of petition, praise and thanksgiving.

Appreciation of creaturehood is perhaps the central belief in Arapaho and all of Indian religion. We can find numerous examples of this, with ramifications that spread out into worship and ethical conduct. Thus for example, we read the prayer of Hawkan before the erection of the Offerings Lodge for the 1902 rite, a prayer very much like those recited today:

> My father, Man-Above, we are sitting here on the ground in humble spirit and of poor heart, and ask your tender mercy upon us, one and all. Through the merits of your children who taught us this law of the Sacred-Offerings-lodge which we are about to locate, may we do it in such a manner as to obtain your favor and increased good spirit, to the end of the lodge! Give to us all our spirit and abundant mercy, and let us unite in one spirit toward you, who made us and ordered these things! My Grandfather, the Light-of-the-Earth, please look down this day upon your poor and needy people, that whatsoever they may do in their behalf may be pleasing to you! Now, my Mother-Earth, take pity on me, poor creature, and guide me straight! Let me do these things right, in the way your servants used to do![17]

•　　•　　•

WORSHIP

To separate worship from morality, especially from community, is impossible in the study of Indian religion. While one cannot learn all of Indian tribal morals and ethics from worship ceremonies, it is possible by examining them to arrive at the fundamentals of moral conduct. *De facto*, most Indian tribal customs and sanctions have been radically altered by the breakdown in culture, whether a Christian would consider this to the good or not. What we are concerned with here are attitudes rather than specific practices, and we shall therefore examine Arapaho worship before we discuss the ethical and communitarian attitudes connected with it. It is in the notion of tribal solidarity that we find the seeds of communitarian life and worship.

The most elaborate and carefully prepared ritual among modern Arapahos, and the one we shall concentrate on here, is the "Sun Dance," now carried out in the Arapaho tribe only by those resident in Wyoming....

..."Sun Dance" is a misnomer for this rite, although the title can be justified in light of the Sioux practice of calling it a "dance facing the sun." In Arapaho, the service is called *hasiha^nwu*, or "Ceremony of the Offerings Lodge,"[18] the term "offering" being more inclusive and expressive of all that occurs during the three-day period. The dance is an affair that follows three or four previous days of the aforementioned "Rabbit Lodge," a commemoration of the hunt and the Indian closeness to nature and what it offers him. Around midnight on Thursday, the dancers, all men who have made a vow to carry out the ritual (there were thirty-six in 1970), enter into the previously constructed Sun Dance lodge—a circular structure some forty feet in diameter, made from cottonwood trees and branches and other foliage. The description and photographs in Dorsey's work show a very close similarity to the lodge of 1970. The dancers have now begun a three-day total abstention from food and drink. They don elaborate paint and costumes, painstakingly prepared by mothers, wives or grandmothers and applied by a sponsor or "grandfather." The honor of one who completes the ordeal is felt by his entire family, the reward of what has been perhaps a year-long series of preparations.

The dancers move into a circle around the lodgepole, decorated for the present with offerings of sage, sweet gums, colored clothes, and a symbolic buffalo skull.[19] A fire burns a short distance away. This religious dance, unlike the rapid and athletic dancing done by the men at a social pow wow, is stationary and sedate—a mere rhythmic raising and lowering of the body on the balls of the feet to the beat of drum, chants and rattles. The dancers hold eagle-bone whistles in their mouths and blow on these to the beat of the drum. During all the dancing, one of the two chief dancers—the yearly sponsors of the lodge—waves a carefully constructed sacred wheel[20] in the direction of the pole. All gestures made to the pole—whistling, dancing, waving of the wheel or of eagle feathers—are a prayer of petition for courage and strength from the Tree of Life and ultimately from the Creator.

On the first night, dancing ceases around 2:30 A.M., and the dancers retire to sleep within the lodge on beds of reeds, wrapping themselves in large ceremonial quilts and still wearing their ritual paint of the day. Shortly before sunrise on the following day, and also on Saturday and Sunday, the celebrants are awakened, don their garb once more, and stand alongside their "grandfathers" in a horseshoe formation, facing out of the east entrance, in the direction of the rising sun—the noblest of divine gifts to man. A clergyman then steps into the center of the lodge, faces the pole, and prays aloud for the dancers and their intentions. The drums then begin their solemn beat, the dancers extend their arms toward the sun, and begin once more the vertical swaying of the Sun Dance rite, again "whistling to the sun" as they dance. The medicine wheel is now waved to the sun, which begins to rise over the horizon and slowly bathes lodge and painted dancers with its rays. There were many spectators, both white and Indian at the ceremonies of this year, and all were silent. Speech now would be profane indeed, as all things become relativized to the praise of the Creator who sends daily life to man, who renews the seasons, cleanses men from their sins, and accepts the offerings of men of good will. With such a tradition behind him, the Indian might well be the silent one he is reputed to be. Especially in the realm of mystery, symbols and gestures put all speech to shame as mere chatter. The dance then ceases once the sun is full in the sky, and the participants retire to rest for most of the morning.

.   .   .

ETHICS

It is in reflecting on the above sketch of the Sun Dance rite that one comes to see the interweaving of the cultic and the ethical in Arapaho religion. The Ceremony of The Offerings Lodge is above all a ceremony of recreation, a Lent of suffering, undertaken because of a vow, to seek a grace, amend a fault or render thanks, and it ends in a resurrection celebration of emergence from the lodge. Just as the Arapaho dance to pray a requiem for their dead, so too they dance to seek physical and spiritual regeneration. The author, during a discussion with several veterans of the Sun Dance (a man may enter the lodge four times, and three more by special indult), was given to understand that Arapaho symbolism of creation is directed at spiritual and moral rebirth. "Communal penance" is built into this ritual, without, however, a public confession of sins as often takes place during a peyote rite. One participant remarked on his decision to overcome a drinking problem while alone with his thoughts in the Offerings Lodge.

Walter Eichrodt has discussed the prophetic message of the Old Testament as being an attack on both magicalism, which seeks automatic results through ritual, and "moralism," which eliminates all cult in the name of priggish ethical preachments.[21] The Indian possesses the germ of such prophecy deep in his tradition, and it is in one sense unfortunate that the tradition is only an oral one, because numerous prophets have emerged from arduous "vision quests" to lead their people.[22] Magicalism and moralism are both prophetically avoided in Arapaho ritual. Rites are carried out exactly, as the author was told, not out of the fear of an angry God, but because things should be done "just so" out of respect for order. (Ritual, as we know in the case of alcohol among the Jews and peyote among the Indians, seems to prevent the abuse of these elements.) Neither is sacrifice considered a form of what Lutherans would call "works righteousness," at least not when properly performed. When dancers fast, or when they formerly pierced their flesh or gashed it, they were not "bribing" the Deity, but surrendering their flesh to Him, rendering back part of that which was given to them.[23] Alexander compares such rites to the "freeing from the flesh" of Christian tradition.[24]

In all things the Indian tradition seeks unity for man with God, with man himself, with the universe, and with one's fellow man.[25] All symbolism manifests this search for integrity. The sacred numbers and colors used in ritual and decoration are aimed at this search. The number 4 among the Arapaho signifies perfection,[26] and the numbers 5 and 7 develop it. Figures like the rhombus, square, cross and circle indicate perfect wholeness, as when prayer is made to "The Four Old Men," or the four directions and the four elements of summer, winter, day and night.[27] Kroeber writes,

Of course, this connection is given in nature by the four quarters determined by the sun, whose manifestations form the greatest visible phenomenon in the world, and there probably is more or less causal relation; but the connection extends to human matters, not in any direct relation with nature.[28]

Even the fertility rite formerly connected with the Sun Dance was itself a search for this integrity with nature and its cycles. Everything that is done in ritual, writes Alexander, is part of a search for that purity of heart that will see visions.[29] Without being conscious of it, Indian religion is naturally "ecological"; harmony with and respect for nature are essential, and this must extend to harmony among men. Alongside the rather flamboyant fairy tales about Nih'a^{n}ca^n, we also find fables about the Badger-Woman, condemning adultery and deception and other antisocial actions.[30]

Let me emphasize that, as in all traditions, abuses can be widely observed. The Indian's harmony with nature is soured at times by a discordant note as one sees the litter and wreckage on the reservation. Indian tradition was not equipped to cope with technology and artificial waste. In human ecology, alcoholism is a grave problem, and family breakdown is not uncommon. A great number of modern Indians themselves seem to have little reverence for ceremonies like the Sun Dance, and the problem of a carnival atmosphere on the premises must be coped with. But solutions to these, we might suggest, will not likely be found by imposing white Christian versions of metanoia on the Indians, but by helping them to rediscover their own culture, religious symbols and mores, in dialogue with the modern world in which they must live. The melancholy of man's fate, wrote Martin Buber, is that he must objectify and depersonalize his relationship with nature if he is to make progress as a person. But he must also develop a higher I–Thou relationship with nature as well. It may not be too late for pragmatic and objectivist white society to learn something from Indian history about this problem.

EXPRESSION IN FELLOWSHIP

Community is the goal of morality as well as of religion. We have spoken of community with God and nature thus far, and it remains to discuss more in detail how this sense of God—man—nature—fellowship complements and spills over into a human fellowship and solidarity. In some respects, modern society can probably never return to or encourage the close simple tribalism of former days among all Indians in a tribe and among tribes. Yet it can learn much from such solidarity, and Christian "missionaries," whatever their *modus agendi* in the future, will have to be ruthlessly self-denying in their attitudes and their efforts to understand....

The closeness of man to God, world, fellow man and to his own self is illustrated in a typical Arapaho prayer quoted by Kroeber—a prayer before eating:

Our Father, hear us, and our grandfather. I mention also all those that shine (the stars), the yellow day, the good wind, the good timber, and the good earth. All the animals, listen to me under the ground. Animals above ground, and water-animals, listen to me. We shall eat your remnants of food. Let them be good. Let there be long breath and life. Let the people increase, the children of all ages, the girls and the boys, and the men of all ages and the women, the old men of all ages and the old women. The food will give us strength whenever the sun runs. Listen to us, father, grandfather. We ask thought, heart, love, happiness. We are going to eat.[31]

Worship enters integrally here, without artificiality or intrusiveness. Solidarity is realized because men and women share in the elements of nature, and the sharing may or may not follow a religious event. Hospitality is given the greatest attention, and sharing is an essential note of Arapaho gatherings. St. Paul would never have to rebuke these assemblies as he did those in Corinth in I Cor. 11—at least not when the Indian feasts are conducted according to tradition.

.   .   .

CONCLUSION

This article has merely scratched the surface of the vast potential for Indian–Christian dialogue as a replacement for imperialism, which in generations to come will be doomed to failure even if attempted. Hopefully I have emphasized the most obvious sources for rapport in thought and symbol, worship and social conduct, and encouraged an opening of attitudes that would make the practice of Indian rites a possibility for Christian Indians. This should not be done uncritically, of course, but there seems to be no reason why such rites as the Sun Dance, Pipe Covering, and Sweat Lodge, as practiced by the Arapaho, should not be considered as possible "para-liturgy," and even as cultural settings for Christian worship for Indians who so choose. Such an opening of interest on all sides could then lead interested persons into further comparative study of symbols, archetypes, myths and goals of history. This is already being discussed and experimented with in some quarters by Christians on traditional Indian missions. The position of a tribal religious leader, for example, might be fertile soil for the introduction of a new form of diaconate, according to Indian culture and rituals. But the word "ecumenism" is used here designedly; white–Indian relations indicate a two-way street, and Indian religion offers insights to Christians that might have been long neglected. Recent attempts at liturgical celebrations of Earth Day, and efforts to develop more esthetic and sensually pleasing worship are cases in point. Thus, we should not think merely of "Christianizing" Indian rites, and of imposing a clerical dominance on them. It will be far more authentic if these become rituals practiced by Indians who are Christians, with clergy at most in a guest role, or responding to invitation to include Christian sacramental ministry within certain cultural settings.[32]

I wish to close this work with several important references to the book of H. B. Alexander. What struck this great philosopher-anthropologist was the sweep of thought and symbolism within native American cultures. He observes the readiness of Indian religion for rapport with all great religious traditions. With men like James and Huxley, the American Indian sees through the material world to its Ground:

> It is not a material labyrinth in which the soul of man has been incidentally trapped, but it is rather a sense-born phantasm, as Plato held it to be. Nothing is more obvious in Indian thinking than his belief that the Powers are the Realities, and that shapes and functions of things are primarily the exercise of those powers.... In the language of our own metaphysics, the Indian is an idealist, not a materialist.[33]

One might not choose to accept this "system" of thought. No Indian would, if he gave it consideration, argue over the defense of idealism, for to him the world is very real, however impermanent. All that genuine Indian religion, when given its true scope, endeavors to remind us of is that we must look beyond the *phenomena* to the *gignomena*, as Alexander writes, to a life that is not merely physical but moral.[34]

. . .

NOTES

[1] The Arapaho are a tribe of Algonquian linguistic stock, who migrated westward from the Minnesota area some three to four hundred years ago. They are closely related to the Gros Ventres and the Northern and Southern Cheyenne. There are approximately 3500 Northern Arapahos sharing the Wind River Reservation in central Wyoming with the Shoshone tribe. This tribe has been more active in conserving the Arapaho religious tradition over the last fifty years. Another portion of the tribe has lived in Oklahoma since the late nineteenth century, and is statistically listed with the Southern Cheyenne, with a combined population approaching 5000. These statistics can be found, along with other valuable information about the social and economic status of American Indians in: *American Indians, Facts and Future: Toward Economic Development for Native American Communities* (New York: Arno Press, 1970), p. 435. This is a publication of the Joint Economic Committee of the U.S. Congress.

[2] VINE DELORIA, *Custer Died for Your Sins: An Indian Manifesto* (New York: Macmillan, 1969), pp. 101–104 especially.

[3] The author had intended a discussion of the Peyote Cult and its place in Indian religion as part of this article, but since there was no opportunity to experience a meeting, this will not be included, even though informants imparted to me their fund of factual knowledge and experience. For a full study of the peyote matter, cf. WESTON LABARRE, *The Peyote Cult* (Hamden, Conn.: The Shoe String Press, 1964, enlarged edition), and MOLLY STERNBERG, "The Peyote Cult Among Wyoming Indians," Laramie, 1945. This latter is a master's thesis for the University of Wyoming, and goes into great detail. The author of this work personally shared in a meeting before the founding of the Native American Church in Wyoming. My own evidence from this and other data is that, while peyote is not a traditional part of ancient Indian religion, it would be most unwise for either political or ecclesiastical authorities to try to suppress it. Some evidence indicates that it is a very positive force for unity among tribes.

[4] DELORIA, p. 123.

[5] There is clearly here a hearkening back to an old danger of national churches and their attendant separatism. However, at times such groups seem to be a strong identifying factor and to serve as a transition aid to full and equal entry into the mainstream of a culture.

[6] HARTLEY BURR ALEXANDER, *The World's Rim: Great Mysteries of the North American Indians* (Lincoln: University of Nebraska Press, 1969), p. 232. For additional Indian background, see also Alexander's *North American Mythology* (Cambridge, Mass.: The University Press, 1916).

[7] Ibid., pp. 34–35.

[8] JOHN F. BRYDE, *Acculturational Psychology or Modern Indian Psychology* (United States Department of the Interior, Bureau of Indian Affairs, 1967), pp. 7–8.

[9] ALEXANDER, p. 43.

[10] Ibid., p. 78.

[11] Ibid., p. 111.

[12] Ibid., p. 126.

[13] Ibid., p. 184.

[14] Ibid., p. 222.

[15] Cf. JOACHIM WACH, *The Comparative Study of Religions*, ed. Joseph M. Kitagawa (New York: Columbia University Press).

[16] Cf. the various prayers in GEORGE A. DORSEY, *The Arapaho Sun Dance: The Ceremony of The Offerings Lodge* (Chicago: Field Columbian Museum, 1903).

[17] Ibid., p. 79.

[18] ALFRED KROEBER, "The Arapaho, Part IV: Religion," *Bulletin of The American Museum of Natural History*, Vol. XVIII, pp. 279–454, New York: May, 1907. p. 280. This entire volume of the Bulletin is devoted to the work of KROEBER on the Arapaho—their general description, art and religion.

[19] Cf. DORSEY, p. 112, for details. ALEXANDER, pp. 150–151, makes much of the Tree of Life symbolism here. Some modern Arapaho of Christian persuasion refer to the central pole and its twelve extended beams as representing Christ and the twelve apostles. This adaptation is not far-fetched, since DORSEY, in this work (p. 112) says that the pole also stands for Man-Above.

[20] DORSEY, pp. 12–13, explains the symbolism of the wheel perhaps being the serpent surrounding the earth at creation. Symbolism differs according to different accounts. On pp. 142–143, Dorsey describes the dance with the wheel, and this has not changed noticeably since 1903.

[21] WALTER EICHRODT, *Theology of The Old Testament*, trans. J. A. Baker (Philadelphia: The Westminster Press, 1961), pp. 364–369.

[22] On prophecy among Indian peoples, cf. ALEXANDER, pp. 186 ff.; WILLOYA and BROWN, *passim*; HARRY W. PAIGE, *Songs of The Teton Sioux* (Los Angeles: Westernlore Press, 1970), *passim*, and pp. 133–178.

[23] WILLIAM SHAKESPEARE, "The Northern Arapaho," unpublished paper delivered at workshop in Lander, Wyoming in August, 1969, p. 45.

[24] ALEXANDER, p. 148.

[25] Cf. BRYDE, pp. 7–8 and *passim* on this.

[26] KROEBER, p. 412.

[27] DORSEY, p. 113 goes into detail on the symbolism.

[28] KROEBER, p. 413.

[29] ALEXANDER, pp. 164–167. DORSEY gives a description of the modified rite.

[30] DORSEY and KROEBER, pp. 190–203.

[31] KROEBER, p. 314.

[32] Leaders of contemporary Indian festivities on the Arapaho Wind River Reservation, as a matter of fact, generally encourage their charges to bear witness to their good will by a faithful practice of their Christian religion, if they are such. Most Christian pastoral effort concentrates now solely on Indians who are Christian.

[33] ALEXANDER, p. 230.

[34] Ibid.

Saving the Earth: A Challenge to Our Religious Traditions

EDWARD B. FISKE

Several months ago a group of students at San Jose State College, in California, pooled $2,500, bought a shiny new yellow sports car and ceremoniously buried it, to the sound of taps, in a freshly dug grave in the center of the campus. This expensive ritual dramatized the students' belief that the automobile, polluter of the environment, represents a "grave danger to the survival of mankind."

But the students also recognized the car as something more—a symbol of the American Way of Life. As one young woman said: "We're not burying just a piece of metal, but a lot of other things with it."

By their actions the students showed that they know what most of us are beginning to realize in the haziest way: that the current ecological crisis requires not only a few more laws against air pollution, but also a fundamental overhaul of our most basic national values and drastic changes in our daily lives. In choosing the traditional burial ceremony to express this the students symbolized too, perhaps unknowingly, the deep connection between ecology and religion and the fact that ecology has become the most crucial religious issue of our day.

Like all cultural and economic systems, ours has been built on a foundation of religious values. Our attitude toward ourselves and our fellow men, our response to the natural world, all are derived from our Judeo-Christian heritage. We believe, for example, in our inherent right to use land, air and water as we choose, to "have dominion over the earth"; in our freedom indeed, our duty to have as many children as we desire, to "multiply and replenish the earth"; in our privilege to acquire as many material belongings as we wish, convinced that the "upright man shall have good things in possession."

· · ·

Some experts have argued that the beginning of the problem dates from the victory of Judaism, and subsequently Christianity, over paganism. While pagans believed that all objects in nature were endowed with life, and thus had profound respect for the natural order, Jews and Christians placed God in

---

Edward B. Fiske is Religion Editor of *The New York Times.*

the heavens. The result, according to Lynn White, Jr., a historian at the University of California at Los Angeles, was that "Christianity made it possible to exploit nature in a mood of indifference."

While it is true that the Judeo-Christian tradition also contains themes of reverence for the created world, these have not been dominant. Inherent in solving the ecological crisis, therefore, is the development of a fundamentally new religious outlook with new priorities.

The most important element of the new religion must be the recovery of respect for nature. Here we can learn a good deal from the Eastern religions —especially Buddhism, which teaches reverence for all living creatures, and Taoism, which stresses man's harmony and unity with nature. We should concentrate on rediscovering certain of these Eastern attitudes that are latent in our Western heritage. The Creation narrative, the Psalms, the concept of a Sabbath day of rest—all contain positive values of responsibility, stewardship and respect for nature.

Second only to a respect for nature must come a humbler view of man. The Judeo-Christian tradition has emphasized the glory of man, created "in the image and likeness of God" and placed highest in the order of creation. Unfortunately this has carried with it the unquestioned corollary that man is far removed from other forms of life, that plants and animals have value and nobility only insofar as they satisfy human needs. Ecology is now show-ing us that this view is not only narcissistic, but also potentially suicidal. "To struggle to defend the dignity of man," said theologian Gabriel Fackre, "does not mean one has to denigrate the earth."

A third element of the new religious value system must be a different concept of the relation of man to nature. If man views himself with more humility and views nature with more respect, the two then can coexist as partners, rather than as master and servant. As William McElvaney, a Meth-odist pastor, put it: "Nature will become man's biospheric colleague, not an environment to be conquered and thoughtlessly exploited." Others have suggested a spaceship metaphor: man and his environment traveling through space on an unknown journey, the functioning of both depending on close cooperation and the constant recycling of limited resources.

Here we might point out that the ecological crisis has emphasized one religious theme that has received little attention in recent time: divine judg-ment. We do not need a theology of heaven and hell to realize that violation of God's commands to honor His creation carries built-in penalties.

Finally, a religious system capable of meeting the ecological crisis must contain a radically new ethic. For one thing, it has to bring into question our traditional emphasis on individualism. No longer can ethics and law be organized primarily around preserving the rights of individuals. We must recognize crimes against nature and society; we must weigh personal comfort against ecological realities. We must, as we have already noted, challenge the right of every couple to decide how many children to have, in view of the urgent need to control population. We must question an individual's prerogative to utilize limited natural resources, such as seashore property, for private rather than for public use. We must restrict an individual's freedom to possess goods, such as alligator belts and redwood lawn furniture, in order to preserve animal and plant life. In short, we must begin to live by the golden rule, and apply it to our neighbor as well as to the natural world.

·　　·　　·

The ecological crisis has arisen largely because we have thought primarily in individualistic terms, isolated ourselves from each other as well as from the world around us and compartmentalized our experiences. Institutional religion too has allowed itself to become fragmented over minor doctrinal issues: it has lost sight of common fundamental truths and reduced its ideology to formulas that have little relevance to life as it is actually lived.

But at its best religion is profoundly ecological, for it embraces the totality of an individual's relationships—to himself, to others, to the universe itself—and gives them the unified meaning ecologists say is necessary for the survival of the human race.

Right now, more than any time in recent history, people are searching for religious values that will give meaning to their lives.

Ecology has given our own religious tradition a new and urgent task—to provide the symbols and rituals that will accompany the new values. This should not be a difficult task—traditional religious symbols, like the Garden of Eden, the bread and wine of Holy Communion, can easily be infused with new meaning and made relevant.

Religion and ecology ultimately meet because both stand in judgment against all that is life-denying. Perhaps the mandate they share is that proclaimed by the Lord to Moses in Deuteronomy 30:19: "I call heaven and earth to record this day against you, that I have set before you life and death, blessing and cursing: therefore choose life, that both thou and thy seed may live . . ."

✛✛✛

Toward A Feminist Theology

SHEILA D. COLLINS

Throughout history—so textual critics and anthropologists agree—societies have elevated certain of their social infrastructures to the realm of belief; and such belief systems in turn have become the justification for the continuation of the social structures from which they sprang. As sophisticated Christians, I think we all realize that Christianity, though revelatory, has not been without its cultural taint.

What has been dismaying churchwomen of late is the failure of male theologians even today to distinguish between the essence of the faith and some of its most blatant cultural accretions. Just as the theory of the divine rights of kings served to legitimize a feudal system which kept a vast majority of the people in subjection and poverty, so the system of male-oriented symbols, doctrines and taboos in the Judeo-Christian tradition has served to keep females in subjection to men and in spiritual, if not always physical, poverty.

UPSETTING THE APPLECART

The women's liberation movement has awakened women theologians, seminary students and churchwomen to the need to rethink theology in radical terms. Starting with an analysis of the patriarchal society out of which Judaism and, later, Christianity developed, these women are developing new models of Christian consciousness, based on an egalitarian ethic of liberation, and are attempting to replace outmoded symbols which give meaning and vision to the experiences of all people. They are not attempting to appropriate male religious symbols for themselves, but to right an imbalance in the system which has shaped religious consciousness since the time of the patriarchs. But in order to right this imbalance they must first upset the applecart; which is to say that the feminist theologians are not reformers but revolutionaries, who attack even the theology of hope as being tied to old patriarchal symbols.

Who are these new feminist theologians and what are they saying about Christianity? Surprisingly enough, the vanguard of this movement is to be found in the Roman Catholic Church. Three of today's prominent women

Sheila D. Collins is a member of New Women and of a Task Force on Women's Liberation of the New York Conference of the United Methodist Church.

theologians are Catholic—Mary Daly, Rosemary Reuther and Elizabeth Farians. (The man who has made the most important background contribution to this movement is also a Catholic—Leonard Swidler of Temple University, who in his article "Jesus Was a Feminist," in the January 1971 *Catholic World*, argues convincingly that Jesus himself was one of the "new" feminist theologians.) Protestant women theologians—notably Letty Russell, Peggy Way and Nelle Morton—have also picked up the gauntlet and are busy exploring these new avenues and adding to the growing body of literature on the subject.

The feminist theologians see in the religion of the Scriptures as it has been transmitted by the church a reflection of the male experience of the world. In both Old and New Testament times women were regarded as an inferior species to be owned like cattle, as unclean creatures incapable of participating in the mysteries of the worship of Yahweh. For whatever historical reason— perhaps out of violent reaction to the excesses of the more female-oriented Canaanite fertility cults—ancient Hebrew society was blatantly misogynist and male dominated. No wonder that in such a society God became male— "King," "Father," "Lord," "Master." "So God created man in his own image, in the image of God *he* created *him*." Or was it the other way around?

Of course, sophisticated thinkers have never identified God with an elderly male parent in heaven. We like to think we are beyond such anthropomorphism. But what happens to us when we change the words around? God created *woman* in *her* own image, in the image of God *she* created *her*. As linguist Benjamin Lee Whorf has observed: "The limits of my language are the limits of my thought." Theological language was fixed in the era of the early patriarchy and has never shaken itself loose, in spite of our changing conceptions of reality. Images, solidified in language, have a way of surviving in the imagination so that a person can function on two different and often contradictory levels. One can speak of the abstract conceptualization of God as spirit and still imagine "him" as male.

PAUL, AQUINAS, AND LUTHER

When God was identified as male, a hierarchy of values was established. Since man was made in God's image and God was male, females were excluded from participation in that image. We may express what happened in an equation: Man is to God as woman is to *not God*. Paul puts it plainly in I Corinthians: "For a man ought not to cover his head, since he is the image and glory of God; but woman is the glory of man. For man is not made from woman, but woman from man." Since all that was not God was sinful, woman became identified with sin; and this identification was reinforced by the myth of Adam and Eve.

With the incorporation of Hellenistic dualism into Christian theology, a further dimension was added to the growing alienation of man from woman and woman from God in the Christian imagination. Hellenism brought with it an identification of sin with the body. And since in Hebrew culture woman was already identified (because of child-bearing and menstruation) with unclean bodily functions, it was but a natural extension to identify her with this new dimension of sin. Thus woman became the temptress, the devouring Earth Mother, the witch whose very existence threatened the spirituality of theocratic man. The patristic commentators on Genesis interpret the Fall as a succumbing to bodiliness, to femaleness, to sexuality. It is no historical accident that Ann Hutchinson, who dared to counsel self-determination for women in spiritual matters, was banished from the Massachusetts Bay Colony as a witch.

The effect of elevating patriarchal structures to the realm of belief was to put those beliefs in the service of the hierarchical, inegalitarian infra-structures of the society. Thus St. Paul could counsel women to be quiet in church and to obey their husbands because this was ordained by God, this was the nature of creation (Eph. 5:24; I Cor. 11:3). Despite his insight that we are all one in Christ Jesus, Paul was very much a man of his times.

So was Thomas Aquinas, who declared in the *Summa Theologica*: "Woman was made to be a help to man. But she was not fitted to be a help to man except in generation, because another man would prove a more effective help in anything else." The Roman church's veneration of Mary as virgin and mother can be seen as an attempt to make sense out of a theological system which had become alienated from existential reality. To reconcile the fact of and the necessity for procreation with a theology which declared that everything having to do with the body—therefore sexual/procreative activity—was unclean and evil, the church simply asserted that God incarnate was not conceived in a "natural" way and sentimentalized the role of Mother so that it no longer needed to be tied to natural bodily functions.

Centuries after Aquinas, Martin Luther held to the old patriarchal view. His "priesthood of all believers" challenged the hierarchy of the Roman church, but he did nothing to reform the hierarchical relationship between men and women. Indeed he declared: "Women are on earth to bear children. If they die in child-bearing, it matters not; that is all they are here to do." Even in our own day a theologian of the stature of Karl Barth holds to the same revelatory religion which has always excluded the existential experience of women. "Women," he wrote, "are ontologically inferior to men."

As Rosemary Reuther points out, modern psychoanalysis sees such theological formulations as the result of an alienation within the human psyche, as projections onto another of the fear in one's own unconscious. Man, fearing his own sexuality, passivity and emotionality, projects them onto woman, thus doing away with the need to deal with that part of his nature. (Just so white society projected similar attributes onto the black population it held inferior.)

The results of such psychic alienation are widely visible today. Thus the Roman Catholic and Episcopal churches refuse to ordain women; the Protestant churches fail to take women's intellectual and moral gifts seriously;

many congregations insist that female ministers would be sexually distracting or would lack the image the ministry needs if it is to be an effective interpreter for God. But perhaps the worst result is the internalization by many women of their own inferiority to men. This limits their life options and their potential, so that they can see themselves as baking cakes for the women's society but not as head of the board of trustees or the council on ministries.

JESUS AND WOMEN

Having torn down the symbols which have kept them oppressed, what would the feminist theologians substitute?

The first step is to go back to the roots of the faith to see what is meaningful in them once they are shorn of their cultural outgrowths. One of the most important contributions to this stage of inquiry has been the re-examination of Jesus' life in terms of his relationships with people. In the Gospels Jesus appears as a man at odds with his time and culture—so much at odds that even his disciples (and much less his later followers) did not often understand what he was doing.

In the article cited above, Leonard Swidler offers evidence that, flouting the social and religious mores of his time which kept women strictly cloistered and in bondage to their husbands, Jesus went out of his way to treat women (and the other pariahs of his time) as complete human beings, equal to men and capable of being spokeswomen for God. In view of the fact that the Gospels must be seen through the lens of first century Christian communities which, obviously, shared the antiwoman culture then prevailing, it is all the more extraordinary that the Gospels reveal no negative attitude toward women on the part of Jesus. As Dorothy Sayers has so beautifully said it: "There is no act, no sermon, no parable in the whole Gospel that borrows its pungency from female perversity; nobody could possibly guess from the words and deeds of Jesus that there was anything 'funny' about woman's nature."

Seen in this light, Jesus' life and its meaning take on new dimensions and bring us to a clearer understanding of Paul's truly prophetic passage:

> Now before faith came, we were confined under the law, kept under restraint until faith should be revealed. But now that faith has come we are no longer under a custodian; for in Christ Jesus you are all sons of God, through faith. There is neither Jew nor Greek, there is neither slave nor free, there is neither male nor female; for you are all one in Christ Jesus [Gal. 3: 23–28].

Though but fleetingly, Paul saw that the Hebrew laws regarding the ordering of persons—among them laws which stipulated that women were ritually unclean, that they could not be seen or talked with in public, that in adultery they were more guilty than their male partners, and that they were the property of their husbands—were all made irrelevant by Jesus and were ignored by him in his relationships with people. It is a sad commentary on the history of Christian thought that scarcely a single theologian, beginning with Paul, picked up this unique aspect of Jesus' ministry.

Here is Karl Barth, acknowledging (in his *Church Dogmatics*) not Jesus but Paul as his mentor and basing his contentions about God's will for men and women on Paul's culturally biased views:

> The command of God will always point man to his position and woman to hers. In every situation, in face of every task and in every conversation, their functions and possibilities when they are obedient to the command, will be distinctive and diverse and will never be interchangeable.... Why should not woman be the second in sequence, but only in sequence? What other choice has she, seeing she can be nothing at all apart from this sequence and her place in it?

The feminist theologian is bound to ask Barth: Who decreed the ordering of creation into superior and subordinate, into first and second? Was it laid down by divine fiat, or by a male theologian so blinded by cultural stereotypes (which were even more blatant in the German Swiss milieu he grew up in) that he couldn't see that Jesus' relationships with people led in the opposite direction?

A PLURALISTIC SCHEMA

Feminist theology, then, rejects the tradition of hierarchical orders of creation in favor of an egalitarian, pluralistic schema. It finds its corroboration in the life and ministry of Jesus, who repudiated such elitist practices and attitudes and called all people—men and women, beggars and merchants, tax collectors and poor widows—to be true to the God within them. Feminist theology rejects the Adamic myth as bound to perpetuate the alienation of men and women from each other and from themselves. It prefers the priestly version of the creation story, which (in spite of some problems with language) emphasizes the androgynous nature of God's creation and the care which humans are to have for the earth and its creatures.

Feminist theology does not hypostasize sin as an event that *happened* or as something that people *do*. Rather, it defines sin as a basic alienation within the psyche—a failure to lay claim to that part of one's humanity that one then projects onto an "other." The male's failure to claim his own emotionality, his insecurities or creatureliness, his capacity for nurturance and his need to be creative, as well as the female's failure to recognize her own aggressiveness, power, competence and intellectuality are examples of such psychic alienation. Many feminists, not just theologians, contend that this phenomenon accounts for many social ills, including war. We project our individual or group fears onto an "other," a "not me"—be it females, an ethnic minority or "the enemy" we hear so much about from our government officials.

Just as man is alienated from himself and from woman, so Westerners, conditioned by the Judeo-Christian tradition, are alienated from that part of themselves which belongs to the earth. Our failure to see that we are intimately tied to the rivers, the air, the land we are polluting is another form of sin which is already becoming disastrous for all of God's creation.

OVERINDULGING IN HUMBLE PIE

Sin, then, is not so much a falling away from God or a deliberate transgression of a divine being's orders as it is a failure to recognize the God within us and our fellow creatures. Feminists are therefore more likely to stress immanence rather than transcendence. They hold that sin is institutionalized wherever hierarchies are established; for hierarchies inescapably separate persons from one another or from part of themselves.

Because peoples have had different histories, sin takes different forms for different people. Herein feminists enter a crucial critique of traditional Christian ethics. Mary Daly states (in an article in the March 12, 1971, *Commonweal*) that "much of traditional Christian virtue appears to be the product of reactions on the part of men—perhaps guilty reactions—to the behavioral excesses of the stereotypic male." Christians have always been counseled to be meek, obedient, self-sacrificing and humble, to live a life of charity toward others, etc. This emphasis may have been necessary to counteract excessive aggressiveness, pride, and exploitative tendencies which characterize a male culture. The trouble was that these virtues were preached to women, for whom meekness, humility and self-sacrifice were already a way of life. Man's sin is that he has not had enough humility, woman's that she has had too much of it. It is as if, by letting women carry the burden of being humble and pious for them, men have got rid of any need to appropriate these virtues for themselves and so have felt free to visit aggression on the world. Here again, Jesus' relations with women are revealing. He did not speak to their weaknesses or coach them to eat humble pie. Remember, he said that Mary, not Martha, had chosen the better part! Jesus spoke to the capacity of women for real faith and courage and for carrying out decisions.

It is in this understanding of sin and in the critique of Christian ethics that feminist theology converges with the growing theologies of other oppressed groups, such as black theology. If we, as affluent Christians, counsel an underdeveloped people or an exploited underclass to be patient, meek and forever self-sacrificing, we commit the very sin we hope to avoid. Christ did not counsel the beggar to sell all he had, but he did so counsel the rich young ruler.

Many Christians have written at length about the "new man," the "new humanity," that Christ came to bring about. Few, however, have explained what it means to be "new." Feminists see the man-woman relationship as the key to the new humanity. The alienation between man and woman, they say, is the primordial one from which all other false or unjust relationships derive. Lest any accuse us of exaggerating the man-woman thing out of all proportion, let them recall Gunnar Myrdal's discovery that when, 200 years ago, laws were needed to justify the enslavement of black Africans, the slave-holders took as their models the English laws of the time which restricted the rights of women. How can we hope to be for reconciliation with our black or poor brothers and sisters if we cannot achieve reconciliation with that other half of ourselves?

A TRULY LIBERATING PARTNERSHIP

For the feminists, salvation is that discovery and celebration of the "other" in ourselves. When men discover their femininity and women their mas-culinity, then perhaps we can form a truly liberating and mutually enriching partnership. And then perhaps we can discover our own "blackness" and "whiteness," our own poverty and affluence, which we have so long kept hidden from ourselves. The new humanity is a humanity which is becoming, impelled by a revelation that is not located in the distant past but is only now becoming manifest in the clamor for dignity and liberation on the part of underdeveloped peoples.

Feminist theology calls for a repudiation of the old male-oriented hierarchical symbols—God as Lord, King, Master and Almighty Father—in favor of something like Tillich's notion of the "ground and power of being" or White-head and Hartshorne's conception of a feeling, responding, relational God. Or if we must anthropomorphize, why not God as mother/father—"she" as well as "he"?

Mary Daly points out that religious symbols die when the cultural situation that supported them ceases to be acceptable. This is happening today with the emergence of the women's liberation movement and of Third World peoples. But this development, Daly says, should pose no problem to authentic faith, for such "accepts the relativity of all symbols and recognizes that fixation upon any one of them as absolute is idolatrous."

Feminist theology calls also for a rethinking of the traditional doctrines of sin, incarnation and salvation in the light of our new understanding of the Gospels and of our conviction that such doctrines must speak to and be consonant with the existential experience of all people, not just of white, Western males. And, finally, feminist theology calls for an ethic based on the responsible self-actualization of every person so that we may achieve deeper awareness of the ties that bind all of creation together.

76 77 9 8 7 6 5 4 3